The McGraw-Hill Guide to Managing Growth in Your Emerging Business

The McGraw-Hill Guide to Managing Growth in Your Emerging Business

Guidelines for Transforming Your Small Business into an Exceptional Enterprise

Stephen C. Harper

McGraw-Hill, Inc.

New York   San Francisco   Washington,D.C.   Auckland   Bogotá
Caracas   Lisbon   London   Madrid   Mexico City   Milan
Montreal   New Delhi   San Juan   Singapore
Sydney   Tokyo   Toronto

Library of Congress Cataloging-in-Publication Data

Harper, Stephen C.
  The McGraw-Hill guide to managing growth in your emerging business
  : guidelines for transforming your small business into an
  exceptional enterprise / Stephen C. Harper.
        p.   cm.
  Includes index.
  ISBN 0-07-026689-1
  1. Small business—Management—Handbooks, manuals, etc.
  I. Title. II. Title: Guide to managing growth in your emerging
  business
  HD62.7.H376   1994
  658.02'2—dc20   94-17607
                                                                      CIP

The author has been unable to locate the original source and artist for the "dancing elephants." The elephant in the epilogue was drawn by Taylor C. Harper.

1 2 3 4 5 6 7 8 9 0   DOC/DOC   9 0 9 8 7 6 5 4

ISBN 0-07-026689-1

The sponsoring editor for this book was James Bessent, the editing supervisor was Jim Halston, and the production supervisor was Donald F. Schmidt. It was set in Palatino by Judith N. Olenick.

> The author believes that the material presented in this book is accurate. The material presented is the product of the author's efforts. Particular attention has been directed to citing the source or author of the material that has been included. In no way is the University of North Carolina at Wilmington to be considered responsible or liable for the book's content.

This book is printed on recycled, acid-free paper containing a minimum of 50% recycled de-inked fiber.

Contents

Acknowledgments

I would like to acknowledge Henry Wyche, former executive vice president of what is now United Carolina Bank—a midsize, multistate bank. In addition to his managerial prowess and keen sense for the real issues at play in business situations, Henry was an accomplished artist. Years ago, I asked Henry if he would donate one of his paintings to the boardroom in our school of business. He agreed with the provision that its name be prominently displayed on the frame.

The watercolor was of a small and rustic gas station and general store situated at a crossroads in rural North Carolina. Henry titled the painting, *Capitalism*. He attached a note indicating that the painting and its title were to serve as a reminder that nearly every successful enterprise had originated with one person, one idea, and one location. Even today's largest firms came from a modest beginning. The difference between businesses that blossom and thrive and those that wither and die boils down to how well they are managed! This book is about how to develop a business that will thrive in the years ahead.

Henry's watercolor also indicates the impact economic and government systems can have on the creation and development of business ventures. We are fortunate to be alive at a time when democracy and the spirit of free enterprise are valued. This country's founders recognized that the standard of living and society's quality of life are directly related to whether business enterprise is encouraged or inhibited. It is refreshing to see people throughout the world also recognize the importance of this symbiotic relationship. I would also like to recognize a number of people I have known over the years. Their ideas, enthusiasm, and perseverance have had a major impact on my views about business. These people include: Herb McKim and Mike

Creed of McKim & Creed Engineers, Ed Mayorga of R & E Electronics, Tom Long of Maricultura, Bill and Mercer Rowe—formerly of South Atlantic Services, Dave Valliere of Dove Computer, Chuck and Dorothy Noe of Dorothy's Ruffled Originals, Fred Sancilio of Applied Analytical Industries, Russell Carter of Atlantic Corporation, Jim Rouse and Alan Zimmer of Reed's Jewelers, Bob Warwick of McGladrey & Pullen CPAs, Fred Eshelman of Pharmaceutical Product Development, Jon Vincent of JTV Business and Management Consultants, and the other "capitalists" who wrote the minisections of this book.

I would like to thank Suzanne Morgan and Holly Rotalsky. As graduate assistants, they provided valuable research for this book. I also want to thank Dan and Betty Cameron as well as Bruce and Louise Cameron who created the endowment for the Cameron School of Business at the University of North Carolina at Wilmington. The Cameron School of Business faculty research and development fund helped make this book possible. Jim Bessent, senior acquisitions editor for McGraw-Hill, also needs to be recognized. He was very supportive of my last book, *The McGraw-Hill Guide to Starting Your Own Business*. His encouragement and persistence made this book a reality. I also want to thank Keith Davis who was one of my professors at Arizona State University. Keith also served as management textbooks editor for McGraw-Hill. As the author of leading books in the field of human relations and social responsibility, his encouragement to "write for the reader" continues to influence me today.

Finally, I want to acknowledge my grandfather and two women in my life. My grandfather, H. M. Harper, created a company from scratch. When it was acquired by I.T.& T. in 1971, it had grown into a publicly-traded firm that employed over 1000 people. He showed me the fruits of free enterprise. My mother, Ellen, and my wife, Marshall, continue to demonstrate that with the proper guidance and a supportive environment—two of the qualities required to manage a growing business—almost anything is possible. Their values and their sense of patience have served me well over the years.

Forward!

*In every economy, there is one crucial and
definitive conflict ... the struggle between the
past and the future, between the existing
configuration of industries and the industries
that will someday replace them.*

GEORGE GILDER

We live in a time when it would be easy to join the procession of
"doomsayers" who offer little hope for the future of business enterprise in
the United States. In an era characterized by corporate "downsizing,"
growing foreign competition, and volatile capital markets, all is not gloom
and doom. There is a ray of hope for the future of American enterprise and
the overall quality of life that is inextricably tied to it. A platoon of relatively
new ventures is already trying to liberate our economy from the forces of
complacency, arrogance, and mediocrity that have taken the United States
to the brink of total noncompetitiveness.

These new ventures capture the spirit of the pioneers who explored and
developed this country. Like the early colonists who had the courage to
break away from Great Britain and other monarchies, these new ventures
often lack the polish of more established firms. In their brashness, however,
they capture a level of excitement, exhibit a desire to experiment, and radiate
a zeal to find new ways to do things and new things to do that few larger and
more established firms demonstrate today.

This book is for people who want their firms to be part of the revitalization of this country's economy and the crusade to bring about a quality of life that will surpass the good old days of the 1950s and 1960s that one's parents and grandparents may still talk about today. Relatively new ventures may not be able to single-handedly turn the whole situation around, but they can provide an example of opportunistic and progressive management for others to follow.

The platoon of relatively new firms can do to their respective markets and industries what Apple and Compaq did to the computer industry. These firms saw emerging market opportunities and capitalized on them. Other firms like Bill Gates' Microsoft and Ross Perot's EDS, identified market opportunities that would come with the inevitable computer revolution. Gateway and Dell recognized that distinct distribution and customization competencies would also provide phenomenal growth opportunities.

Yet firms don't have to be in "high-tech" fields to experience meteoric rates of growth. Opportunities continue to exist for firms that can identify markets that are not being served well or at all by existing businesses. Numerous entrepreneurs have demonstrated that new "Davids" can succeed in a world of corporate "Goliaths."

Sam Walton had the courage to go into retailing at a time when Sears and K-Mart dominated the marketplace. By developing the right retail "formula" and choosing the right locations, he became one of the richest men in America. David Thomas's Wendy's proved the industry analysts wrong who said McDonald's, Burger King, and Hardee's left no room for an additional hamburger franchise. Wendy's shows that the *Field of Dreams* line, "If you build it, he will come" may also apply to new ventures. Wendy's built a hamburger that people could see and taste ... and people did come!

Fred DeLuca sensed the market wanted something other than a hamburger. His Subway franchise has been one of the greatest success stories. Ben and Jerry's illustrates that when you have a sense of humor and offer the market a steady stream of innovative flavors, people will come as well! In each case, these relatively new ventures were the ones that developed distinct competitive advantages over established businesses.

This book is for people who want to transform their small businesses into exceptional enterprises. Growth brings complexity and new challenges. Managing growth is like traversing a minefield ... it needs to be approached in a systematic manner. Too many firms are the casualties of their own growth. They may have grown in size, but they spread themselves so thin that too many things fell through the cracks.

Entrepreneurs often exclaim, "If only I had known...!" This book serves as a guide to what lies ahead. It contains hundreds of ideas and examples of how firms can identify opportunities and capitalize on them. It also contains tips from people who have successfully traversed the minefield. Their insights will let you know what you can expect before you get there. While there are no guarantees for success, this book will definitely improve the odds.

This book is based on the premise that entrepreneurs need to anticipate what lies ahead and prepare themselves and their firms for the challenges associated with growth. As someone said, "Only two kinds of people dance with the elephants ... the quick and the dead!" This book can be viewed as a guide to managing growth so your firm will not be blindsided or trampled to death by other firms, excessive debt, uncontrolled growth, or one's own arrogance.

The McGraw-Hill Guide to Managing Growth in Your Emerging Business

1
Seize the Moment!

*To make a child...easy. To raise the
child...difficult!*

This Chinese proverb captures the essence of this book. For years, the
process of starting a business received top billing in the theater of American
business enterprise. Recently, the thrill of entrepreneurship has been replaced by the cry of anguish, "Now that I've started this business, how do
I keep it going?" The excitement of seeing your business's name in lights,
making your first major sale, and being heralded as the next Henry Ford in
the business pages of your local newspaper has been replaced with the
sobering reality of: "What must I do to ensure that what was once my
dream doesn't become my worst nightmare?"

This book is not about how to keep your business going. There are a
myriad of books about how to manage a small business. This book is not for
caretakers or imitators. It is for people who want to be proactive and who
want their firms to be exceptional. This book is not about getting through
the day. It is for people who are committed to laying the foundation today
for a better tomorrow. This is a book for people who recognize that
business is not a 12-second, 100-meter sprint. It is for people who already
know that business must be viewed as a marathon where only the firms
that are mentally and physically fit will succeed.

Few firms can sustain the hand-to-mouth existence associated with the
start-up stage. For the first year or two, new ventures run on emotion and
sweat equity. The entrepreneur and others involved in the start-up stage
run on the hope that there will come a time when things won't be so crazy
and when there will be enough hours in the day to do what needs to be

done. They yearn for the time when sound management practices will replace seat-of-the-pants decision making. They relish the prospect that someday they will not have to traverse the tightrope without a net.

Your Challenge: To Develop an Exceptional Firm

This book is about managing growth, going the distance, and testing the limits. It is about how to keep the spirit of entrepreneurship alive in your business after the honeymoon associated with the start-up stage is replaced with a marketplace that shows little mercy for firms that don't have their managerial acts together. It is time to be honest with yourself. Your goal wasn't just to start a business—anyone can start a business. A proprietorship can be started in a blink of an eye, a partnership agreement can be drafted in a day, and a corporation can be chartered in less than a month.

Your real goal was to create an exceptional business—one that will continue to provide challenges, financial rewards, and intrinsic satisfaction for years. You started your business for the same reason John Sculley left PepsiCo at the prime of his career to join Apple Computer. After several lucrative offers to lure him away from PepsiCo, Steven Jobs—one of Apple's founders—issued the challenge "Do you want to spend the rest of your life selling colored sugar water or do you want to have a chance to change the world?"[1] When put in that perspective, it was an offer and an opportunity that Sculley and few others could refuse.

This book is about how to manage your business so that it grows to the point where it has the resiliency and strength to withstand economic downturns as well as the entrepreneurial drive to capitalize on the multitude of opportunities that will be available to only the few enterprising firms that are able to seize the moment in good times. This book is intended to help you guide your firm so that it can develop into an exceptional firm—to be the leader in your target market(s) and possibly your industry. It is about how your firm can be the initiator of change rather than the victim of change.

There is an old saying "unless you're the lead dog, the scenery never changes." Warren Bennis captured the value and benefits of being a pathfinding firm in his book, *On Becoming a Leader*. Bennis notes that "for the leader, the scenery is always changing. Everything is new."[2] The leading firm in a market segment is like the lead dog pulling a sled. The lead dog has a broad field of vision. It is also in a good position to navigate around potential obstructions. By virtue of its position, it has some latitude in choosing its path. Life for the rest of the dogs in the team is not as exciting. Any time you are tempted to ease up, to make compromises, or to cut corners remember the consequences of falling behind. If you aren't the lead dog, the view is always the same—and it isn't very pleasant!

Beware: Growth Should Never Be *the* Objective

This book is about how management can identify lasting opportunities, how the firm can profitably capitalize on them, and how to manage growth so that it will not backfire and cause the business's demise. It should be noted that growth should never be an end in itself. Growth should serve as a means to a higher end. Growth should be pursued only if it will strengthen the firm. This book distinguishes between healthy growth and jeopardizing growth. Jeopardizing growth usually comes in two forms: premature growth and excessive growth. Premature growth occurs when management does not have even the slightest semblance of an operating system in place to deal with additional volume. Without established systems and procedures, management is operating almost exclusively on a trial-and-error basis.

Excessive growth jeopardizes the firm because management is "driving beyond its headlights." When you drive beyond your headlights, you are traveling at such a high speed that by the time an object ahead of you is illuminated by your headlights, it's too late to stop. You either have to hit the object or swerve off the road to avoid it. With excessive or uncontrolled growth, management may have certain systems in place, but the rate of growth exceeds management's ability to stay current and to focus on the big picture.

Whenever management is unwilling or unable to control growth, things start falling through the cracks. Instead of saying "whoa!," sales, advertising, expansion, and credit-extending efforts go unbridled. Delivery commitments are made that cannot be honored, people are hired who are not qualified, and facilities are purchased or leased that may not fit the business's size or needs. Before long, product quality, customer service, employee relations, and cash reserves show the strain of uncontrolled growth. Without a plan or blueprint for constructive growth, management is not likely to say "No!" when the marketplace plays its seductive game of more, more, more!

With uncontrolled growth, too many compromises are made. What was to be an exceptional firm now develops a habit of and reputation for cutting corners. Goodwill, which is a fundamental prerequisite for achieving excellence, quickly degenerates into ill will. The firm starts to hemorrhage. Some of the best employees quit, suppliers tighten credit, and key accounts are lost. When management is seduced by delusions of grandeur, it often ends up raping the business of its virtues and its future. Osborn Computer, Worlds of Wonder, Pizza Time Theatres, and People Express are examples of growth gone astray. These four firms were once heralded by the media as outstanding new ventures. Unfortunately, they demonstrate the all-too-common "here today, gone tomorrow" syndrome that usually accompanies uncontrolled growth.

In 18 months, Adam Osborn started his computer company, generated more than $100 million in sales, and watched it career into bankruptcy. Donald Kingsborough's Worlds of Wonder had the distinction of having the most popular toy on the market for two consecutive years. Customers were nearly rioting in the stores because Kingsborough's firm could not meet demand. Worlds of Wonder's stock quickly dropped from $20 a share to 50 cents as it petitioned for financial reorganization.

An enviable 170 percent rate of growth per year over a five-year period put Nolan Bushnell's Pizza Time Theatres on *Inc.* magazine's list of the nation's 100 fastest-growing companies. This distinction came just before the firm went into Chapter 11. Donald Burr liquidated all of his personal assets to create People Express. His firm virtually rewrote the rule book on discount airfares while it captured significant market share from the established carriers. Unfortunately, the only thing that remains today are memories of his exciting concept for an all-new way to run an airline.

All four firms drove beyond their headlights. Their meteoric rise was surpassed only by their free fall into oblivion. Lasting success takes more than just good markets and good products—it takes good management to chart the path and control the throttle.

For every Apple Computer, Wal-Mart, and Microsoft, there are scores of firms that die early deaths. Ironically, corporate autopsies of relatively new ventures reveal death was not caused by factors beyond management's control. They died because management, particularly the founder, failed to prepare the firm for the long journey.

Bill Gates, the founder of Microsoft, is considered to be one of this country's most successful entrepreneurs. He was asked in a recent interview if he thought it was possible for today's start-ups to match Microsoft's success. Gates indicated opportunities like Amgen, Sun Microsystems, Microsoft, and MCI are out there. He stated, "You can hit the home run. But somebody can become quite wealthy creating a $20-million-a-year company. Some opportunities have a certain size and shouldn't be driven past that size."[3] There appears to be an optimal size for each firm where it stands at the brink but is still manageable. The key is to know what that level is and to stay within its tolerance limits.

Staying as Agile as David without Acting like a Goliath

The last few decades have demonstrated that bigger seldom is better. There are few true economies of scale. Classical economic theory may have postulated that economies of scale may exist in the production of goods: the more you produce, the lower the average cost per unit. Reality has shown that any economies of scale in production tend to be more than offset by diseconomies of management. Larger organizations seem to require a disproportionately larger number of managers and staff specialists. It is also apparent that the long-term commitment of funds to the capital equipment needed to achieve any economies of scale may actually jeopardize the future of the business. Any time management commits resources, it restricts the firm's flexibility. Firms that lack the ability to quickly modify their capabilities to meet the needs of an ever changing marketplace and keep pace with the accelerating technological revolution will be more than a day late and a dollar short—they will no longer exist.

Sam Walton sensed the evolving nature of the marketplace. He founded Wal-Mart to fill the gap in the market that larger firms had ignored. He recognized that K-Mart, the leading retailer in the United States at the time, would not establish stores in towns with populations of less than 50,000. Walton knew that with the right "formula" he could make money in towns with as few as 5,000 people. Walton observed there are a lot more towns with 5,000 people in them than towns with populations over 50,000. He also noted that Wal-Mart would be the dominant retail force in smaller towns. In many communities, the announcement that Wal-Mart will be opening a store is considered to be a historic event.

Throughout his tenure as CEO, Walton stressed the need to stay in tune with the changing trends in the market. He also stressed the need to create a retail organization that would blend customer service, employee relations, distribution efficiency, and state-of-the-art technology with strong financial management. He spent most of his time trying to make sure his firm reflected the qualities of smaller businesses rather than the aloofness of most large firms. Instead of building the world's tallest building in downtown Chicago as Sears did, Wal-Mart continued operating out of a one-story office warehouse in Bentonville, Arkansas. He wanted to be sure that his firm, which started out as "David," would not operate like a "Goliath."

Sam Walton made a point of visiting each store in the Wal-Mart chain at least once a year. He wanted to experience firsthand what was happening on the front lines as well as solicit his employees' (called associates) ideas about how Wal-Mart could be even better. He seemed to be obsessed with making sure Wal-Mart was in tune with the marketplace and that it was positioned to capitalize on changes as they occurred. He viewed each store as a laboratory for experimentation and innovation. Just before his death, he was asked if he thought it was possible for a Wal-Mart story to occur again. He responded: "Somewhere out there right now there's probably hundreds of thousands of someones—with enough good ideas to go all the way. It's all a matter of attitude and the capacity to constantly study and question the management of the business."[4]

Aim for Big Bull's-Eyes on Small to Midsize Targets

Economies of scale are usually based on standardization. Mass production worked well when there were mass markets, and everyone wanted the same thing. As Henry Ford put it "You can have any color you want as long as it is black!" With each passing day, the marketplace is moving more and more to a Baskin-Robbins 31 Flavors mosaic of minisegments in which nearly every customer wants—to borrow the Burger King slogan—"to have it their way." Yesterday's sunset of megafirms based on the concept of mass production is being followed by the sunrise of smaller, more entrepreneurially driven firms that are more agile and demonstrate the ability to customize almost everything they do. Ken Iverson's Nucor is a living testament that agility and customization are effective competitive weapons. While the steel industry continues to be plagued with a multitude of serious problems, Nucor's minimill concept has proven that lucrative niches may exist even in the gloomiest industries.

Just as the days of saturation bombing in war have been replaced by the use of "smart" bombs that can hit a specific target with pinpoint accuracy, today's and tomorrow's firms will also need to be able to demonstrate the ability to operate with a neurosurgeon's precision. It is ironic that just twenty years ago, small firms wanted to be like Fortune 500 firms. Today, large firms are desperately searching for ways to capture the qualities of the Inc. 500 firms. Firms that can identify market opportunities, quickly develop the appropriate offering, and have the management infrastructure in place so nothing falls through the cracks are destined to stay way out in front of firms that fail to discontinue past business practices. Entrepreneurially driven, adaptive, agile, "nichemanship" firms are what this book is all about.

Few things are certain about what the future may hold. Two things, however, are clear. First, the future will not be the same as the past. The past will not be prologue to the future. Second, it will not be business as usual! In the 1960s, when IBM was in its prime, Thomas Watson noted "There has never been any future in the status quo. In business, the status quo means inevitable failure."[5] What worked well yesterday will be less effective today, inappropriate tomorrow, and obsolete the day after that.

Future success will be contingent on the firm's ability to develop and sustain exceptional qualities. To develop an exceptional firm you must:

1. Focus on what can be rather than spend all your time celebrating your successes and emphasizing how far your firm has come.

2. Make the most out of what the firm presently has at its disposal and not take your customers, employees, and market position for granted. Be prepared for the long term yet try to make the most out of each day, each product, each territory, and each dollar.

3. Be entrepreneurial but avoid being seduced by short-term opportunities. Don't be tempted to implement quick fixes when you encounter problems.

4. Be committed to excellence. Resist the tendency to make compromises and to cut corners.

5. Recognize that it doesn't take a genius to spot opportunities. Be receptive to new ideas. Your employees and your customers may be the best source for new ideas.

6. Realize that if mismanagement is the number one reason for new venture failure, then mismanagement is probably also the number one reason for the lack of growth for your venture.

7. Be professional but do not create a sterile, emotionless, bureaucratic firm.

Concluding Comments: Let the Dance Begin!

This book is built around the premise that because there are no time-outs and no commercial breaks in business, only the most perceptive, resourceful, and agile firms will succeed. The entrepreneur/chief executive officer (E/CEO) of a relatively new venture faces a multitude of challenges. Because the E/CEO does not have a staff of MBAs or a cast of thousands to delegate projects, activities, and decisions to, there is little opportunity to network with people in or outside one's industry, read articles on the latest management techniques, or monitor emerging market trends. In this book, the ever changing marketplace as well as present and future competitors can be viewed as the elephants. Your immediate challenge is to learn how to dance with the elephants without being trampled to death. Your ultimate challenge is to develop your firm to the point where it is able to lead the elephants on the dance floor!

*If we are to achieve results never before
accomplished
We must employ methods never before
attempted.*   SIR FRANCIS BACON

Carpe Diem!

P.S. There are no road maps when you are out in front of the pack or at the forefront of an emerging market. It is for this reason that each of the following chapters concludes with a section called "Chief Executive Guidelines" by two or more CEOs. These CEOs have demonstrated the ability to dance with the elephants in their respective markets. Hopefully, their tips, insights, and cautions will help you navigate the rapids in your quest to develop an exceptional enterprise.

2

The Nature of New Venture Growth

It is a time for pathfinders and pioneers.
JOHN F. KENNEDY

Business schools have an intriguing way of addressing business growth. First, economists draw a demand curve that depicts the number of units that will be sold at varying price levels. Then marketing professors present the product life cycle, which resembles a bell-shaped curve. The life cycle depicts the introduction, growth, maturity, decline, and death of a product—or for that matter a market or even an industry.

Wait a minute...time out! The real world tells us a few things about business growth. Growth cannot be portrayed or explained with such simplicity. Academic models are nice, but they cannot reflect the dynamics and complexity of today's marketplace. If life was that simple, then all you would need to do is decrease your price to increase your firm's sales.

A number of start-ups fail because of simplistic reasoning. Their E/CEOs may have heard that advertising expenditures averaged 5 percent of sales in their industry. After they spent $10,000 on advertising, they wondered why they did not automatically have $200,000 in sales. The same reasoning may be applied to increasing the level of inventory, the amount of square feet for sales space, and the number of personnel. Increasing one

Portions of the material in this chapter originally appeared in the article "Preventing the Here Today, Gone Tomorrow New Venture Syndrome" by the author in *Business Forum*, Summer 1991, pp. 18–22. Reprinted with permission of California State University—Los Angeles.

or more of these factors will not necessarily produce a commensurate increase in sales.

E/CEOs need to recognize there is no such thing as a commodity! The economists' demand curves give the impression that price is the only factor affecting demand. A multitude of factors including management's actions influence the number of units sold by that firm and for that industry.

Few products, firms, or industries go through the classic bell-shaped life cycle. Products such as washing machines and refrigerators may plateau in the maturity stage for years or even decades. Other products may experience a moderate existence for years and then enjoy a whole renaissance as a result of a change in lifestyles. This was the case with portable radios. Just when everyone thought the market for portable radios was saturated, the people at Sony recognized there was a growing desire for a miniature yet high-quality sound system. Other firms failed to recognize that a growing number of people wanted better quality than was provided by conventional portable tape players. The jogging boom was also going at full speed. Sony came up with the Walkman, which transformed the whole market. The CD Discman that followed the Walkman demonstrated Sony's ability to thrive in a constantly evolving marketplace. Sony management's unwillingness to take the market for granted is one of the reasons why Sony has become an exceptional firm.

Products that have been around for years may experience a brief growth "spike" and then return to a moderate level of existence. This was the case with CB radios in the 1970s. Firms that were able to sense the growing popularity of CBs and capitalize on their widespread appeal enjoyed higher sales. Firms that geared up later than others were more than a day late and a dollar short. Other products and firms may not even leave the launchpad. Firms die when management is not in tune with the marketplace and is unable to make the right decisions.

Preventing the Here Today, Gone Tomorrow New Venture Syndrome

People tend to call a new venture a success when it enters the market with a bang and shakes up the industry. Many firms make it through the first few year's hurdles only to face eroding profitability, cutthroat competition, and waning demand. Unfortunately, their entrepreneurs' hopes of being included in the Inc. 500 and heralded as one of the movers and shakers of the decade are crushed as they are rudely awakened by the fact that success tends to vanish quickly for most firms. To put it in more popular terms, "the thrill of victory" is quickly followed by "the agony of defeat."

Why does success, if achieved, appear to be a here today, gone tomorrow phenomenon for so many new ventures? Maybe success should be defined as "something that is sustained over an extended period of time." For every Apple Computer, there are dozens of firms that crashed and burned soon after gaining celebrity status. Their meteoric ascent was matched by their free fall into oblivion. Relatively new ventures like Osborn Computers, Pizza Time Theatres, and Worlds of Wonder noted in the last chapter represent the tip of a very large iceberg composed of firms that danced momentarily in the media's limelight. They attracted a tidal wave of attention from the investment community but died early deaths or were relegated to a coma-like existence associated with Chapter 11—also known as financial reorganization.

Each new firm has its own story. In some cases, the firm was driven by a market opportunity but sabotaged by the total lack of concern for logistical support. In other cases, the management team failed to test the reality of the assumptions that served as the foundation for their firm's plans for expansion. Whatever the reasons, it is clear that the people at the helm did not prepare most of the here today, gone tomorrow firms for a long voyage. They did not prepare their firms for the inevitable changes that would occur in the marketplace and/or calibrate their firm's infrastructure so the various internal components would be synchronized. Ironically, corporate autopsies reveal death was not caused by factors beyond management's control. They died a premature death because management, particularly the entrepreneur, failed to prepare the venture for the long run.

Proper Positioning Is Essential for Growth

While this book will focus on the nature of business growth, it should be stated up front that each market is unique. Management needs to remember this at all times. If management does not position the firm properly, the firm may never grow. On the other hand, while certain products may enjoy success and then decline in the marketplace, this does not mean that the firm has to decline. If management is perceptive and agile—prepared to dance with the elephants—then it may be able to time its market offerings so that the relatively new venture succeeds. Conversely, unidimensional firms may be subject to considerable risk. If the firm is tied to one product, one customer, one market, or even one industry, then it runs the risk of having all its eggs in one basket. It also can suffer the opportunity cost of not seeing even better opportunities beyond its present efforts. This "management by braille" will be discussed later in the book.

Various scenarios are possible for firms that survive the start-up stage. Firms that make it through the start-up stage may then:

1. Die a quick death
2. Experience a slow death
3. Barely stay alive for years in a hand-to-mouth existence
4. Generate a modest level of profit but not enough to support any real growth
5. Reach a sufficient level of profit to justify the owners' investment and fund growth
6. Attain a high level of growth only to self-destruct from the problems associated with uncontrolled growth
7. Experience a high level of growth but not operate from a position of strength or provide a lucrative return on investment
8. Enjoy sustained growth and strength because management controlled the rate and nature of growth

This book will pay particular attention to how management can increase the odds of being the type of firm cited in the eighth scenario. It will also focus on how to avoid being the here today, gone tomorrow type of firm cited in the first, second, and sixth scenarios.

Controlled Growth Requires Both an External and an Internal Orientation

Controlled growth is two-dimensional. It has offensive and defensive dimensions. The offensive dimension deals with identifying opportunities for growth and anticipating what the firm must be able to do to capitalize on each opportunity before it is time to dance with a new set of elephants. The defensive dimension involves not making mistakes that could jeopardize the firm's existence. Exceptional firms thereby practice what is called "bifocal" management. While management is looking to what may be on the horizon, it also needs to keep one eye on the present so little falls through the cracks.

It should be apparent by now that this book is built on the premise that your firm will develop into an exceptional firm only to the extent you are prepared to manage its growth. Growth will be affected by economic conditions, government regulations, and the nature of competition. But in the final analysis, management will be the primary factor in determining the future success of the venture.

When a firm is experiencing rapid growth, people usually say the firm is fortunate because it is in a "growth industry." Theodore Levitt makes an interesting observation about supposed growth industries. According to Levitt, "There is no such thing as a growth industry. . .Industries that assume themselves to be riding some automatic growth escalator invariably descend into stagnation."[1] Levitt argues that there are no growth industries; there are only industries experiencing a growth stage.

Even though an industry may be in a growth stage doesn't mean every firm in that industry will automatically grow. The saying "all boats rise with a rising tide" does not always apply to business ventures. An improperly positioned or poorly managed firm can fail even in an industry experiencing significant and rapid growth. It is also possible for a business to grow in a mature or even a declining market or industry.

Concluding Comments: Managing Growth Is like Playing Hockey

The key to success is being at the right place at the right time with the right capabilities and the right resources. This can be called the Gretzky approach to managing growth. A few years ago a sports commentator asked Wayne Gretzky to explain how he had become such a successful hockey player. The commentator wondered how Gretzky could be so good. After all, Gretzky wasn't known for being the fastest, the strongest, or the best shooter in the league. Gretzky replied that during play everyone else tends to be playing the puck where it is while he looks at the flow of play and anticipates where the puck *will* be. Then he skates to that point on the ice.

Gretzky suggested that if you anticipate where the puck will be and put yourself there before anyone else, then you usually have a clear shot at the goal. He noted that when you're in that position and have your stick ready, you don't have to be world's greatest shooter to score a goal! This is what controlled growth is all about. This is what this book is all about.

To every man there comes in his lifetime that special moment when he is figuratively tapped on the shoulder and offered the chance to do a very special thing, unique to him and fitted to his talent; what a tragedy if that moment finds him unprepared or unqualified for the work that could have been his finest hour.
WINSTON CHURCHILL

CHIEF EXECUTIVE GUIDELINES

Names: Bobby Kolb, President; and Michael Ingram, Vice President
Company: Preventive Maintenance Inc.
Product/Service: On-line Leak Sealing/Environmental Monitoring/Line Freezing
Sales: $2,000,000   *Number of Employees:* 30

General Guidelines: When it comes to positioning the firm to capitalize on growth opportunities and controlling growth, the E/CEO should keep the following tips in mind:

1. Stay personally involved with all areas of operation within the organization.
2. Plan and set realistic sales budgets and projections.
3. Involve existing staff members in all areas of future growth decisions.
4. Set operation up to operate at maximum performance levels with the least amount of operating expenses.
5. Maintain and update technical and safety training.

Proceed with Caution Guidelines:

1. Don't try to do everything yourself—delegate responsibilities.
2. Establish a savings plan and adhere to it.
3. Do not overstaff support personnel for future growth—use only the bare minimum of personnel involved in growth start-up.
4. Maintain an honest and close relationship with your bank.
5. Establish detailed accounting programs at the onset of the firm.

And I Would Be Particularly Careful Not to:

1. Fool yourself with growth success and waste money—there will be slowdowns!
2. Become so self-absorbed with business as to forget family and personal life.
3. Forget the lean days of start-up operations. You need to approach growth with the same cost savings attitude.

CHIEF EXECUTIVE GUIDELINES

Name: Christopher Fish, Owner
Company: Northwest Industrial Coatings
Product/Service: Industrial Coating Products/Services
Sales: $1,200,000   *Number of Employees:* 22
Awards/Distinctions:

1. Small Business Award for Oregon, 1991

2. Profiled in *Nation's Business* and *Independent Business.*

General Guidelines: When it comes to positioning the firm to capitalize on growth opportunities and controlling growth, the E/CEO should keep the following tips in mind:

1. Budget the company and yourself in regards to: (a) available time; (b) available capital to fund present load; and (c) available capital to fund present product growth

2. Reserve capital to fund new product development

3. Listen to your customer—"The feedback can be eye-opening."

Proceed with Caution Guidelines:

1. Grow slower than we did. We grew at an average rate of 25 percent per year.

2. Expand reserve capital much sooner.

3. Set company policies and procedures for both customers and employees as early as possible.

4. Even though your intent is good, do not over obligate yourself. This may be the hardest thing to learn.

And I Would Be Particularly Careful Not to:

1. Expand at the risk of "loss of quality and service" if word of mouth is to be any part of your marketing.

2. Allow any one customer to become too large in relation to your other customers. Have a diversified customer base. Never have all your eggs in one basket.

3

The Managerial Stages of Growth

*When you are growing very fast, you can't
afford to outdistance your management.*[1]
JIM SINEGAL, CEO OF COSTCO WHOLESALE

In an ideal world, growth would be predictable and occur in a linear fashion. For most firms, however, growth resembles a toddler taking its first steps. While the desire to cross the room is there, the child is destined to teeter, stumble, and fall. The key to controlled growth is the ability to sense in advance what is needed and to develop the ability to function at the new level without major problems.

Managing growth is not a simple process. Growth rarely involves doing more of the same on a larger scale. Growth brings complexity and requires adaptation. Entrepreneurs who successfully navigate their firms through the rapids of the start-up stage find that the rapids of managing growth can be even wilder. Managing growth usually requires an entirely different blend of skills at each stage of evolution. It certainly requires different skills from the ones required in the start-up stage. The Seven Stages of New Venture Evolution model indicates the various levels of business growth. This model will be the basis for the remainder of this and other chapters (see Figure 3-1).

Figure 3-1. The Seven Stages of New Venture Evolution.

Stage One: Entrepreneurship

In the start-up stage, entrepreneurial skills are needed to identify one or more market opportunities. The ability to sense an unmet need in the marketplace, to put together a skeletal business plan, to raise sufficient capital, and to provide a product or service to meet that need are essential skills. The ability to envision a venture where none existed before and then to transform the concept into a living reality are rare and valuable qualities.

No one expects the business to function with the utmost precision or to follow the business plan, if one exists, to its finest detail. The ability to sense what needs to be done and the ability to do it are the two things that matter. This stage places a premium on flexibility and resourcefulness.

Few things go as planned in the entrepreneurship stage. It is for this reason that the entrepreneur needs to wear most of the hats. No one else may have the big picture. Everything is being done for the first time. Perfection is not the issue. Trial and error is commonplace. At this stage, the entrepreneur is merely trying to hit the target (i.e., generate enough revenue to make it through the year). The entrepreneur may not even be trying to hit the bull's-eye (profitability). At this stage the dance with the elephants is more a matter of how to avoid being trampled to death than how to look graceful.

Stage Two: More Hands on Deck
Are Needed to Support Growth

The fact that the firm survived the start-up stage indicates that there must be a market for the firm's products or services—without revenue, the firm would have died. Management's concern now shifts from getting the firm up and running to generating positive cash flow and a sufficient level of profit to finance additional growth. The focus is now on supporting higher levels of sales.

Management now directs its attention to what it will take to fulfill the firm's potential. Survival is not the issue; growth is now paramount. Instead of making any major modifications in its original product or service, the firm attempts to sell as much as it can of what it already offers. The entrepreneur seems to be preoccupied with more, more, more rather than better, better, better!

If the firm has accurately sensed an unmet need, then more people are hired to make or provide the service. The firm's ranks of hired hands grow to meet and/or foster additional sales. The emphasis on securing sales often borders on reckless abandon. Little attention is placed on managing sales. The firm will do whatever it takes to make a sale. No thought is given to saying "whoa!" Everyone works crazy hours, overtime goes through the roof, and overnight deliveries are now the rule.

If fatal flaws existed in the firm's basic business concept, then the firm would not have made it to this stage. Things start falling through the cracks, however, with the increase in sales. Mistakes that were expected in the start-up stage are usually tolerated at this stage. Management is quick to rationalize various things falling through the cracks as an acceptable price to be paid for meeting additional demand. Little mistakes of omission now become habitual. Little mistakes when done often can cause big problems. When the firm is experiencing rapid growth, things like efficiency, quality control, accounts receivable, payroll deposits, and the like usually are not at the center of management's attention. It is easy for a firm as it enters a larger set of rapids to get so caught up in a "paddle, paddle, paddle" frenzy that its management fails to check to see if the raft has been torn and is taking on water.

Many emerging firms do not survive the rapids. Of those that do, few truly benefit from the growth. While the survivors have seen their sales grow by leaps and bounds, few enjoy a commensurate level of profits or overall strength. Some firms are so overextended that they are flirting with bankruptcy. Other firms may have caused so much ill will with their vendors, employees, and customers in the process that they have lost the very qualities that provided the basis for growth in the first place.

Growth must be managed from a two-dimensional perspective. Not only must management prepare for growth; it must also be sure that its house is in order so little falls through the cracks. When management fails to manage growth, management is sowing the seeds for the firm's destruction.

Stage Three: Supervisors Are Hired and Delegation May Begin

This stage represents a major step in the evolution of the firm. It begins when the E/CEO acknowledges that he or she cannot make every decision. It is time for the E/CEO to end the juggling act. The E/CEO cannot be in all places at one time. Other people are needed to supervise the firm's basic activities. The firm has grown to the point where the span of control and the variety of daily and weekly tasks exceed the E/CEO's time and attention.

E/CEOs tend to be reluctant to establish supervisory positions because it means other people will be making decisions that will affect the viability of the firm. The first supervisory position is usually established to oversee the production of goods or the provision of services. This area tends to mirror the growth in volume, so it is the most likely area for the firm's first supervisor. With continued growth, a supervisor may be appointed to coordinate sales personnel. An office manager may also be appointed to oversee all bookkeeping activities, coordinate payroll, and monitor accounts payable and accounts receivable.

The E/CEO may actually be the cause of the firm's problems at this stage. The E/CEO may even impede further growth. If the E/CEO fails to establish supervisory positions, then growth may suffer because too many things fall through the cracks. If the E/CEO does establish supervisory positions, then three other types of problems may arise. First, the E/CEO may not give the supervisors enough authority to do their jobs. If the production supervisor does not have the authority to hire and fire as well as to schedule production, then that person is a supervisor in name only. The same applies to sales activities and the operation of the office.

In most cases, the E/CEO does not want the supervisor to embark on major initiatives. Supervisors are usually expected to operate within a set of parameters set by the E/CEO. In a sense, the supervisors tend to be there to make sure their respective operations make it through the day. Important decisions will continue to be made by the E/CEO.

Second, E/CEOs tend to appoint the best or most senior worker to the position of supervisor rather than hire a veteran supervisor from outside the firm. E/CEOs tend to fall prey to the Peter Principle. Its author, Lawrence J. Peter, notes, "In time, every post tends to be occupied by an employee who is incompetent to carry out its duties."[2] Different positions require different skills. The fact that a person does a good job with a piece of machinery does not mean that he or she will be able to coordinate a group of employees, develop an appropriate schedule, or be current with OSHA, EPA, and EEO guidelines. The same situation is likely to be true when you make a salesperson the sales director and a bookkeeper the office manager. E/CEOs are courting disaster when they promote someone to a supervisory position and give them authority to make key decisions without proper training or prior experience. E/CEOs need to be aware of the Peter Principle when they hire, place, and promote people.

The third problem area arises when additional supervisory positions are established to oversee the sales function and office operations. Supervisors tend to be responsible for their respective areas. The functional division of the firm creates interdepartmental coordination problems. When the E/CEO was in charge of everything, he or she could make decisions on the spot. Coordination problems and turf battles were minimal. This stage of evolution may be a source of considerable frustration for the E/CEO. After all, the supervisors were supposed to make the E/CEO's life easier.

This stage in the growth process has major implications for the future of the firm. If the E/CEO fails to establish supervisory positions, then the firm has little chance for continued growth. The firm will not be competitive if it is run as a one-manager enterprise. While many E/CEOs consider themselves to be all-knowing, no one can be in ten places at one time. If the E/CEO fails to staff the positions with capable people, then the E/CEO and the firm will suffer.

This stage represents the E/CEO's first managerial challenge. Management is defined as "achieving results with and through others." If the E/CEO is unable to delegate decision-making authority to the supervisors or lacks the ability to orchestrate the operating divisions within the firm, then the E/CEO may need to step aside and let someone else run the firm.

Stage Four: Bringing in Professional Managers

When the firm entered the second stage of growth, the E/CEO hired people to serve as additional sets of hands. As the firm approached stage three, it was apparent that the E/CEO needed to establish supervisory positions to oversee the growing number of employees and to minimize the chances that things would fall through the cracks. In stage four, the firm has reached the point where hiring more employees and appointing a few more supervisors will not be sufficient to meet demand and remain competitive. As noted earlier, there are no economies of scale for management.

Three factors now compound the challenges facing management. First, the size and resulting complexity of the firm require a higher level of managerial sophistication. In stage three, the E/CEO may have been able to orchestrate the handful of supervisors and be personally involved in even moderate decisions. The firm is now at the point where the E/CEO cannot stop to make daily operating decisions in each functional area. Moreover, the E/CEO may not have the appropriate knowledge or experience to make those decisions.

Second, the firm may have had a market niche to itself. Other firms may have been so preoccupied with their existing customers and markets that they did not even notice that a segment had been neglected. The firm may now have grown to the size that competitors see it as more than just an upstart. Competition may take note of the gap in the market that the firm is serving. Competitors may now try to capture some of that segment.

As the first firm to enter this segment, the firm did not have to be especially good to attract customers. As someone once said, "If no one delivered pizza to a rural community . . . how good would the pizza have to be if you were the first business to offer delivery?" The answer to the question is: "It would have to be reasonably priced, arrive within an hour, and not be stuck to the cardboard box!" This may also have been the case for the firm up to now.

The firm may have grown due to unmet demand rather than because it was doing an exceptional job meeting the market segment's particular needs. Too many firms are blinded by their rapid growth to recognize that they may not be serving the market well. The firm may have just been providing a "reasonable" offering. Reasonable, however, means that few customers are delighted. The firm was able to capitalize on the market gap because no one else was there to serve that segment.

If the firm is not providing exactly what the market segment wants, then a gap still exists for other firms to enter the market segment. If the market was growing at some astronomical rate, then the entry of additional firms may not have an immediate impact on the firm. In markets that are experiencing a phenomenal rate of growth, most firms concentrate on capitalizing on the growth that comes with additional customers. In most markets, however, a significant part of one firm's growth must come at the expense of other firms. Gaining a larger share of the market only comes from attracting customers from other firms. The less the firm delights its customers, the easier it will be for its competitors to steal them!

Getting the Firm's Managerial Act Together

As the firm enters stage four, it becomes apparent that getting through the day doing a "reasonable job" of serving the market will not assure continued growth or even survival. The firm's honeymoon with the market segment is over—reasonable pizza will no longer cut it. The firm has put out a welcome mat for other firms and has become a target for firms entering the market. The firm now must sharpen its competitive offering.

The firm's increasing size and complexity now require a much higher level of sophistication. The firm needs to be more in tune with the market, and it needs to use a state-of-the-art approach for managing the firm. Until this stage, the firm's management systems were merely what the E/CEO had done and what the supervisors were able to improvise. As Peter Drucker notes, firms that want to prepare for tomorrow must be willing to slough off yesterday.[3] In stage four, the E/CEO must bite the bullet and change the way the firm is managed.

The third factor associated with entering this stage of growth is directly related to the preceding point. Even if the E/CEO recognizes the need to adopt a more sophisticated approach to managing the firm, it quickly becomes apparent that no one in the firm—including the E/CEO—may possess the appropriate level of education or experience. The firm has been run the way a pilot flies a vintage biplane. Flying with one hand on the rudder without instruments at 80 miles an hour will not be good enough to compete in today's global marketplace. Given the electronic and technological revolution, things now take place with supersonic speed. The marketplace will show no mercy to firms that are out of step. While the firm may have been successful enough to make it to the fourth stage of growth, the firm's squadron of supervisors is usually ill-equipped to meet the challenges associated with competing in the fast lane. Because they were brought up through the ranks, they do not have the experience or level of sophistication necessary to develop the management systems needed for the firm to remain competitive.

While the supervisors were busy dancing with the elephants in stage three, they did not take the time to enroll in the evening program of the closest business school or to attend management development seminars. The E/CEO's lack of experience and education may also be showing at this stage. Trial-and-error management must come to an end. It is time for the firm to adopt a "professional management" approach to doing business. It also means that professional managers must be brought into the firm. The increase in size, complexity, and competition associated with stage four will not permit the supervisors to learn on the job. A whole new level of management above them must be created and staffed.

In stage one, the E/CEO did all the selling. In stage two, the E/CEO hired one or more people to assist in selling the firm's products or services. In stage three, a salesperson may have been appointed to supervise sales activities and sales personnel. Now, the firm needs to have a director, vice president, or person of similar caliber to manage the firm's overall marketing efforts. The firm needs the type of person who can work closely with the E/CEO or take the lead in developing the firm's overall marketing program. If growth is to continue, then the firm may need to evolve beyond its one-product/service, one-market orientation. It will need to develop a multidimensional marketing mix orientation. The "sell, sell, sell" mentality must be elevated to a true marketing orientation.

The same situation applies to the firm's production and financial accounting functions. A production manager is needed to provide direction for the supervisor(s) in that area and to synchronize the various production or service-providing components of the firm. Supervision of the work force will continue to be important, but without a professional manager the firm is not likely to move toward a total quality management system, to determine the optimal level of inventory, or to be up to speed with OSHA and EPA statutes. A chief financial officer or controller-level individual may also be needed above the firm's in-house accountant(s). Without a professional manager, it is not likely that pension plans will receive sufficient attention, cash flow carefully analyzed, or the debt structure optimized.

If the E/CEO tries to continue with just the present group of supervisors, then the firm's future may be in jeopardy. It is not likely that an inexperienced sales supervisor will be able to develop and coordinate a marketing program that will take the firm from $2 to $20 million in sales in the next five years.

The firm's future could also be at risk if the E/CEO tries to save a few dollars by cutting corners on talent. The E/CEO of a moderate-sized venture indicated that he would rather hire two young and less experienced managers at $25,000 than spend $50,000 to hire an experienced midlevel manager. That firm seems to be in a perpetual "fire fighting" mode.

Firms that are prepared to invest in talent usually benefit from that investment. The most successful firms invest in talent before they need it so the key people are in place and acclimated when their firms need their knowledge, experience, and skills. These firms are better equipped to maintain the rate of growth. Their people are not intimidated by the five-year sales target of $20 million or competing against larger firms. They are brought on board to establish state-of-the-art systems that will bring method to the madness. Their experience and ideas lay the foundation for the strength that will be needed to successfully meet the market's evolving needs. Only then will the firm have a chance to be the leader in the marketplace. Firms that cut corners are almost destined to continue a crisis-to-crisis type of existence.

Rarely does the process of introducing professional systems go smoothly. Most E/CEOs are reluctant to delegate important decisions. If the E/CEO does delegate various decisions to other personnel, however, it does not mean the E/CEO will automatically agree with their decisions. Different educational backgrounds and experiences usually elicit different perceptions and different decisions. It is not unusual for the E/CEO to insist that all managers sing from the E/CEO's sheet of music when they are hired.

This usually causes some tension between the E/CEO and the professional managers. If the E/CEO has a clear vision of what the firm should be, then there will be fewer differences.

Animosity may arise from the supervisors who do not get promoted to the positions the new "outsiders" now have above them. Problems may also arise when people at lower levels and certain customers who were accustomed to dealing directly with the E/CEO are now expected to go through proper channels. People, including the E/CEO, who dealt with others as the need arose now have to follow standard operating procedures.

Most E/CEOs hire professional managers only as the need or crisis arises. The irony of the situation is that many E/CEOs do not have the depth or breadth of business experience to know which decisions need to be made to move the firm to a higher level. This further inhibits the selection and utilization of professional managers. The infusion of talent also has an immediate impact on the firm's cash flow. Managerial talent doesn't come cheap. Professional managers may also expect a piece of the equity. This may cause considerable problems with people who have been with the firm for some time. A portion of the firm's success may be attributed to their sweat equity. There may also be some animosity by employees toward the people who are hired to work with them. As more people are brought into the firm, the people who have been there all along feel they are being taken for granted. There is also a question of how well and how soon the new professionals will be able to adjust to the firm's specific technology, market(s), personalities, and culture. The E/CEO needs to recognize that there is a tendency for professional managers to manage the firm as they did in their last firm rather than modify their approaches to fit the unique situation they are now facing.

Some people who have been with the firm a while may welcome the more systematic way of doing business. Other people may yearn for a return to the good old days that may have existed just a year earlier. The E/CEO who was once ever present and involved in every decision may now be relegated to spending a considerable time reviewing financial data. Unfortunately, he or she still may not be on top of every dimension of the firm. It is not unusual for the E/CEO to develop an identity crisis at this stage of the firm's evolution.

Stage Five: Building the Management Team

The firm should be in a position to progress to stage five if the E/CEO was able to delegate the key divisional decisions to the professional managers, and if they were able to implement state-of-the-art approaches to strengthening their respective areas. This stage of evolution involves the challenge of whether the E/CEO can get the managers to work together as a team. Résumés and references are nice, but the truest test of professional talent rests in the ability to function as a member of the management team. Until this stage, everything may have been done on a functional basis with each manager addressing his or her respective area. The firm is now at the point where the functional systems need to be integrated into an overall business system. Each manager may have been hired for a special orientation; now they need to work together. Management may now attempt to lay the foundation for the firm's first comprehensive business plan. Decisions need to be made according to a plan rather than relying as before solely on the perspective of the E/CEO.

The comprehensive business plan also represents a deliberate effort to change from what may have been a reactive approach to doing business to a systematic and proactive way of doing business. Stage four dealt with hiring professional managers so that each functional area would get its act together. Attention was directed to reducing the points where the firm may have been vulnerable to competition or susceptible to major operating mistakes. In stage five, attention is directed to getting the whole firm's act together so that it can operate from a position of strength. Synergy is the issue in this stage. Every effort is directed to assuring that each area is functioning to its potential and that all the functional areas are integrated in a synergistic fashion.

The E/CEO and the management team now may spend some of their time together fixing the operational side of the firm that has eluded the E/CEO's attention. These areas include but are not limited to developing retirement or pension programs, initiating training and development processes, conducting performance reviews, evaluating various types of incentives, and analyzing the overall pay scale. However, it is at this stage that the management team should direct more attention to managing by objectives, analyzing markets, identifying staff requirements, and estimating future capital needs. The E/CEO may have been able to dance with the elephants in the early years; now it is time for the management team to learn how to dance with them as well.

The E/CEO must serve as the firm's chief executive officer at this stage of the firm's evolution. The challenge is whether the E/CEO has the managerial wherewithal to gain the respect of the professional managers. Hiring them and letting them run their respective departments in stage four may have challenged the E/CEO's ability to delegate. In stage five, the E/CEO must demonstrate that he or she is qualified to serve as the firm's chief "executive" officer.

If the E/CEO lacks the ability or the desire to serve as the firm's chief executive officer, then he or she should step aside and bring in someone who can serve in that capacity. Many E/CEOs hire a general manager to help coordinate the firm's various operations. As noted in Chapter 1, this is what happened when Steven Jobs, the cofounder of Apple Computer, recognized the need to bring John Sculley in from PepsiCo to orchestrate the firm's management team. Sculley's executive-level experience and skills were critical to Apple at that stage of its development. Jobs's awareness of the need to make the management change and the decision to have Michael Spindler succeed Sculley years later demonstrate the importance of having the right person at helm at the right time.

Stage Six: Managing the Strategic Side of the Firm

If the E/CEO is successful in getting the professional managers to manage the firm as an integrated whole, then the E/CEO may believe that he or she has fulfilled the responsibility of being the firm's chief executive officer. The firm's operating systems may be taking growth in stride, and few things may be falling through the cracks. The E/CEO may be tempted to relax because the firm now has its managerial act together. Management has made the transition from getting through the day without a major crisis; now it is concerned with implementing the firm's annual operating plan.

Many E/CEOs feel that when they have made it through stage five their job becomes one of making sure that things remain smooth. It would be easy for the E/CEO to sit back and say, "I have learned to dance with the elephants!" But as John Gardner points out, "Self-congratulation should be taken in small doses."[4] If the firm wants to evolve to a higher plane of strength and success, then the E/CEO must learn a new dance. To paraphrase Peter Drucker, "Firms that fail to plan for the future will have no future."

Management's efforts in stage five were designed to make sure everything in the operational side of the firm was being done right. This is why the firm developed its annual business plan. Stage six involves moving from an annual perspective to a multiyear or what is termed a "strategic management" perspective.

The challenge in stage six is centered around whether the E/CEO can develop a strategic orientation to complement the firm's operating systems. The professional managers may have a good idea of how to run their respective operations. They may even be functioning as an integrated management team. The E/CEO now must develop a strategic orientation. The E/CEO then needs to be able to blend strategic management with operational management so the firm utilizes bifocal management. The firm will continue to grow only if the E/CEO can blend these two perspectives.

If the E/CEO and the management team lack a strategic orientation, then the firm may be relegated to the status of a follower or a merely reactive type of existence. Fine tuning may be essential to maintaining a competitive edge in stable markets, but in what Peter Drucker describes as this "Age of Discontinuity," firms that want to be leaders will need to make major changes, launch bold initiatives, capitalize on emerging opportunities, and do what is necessary to prevent or minimize potential problems.

Economists have an interesting way of differentiating time horizons. In the short run, few things can be changed. All management can do is make the most out of what it already has. The firm needs to make the most of its present products or services, markets, people, and financial resources. In the intermediate term, some things can be changed. The firm may expand into additional territories, add new models and services, and hire new people. The present work force can even receive additional training. In the long run, however, anything is possible because everything can be changed. The firm can enter entirely different markets, develop and utilize new technology, and completely transform the nature of its business.

Without a strategic orientation, the firm may be destined to continue doing tomorrow what it is doing today. If the world was totally static, this might not be that bad. However, today's marketplace is anything but static. As noted earlier, management must recognize the fact that what worked well yesterday will be less effective today, inappropriate tomorrow, and obsolete the day after tomorrow.

Strategic management forces management to ask "What business(es) should we be in?" Most firms use a linear or incremental growth strategy. They tend to use what they are presently doing as the foundation for what they will do in the years to come. Unfortunately, this strategy doesn't work well in times of discontinuity. Most firms are now in mature industries. There may be pockets of opportunity in mature markets, but it is apparent that in the years ahead it will be more difficult for firms to prosper in saturated markets where competition may look like hand-to-hand combat.

The E/CEO Must Change the Way the Firm Is Managed

Stage six involves three specific changes in the way the firm is managed. First, management must adopt a strategic orientation. Second, management must blend strategic and operational management into bifocal management. The third area involves the role that the firm's board of directors should play in the direction of the firm. The board has not been discussed until this point because this tends to be one of the most ignored aspects of managing a firm. If a firm is incorporated, then it is required to have a board of directors. State statutes require only the most rudimentary functions be performed by the board. While boards may be required to draft bylaws, hold meetings, and keep minutes, no statute requires the board to adopt a strategic perspective or ensure that the firm is a leader in its field.

The role of the board of directors and its relationship with the firm's E/CEO will be discussed in Chapter 9. It needs to be pointed out here, however, that without a fully functioning board of directors the firm is not likely to have a strategic orientation, maintain its competitive edge, and fulfill its potential. Even if the venture is not incorporated, an advisory board should be established to function in the same manner as a board of directors.

Most E/CEOs are hesitant to have the type of board their business needs because boards should function as a reality check. If the board is properly charged, then it should ensure that: (1) there is a clear sense of where the firm is to be in five to seven years, (2) the firm has a comprehensive business plan for getting there, (3) the firm's plan is being updated on a regular basis, and (4) the desired results are being achieved.

The board is there to add value to the management of the firm. While the board should not be directly involved in operating matters, it can help the E/CEO identify opportunities and anticipate problems that may be just around the bend. The board thereby represents an essential component of the sixth stage of growth.

The sixth stage represents a new challenge for the E/CEO. If the E/CEO is unable or unwilling to evolve, then the firm will not evolve. If such a situation arises, then the E/CEO should step aside so someone else will guide the firm. If the E/CEO doesn't see the light, then the directors should act as trustees for the firm and replace the E/CEO. This may seem a bit rash, but if the firm is serious about being a leader, then it needs to have a CEO who is able to lead the firm.

Stage Seven: Regaining the Entrepreneurial Spirit

The seventh stage of growth will be discussed briefly in this chapter because few firms evolve to this level. Most firms either level off and operate at one of the earlier stages or they experience a crisis that causes their demise. The seventh stage represents a major point in the evolution of the firm. While the linear or incremental strategy may be an effective avenue for continued growth, strategic management usually dictates that at least part of a firm's future growth will have to involve significant change.

E/CEOs who are serious about preparing their firms for the future need to recommit themselves and their firms to the entrepreneurial growth strategy that characterized their firms when they were conceived. The firm may need to look for emerging markets and emerging technology rather than try to milk some marginal existence from saturated markets if it is to sustain or regain a high level of growth.

The last few stages have emphasized the need for the firm to professionalize its approach, develop the management team, and balance strategic and operational management. While these endeavors are important, sustained growth and success in the years ahead, however, may be directly related to whether the firm can restore or preserve its original entrepreneurial qualities. If the E/CEO wants the firm to be recognized as a true leader in the marketplace, then the firm will have to be at the leading edge. It cannot operate in the shadow of other more entrepreneurial firms.

It is ironic that the firm that once needed to professionalize its approach to doing business now tries to regain its entrepreneurial flair. There seems to be a catch-22 when it comes to the managerial evolution of the firm. Management's efforts to professionalize the firm often squash the entrepreneurial spirit. This is why so many Fortune 500 firms have been trying to be more "intrapreneurial" in recent years.

It is difficult to regain the entrepreneurial spirit once it has been lost. To paraphrase Thomas Watson, as CEO of IBM, "You can tame a wild duck but you can't make a tame duck wild." Continuous entrepreneurial capability will be directly related to whether the venture adopts an entrepreneurial rather than a linear or incremental growth strategy. Success will also depend on whether management is able to create or maintain a corporate culture that supports entrepreneurial endeavors.

Entrepreneurial endeavors take considerable time and resources. If the E/CEO and the management team are spending all their time dancing with strategic and operational elephants, then it is unlikely that their attention will also be directed to entrepreneurial endeavors. This is unfortunate because opportunities only knock once. Opportunities do not wait for firms to get their acts together. It is a shame that firms that may be seeking avenues for growth may not be in a position to see the windows of opportunity opening and closing around them.

The major challenge facing the E/CEO at this stage is similar to the challenge of the initial entrepreneurship stage. E/CEOs may have the entrepreneurial spirit, but if they are unable to operationalize that spirit by developing tangible avenues whereby opportunities are identified and action plans are developed, and resources committed to capitalize on them, then life will be frustrating for everyone.

Concluding Comments: The Dance Never Ends!

Two major points should be evident in this chapter. First, the firm must evolve if it is to be able to cultivate and capitalize on the almost unlimited number of opportunities that lie ahead. Second, the E/CEO's perspective, skills, and approach to managing the firm and the people in it will have to evolve if he or she is to lead the firm. E/CEOs are advised to anticipate emerging opportunities and to prepare for them before they arrive. E/CEOs also need to be objective about their own abilities so that when the Peter Principle starts to apply to them, they either rise to the occasion by gaining the skills they need to lead the firm or they have the sense to get out of the way.

The best executive is the one who has sense enough to pick good men to do what he wants done, and self-restraint enough to keep from meddling with them while they do it.
　　　　　　　　　　　　　　THEODORE ROOSEVELT

CHIEF EXECUTIVE GUIDELINES

Name: Ed Mayorga, President
Company: R & E Electronics Inc.
Product/Service: Voice/Data Telecommunications Services
Awards/Distinctions:

1. Ernst & Young "Entrepreneur of the Year"

2. Chivas Regal National "Entrepreneur of the Year"

3. U.S. Small Business Administration District "Small and Minority Business Person of the Year"

General Guidelines: When it comes to managing a growing firm (developing a management team and how he or she spends his or her time), the E/CEO should keep the following tips in mind:

1. Be realistic in setting goals: no wish lists.
2. Establish and maintain the corporate culture.
3. Hire those individuals today who can address tomorrow's three-year plan.
4. Stay lean.
5. Give responsible people responsibility.

Proceed with Caution Guidelines:

1. Spend more time and effort on ensuring proper capitalization.
2. Ensure better communication within the management team.
3. Of the hours you allocate for business, spend more in areas that would make the business money.
4. Stay focused.
5. Establish more partnerships and teaming agreements.

And I Would Be Particularly Careful Not to:

1. Be convinced that the company must buy into a project for the prestige, track record, and so on.
2. Ignore cash flow.
3. Accept a financial pro forma without asking tough questions.
4. Be overconfident.

CHIEF EXECUTIVE GUIDELINES

Name: Mike Weaver, Chairman and Chief Executive Officer
Company: Hand Held Products Inc.
Product/Service: Custom Portable Computer Products
Awards/Distinctions: Profiled in *Nation's Business.*

General Guidelines: When it comes to managing a growing firm, the E/CEO should keep the following tips in mind:

1. The E/CEO is responsible for an integrated vision for the future. It is easier to hire good managers to grow the business when needed than it is to hire a good visionary. Expect to be the visionary for your

company until you retire unless you are fortunate to grow some in house over the years. When you discover visionaries in house, back them in every way possible. They are your future.

2. Remember that a company is really a process that is evolving not only in terms of size of sales, number of people, and the like but in terms of what the company does to add value to the world. Technology changes, visions improve, new opportunities increase with age and exposure, and your company must evolve to take advantage of new opportunities when they fit your vision.

3. Never stop being opportunistic. No matter what your size, you can grow by staying alert for market or customer opportunities that add significant value to your company. They sometimes just appear. You need to be able to recognize them and act in a timely manner.

4. The customers have the money you need to succeed, and they expect you to add value in exchange for it. Know where your value-added originates in the perception of your customers, and know how each element of your company builds it either directly or indirectly. Communicate that knowledge through your management clearly and often.

Proceed with Caution Guidelines:

1. As your span of management exceeds five to seven, expect challenges. When you are forced into "middle management," expect more challenges. The trend continues as you grow. Communicate your vision and value-added guidelines throughout the organization regularly. That is the glue that helps keep things together over time. Eventually the process evolves into a corporate culture.

2. When you feel something is out of line, trust your instincts and check it out carefully. Challenge your managers to provide details supporting their recommendations. You do your homework so make sure others do likewise. It is a mind-set that must be reinforced regularly.

3. Avoid sales opportunities lacking in the margins you need. You cannot buy business and sustain growth.

And I Would Be Particularly Careful Not to:

1. Employ a set of hands rather than a mind.

2. Change either your vision or concept of value-added without clearly understanding why it is right to do so.

3. Ignore your cash flow at any time.

4. Think you can do it all by yourself. There are not enough hours in a day for that to be true.

5. Burn out physically or mentally.

6. Forget why you are doing all this in the first place.

4

Problems Associated with Growth

*Prudence sometimes dictates easing back on
the corporate throttle to give employees and
internal systems time to adjust.*[1]
WILLIAM E. SHEELINE

Growth, especially rapid growth, is rarely a smooth and uneventful journey. Numerous factors and forces can derail the firm's efforts to become an exceptional enterprise. E/CEOs who are aware of the problems and pitfalls associated with growth will be in a better position to minimize their likelihood and consequences. This chapter identifies many of the mistakes that impede growth. With sufficient lead time, resourcefulness, and self-discipline, E/CEOs of emerging firms may be able to experience the benefits of controlled growth rather than be left saying "If only I had known!"

When you try to identify why emerging firms fail to sustain their rate of growth, you hear a whole range of explanations and excuses. While most E/CEOs would like to attribute their firm's lack of sustained growth (or its demise) to factors outside the firm, it is apparent that lack of growth (or success) may be attributed to the E/CEO's inability to meet the challenges associated with growth.

This chapter profiles the views expressed by sixty E/CEOs across the country, who participated in a survey for this book. They shared their views about the challenges that lie ahead as well as problems that come with growth. The problems associated with growth range from the lack of sufficient resources all the way to management's belief that it can do no wrong. Particular attention is directed to identifying pitfalls to avoid and indicators that the firm's growth may be in jeopardy. The following problems and pitfalls may not represent a complete list, but they do represent a fair sample of what can go wrong. Moreover, the areas have not been presented in their order of likelihood. Each firm is likely to experience its own unique blend of problems and pitfalls.

Overexpansion: Driving beyond One's Headlights

Most emerging firms drive beyond their headlights at one time or another. E/CEOs need to recognize that when they make commitments to do things beyond their available resources, they are driving beyond their headlights. By the time they see what is in front of them, it is too late to stop. They either hit the object or have to swerve off the road to avoid it. Both situations can have a devastating effect on the firm. The more rapid the growth, the higher the likelihood management will be driving the firm beyond its available resources.

Robert Patterson, CEO of Celebrity Inc., notes that fast-growth companies must watch that they do not "outstrip" their capital base. He suggests that allowing the firm's debt to rise too fast may be the most significant problem for E/CEOs to avoid. C. Lawrence Decker, M.D., president of Ambulatory Medical Care Inc., shares Patterson's observation. He claims that through overexpansion an emerging business can actually "grow itself into bankruptcy."

When the firm spends its cash in anticipation of growth, it is committing its limited resources to a very uncertain future. Russell Gentner, CEO of Gentner Communications Corporation, indicates that growth can cause a vicious cycle. He notes that undercapitalized emerging businesses frequently get caught in a cycle in which management feels it needs to invest in its employees, inventory, and the like to enable the firm to grow. Profitability then suffers because management is "investing in the future." While the level of sales may increase, the lack or low level of profitability contributes further to the firm's cash flow problems. The whole dilemma is then magnified when management concludes it must invest even more money in employees, inventory, advertising, and other areas so the firm may become profitable.

Gentner claims that most firms that get caught in the undercapitalized "growth trap" continue in the cycle until they reach the meltdown stage. This situation is similar to falling into quicksand. The more you try to free yourself from it, the more you are engulfed by it. Ironically, experts say that when you find yourself in quicksand you should move very slowly and try to float. This strategy, however, may take a level of discipline and patience that few E/CEOs of emerging firms possess.

Undercapitalization: Operating without a Net

If management fails to have a sufficient level of resources in reserve to meet unexpected setbacks, then it is setting the firm up for a fall. Undercapitalization is like an acrobat operating without a net—sooner rather than later something will not go as planned, and the firm will experience a major setback. The greater the volatility in the marketplace, the greater the need to have resources in reserve to weather the storm. Just as the firm needs to have contingency plans available to adjust its efforts when things do not go as expected, it needs to have resources in reserve to meet the challenges associated with growth. This is particularly true when the growth bubble bursts or when uncontrolled growth drains the firm of its cash.

One CEO, who chose to remain anonymous, indicated emerging firms are vulnerable when they "fail to maintain financial strength and liquidity with a clear strategy to survive downside (or doomsday) scenarios." That executive noted that downside scenarios need to be reviewed so management can determine specific levels of financial strength that will be needed. He also advised, "Discipline must be exercised."

Undercapitalization tends to occur in two ways. First, the firm may start off undercapitalized. When this happens, the firm will have a difficult time keeping its head above water. Second, firms may underestimate the capital required to meet growth's demands. Most veteran E/CEOs recognize that cash usually leaves the firm much quicker than it returns. E/CEOs need to prepare themselves for this problem. When it comes to cash, they cannot afford to have too little or permit it to be too late.

Undercapitalization Can Also Apply to Human Capital

When most people think about undercapitalization, they usually think about the lack of financial capital. Undercapitalization can also apply to firms when they don't have the right number of people in the right place with the right capabilities at the right time. If the E/CEO fails to properly

staff the firm to meet the challenges associated with growth, then things
will start falling through the cracks.

The firm will also suffer when the E/CEO fails to develop and utilize the
talents of the firm's present human resources. Ronald Manganiello, CEO of
Hanger Orthopedic Group Inc., believes "micro-managing" can be a real
pitfall for the emerging firm. He notes that the failure to delegate responsibility to middle managers can be a real problem. A. E. Wolf, CEO of
Checkpoint, indicates that the E/CEO must guard against strangling potential by overcontrolling the firm's people and operations. Gary Yancey,
CEO of Applied Signal Technology Inc., considers "not delegating responsibility downward rapidly enough" to be the most significant pitfall to
avoid for an emerging business.

Julian Lazrus, president of Bowles Fluidics Corporation, notes that the
firm can quickly get into trouble when it lacks a cadre of capable people to
whom to assign new projects and products. Daniel Glassman, CEO of
Bradley Pharmaceuticals Inc., expressed a related concern. He argues that
the E/CEO needs to make sure the firm does not expand into areas where
there is a "knowledge shortfall." Glassman also notes that the inability to
hire the people necessary to manage the growing company may be one of
the first indicators that the firm's growth may be in jeopardy. Rapid growth
does not give managers, especially inexperienced managers, the time to
learn on the job. As someone once observed, "It's pretty difficult to change
a tire on a car that is going 50 m.p.h.!"

Beware of the Midas Touch Syndrome

While some E/CEOs recognize that they don't have a sufficient supply of
managers to meet the challenges associated with growth, other E/CEOs
operate with the belief that they can do no wrong. For some E/CEOs, the
confidence that comes with initial success develops into a severe case of
managerial arrogance. This can spell disaster. These E/CEOs believe that if
they can be successful in one area of business they can succeed in almost
any situation. Marshall Chiaraluce, president of The Connecticut Water
Company, believes emerging firms are courting disaster when they stray
away from their core business and into areas where management does not
have the expertise to succeed. Michael Weinstein, president of Ark Restaurants Corporation, stresses the need for the firm to "stick to the knitting."
He cautions E/CEOs not to go into areas they are not profoundly knowledgeable about.

Raymond Hemmig, CEO of ACE—America's Cash Express, observes,
"Most entrepreneurs of emerging businesses . . . must approach most chal-

lenges with a certain amount of self-confidence . . . and a certain amount of self-doubt and anxiety about new and continuing opportunities." He cautions E/CEOs of emerging companies: "Whenever self-confidence or self-doubt occupies a disproportionate share of influence over their decisions . . . mistakes increase as a result. The key factor in avoiding these pitfalls is to keep these opposing factors in balance . . . not letting one overshadow the other!"

Don't Fall Prey to the Five Managerial Sins

E/CEOs need to recognize that their egos can have a tremendous impact on the way the firm is run. They must be vigilant that they do not fall prey to the five managerial sins: arrogance, ignorance, complacency, denial, and ineptitude. E/CEOs need to be particularly cognizant of the potential to have delusions of grandeur or to believe they have the Midas touch.

E/CEOs frequently get caught up in delusions of grandeur. They start adding nicer furnishings, fly first-class, and replace their practical sedan with a new top-of-the-line Mercedes. Most E/CEOs get so caught up in enjoying their perks and projecting the right image that they lose their focus on running the business and deplete the firm's valuable working capital. The symptoms of the "delusions of grandeur syndrome" may not be that visible at first. The E/CEO is just spending "a few more dollars" for this and "a few more dollars" for that. After a while, however, the small stream turns into a raging river.

The delusions of grandeur syndrome reaches the terminal level when the E/CEO hires an architect to design the firm's new corporate headquarters. When this happens, the E/CEO's desire to build a monument to his or her entrepreneurial prowess usually preempts the need to diligently manage the firm's capital. Planning the firm's new headquarters not only robs the firm of its limited funds, it also diverts the E/CEO's attention away from what it takes to create and maintain customers for a profit.

The Midas touch syndrome tends to be accompanied by a sense of invulnerability. Many E/CEOs believe growth will never end. E/CEOs who believe their firms are destined to maintain their meteoric ascent into the Fortune 500 tend to lose touch with the world around them. W. Philip Woodward, president of Chalone Wine Group, believes the firm is likely to encounter serious problems when the E/CEO thinks that double-digit growth can always happen. Gary Yancey, CEO of Applied Signal Technology Inc., suggests that the first "indicator" the firm's growth may be in jeopardy is when "top management thinks they have it made."

Arrogance has a tendency to turn into ignorance. When this happens, E/CEOs get out of touch. Before long, their firms are no longer in tune with the ever evolving marketplace. When management loses touch with what the firm's customers really need and with what competitors are doing to meet those needs, it is just a matter of time before the firm loses its appeal and competitive edge. One anonymous CEO advises that E/CEOs need to pay particular attention when their firms begin to lose market share even though revenues continue to increase: this is the first indicator the firm's growth may be in jeopardy.

E/CEOs who fall prey to ignorance and complacency either fail to recognize the turn in the firm's position or they rationalize away the various indicators that something may be amiss. Ignorance is not bliss. R. Terran Dunlap, CEO of Go Video, believes the first indicator the firm is in jeopardy is "when your management team tells you everything is OK!" The tendency to deny reality is even worse than ignorance. Russell Gentner of Gentner Communications Corporation holds that the firm's growth is in jeopardy when management continues to make excuses for the lack of profitability while cash flow continues to deteriorate.

When management loses touch with the set of factors that comprise the firm's unique situation, then it is destined to operate in an inept manner. Plans will not be developed, decisions will not be made the right way or at all, and new products will not be developed. Richard F. Demerjian, CEO of Commerce National Bank in Montebello, California, notes that the lack of a business plan can be a major pitfall for the emerging business. When you are going where you haven't gone before, you need to follow a road map.

Growth without focus and direction will quickly place the firm in jeopardy. Charles Hood, CEO of Advantage Media Group Inc., considers "weak or nondecisive management personnel in any capacity" to be the most significant problem to avoid. Another anonymous CEO observed that the first indicator the firm's growth may be in jeopardy occurs when there is no consistency in communication of strategy and priorities in the firm.

While not having a plan can be a problem, not sticking to it can be another problem. Howard Hawkins, chairman of Hawkins Chemical Inc., considers "making a move on impulse instead of thinking it over" to be the most significant pitfall for the emerging business. Neal Patterson, CEO of Cerner Corporation, believes the most significant pitfall to avoid occurs when management fails to "adjust for a change in a major assumption."

Avoid Ostrich Management

E/CEOs who fail to stay in tune with the changes that are taking place around their firm run the risk of developing a terminal case of "ostrich management." Awareness precedes change. Their firms are destined to be more than a day late and a dollar short. E/CEOs are setting their firms up for disaster when they fail to recognize the need to change what their firms are doing or when they are unwilling to make the changes that must be made. Firms that operate without plans, timetables, customer satisfaction indicators, budgets, and targets or goals are not likely to notice unfavorable trends when they begin. Raymond Hemmig, CEO of ACE—America's Cash Express, notes that the "numbers" may be the first indicator the firm's growth may be in jeopardy. He states that many businesses fail to track the key indicators (sales, expenses, income, customer counts, and so on) often enough to note unfavorable trends . . . many emerging businesses discover in hindsight that trends are always visible. He noted that the "tip of the decline" can be observed if management is monitoring the numbers on a timely basis.

Other CEOs who participated in the survey shared Hemmig's observation about the need to be on top of trends. They identified a whole range of factors that may be seen as the first indicator the firm's growth may be short-lived. The following lists of quantitative and qualitative factors may serve as warning signals to E/CEOs that their firm's growth may be in jeopardy. The indicators are not listed in their order of occurrence or relative importance, which will vary from firm to firm.

Ten Quantitative Indicators that Growth Is in Jeopardy

1. Not realizing sales forecasts (Neal Patterson; Cerner Corporation)
2. Employee turnover (Ronald Manganiello; Hanger Orthopedic Group Inc.)
3. Increasing overhead without a corresponding rise in sales (anonymous)
4. Unsubstantiated decline in earnings per share (Stanley Stein; American Health Corporation)
5. Profit ratios and efficiency ratios begin to fall below superior levels (Hjalma Johnson; East Coast Bank Corporation)
6. Missing key milestones (Patrick Leonard; Cambridge Biotech)
7. Not able to meet delivery schedules (L. C. Martin; Aztec Manufacturing Company)
8. Loss of market share even though revenue gain looks OK (anonymous)

9. Negative cash flow trends (James Fore; Communication Cable Company)

10. Beginning to discount and accept marginal business (William W. Neal; Broadway & Seymour)

Ten Qualitative Indicators that Growth Is in Jeopardy

1. Direction is unclear (anonymous)

2. New product stream dwindles or dries up (Paul Saxton; General Housewares Corporation)

3. Predatory competitors enter the market (Barry Hall; California Amplifier, Inc.)

4. People missing deadlines (John Schwager; Alamco Inc.)

5. Declining customer enthusiasm for the company and product (Joseph Kelly; Crop Genetics International)

6. Complacency among employees (anonymous)

7. Visible slowdown in people's pace (Howard Yenke; Boca Research Inc.)

8. Whiffs of defeatism (anonymous)

9. Inability to come up with new managers (Daniel Glassman; Bradley Pharmaceuticals Inc.)

10. Realizing (if you ever do) that the business has become a nonresponsive bureaucracy (Richard F. Demerjian; Commerce National Bank)

Concluding Comments: An Ounce of Prevention Is Better than a Pound of Cure

Managing rapid growth is like traversing a minefield. One wrong step and the firm may be history. E/CEOs need to be particularly vigilant about the potential pitfalls and problems that may lie just below the surface. Sustained growth will require a commitment to closely monitoring what is going on outside the firm as well as what is going on within it.

*The fast lane is paved with the wreckages of
businesses that failed to spot the hazards in
time.*[2]

WILLIAM E. SHEELINE

CHIEF EXECUTIVE GUIDELINES

Name: Jerry A. Graham, President
Company: Data Medical Associates Inc.
Product/Service: Clinical Diagnostic Products Manufacturer
Number of Employees: 45
Awards/Distinctions:

1. Profiled in *Entrepreneur* magazine

2. 1992 "Exporter of the Year" Regional Award from the U.S. Small Business Administration

3. "Exporter of the Year Top 40" by Arthur Anderson for Tarrant County

General Guidelines: When it comes to managing a growing firm, the E/CEO should keep the following tips in mind:

1. Conserve your cash, don't buy nonproductive assets such as fancy office furniture, decorations, and the like.

2. Buy insurance.

3. Be realistic in setting your objectives for the business. Do not commit the business beyond your resources.

4. Plan your business operations in detail, and refer to your plan frequently during the course of the year.

5. Stick to your plan. Do not be tempted to "take advantage" of an unforeseen and unplanned "opportunity."

6. Hire the best people you can find. Bring their experience and knowledge into your business, and reward them.

7. Give your employees an opportunity to contribute to and grow with the company.

8. Hire the best service firms you can find, e.g., insurance agents, lawyers, printers, and so on. Don't go to the new accountant because you are both starting out in business at the same time. You need the benefit of the experience and knowledge of an established firm.

9. Monitor your operations closely. Make sure that you have accurate and timely financial data. Count your current assets including your cash balances daily.

Proceed with Caution Guidelines:

1. Don't be too trusting. Check the references of the people you are doing business with.

2. *Read* every line and understand it before you sign it. During the signing process for an SBA loan, given only the small corner of a secretary's desk for the papers and pressured by a frenzy of activity during the signing, I discovered a document that assigned all of my stock holdings in the company along with the voting rights to the president of the bank for the seven-year duration of the loan. I didn't sign it, and I got the loan anyway.

3. Don't get too caught up in the rapture of the deal. Enthusiasm and optimism are necessary ingredients to your venture, but realism must prevail.

4. Remember: "There ain't no free lunch." You must understand the motivations of the people that you deal with.

CHIEF EXECUTIVE GUIDELINES

Name: Dave Valliere, Chief Executive Officer
Company: Dove Computer Corporation
Product/Service: Computer Peripherals for MacIntosh Computers
Awards/Distinctions: *MacWorld* "World Class Award" 1991 and 1992

General Guidelines: When it comes to managing a growing firm, the E/CEO should keep the following tips in mind:

1. Never let satisfying the organization or any one person in the organization become more important than your customers.

2. The CEO sets the pace of the organization, particularly in the early growth phase. Teach by example.

3. Never fail to recognize your own importance, no matter how large or how small the organization. Set your expectations by example, and remember others are always trying to verify their beliefs about where

and what and why the organization "is" by watching and listening to you.

4. Always demand exceptional performance from your key personnel without exception. Start-ups and high-growth companies cannot afford the time to train key players, no matter how conscientious you are about training. If a key management team player has to be taught or told how to execute his part of the plan, he is the wrong person for the job.

5. Always accept an offer for additional working capital when it comes. A bird in the hand is always worth two in the bush. Equity and even loan offers rarely occur before 120 to 180 days of relationship-building and due diligence have passed, so think long and hard before turning down an offer. Doing so usually ensures an additional six months to one year of doing without. The typical growth company has very little reserve momentum. What may look good today might look completely different tomorrow.

Proceed with Caution Guidelines: Things to Do

1. Overestimate working capital requirements and set an absolute "go" or "no go" amount.

2. Create a nonpreferential "rewards for results" pay system with many miniobjective-based bonuses for jobs well done. Avoid "perverse incentives" that encourage damaging business practices or ethics.

3. Set up a system for continually measuring customer satisfaction early.

4. Act swiftly to fix management team performance issues objectively and nonemotionally.

5. CEOs are rarely "liked" by everyone: accept this fact and expect to make enemies as well as friends. Because you are the highest authority to most people who are involved with the company, to most of them you become the cause of many successes and, unfortunately, the reason for many failures.

6. Beware of friendships. They often prolong or even prevent addressing a performance issue until it is too late to preserve the friendship or business relationship.

Proceed with Caution Guidelines: Things Not *to Do*

1. Never use debt or other leverage as a sole source of capital.

2. Never be intimidated by the demands of a single outspoken shareholder, director, and so on. You are the CEO of the business because

you are qualified to be in that position. Be respectful and listen but still determine a course of action based on all available information.

3. In general, never personally guarantee anything unless the liability goes away if you are not directly involved.

4. Never take action while angry. Cool heads always make better decisions. If nothing else, listen to the other side of the story before taking action.

5. Always be consistent, fair, and honest in dealing with everyone.

6. Don't get caught in the "emperor has no clothes" situation. Growth organizations usually have a high percentage of positive attitude, success-driven personalities. There is an inclination to always focus on the strengths of the organization and to overlook its shortcomings. CEOs can easily become victims of their organizations continually telling them how great they are. To avoid finding yourself stark naked when you thought you were dressed to a tee, demand to know what problems exist and never, ever chop off the head of the messenger. Establish regular "What can we do to improve?" discussions with customers, suppliers, employees, and bankers. Don't be the emperor, it's too embarrassing.

5

Prerequisites for Sustained Growth

He who stops being better stops being good.
OLIVER CROMWELL

While Chapter 4 may have provided insight into the problems and pitfalls that E/CEOs need to avoid, it should be noted that success involves more than just preventing problems or minimizing their consequences. There is a big difference between surviving and succeeding. People in the medical field acknowledge that the absence of illness should not be confused with being healthy. People who lose weight and stop smoking should be congratulated, but they should also recognize they will not be healthy until they eat nutritious foods, exercise regularly, and keep their minds active by engaging in new and challenging pursuits. Health is never an accident. It is the result of a deliberate and never-ending commitment to getting the most out of one's life.

This chapter identifies the factors that are prerequisite to achieving and sustaining corporate health. Emerging firms demonstrated their ability to beat the odds when they made it through the start-up stage. In a sense, they have completed the 100-meter dash without falling down. Yet the realities of the marketplace do not offer them any time to catch their breath...now they must face the challenges associated with running the marathon.

Achieving sustained growth is like a marathon. While some firms are able to go the distance, only exceptional firms win marathons. The same principle applies to emerging firms. Many may succeed but few experience exceptional growth and success. In statistical terms, exceptional firms are the ones that operate three standard deviations from the mean!

In the survey conducted for this book, sixty chief executives from across the country who have directed their firm's growth were asked to identify the prerequisites to sustained growth. The following list highlights the factors they identified. The factors are not provided in any particular order. Instead, they are intended to serve more as a checklist than as a ranking of relative importance.

Prerequisites for Sustained Growth

1. A Commitment to Building Strength Rather than Size
2. Being in Markets where Lasting Profit Opportunities Exist
3. The Ability to Create and Maintain Competitive Advantages
4. Strong Leadership and an Effective Management Team
5. A Unified Vision and the Ability to Maintain Focus
6. Effective Systems for Planning and Controlling Operations
7. Highly Motivated and Resourceful Employees
8. The Ability to Sense the Need to Change
9. A Commitment to Customer Satisfaction
10. A Sufficient Supply of Capital

Prerequisite No. 1: Don't Confuse Growth with Strength

Numerous factors must be in place if the emerging firm is to thrive in the years that follow the start-up stage. There may be no guaranteed formula for becoming an exceptional firm, but certain prerequisites must be met. The first prerequisite is more a matter of perspective than a tangible ingredient. E/CEOs must recognize that growth should not be viewed as an end in itself. Tom Richmond notes, "When entrepreneurs and CEOs forget that growth is only one measure of business success among many—when they become fixated on growth and feel compelled by pride or ambition to emulate or top the growth of others—that is when they get into trouble."[1]

There is a big difference between random, uncontrolled growth and managed, healthy growth. Growth strategies should be undertaken only when being larger will help the firm be better. If growth will: (1) help the firm provide consistently better products at lower prices to the firm's customers: (2) improve the firm's financial position so it can be more innovative and reward its employees and investors: and (3) position the firm to weather life's inevitable setbacks, then growth should be pursued. E/CEOs who know the difference between growth that develops strength and growth for the sake of growth have taken the first step in their firm's journey toward becoming an exceptional enterprise.

Prerequisite No. 2: Operate in High-Growth Markets

People who catch fish for a living operate with a very simple principle, "You need to go where the fish are." A number of CEOs stated that being in a high-growth market may be the greatest prerequisite for sustained growth. L. C. Martin, CEO of Aztec Manufacturing Company, believes that emerging firms should operate in an expanding market. He cautioned E/CEOs from operating in mature markets because predatory pricing is more prevalent in mature markets.

Steven Jobs once noted that if you are going to start a business, you might as well go after a big opportunity because it takes about the same amount of effort to start a business to capitalize on a large opportunity as it does a small opportunity. Jobs's observation may apply equally well to emerging businesses.

Prerequisite No. 3: Create and Maintain a Competitive Advantage

Another CEO, who chose to remain anonymous, indicated that it would be all right if the firm was in a mature market if the firm had a significant competitive advantage. Creating and maintaining competitive advantages is of paramount importance regardless of whether the market is growing or mature. E/CEOs of rapid-growth firms seem to have the ability to identify growing markets, enter lucrative niches, and develop competitive advantages that enable their firms to create and maintain customers for a profit.

Patrick Leonard, CEO of Cambridge Biotech, put these factors in perspective when he said the firm must be able to provide "a continuing stream of products which meet customer requirements in an expanding market."

The firm will only be able to maintain its competitive advantages if it is synchronized with market conditions. Donald Goldberg, CEO of GeoEnvironmental Technologies Inc., states that CEOs must "understand that your role is to fulfill a need...and as needs keep changing, products must change." A. E. Wolf, CEO of Checkpoint, believes success will only be possible if management maintains "a constant vigilance over market trends."

Firms that are unable to offer the market what it values in a manner that is better than its competitors are destined to fall by the wayside. If the firm cannot provide superior products, better service, proprietary technology, lower prices and/or higher quality than its competitors, then it should put the business up for sale while there is still something left to sell.

Prerequisite No. 4: Demonstrate Leadership and Develop a Strong Management Team

If a chain can only be as strong as its weakest link, then the firm can only be as strong as its people. No links are more important in the chain of management than the links at the top. Charles Hood, CEO of Advantage Media Group Inc., believes the firm must have "qualified leaders in all skill positions—particularly in sales, marketing, and finance."

The development of an effective management team was emphasized by numerous CEOs. Robert Patterson, CEO of Celebrity Inc., considers "developing competent management to carry out functions previously performed by the chief executive" to be the most important prerequisite for sustained growth. He believes, "The CEO must be free to continue to develop the business from a growth aspect as opposed to doing mundane functions that lower management can properly handle."

Two other CEOs also stressed the need for E/CEOs to have people on their management teams who add value to the enterprise. One CEO, who wanted to remain anonymous, stressed the need for "enthusiastic, engaged, committed, nimble thinkers." This emphasis on nimble thinking was shared by A. Charles Lubash, CEO of Astro Sciences Corporation. He not only encourages E/CEOs to select the best people as subordinates, he also advises, "Always try to secure more talented people than you, thus you become a better executive. The company with the best executives will always win."

Prerequisite No. 5: Have a
Unified Vision and Maintain Focus

Growth without direction is like trying to sail a ship without a rudder. E/
CEOs with a clear vision are less likely to be seduced by short-lived
opportunities that tend to rob their firms of valuable resources. One CEO
considers "leadership that provides the vision and inspiration to achieve
the desired results" to be the most important factor for sustained growth.
Howard Yenke, CEO of Boca Research Inc., echoes that notion. He believes
CEOs "need to change when change is required, but [they] must remain
disciplined and focused." Managers with a clear vision know what business they are in and where they are going. This aids decision making
because everyone knows what is right and what needs to be accomplished.
Firms that operate without vision and focus are destined to aimlessly drift
until their resources are depleted.

Prerequisite No. 6: Planning
and Control Systems Need
to Be in Place

A clearly articulated vision can serve as the foundation for the development of the firm's strategic plan. The firm's strategic plan, in turn, provides
the basis for developing the firm's operating plans, timetables, and budgets. The firm's vision represents the target everyone is shooting for. Plans,
timetables, and budgets represent the bull's-eye in the center of the target.

Effective planning and control systems permit management to practice
what David Burch calls "real-time decision making." Firms with good
management information systems are in a better position to monitor key
performance areas and make the appropriate changes to keep the firm on
course. R. Terren Dunlop, CEO of Go Video, stresses the need to "stay
focused on what your company knows best...control your growth, don't let
it control you."

Prerequisite No. 7: Highly
Motivated and Resourceful
Employees Are Essential

Success is contingent on having the right number of people in the right
place at the right time with the right capabilities. Raymond Hemmig, CEO
of ACE—America's Cash Express, puts the importance of having good

people in perspective. He says, "There are only two assets in any business that are really important...cash and people...of which most important is people! Clearly businesses must have a product or service that is of sufficient quality to sustain growth...but I assert that a business's ability to attract, retain, and motivate its people is the requirement of the first order."

John Williams, CEO of Communications Systems Inc., notes that emerging firms will be in a position to sustain growth only if they "develop a cadre of excellent, talented, excited people." John Raycraft, CEO of First American Health Concepts, shares Williams's view. He states, "Hire the best people, let them do their jobs, and pay them for results." Ronald Olson, CEO of Grow Biz, notes the role that quality personnel and timing can play in the firm's ability to grow. He stresses the need to "develop your organization with the best possible people and never take second best." He also states, "Planning your people needs in advance will help give you the time to find the right person."

Prerequisite No. 8: Anticipate the Need to Change

Success will be contingent on management's ability to anticipate change and to position the firm to benefit from it. This is the underlying principle of proactive management. Craig Hickman and Michael Silva have an interesting way of looking at the nature and rate of change. In their book, *Creating Excellence,* they note that change can be viewed as a distant object bearing down on the firm. If management spots it early, then management will be able to monitor its speed and direction. As the object gets closer, management should be in a position to determine if the object is a threat or an opportunity. If management identifies the nature of the object early enough, then it may have sufficient lead time to deal with it. If the firm is the first to see it as an opportunity, then management should be in an excellent position to capitalize on it. If it turns out to be a threat, then management may have time to step aside and watch it hit its competition head on—who never saw it coming![2]

All firms operate in the same world. The difference between successful emerging ventures and those that stagnate and die is that the emerging firms have the lead time to capitalize on the opportunities that come with change—reactive firms are left wondering what hit them! Judith Kaplan, CEO of Action Products International Inc., shares this view about change. She notes E/CEOs of emerging firms need to have "the instinct to know what is right at the moment."

Marketplace savvy appears to be particularly important for emerging firms. Daniel Glassman, CEO of Bradley Pharmaceuticals Inc., believes the most important prerequisite for sustained growth is management's ability to "successfully anticipate the industry's future." Hal Lieberman, CEO of HemaCare Corporation, notes that "knowledge of your marketplace and making good strategic choices as the marketplace changes" are essential for sustained growth. Kenneth Brown, CEO of Citation Computer Systems Inc., recognizes that management must do more than just recognize the need for change. He notes that for the firm to grow, management must also have the "willingness to gamble on new approaches."

Prerequisite No. 9:
Customer Satisfaction
Should Not Be Compromised

The ability to "create and maintain customers for a profit" is the lifeblood of the emerging firm. John Raycraft, CEO of First American Health Concepts, notes that emerging firms must "never forget who the boss is...the customer!" Gary Yancey, President of Applied Signal Technology Inc., echoes Raycraft's point when he emphasizes the need for everyone in the firm to focus their attention on "customer satisfaction through the stellar work ethic." An anonymous CEO voiced a similar belief that sustained growth will be possible only if the firm demonstrates the "continued ability to service clients at a sustained high level." Brian McAuley, CEO of Nextel Communications, Inc., recognizes the relationship between the ability to sense change and customer satisfaction. He believes that if emerging firms are to serve their customers well, then they must anticipate customer needs.

Prerequisite No. 10: Capital
Must Be Available

Capital plays such a critical role in sustaining growth that it should not surprise anyone that it appears on the list of prerequisites. Some CEOs stressed the need to have a sufficient supply of capital. Other CEOs indicated that having cash on hand was not as important as the ability to raise and access it when the need arises. The CEOs made it clear, however, that the firm would be able to continue growing only to the extent that it is able to generate a healthy cash flow and produce a reasonable return on the money invested in the enterprise. The CEOs noted that if firms are to be successful they will need to heed the words of the Smith Barney ad, "We make money the old-fashioned way...we earn it!"

Concluding Comments:
Successful Emerging Firms Have
Wisdom beyond Their Years

The CEOs who shared their thoughts on the prerequisites for sustained growth were far from reaching a consensus. Instead, they identified a whole range of factors that need to serve as cornerstones in building an exceptional enterprise. A closer look at their responses, however, indicates that one word may capture what separates the best emerging firms from the pack. That word is "precocious."

Precocious is defined as "an unusually early development or maturity." The most successful emerging firms seem to have developed the ability to size up the worlds around them, the perceptiveness to anticipate what the future may hold, and the resourcefulness to capitalize on opportunities that arise. Simply stated, they have "learned how to learn." They have developed healthy patterns for addressing situations. They have evolved beyond the trial-and-error processes that characterize most new ventures. When they are faced with a challenge, they know how to "land on their feet."

Resiliency and the ability to learn from one's experiences are vital qualities for emerging firms. According to William Sheeline, "The real challenges of rapid growth come when a company hits its first rough stretch of highway."[3] Successful ventures constantly renew themselves, and they consistently rise to the occasion. Their E/CEOs have what is referred to as "tolerance for the turbulence." As one CEO put it, "You've got to have ice water in your veins!"

*Accept the challenges so that you can feel the
exhilaration of victory.*
GENERAL GEORGE PATTON

CHIEF EXECUTIVE GUIDELINES

Name: Michael Fitzgerald, Chief Executive Officer
Company: Sunrise Publications Inc.
Product/Service: Greeting Cards and Paper Products
Sales: $25,000,000   *Number of Employees:* 320
Awards/Distinctions:

1. Profiled in *Nation's Business*

2. Keynote speaker for 1993 Indiana Governor's "Entrepreneurs Day" symposium

3. Author of various business and legal articles

General Guidelines: When it comes to the prerequisites for sustained growth, E/CEO should keep the following guidelines in mind.

My job as CEO is defined by only two responsibilities: strategic growth planning and opening up "bottlenecks" in the organization. The key strength of our business is our "people." Any successful business is only as good as its "people." Even if the CEO is the successful mind that can conceive excellent growth strategies, the CEO cannot execute all of the necessary changes without the effective cooperation and coordination of the entire body. Your team of people are the body of the business. Put another way: you must rely on others. If you try to do it all yourself, you will either fail, ruin your health, or have only a very small business without real growth potential. An understanding of the effects of growth on people is therefore important in order to select the right team.

Sustained growth means continual change for any organization. An oriental language that uses ideograms defines "change" as a combination of two characters: the symbol for "opportunity" and the symbol for "danger." Communicating and balancing both of these characteristics to everyone in your company is the most important element in managing successful change. Certain key employees will fall into the group that see change as only an "opportunity," while many other employees will see change as a continual "danger" to their comfortable job description. A successful entrepreneur must create a team in which virtually everyone realizes that there will always be a certain amount of controlled chaos as the company tries to balance the changes. This theory may sound nice, but what about practical applications?

The practical danger is that no one department is so far ahead of, or behind, all the other departments that the process breaks down or causes unacceptable human friction. Every department must be maintaining day to day profit generating responsibilities while anticipating the changes and therefore planning for the next phase of growth. This places a remarkable stress on key employees because their jobs are always changing in an ever changing interaction with ever changing jobs in other departments. Problems are compounded if your key personnel are incentivized on performance for just their area of responsibility. We have found it very important to create financial incentives that foster teamwork between all departments and not a focus on just one area.

You also must balance incentives on both short and long term goals because it is evident that changes for growth cost the organization in terms of lost productivity, as well as additional expenses in view of longer term results. If you have only short term incentives, then your key personnel will resent change because it reduces this year's earnings. Therefore prepare a well written and comprehensive business plan and update it yearly so that all key team members will understand your short and long term goals.

Create an atmosphere that encourages communication among all of your people because only communication can prevent major human relations problems. Unless everyone on your team can grow both personally and professionally as your business grows, you will have human problems that will prevent your success. Over the years, I had to fire some of the most talented people who I have ever worked with because they could not delegate responsibility to others and treat others with the necessary human respect. In these cases the results were a substantial improvement in morale and productivity. In all our key job descriptions we now state that maintaining collegial relations and communication with all other personnel is an equal criteria of employment.

There are many programs, policies and publications that we have used to communicate our "philosophy" to all of our people, starting with our employee handbook, entitled, "People." Every business will be different, but change always brings both the danger and the opportunity. If you surround yourself with the best people, delegate responsibility with matched authority, communicate your vision effectively and then work with your key team members to understand their problems and open up their bottlenecks to performance, you will have established the prerequisites for sustained growth.

CHIEF EXECUTIVE GUIDELINES

Name: Garry Snook, Chief Executive Officer
Company: Performance Inc.
Product/Service: Retail Stores and Direct Marketing of Cycling Products and Accessories
Sales: $70,000,000   *Number of Employees:* 700
Awards/Distinctions: Profiled in *Inc.* Magazine

General Guidelines: When it comes to the prerequisites for sustained growth, the E/CEO should keep the following tips in mind:

1. Most entrepreneurs recognize the need to operate in niche markets. Niche markets, however, may have narrow boundaries that will constrain growth. Find a niche market that has the potential to sustain growth.

2. There is a tendency for entrepreneurs to cut corners on payroll—this limits the caliber of people the firm will be able to attract and keep. If you want quality people, then you must be willing to pay for them.

3. You must have a "customer" viewpoint. You have to see the world through the customers' eyes. You also need to recognize that the customers' views will change over time. Your firm cannot afford to be static.

4. Today's customers are far more educated than in the past. You have to do a lot more than just open your doors and assume your products will sell themselves.

5. Sustained growth requires profit. While you may need more than profit to finance growth—you must be profitable to get the financing.

Proceed with Caution Guidelines:

1. Pay close attention to profitability. While we have been profitable every year since the firm was founded—it is easy to get caught up in sales growth and market share.

2. Bring in more talented people earlier. Most entrepreneurs have a tendency to do things a little later than they should. This is particularly true with talent.

3. Entrepreneurs usually prefer "starting" things and new endeavors. They usually don't like fine-tuning things and dealing in operational matters. If the entrepreneur doesn't have the time, the patience or the desire to do the fine-tuning and to oversee operational matters, then

he or she should bring someone in who will take care of these dimensions of the business.

And I Would Be Particularly Careful Not *to:*

Lose your focus. Look carefully before being tempted into new areas that may be beyond your core business. Diversions dilute your effort, your management, and your capital.

6

Perceptive Timing Can Provide a Competitive Edge

*I owe my success in life to having always been
a quarter of an hour beforehand.*
ADMIRAL HORATIO NELSON

It has been said that it may be more difficult to maintain excellence than it is to achieve it. The same may also be true for new venture success. Success needs to be viewed more as a marathon than a 100-meter sprint. The annals of sports are full of Heisman Trophy winners who never made it to the Pro Bowl and of rookie batters who hit .300 and then vanished from the majors within a few seasons. The same appears to be the case for many new ventures. Almost overnight, they go from being celebrated in the business pages to being listed in the corporate obituaries.

A closer look at here today, gone tomorrow firms reveals that their initial success can be attributed to their entrepreneurs being in the right place at the right time with the right product or service. All the conditions were right. As conditions changed, however, their firms were no longer in a position to capitalize on market opportunities. As their markets evolved,

Portions of the material in this chapter originally appeared in the article, "Preventing the Here Today, Gone Tomorrow New Venture Syndrome," by the author in *Business Forum,* Summer 1991, pp. 18-22. Reprinted with permission of California State University—Los Angeles.

their firms were out of synch with new realities. In their dance with the elephants, here today, gone tomorrow firms made too many wrong steps.

When the here today, gone tomorrow ventures were created, market demand may have been so strong that consumers would have bought almost anything that would meet their needs. As their markets grew and then matured, competitors entered the scene that were more in tune with changes in the marketplace. Entrepreneurs of "first-to-market" firms may have been perceptive and recognized what the market wanted initially, but many lacked the resources and/or managerial wherewithal to support their firm's rapid growth. Hence, many new ventures implode.

Postmortems of here today, gone tomorrow firms reveal that lasting success requires numerous factors. Firms that are driven by a single market may be destined to fail. Peter Drucker notes that if you stay in one business long enough, you will go out of business. Lasting success is contingent on being able to keep up with changes in the marketplace as well as being able to calibrate the firm's infrastructure to support sustained growth. Perceptiveness, agility, resourcefulness, and stamina are valuable talents in the dance with the elephants. When the rate of change is accelerating and uncertainty is the rule, the ability to turn on a dime may keep the firm from being trampled to death.

A Keen Sense of Timing Is Essential for Sustained Growth

Entrepreneurship is usually associated with identifying an emerging opportunity. The ability to capitalize on the market opportunity may provide a new venture with the avenue for initial growth. To maintain growth, however, management must develop a strategy that makes sustained growth possible. The need to identify market opportunities tends to overshadow the importance of having a keen sense of timing. The Wayne Gretzky approach to doing business presented in Chapter 2, however, suggests the role that timing can play in the competitive arena.

Numerous new ventures fail not because they do not have good ideas; they fail because their entrepreneurs do not have a good sense of timing. The timing of initiatives continues to play an integral role in the success of an enterprise long after the start-up stage. There are at least six types of timing initiatives that need to be addressed during the life of a new venture. They are:

1. When to start the venture?
2. When to initiate major expansion?
3. When to consolidate operations?

4. When to exit existing markets?

5. When to enter emerging markets?

6. When to sell all or part of the venture?

Timing is particularly important if the firm is to continue growing. Lasting success is contingent on knowing when things need to be done as much as it is on knowing what needs to be done.

The formula for business success has not changed over the years. Firms that are in the right place at the right time with the right capabilities and resources are more likely to succeed. The accelerating rate of change in the marketplace, however, has placed a premium on having foresight and the ability to quickly modify the firm's capabilities. While it may be true that there may be more opportunities than at any time in the past, E/CEOs also need to recognize that windows of opportunity may be opening and closing more rapidly than at any other time. Competition is quick to jump on the bandwagon of markets that show promise. The challenge is amplified by the fact that it may take more lead time to develop competencies to meet the needs of a more sophisticated market.

Anthony Carnevale captured the essence of timing. He notes that in today's economy, there are four races against the clock in which organizations compete:[1]

The First Race: Developing innovations in technology, products, or work processes.

The Second Race: Getting innovation off the drawing board and into the hands of consumers.

The Third Race: Increasing the efficiency or quality of the innovation or developing new applications

The Fourth Race: Using what has been learned in the previous steps to move to another innovation

One of Kenny Rogers's songs about playing poker highlights the importance of timing. To paraphrase Rogers, success comes from knowing "when to hold and when to fold." When Nolan Bushnell reflected on his life as an entrepreneur, he indicated that while his ideas were good, his timing was off: he got out of Atari too soon and out of Pizza Time Theatres too late.

The word *entrepreneur* is derived from the French term *entreprendre,* which means to initiate something. New venture success may be tied just as closely to knowing when to *exit* a market. If the venture is to continue growing, then management must be willing to explore new opportunities. For this to happen, management must be willing to venture away from its present position regardless of how comfortable it may be. The firm must also possess chameleonlike capabilities so it can be transformed into what it needs to be rather than what it has been.

Success May Be Temporary

Too many firms focus their attention on their present market(s). This practice is not only myopic, it may jeopardize the firm's very survival. Entrepreneurs frequently use their firm's present market(s) as a security blanket. While a security blanket may be comfortable, it can easily suffocate the firm's ability to adjust to a rapidly changing marketplace. Too often, entrepreneurs wait until their firms are in serious trouble before they begin to look for ways to keep their firms afloat. One of the things that separates the successful new venture from the others is that management does not wait for major problems to arise before it starts looking for ways to strengthen the firm.

Successful new ventures tend to exhibit a longer-term time horizon. This gives them two strategic advantages over other firms. The longer-term time horizon enables management to have a more objective view of where the venture is and what its future may hold. Managers who live only in the present frequently assume that today's markets and the firm's competitive advantage(s) will last forever. Managers of successful new ventures recognize no market lasts forever. Ted Levitt's comment cited in Chapter 2 warrants repeating here. Levitt observed, "There is no such thing as a growth industry. There are only companies organized and operated to create and capitalize on growth opportunities. Industries that assume themselves to be riding some automatic growth escalator invariably descend into stagnation."[2] The same reasoning also applies to markets, customers, locations, products, processes, and services. Those at the helm of their firms must recognize that nothing lasts forever. As Alvin Toffler so aptly put it, "The future has a habit of invading the present."

A longer-term time horizon also permits management to look beyond the firm's present market(s). Successful E/CEOs recognize that almost anything is possible. They live by Ferrari's motto, "If you can dream it, we can make it." If the firm has sufficient lead time, it can develop new products, processes, and competencies and expand into new territories. The longer-term time horizon may also provide the impetus needed for the firm to move into an entirely different industry! In its truest sense, a longer-term horizon may even permit management to adopt a visionary perspective. To borrow and modify the prelude to *Star Trek*, the new venture may be in a position to "boldly go where no firm has gone before!"

Nicholas Murray Butler observed, "There are three types of people in the world: those who make things happen, those who watch what happens, and those who wonder what happened." His distinction between types of people may also apply to emerging firms. In this case, however, there can be four types: laggard ventures, reactive ventures, proactive ventures, and visionary ventures.

The Laggard Firm Is Destined to Fail

One of the most important dimensions of emerging venture strategy is when the management team starts looking for growth opportunities. Laggard firms depicted in Figure 6-1 tend to wait until they are well into the decline stage of the market life cycle before they start searching for some way to stay alive. After two consecutive declining quarters or years, management begins to take a closer look at the firm's operations and the appropriateness of the firm's market offering. Managers in laggard firms miss or ignore the first signs of a declining situation. They may even rationalize away the signals and attribute their firm's declining sales to a "soft economy." It usually takes a major crisis to get management to acknowledge the need for things to change. Their acts of desperation, however, tend to be too little and too late.

Even if management's last-minute strategies work, they merely postpone the firm's demise. These firms resemble the gamblers who place and keep their bets at the roulette wheel on the color red with each spin of the wheel. The wheel may stop on the red for a time or two, but sooner rather than later the wheel will stop on the black. In the long haul, success will be based on good management rather than good luck. The marketplace shows little mercy to firms that fail to keep pace.

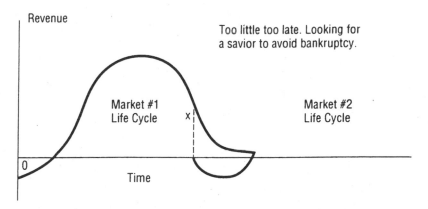

X = Awareness of the need for change and the beginning of the effort to reposition the firm. This usually occurs after the second consecutive period of declining revenue.

Figure 6-1. The Laggard Firm.

Reactive Firms May Stay in the Game But They Do Not Prosper

The reactive management team tends to start looking for growth opportunities at the first signs of a declining market (Figure 6-2). Management does not wait for the second consecutive period of declining sales to assess the appropriateness of the firm's market offering. Management looks for declining margins and lack of repeat purchases. Management also recognizes the firm is having to increase its advertising and sales efforts to maintain its level of sales. This gives the reactive firm more time than the laggard firm to modify the firm's strategy. Managers of reactive firms recognize price competition can be intense in saturated markets. While sales may continue increasing for the overall market, profit margins are already deteriorating.

While laggard firms don't know what has happened until it already has, reactive firms at least are monitoring key performance indicators. Even reactive firms acknowledge the Merrill-Lynch commodity trader's maxim, "It's not just how much you know. It's how soon." The earlier awareness of the reactive firm may give its management enough time to come up with a strategy to keep the firm's head above water before it runs out of capital.

Most successful E/CEOs agree that cash flow is not a leading indicator of problems. They say that by the time cash flow problems occur, it may be too late to turn the situation around. They also know that cash flow problems are seldom the real cause of the firm's financial problems. Cash flow problems are the result of more fundamental problems.

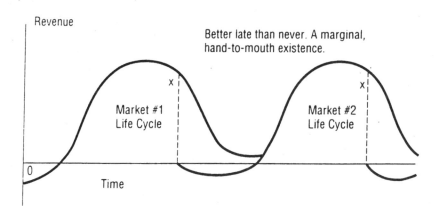

X = Awareness of the need for change and the beginning of an effort to reposition the firm. This usually occurs when revenue begins decreasing at an increasing rate.

Figure 6-2. The Reactive Firm.

The Proactive Firm Recognizes Nothing Lasts Forever

One of the major differences between the proactive and the reactive firm is management's sense of timing. Proactive managers recognize the need to start thinking about repositioning their firms earlier in the market life cycle. Proactive managers closely monitor the rate of growth during the growth stage. At the point of inflection, the market may still be growing but it is growing at a slower rate. By starting the search earlier, proactive firms have additional time to identify emerging opportunities (Figure 6-3).

Additional lead time gives proactive firms a chance to test an emerging market rather than to jump in with both feet. Rosabeth Moss Kanter of the Harvard Business School noted the relationship between an opportunity-driven firm and a sales-driven firm. According to Kanter, "Staying ahead of change means anticipating new actions that external events will eventually require and taking them early, before others, before being forced, while there is still time to exercise choice about how and when and what—and time to influence, shape, or redirect the external events themselves."[3]

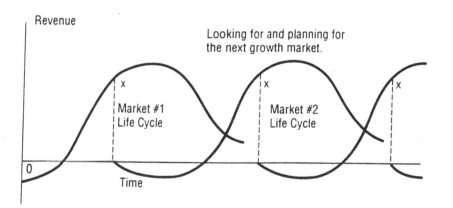

X = Awareness of the need for change and the beginning of the effort to reposition the firm. This usually occurs when revenue is increasing at a decreasing rate.

Figure 6-3. The Proactive Firm.

The Visionary Firm Plans "Two Racks" Ahead

Proactive firms may be less reactive, but they are not visionary. Firms that exemplify the visionary mode almost always have a jump on the competition. They don't wait for the signs of market maturity to initiate their search for growth opportunities.

Visionary management teams are constantly scanning the horizon for growth opportunities (Figure 6-4). They are looking for trends, cues, and clues for what may be just over the horizon. They recognize that the first-to-market firms usually reap the greatest reward. As someone has said, "The first bite of the apple is usually the best." Visionary firms tend to spend considerable time and resources scanning the horizon for "fresh" opportunities. They are not only looking for ripe apples, they are also looking for fertile fields so they can plant orchards to harvest in the future. This way, they are almost assured of having a bountiful supply of fresh and juicy apples for the decade to come.

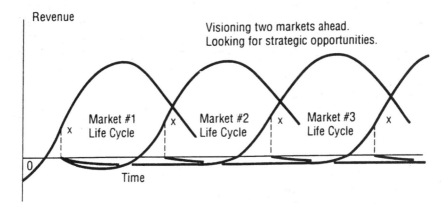

X = Awareness of the need for change and the beginning of the effort to reposition the firm. This usually occurs when revenue is increasing at an increasing rate.

Figure 6-4. The Visionary Firm.

The visionary firm operates with at least twice as long a time horizon as the proactive firm. While the proactive firm is preparing for the next market life cycle, the visionary firm is directing some of its attention and resources beyond the next market life cycle. The proactive firm may be looking for an emerging market; the visionary firm is looking for a market or industry to create!

Quite a few executives have difficulty conceiving how visionary executives can think that far ahead. Interestingly enough, there may be a close parallel between the managers of high-growth ventures and the top pool players. Years ago, the champion pool player was interviewed about how he plays the game. He admitted that when he is taking his first shot to "break" the rack of fifteen balls, he is already planning where he wants the cue ball to be positioned when he breaks the next rack so when he finishes that rack he will be in the best position to start the third rack.

The visionary E/CEO is similar to the champion pool player who thinks "two racks" ahead. The visionary mode of playing "two markets ahead" gives the management team a clear vision of the type of game the firm needs to play. It also notes that everything may need to be changed to create, cultivate, and capitalize on future growth opportunities.

One of the reasons 3M Corporation has been such a successful firm for the last few decades is that it has continued finding new business opportunities. One of 3M's goals is to have 30 percent of the firm's sales five years from now come from products that don't exist today. Looking for and capitalizing on opportunities is more than a dream or a slogan at 3M; it has operationalized the development of new products to the point that it is a way of corporate life.

Visionary E/CEOs recognize that playing "two markets ahead" is not a luxury that only larger firms can afford. They realize that continuous entrepreneurial efforts may be the fuel that feeds the fire of sustained growth. While the visionary firm may be milking its present markets, it is already preparing its entry into the next market(s) and putting together a team of people to explore opportunities that will be two markets ahead.

Most firms commit all their resources to present markets. Visionary E/CEOs carefully calibrate their firm's investment in present markets. Peter Drucker notes that firms need to have a clear idea of what are yesterday's breadwinners, today's breadwinners, and tomorrow's breadwinners. Drucker also notes that management needs to discipline itself so that its attention and the firm's resources are allocated accordingly. The visionary firm makes a deliberate effort to redeploy some of the revenues from the early growth stage of relatively new efforts to fund initiatives that will be directed to tomorrow's breadwinners.

Laggard firms may commit nearly all their resources to yesterday's breadwinners. Reactive firms divide their resources between yesterday's and today's breadwinners. While proactive firms may commit some resources to exploring new opportunities, almost all of their resources are allocated to today's breadwinners. Visionary ventures may even go so far as to have guidelines that no more than 70 percent of their firm's resources will be committed to their present markets. Twenty percent of the visionary firm's resources may be committed to tomorrow's breadwinners. The final 10 percent of their resources may be invested in tomorrow's tomorrow! The visionary strategy helps foster a corporate culture that places a premium on the firm's human resources. Firms that exhibit the visionary mode tend to attract, motivate, and retain people who are innovative and who want to be part of the "vanguard" type of firm that is positioned to

Allocation Chart of Management's Attention and the Firm's Resources

Type of firm	Percent of Attention and Resources			
	Yesterday's breadwinners	Today's breadwinners	Tomorrow's breadwinners	Tomorrow's tomorrow's breadwinners
Laggard	100	0	0	0
Reactive	80	20	0	0
Proactive	0	80	20	0
Visionary	0	65	25	10

explore new markets and develop new products or services to meet emerging needs.

The visionary firm must have a keen sense for when the window of opportunity is about to open. To jump through the window before it is open could be as disastrous as jumping through it after it has closed. Success may be contingent on anticipating when the window will open. Akio Morita, founder of Sony, captured the essence of visionary leadership when he said, "We should always be the pioneers with our products—out front leading the market. We believe in leading the public with new products rather than asking them what kind of products they want."

Visionary leadership is like skeet shooting. If you aim where the clay pigeon is, then the shot will be behind it. If you lead it too much, then your shot will pass before the clay pigeon. Management needs to be sure that in its zeal to bring the firm's innovations to market, it doesn't introduce its product-service offering before the market is ready. The old saying "If you build a better mousetrap, the world will beat a path to your door" applies only if mice are around and potential customers know about your product. Morris Siegel, as president of Celestial Seasonings, recognized that his firm had developed its line of flavored teas before the health boom had taken hold with the general public. He sought distribution through health food stores until grocery stores and supermarkets would carry his firm's products.

The Celestial Seasonings example brings up an interesting point. Visionary firms should seek out visionary customers. If the emerging firm wants to be the "leading edge" provider of products or services, then it should try to develop symbiotic relationships with "leading edge" users. Visionary firms succeed because they see themselves as "customer problem-solvers." By working closely with potential customers, the firm is almost certain to generate early sales. A number of emerging firms have even formed alliances or joint ventures with other firms to capitalize on emerging needs.

Concluding Comments: Timing Makes a Difference in the Dance with the Elephants

In the years ahead, growth and success in emerging ventures will be contingent on whether management is able to keep pace with rapidly changing markets. Management teams must refine their ability to anticipate emerging markets. They will also need to be more agile in the dance with the elephants—the elephants are destined to be leaner and meaner. Emerging ventures may not be able to take the lead on every occasion. Things are changing so quickly that it is impossible to anticipate everything that may happen. In those instances, quick response time may be the difference between survival and success.

Firms that spend their time celebrating their present successes will not notice the signs that their markets are already starting to erode. Moreover, firms that are unwilling to slough off yesterday will not be prepared for a different tomorrow. E/CEOs of emerging ventures need to recognize that if their firms aren't the initiators and beneficiaries of change, then they will be the victims of change.

Emerging firms that demonstrate visionary prowess will reap the benefits that will come with the myriad of opportunities that tomorrow and tomorrow's tomorrow will bring. Visionary firms not only start looking for growth opportunities earlier than other firms, they also make a serious investment in their future. E/CEOs of new ventures must recognize that while they are trying to improve on the present, they must also be preparing for new markets. Likewise, the management team cannot afford to spend all of its time on operational matters. Instead, it must maintain the entrepreneurial mode by religiously committing its time to scanning the environment, monitoring market trends, anticipating emerging opportunities, and reallocating resources from present product-service offerings to develop future product-service offerings.

The best way to predict the future is to invent it.
ALAN KAY OF APPLE COMPUTER

CHIEF EXECUTIVE GUIDELINES

Name: Jon T. Vincent, CPA, President
Company: JTV Business and Management Consultants
Product/Service: Professional Consulting Services and Providing Financial Services to Franchisees.
Sales: $10,000,000   *Number of Employees:* 500
Distinctions/Awards: Nominated for the "Accountant of the Decade" Award for Delta State University by its Department of Accounting.

General Guidelines: When it comes to timing when the firm should introduce new products and services as well as enter new markets, the E/CEO should keep the following tips in mind:

1. Know your competition. What are their strengths and weaknesses? How and when do you capitalize on their weaknesses, and how do you overcome their strengths?
2. Realize your window of opportunity does not remain open forever.
3. Carve out your niche and promote it with a winning attitude.
4. Plan your promotion and be prepared to handle your sales. A poorly planned promotion is a sign of a poorly managed business. Needless to say, a new product does not need to enter the marketplace tainted from the beginning.
5. Before introducing a new product to the market, picture yourself as the consumer. How does the consumer perceive your product and/or service?

Proceed with Caution Guidelines:

1. Listen to your customers. This can be done through a survey or a conversational gathering of selected consumers. Listen carefully to their comments.
2. Don't attempt to ride a dead horse in hopes that he will come alive again. If your product does not fly, do not continue to waste money funding your hopes, dreams, or ego.
3. Analyze your choice of location very thoroughly. Study the demographic makeup of your target market and try to locate geographically to your customer base.
4. Be sure not to waste marketing dollars on a product the market does not respond to.
5. Don't attempt to gain market share through unit penetration without first developing a successful model to expand from.

And I Would Be Particularly Careful Not to:

1. Introduce a product with inadequate capital to promote it properly.
2. Try to save location cost by choosing a secondary versus a primary site location.
3. Open a business with inadequately trained personnel.
4. Confuse desire to succeed with your instincts that tell you otherwise.

CHIEF EXECUTIVE GUIDELINES

Name: Thomas Venable, Chairman and Chief Executive Officer
Company: World Technology Group, Inc.
Product/Service: Strategic Alliance, Licensing and Technology Transfer
Awards/Distinctions:

1. Business Man of the Year—U.S. Small Business Administration
2. Profiled in *Inc.* and *Fortune* magazines
3. Founder of Spectrum Control Inc. and Bioinfinity International Inc.

General Guidelines: When it comes to timing when the firm should introduce new products and services as well as enter new markets, the E/CEO should keep the following tips in mind:

1. Release new products frequently: each major product line must release at least two major new products or new product innovations each year. For a small company that means two or three products per year.

2. Release your products with fanfare: schedule and time your releases concurrently with major trade shows, the holidays for consumer products, or as the focus for your annual sales meeting. Proper timing and communication to the local, national, and international press trade and general press is critical to assuring a successful product launch.

3. Know your market prior to release: the CEO must routinely attend trade show conventions and technical meetings to obtain a firm sense of market trends. Arrange to meet with your major customers several times per year and listen very closely to what they are really saying about your company, your products, and their needs.

4. If you are entering a new market: a new market can simply be a lateral or an up-and-down move on the vertical integration track, but carefully study the distribution system, the market channels, and the "traditions" or "culture" of the new market. Prior to release into a new market, recruit a successful marketing and sales executive who has a thorough knowledge of what it takes to be a winner in the new market—follow his or her advice and leadership.

5. Don't wait to start digging the well when you are thirsty: many products have a very long product life cycle, but the CEO cannot wait until a downward trend in revenues and profits is occurring before initiating the product development cycle.

Proceed with Caution Guidelines:

1. If your product is not patented or proprietary, establish the selling price to the user or consumer with a reasonable profit margin. Don't allow too large a margin, as it will encourage competition and allow competition to amortize the start-up and tooling of reverse engineered products.

2. Do not wait for declining market share prior to releasing your new products.

3. Do not withhold products from the market that will obsolete your existing products—if you don't do it your competition will.

4. Do not allow the release of a product that misses the target market, i.e., is too big, too small, too expensive, the wrong color, too slow, too fast, too complicated, and so on. Sometimes the development effort falls short, so don't compound the problem by market-releasing something just because it's complete, if it doesn't meet the market need.

And I Would Be Particularly Careful Not to:

1. Release the product to the market if your manufacturing process does not consistently build good products.

2. Release the product to the market if your manufacturing equipment throughput is inadequate to meet the expected production ship rates.

3. Release the product if you do not have a sufficient raw materials flow to meet your customer needs.

4. Release the product to the market if the product fails your qualification tests or, worse yet, if you do not have a meaningful qualification test program in place.

7

"Conventional" Growth Strategies

America is in a product war, and the management of innovation is a strategic weapon...Our ability to get better at the innovative process—to drive products from idea to market faster and with fewer mistakes—is the key to winning the war.[1]
ROBERT G. COOPER

Growth opportunities for new ventures have never been so abundant. This is a time of emerging markets and technological breakthroughs. Yet this is also an era of contrasts. It is an era marked by the sunset of a number of firms and industries that once were an integral part of the Fortune 500. It is also an era marked by the dawn of Inc. 500 firms as new ventures are being created and new industries born.

For many firms, this is a time for getting one's act together. For other firms, it is a time for embarking in new directions. In football, a good defense may keep a team in the game, but it usually takes a strong offense to win. The same is true in managing an emerging venture. If management spends all its time making sure nothing falls through the cracks, then it may never see emerging opportunities. If firms are to grow and remain vibrant,

Portions of this chapter originally appeared in the article "Developing a Corpreneurial Strategy for Fostering Business Growth and Revitalization" by the author in *Industrial Management,* July/August 1992, 19-25. Used with permission of the Institute of Industrial Engineers, Norcross, Georgia.

they must be able to identify, cultivate, and capitalize on the multitude of opportunities that lie ahead. The traditional "incremental" approach of making minor modifications in present products, services, processes, and markets will not guarantee growth; it may not even assure survival. Firms that are committed to growth will have to be more innovative, venturesome, and entrepreneurial.

There are only a few ways for a firm to grow. In very simple terms, the firm can increase sales by using any of the three "U's" of growth. First, the firm may grow by increasing the number of "users." With this strategy, the firm simply tries to find more customers. These customers may be similar to the ones the firm is already serving. The firm can also try to attract different types of customers. McDonald's used this strategy a few years ago when its television ads appealed to consumers in their "golden" years. McDonald's marketing research indicated a disproportionately low percentage of elderly people frequented fast-food restaurants.

The second "U" involves trying to increase the "usage" rate by the firm's existing customers. Orange growers in Florida have used this approach. They now promote orange juice as a beverage that can be consumed at any time of the day instead of just with breakfast.

The third strategy involves finding additional "uses" for the firm's products and services. Arm & Hammer may get the award for this strategy. Arm & Hammer's ads indicate that its baking soda can also be used to reduce odor when it is poured down the sink. It also promotes its baking soda as an air freshener for the refrigerator and freezer. Some people even use baking soda to clean the posts of car batteries!

Economics offers the "elasticity" theory for increasing revenue. According to this theory, the firm may be able to grow by either raising or lowering its prices. First, it may be possible for the firm to grow by reducing the number of units it sells. According to the elasticity equation, the firm's revenues will increase if the percentage increase in price is greater than the percentage decrease in the number of units purchased. Second, the firm may be able to increase sales by reducing its prices if the percentage by which it lowers its prices is less than the percentage increase in the number of units it sells.

The elasticity formula makes sense, but it is fairly simplistic. Any time a firm raises prices, it risks losing a larger percentage of its customers. Managers frequently become arrogant as their firms grow. They assume they have a monopoly on their customers. Unfounded price increases can be seen as an open invitation for competitors to court the firm's customers at a lower price. Conversely, the firm is taking a risk whenever it lowers its prices to attract customers. Competitors may follow suit and start a price war. It should be apparent that the firm's growth strategy needs to take a multitude of factors into account.

The "elasticity" concept and the three "U's" provide a few ideas for enhancing growth that do not require much time or the need to change the firm's product-service offering. If management is willing to consider strategies that go beyond making minor modifications, then it may consider different product-service offerings appealing to different segments and entering different geographic areas.

Choosing the Appropriate Growth Strategy

There are a number of avenues available to firms that desire to grow and strengthen their financial positions. These strategies range from the traditional avenues of geographic expansion and vertical integration all the way to bold initiatives that involve entering emerging markets with revolutionary products that incorporate first-generation technology. Some strategies can be implemented with less risk, fewer resources, and in a short period of time. Other strategies require considerable commitment of time and capital.

Most growth strategies can be found in H. Igor Ansoff's Product-Market matrix.[2] The matrix identifies four strategies for business growth (see Figure 7-1). Firms may grow by:

Market penetration—trying to get more mileage from their present products-services and present market(s).

Market development—taking present products-services and finding additional target markets for them.

Product development—developing additional products-services for present target markets.

Diversification—developing additional products-services and entering additional markets.

	EXISTING PRODUCTS	NEW PRODUCTS
EXISTING MARKETS	MARKET PENETRATION	PRODUCT DEVELOPMENT
NEW MARKETS	MARKET DEVELOPMENT	DIVERSIFICATION

Figure 7-1. Ansoff's Growth Matrix.[2]

These strategies were very effective in the 1960s when nearly every market was expanding. While most markets have matured since that time, these strategies continue to be effective for many ventures. They will be discussed in this chapter. A set of more venturesome strategies will be presented in Chapter 8.

Market Penetration Is the Most Conventional Growth Strategy

Market penetration strategy involves trying to do "more of the same" on a larger scale. For this reason, it is frequently called the "concentration" strategy. The firm continues to concentrate all of its efforts on what it has been doing. The firm simply attempts to increase sales by getting its present customers to buy more of its product-service offering. The firm also tries to find additional customers.

The firm may increase its advertising, lower prices, or provide additional brands of the same product. It may also make its product-service offering more accessible to existing and potential customers in its present geographic market. The firm may even consider entering additional geographic territories by opening additional stores or distribution channels to appeal to potential customers beyond its present reach.

Market penetration strategy appeals to many firms because it does not appear to have much risk. The firm just has to find more customers who have the same needs and desires as the ones it is presently serving. Market penetration is a linear and incremental growth strategy. The firm is continuing what it already knows (linear), and it involves minimal (incremental) change. Management tends to favor this strategy because it is merely an extension of the strategy the firm used at its inception. The firm continues fine-tuning its operations with the market penetration strategy. This should reduce the likelihood that things will fall through the cracks. It may reduce the firm's vulnerability to competition. Market penetration strategy should also enable the firm to operate more efficiently, which will give it a price advantage in the marketplace.

Chain stores and franchises frequently use the market penetration growth strategy. If a business wants to maintain control and ownership over its operations, then management may consider establishing a "chain" of nearly identical businesses. Charles Lazarus, who founded Toys-R-Us, positioned his firm to reap the rewards of a well-orchestrated market penetration strategy. Some analysts believe that Lazarus's firm is in a position to capture nearly 50 percent of retail toy sales. Lazarus did not have to hold his breath very long to enjoy the benefits of rapid growth. A few years ago, he was listed as the highest-paid executive in the United States. His salary, when combined with his stock gains for the year, exceeded $80 million. Starbucks Coffee Company also demonstrates the value of establishing a chain of small retail outlets. The company, which specializes in coffee sales, grew from five stores to over two hundred stores in just ten years. Starbucks is opening one new store each week.

If management is in a hurry to enter certain markets, then it may acquire or merge with existing businesses in its target markets. This form of penetration is frequently called "horizontal integration." The merger and acquisition strategy is particularly useful in service businesses where customer goodwill is essential and where it might take years to establish a strong position in those territories. The merger or acquisition strategy has one other benefit over setting up a chain outlet or branch office in that community. By acquiring an existing business, you have just eliminated a firm that would have been a competitor had you gone in with your own outlet.

Franchising your business concept and licensing your business's name or technology represent other avenues for increasing the size of the business. In licensing, you may sell another business the right to use your name or technology for a period of time in return for a fee. In franchising, your firm would become the "franchisor." It would grant other businesses the right to use your name and business concept. Franchising represents an avenue for quick and widespread geographic expansion that may not be possible for a firm with limited resources. While the franchisor may only get a fraction of the revenue generated by each franchisee, the potential of having a franchise outlet in almost every neighborhood in the United States and abroad may have considerable appeal.

Franchising is attractive to firms that have a great concept but lack the resources to cover a large geographic area in a short period of time. Fred DeLuca recognized the merit of the franchise growth strategy soon after he set up Subway. It would have taken him a lifetime to establish an international chain of Subway sub shops. The franchise strategy has permitted him to establish thousands of sub shops. Subway is presently opening nearly three outlets each day. A drive down any major thoroughfare or walk through any major mall demonstrates the widespread use of market penetration strategy by retail and service firms.

Market penetration strategy is not without its shortcomings. The strategy seems to be based on the "If it ain't broke, don't fix it" mentality. Market penetration strategy is nothing more than "management by braille." By concentrating only on its present products-services and present markets, the firm is only dealing with what it can touch, what is within its reach.

Firms adopting the market penetration growth strategy should be aware of at least four types of risk associated with it. First, the firm is likely to encounter intense competition as the market matures unless it has a strong proprietary position. Second, the management team tends to get caught up in operational matters rather than spend its time searching for emerging opportunities and dealing with strategic issues. Third, a major shift in consumer interests could cause the market to dry up. Peter Drucker notes that if you stay in one business long enough, you will go out of business! Fourth, a major technological breakthrough could render the firm's product-service offering obsolete almost overnight.

The fourth type of risk was particularly evident when the quartz movement for watches was invented. Until 1967, the mainspring watch controlled 65 percent of the world market. One year later, only fifteen thousand of the sixty thousand Swiss watchmakers still had their jobs.[3] The quartz breakthrough may not be an everyday occurrence, but it does illustrate the devastating effect innovation can have on firms that are out of touch with technology and market trends. The same could apply to changes in laws, political unrest in certain countries, and population shifts. Managers who say, "That couldn't happen in this business" should be reminded that the phrase "He didn't think the gun was loaded" appears on numerous tombstones! Market penetration may have considerable merit in the short run, but it surely wouldn't hurt for management to explore other possibilities.

Market Development Targets New Segments of Customers

The market development strategy is more venturesome than the market penetration strategy. Even though the firm may not be making any major changes in its original product-service offering, management is making a deliberate effort to increase its revenue by appealing to a whole new target market. Firms using this growth strategy rarely turn their backs on the markets they have been serving all along. Instead, they are broadening their reach to include a different set of potential customers. The firm's product-service offering may not be modified much but other aspects of its marketing mix will probably be tailored to meet the targeted segment's needs.

Market development frequently involves finding new types of users or uses for the firm's existing product-service offering. The classic example would be for the firm that has developed a product for individual consumers to try to market the product-service to government agencies and corporations. Most electronic appliances were developed for household use. Marketing was done through retail stores. As the consumer market started to mature a number of the appliance manufacturers began to search for other types of consumers. Manufacturers quickly found that hospitals, hotels, schools, corporations, and the military were lucrative markets that required little change in the product's basic configuration.

Smaller, emerging firms also can benefit from the market development strategy. Nancy Abt came to the conclusion that there must be a better way to help people cool off in the heat of summer. Her firm developed and received a patent on "The Cool Advantage." Her product holds blocks of foam that are soaked in salt water. When the blocks, which are in polyurethane insulating bags, are frozen, they are colder than regular ice. Her product comes with a cloth cover seamed with Velcro strips, which allows people to wear it while playing tennis or any other sport. By using the market development growth strategy, her firm is exploring other target markets, particularly people who may need heat or muscle relief. Chefs or people who suffer from multiple sclerosis are potential targets.[4]

Market development encourages management to adopt a much broader perspective on what the firm's product-service offering can do. Market development encourages management to view the firm as a "customer problem-solver" rather than as a business that "sells products-services." By looking for different uses and different users in its formative years, the firm will reduce the likelihood that it will be caught in the quicksand associated with being a one-product, one-market business. In many cases, the "supplementary" markets may be more lucrative and lasting than the firm's original market. Perceptiveness and flexibility may be more important than inventiveness in many markets.

A note of caution may be appropriate here. While the firm may search for new markets that offer different uses and different users, management should not overlook the need to update and/or improve its product-services. To do so would be like laying a welcome mat for the competition. The firm would also be running the risk of being blindsided by technological obsolescence. Firms that choose the market development strategy must ensure their products remain competitive.

Product Development Broadens the Firm's Offering

The product development growth strategy is a unidimensional growth strategy like the market development strategy. Instead of trying to find a new set of customers for its existing product-service offering, the firm directs its attention to broadening its product-service offering. This strategy is based on the premise, "Since the firm already understands its present customers, then it should be able to develop additional products to meet one or more of their other needs." The firm prefers to accept the risk that its offering may not be exactly what its present target market desires rather than accept the risk associated with a market penetration strategy wherein the firm's future is tied to a single product or service.

Numerous firms have adopted the product development strategy. Retail stores that began offering one particular product to the market and then slowly added different products are classic examples. Some stores took this strategy to the extreme and became department stores. Stores that started selling clothes now offer their customers computers, lawn mowers, cut flowers, and almost everything else their segment of customers would buy from other stores. Even service firms have adopted the product development strategy. In addition to renting a video, video stores now offer popcorn, soft drinks, video-player rentals, and a number of other products and services. Bill Gates's Microsoft may be the best example of the product development strategy. He has become one of the wealthiest men in the United States by focusing on providing the most popular software and computer operating systems in the world.

Product development is based on two premises. First, if management believes it will be more difficult in terms of risk, time, and resources to attract more customers, then the firm should focus its attention on broadening its product-service offering for its present target market. Management has to find ways for the firm's present customers to spend more money with each visit.

The second premise for product development sounds a bit greedy. In a sense, the firm operates with the attitude, "If each customer has a specific amount of money available to spend for various products and services, then let's see if we can broaden our product-service offering so that we get a larger portion of each customer's budget." Most firms try to grow by gaining a larger share of the market. Firms using the product development strategy attempt to grow by gaining a larger share of the customer. Gerber demonstrates this approach very well. Gerber's slogan is "Babies are our only business." Gerber recognizes that a family will spend a certain amount of money on a child in its first few years. If Gerber can't increase the birthrate, then all it can do is try to increase its share of what families spend on baby-related items.

Part of Disney's spectacular growth can be attributed to its use of product development. Disney recognized that its customers were spending more money on overnight accommodations at neighboring hotels than at the Disney parks. Disney tripled the number of its on-site hotels, which provide a wide range of amenities. Disney also broadened its product offering so it could gain a larger share of its customers' cash and credit cards.

Disney's recent use of product development strategy is evident in its combination "Disney World—Premier Cruise Line" package. Disney recognized the growing interest in cruises and the desire for parents to take their kids with them. Most cruise lines are geared to retirees or young singles. Disney was able to bring its talents in appealing to kids and families into the cruise market business. This strategy builds on the experience and goodwill the firm already has established with its customer base. In most cases, the firm using the product development strategy has a distinct advantage over other firms because it is already in contact with its target market when it attempts to sell additional products and services. Product development is based on the premise that it is easier to sell an existing customer a second item than it is to create a customer in the first place.

Product development has merit because it reduces the risk of technological obsolescence. It also encourages the firm to experiment. This strategy may also bring new people into the firm who may have different perceptions of what the future may hold and where the firm should go. Product development is not without its drawbacks. The firm still has limited its perceptual field. The firm's potential will always be limited by the opportunities that can be found in one set of customers. The most significant drawback associated with this strategy is the possibility that the market will wane. If there are fewer customers altogether or if their disposable income drops, then the firm's revenue will almost certainly decline. Changing consumer interests also may affect the firm's growth.

The firm must also guard against spreading itself too thin. This is what has happened to a number of department stores. They carried products they did not understand, and they did not monitor their inventories well. By spending so much time on a diverse product-service line, they lost sight of their customers' needs. These firms became "product and inventory-driven" businesses rather than "customer-driven" businesses.

Product development strategy is effective only to the extent the firm can maintain its commitment to being the best firm available for meeting its customers' needs. Whenever management ponders product development strategy, it should avoid getting so caught up in finding new products that it loses sight of the extent the firm is satisfying its customers' needs. In its desire to offer new products management frequently forgets that products are merely the means to the end. Achieving an even higher level of customer satisfaction is the end! Another drawback for firms using this strategy needs to be noted. Management needs to recognize that by pursuing product development, it is incurring the opportunity cost associated with not pursuing other markets, particularly emerging markets, which may have more potential than the firm's present segment(s) of customers.

Diversification Is a Two-Dimensional Growth Strategy

Diversification is more venturesome than the three previously discussed avenues for growth. With diversification, the firm tries to increase sales by appealing to different markets with different products-services. The firm is broadening its reach in two dimensions. This strategy appears to involve greater risk than the other growth strategies. In market penetration, the firm tries to do more of what it was already doing. In market development, while the firm tries to appeal to a different segment of customers, at least it is offering a product that it knows well. With product development, the firm may be venturing into different products, but it is still dealing with a familiar set or type of customers.

Diversification involves going where the firm has not gone before. It is like a general attacking on two fronts. Diversification usually places considerable strain on the firm's cash flow and profitability. The firm is also more likely to make mistakes. Diversification requires learning about different markets and developing different products-services. Few firms develop the "one best way" on their first attempt. Diversification tends to work best when the firm ventures into related markets and deals with a related technology, product, or type of service.

Safety-Kleen Corporation serves as a good example of diversification. Safety-Kleen originally delivered a device to service stations for degreasing parts. The company was losing money on that product. Management, however, found there was an opportunity to recycle substances like antifreeze and transmission fluid that could not be dumped anymore. It also found an opportunity in supplying cleaning agents. The company now supplies 60 percent of the dry cleaners in its territory with cleaning agents. Safety-Kleen's mission statement has even been changed to reflect the change in its products, services, and customers. The company's new mission is "To become the world's biggest processor of hazardous waste fluids." Safety-Kleen is making progress in fulfilling its mission. Before it diversified, the firm was losing money on $1 million in sales. Sales now approach $700 million![5]

The Firm May Use a Combination of All Four Strategies

Kindercare provides an interesting example of a firm that used all four growth strategies. Kindercare started with a market penetration strategy by expanding its day-care facilities throughout the United States. In the early years, most of management's attention was directed to identifying new locations, improving its operations, and keeping costs down so it could gain market share. The firm then used a market development strategy when it developed its "Kindustry" program. Instead of appealing just to parents, Kindercare went after institutions for their business. Its

"Kindustry" program worked directly with major employers to meet their employees' child care needs by building day-care facilities near the entrances to their businesses. Kindercare then demonstrated the product development strategy through the acquisition of Sylvan Learning Systems. Sylvan specializes in tutoring youth as a supplement to regular schooling. Kindercare took its knowledge of establishing facilities that provided services to youth and applied it to older children.

Kindercare then took a quantum leap in its product development growth strategy by buying a children's shoe store chain. While top management may have known something about children, the skills required to operate retail stores differ considerably from those for operating service businesses. The challenge was magnified by the intense competition that came with the maturity of the shoe store market.

Kindercare then dabbled with diversification by acquiring a savings and loan in Florida. This venture illustrated all the risks associated with diversification. Not only was managing a financial institution different in terms of products, services, customers, competitors, technology, and regulations; Kindercare's timing was inopportune. When all was said and done, Kindercare's management transformed a firm that had become the leader in providing child care in the free world into a firm that looked like a carcass that had been picked over by "financial reorganization" vultures. The irony of the situation was that Kindercare did not need to veer from its original penetration strategy for decades. Even though it had over a thousand franchise units in the United States and Canada, it had less than 5 percent of the overall market. Had it stayed exclusively in the day-care business, it could be what Toys-R-Us is to retail toy sales today.

If diversification is attempted, then it needs to be done in an evolutionary manner. Diversification is similar to the concept of "planning one or two markets" ahead discussed in the last chapter. Most successful new ventures that use the diversification strategy do so only after they are established and have sufficient resources to fund this two-dimensional growth strategy. Diversification usually works best if it is done on a moderate level rather than as a "bet the farm" type of endeavor. It is always better to test the temperature and depth of a body of water with your big toe than to jump in with both feet.

Diversification works best when it is done as an incremental strategy that may offer a 10 to 20 percent increase in revenue rather than an effort to double the size of the firm in twelve months. If it is done in a gradual way, the firm should be able to develop competitive proficiency in the markets it enters. It should also be in a position to gracefully phase itself out of the markets it was originally in as they enter the late maturity or decline stage of their respective market life cycles.

The Firm's Growth Strategy Can Also Include Vertical Integration

This chapter would not be complete without a discussion of the merits of vertical integration. Vertical integration can take two forms. Reverse vertical integration occurs when the firm gets involved in doing what its suppliers have done. Forward vertical integration exists when the firm gets involved in the manufacturing or distribution stage that follows what the firm has traditionally been doing. Vertical integration usually is undertaken to give the firm additional economies, better control over quality, or an exclusive source of supply or distribution. Some firms have undertaken both forms of integration.

Three Buoys provides an interesting example of vertical integration. This Canadian business was started by three guys just after they graduated from college. They found there was growing interest in houseboat rentals on one of Canada's lakes. Soon after they started renting houseboats, they realized the boats were not "user-friendly." They also found the existing line of boats was difficult to clean. The first drawback affected demand and revenue. The second factor increased cleaning costs. Three Buoys approached a boatbuilder to build a houseboat for them that would meet their needs. Demand for their houseboats quickly exceeded their supply. Three Buoys then put together an investment syndicate to buy all the boats they needed. Three Buoys then vertically integrated into the boatbuilding business. Before long, Three Buoys had developed the second-largest fleet of boats in Canada. Now, only the Canadian government has more boats.

Three Buoys then vertically integrated in the other direction. They bought resorts where they could dock their boats. The resorts also provided bases for selling grocery items and other products and services. Three Buoys was last seen eyeing U.S. locations that offer an even larger population and a longer rental season. It is amazing how a relatively simple boat rental business can grow in so many directions.

Concluding Comments: The Firm Needs to Have a Deliberate Strategy

Management cannot afford to leave the firm's growth to chance. In the dance with the elephants, management needs to have a game plan so that it knows what it is doing. With the passage of time, changes in the marketplace will require changes in the firm's strategy. Hopefully, management will see the trends early enough to have sufficient lead time to modify the firm's strategy or to adopt another strategy that will capitalize on the opportunities that come with the changes.

Don't wait for extraordinary opportunities.
Seize common occasions and make them great.
ORISON SWETT MARDEN

CHIEF EXECUTIVE GUIDELINES

Name: Dorothy Noe, President
Company: Dorothy's Ruffled Originals Inc.
Product/Service: Custom Home Fashions, Curtains, Bedding, and Related Products
Sales: $10,000,000   Number of Employees: 200
Awards/Distinctions:

1. "Small Business Person of the Year Award" by the U.S. Small Business Administration
2. "Entrepreneurial Excellence Award" for North Carolina by Governor James Martin, 1985
3. *Inc.* Magazine's "One of America's Fastest-Growing Privately Owned Companies," 1986 and 1987
4. North Carolina's "Entrepreneur of the Year" by *Entrepreneur* magazine, 1989

General Guidelines: When it comes to the need for and process of introducing new products and services and expanding the firm's geographic markets, the E/CEO should keep the following tips in mind:

1. Listen to the creative ideas and support them.
2. Listen to the customer daily and believe the information.
3. React to the customers' needs.
4. Move ASAP on the best ideas. Only the savvy entrepreneurs manage to sustain a growth company long after the white-hot product burns out.
5. Set the company culture for fast implementation of new ideas.

Proceed with Caution Guidelines:

1. Limit new products to "focused" best ideas.
2. Look at geographic markets as segments with different needs.
3. Move much faster with changing market needs based on customer needs.
4. Improve training of salespeople in new products.
5. Provide a route to get new ideas from employees and customers, and act on information.

And I Would Be Particularly Careful Not to:

1. Stifle creativity.
2. Ignore new ideas and trends suggested by others.
3. Try to do everything and be everything for all people. You need to be more focused.
4. Forget the customers' needs.

CHIEF EXECUTIVE GUIDELINES

Name: Edgar B. Harris, President and Chief Executive Officer
Company: Comprehensive Home Health Care
Product/Service: Home Health Care
Sales: $36,000,000   Number of Employees: 750
Awards/Distinctions:

1. First "Male" Honorary Chairman of the YWCA "Women of Achievement" Awards for the Wilmington Region, 1993
2. The largest home health company in the Carolinas
3. The first private home health company in the U.S. to be accredited by the Joint Commission on Accreditation of Health Care Organizations (JCAHO)

General Guidelines: When it comes to the need for and process of introducing new products and services and expanding the firm's geographic markets, the E/CEO should keep the following tips in mind:

1. Know your product/subject matter/business better than anyone else.

2. Know your competitors.

3. Keep it simple—simplify, simplify, simplify.

4. Hire quality employees, educate and train extensively and continuously, and test for understanding.

5. Communicate, communicate, communicate.

6. Manage, manage, manage.

Proceed with Caution Guidelines:

1. Forge ahead—move quicker.

2. Practice my philosophy: "The best offense is a good offense."

3. Remember that cash management is more important than the bottom line.

4. Have an expansion team always ready to move.

5. Hold staff accountable for actions and responsibilities—both individually and as a team.

6. Go with your "gut feelings" when in doubt.

And I Would Be Particularly Careful Not to:

1. Listen to accountants too much.

2. Listen to attorneys too much.

3. Listen to consultants too much.

8

"Corpreneurial" Growth Strategies

*A capitalist economy grows by a process
called creative destruction—whereby
entrepreneurial innovation combines with
technological investment to create new
growth industries which inevitably inflict
pain and distress on older, less dynamic
businesses they displace.*

JOSEPH SCHUMPETER

The last chapter identified four conventional growth strategies. This chapter will address five "corpreneurial" growth strategies. The term *corpreneurial* is used because it suggests a more venturesome approach to exploring growth strategies. Corpreneurial implies an entrepreneurial approach to managing an existing venture. Corpreneurial growth strategies may involve going wherever the opportunities may be without regard for where the firm has been before.

Executives who want their firms to thrive in the years ahead must be willing to look beyond the traditional growth strategies. All four of Ansoff's strategies profiled in the last chapter are more incremental than entrepreneurial. Diversification even tends to be an incremental strategy. Most

Portions of this chapter originally appeared in the article "Developing a Corpreneurial Strategy for Fostering Business Growth and Revitalization" by the author in *Industrial Management,* July/August 1992, 19-25. Used with permission of the Institute of Industrial Engineers, Norcross, Georgia.

management teams view it as something to do in addition to what the firm is already doing. The amount of time and resources that management commits to diversifying the firm's reach tends to be limited.

Firms with high expectations for growth need to instill the spirit of corpreneurship. It should be noted here that corpreneurship is not the same concept as Gifford Pinchot III's concept of intrapreneurship. Intrapreneurship tends to be viewed as an effort to improve corporate performance by unleashing the innovative talents of the firm's human resources. In many cases, intrapreneurship represents management's efforts to improve the firm's internal operations rather than capitalize on external opportunities or develop technological breakthroughs. Intrapreneurship also tends to have an incremental theme to it. Attention is directed to finding better ways to do things the firm is already doing.

Corpreneurship is more entrepreneurial than intrapreneurial. It means management is prepared to slough off yesterday and today in its efforts to capitalize on a different tomorrow. Intrapreneurial managers concentrate their attention on improving the firm's present situation. Corpreneurship is based on the premise that there is always something better to do. Corpreneurial managers concentrate their attention on creating the firm's future. Intrapreneurship fine-tunes the firm's present products and processes.

Corpreneurship involves creating corporate teams to capitalize on emerging market opportunities and to develop new technologies. Just as the entrepreneur creates a business to capitalize on an untapped opportunity in the marketplace, the corpreneurial firm creates new business units to enter new markets and to develop revolutionary products, processes, and services.

While the intrapreneur does things that the firm has not done before, the corpreneur does things that no firm has done before. The entrepreneur and the corpreneur operate with a similar philosophy. They exemplify the prelude to *Star Trek*; they are committed to "boldly go where no one has gone before!"

Just as there is a clear distinction between people who start a business and the true entrepreneur, there is a fundamental distinction between traditional growth strategies and corpreneurial growth strategies. Most new ventures are clones of existing businesses. They rarely bring anything markedly innovative to the marketplace. Entrepreneurs stand out from the crowd because they bring something new to the marketplace. Their new ventures are more than a repackaging of existing components. Entrepreneurs add "value" to the marketplace by shaking it up. Corpreneurial firms through their perceptiveness and innovative capabilities change the way the game will be played.

Entrepreneurs accept the risk associated with introducing something that is much more than a minor modification of the present. The same is true for corpreneurs. They are committed to being at the cutting edge and are willing to accept the risk associated with breaking new ground by going where no firm has gone before.

Chapter 3 identified the various stages or phases of new venture growth. The seventh or ultimate stage involves reestablishing the entrepreneurial spirit. Corpreneurship represents the operationalization of the seventh stage. A few years ago, *Business Month* profiled Alcan Aluminum Corporation. Timothy Tuff as president of Alcan in 1989 demonstrated many of the qualities that must be infused into more traditional corporations if they are to capitalize on the opportunities that lie ahead. Tuff developed a team to foster an entrepreneurial culture, promote new ideas, and make product development as simple as casting an ingot. *Business Month* reported that Tuff's team was responsible for finding the technology, funding the project, and designing products that did not yet exist. Alcan set a goal of having 25 percent of total corporate revenue by 1995 come from its new ventures. Tuff's team spurred the development of dozens of such ventures.[1]

Adding Corpreneurial Strategies to Ansoff's Model

Ansoff's model worked well during the period of dramatic, across-the-board, global economic growth. Firms could grow by modifying existing products and moving into related markets. There was little need to be corpreneurial. Times have changed and new strategies may need to be initiated to capitalize on new and different opportunities. Ansoff's model has been updated and modified for this chapter to incorporate the dynamics of emerging markets, changing consumer and institutional needs, and the accelerating rate of technological change (see Figure 8-1). The 2 × 2 matrix has been expanded to a 3 × 3 matrix to incorporate five corpreneurial growth strategies.

	Existing Products	Different Products	New Products
Existing Markets	MARKET PENETRATION	PRODUCT DEVELOPMENT	PRODUCT INNOVATION
Different Markets	MARKET DEVELOPMENT	DIVERSI-FICATION	PRODUCT INVENTION
New Markets	MARKET TRANSFER	MARKET CREATION	PURE CORPRE-NEURSHIP

Figure 8-1. Ansoff's Growth Matrix Modified to Reflect Corpreneurial Growth Strategies.

The headings for the rows and columns have been modified. Ansoff's original matrix had "existing" and "new" headings. The 3 × 3 matrix continues to use the "existing" heading; however, it replaces Ansoff's "new" with the word "different." In the original matrix, anytime the firm did anything it had not done before, the matrix classified that behavior as new. The 3 × 3 matrix distinguishes "new" from "different." If the firm is to embark in a direction that already exists in the marketplace, then the firm is merely doing something different from what it had done before. If, however, the firm is embarking in a direction where no firm has gone before, then this is truly something that can be considered to be new—it is new altogether. The distinction is significant. Just because a firm does something different from what it has done before does not mean that the marketplace will reward it.

When McDonald's decided to offer drive-in services and prepackaged salads, the marketplace did not herald McDonald's as the most innovative fast-food franchise. Most of the other fast-food franchises had already provided these products and services. While it may have been different for McDonald's, these changes were not "new" to the marketplace. The "new" heading in the 3 × 3 matrix indicates that a service, product, or a process is provided for the first time altogether, and the firm is at the leading edge associated with truly entrepreneurial endeavors.

Product Innovation Strategy Adds Considerable Value to the Market

The product innovation strategy goes beyond the traditional product development strategy. The firm may still be directing its attention to the needs of the people or institutions in its present target market, but it attempts to introduce a markedly superior product or service by developing new technology. The basic product or service may have been around for years, but the corpreneurial firm uses state-of-the-art technology to create a new generation of the product.

Yamaha provides an excellent example of product innovation. Yamaha had 40 percent of worldwide piano sales, yet overall demand was declining by 10 percent per year. Instead of settling for a stagnating or declining market, Yamaha's executives sought ways to foster growth through technology. They knew growth would need to come by offering the market a piano that could do things no other piano could do. Yamaha combined digital and optical technology to develop the means whereby a conventional piano can be retrofitted for $2500 to play great works. Yamaha took the original player piano concept and matched it with state-of-the-art technology. A 3.5-inch diskette stores recorded music and programs the piano.

Yamaha was already committed to the production and marketing of pianos and other musical instruments. Management chose product innovation as its primary strategy for revitalizing the market. Yamaha did not pursue the usual routes for turning its situation around. Kenichi Ohmae indicated, "It didn't buckle down to prune costs, proliferate models, slice overhead or all the other typical approaches. It looked with fresh eyes for chances to create value for customers."[2] According to Ohmae, Yamaha was perceptive enough to recognize that people's interest in and appreciation for the piano has continued to grow over the years. The decline in piano sales had come from the reluctance to spend years learning how to play it. Yamaha therefore looked to technology as a way to speed the learning process and highlight the true beauty of the piano.

Yamaha demonstrated that product innovation relies more on perceptiveness than extensive research and development. The piano already existed as did the technology. Yamaha was merely the first firm in the piano field to combine them to offer the market something "new."

Kodak demonstrated the product innovation strategy with its photo CD system. With this system, a person can save pictures taken with an ordinary camera onto a CD. From there, one can view them on the TV set, retouch them on a PC, and send them over the optic-wave phone line to anyone with a CD-ROM reader. Kodak merely recognized a need that could be addressed by combining available technology.

Air-Mouse Remote Controls demonstrates how smaller firms can utilize product innovation strategy. Air-Mouse has provided a major innovation in the way PC users can operate their mice. Air-Mouse developed a mouse that does for the computer what the "remote" did for the TV. Air-Mouse's presentation device works without a wire. When you point it at the projected image on the computer monitor, its base unit interprets the location of the image via infrared light. Product innovation permits the Air-Mouse to function like a pointer flashlight. This mobility provides a level of freedom that was not available with equipment that was based on conventional technology. How's that for creating a better mousetrap?

Putting technology into a new "package" is what makes product innovation an effective strategy. As Robert Allio, author of *The Practical Strategist*, observes, "Technology is a powerful ally in the global game, particularly if it enables a business to improve its product offering."[3] Allio notes that in the competitive arena, "Losers hang on to old technology in the mistaken belief that incremental improvements can forestall the effect of a technological breakthrough."[4]

Product Invention Introduces
a First-Generation Product

The product invention strategy is more corpreneurial than the product innovation growth strategy. Whereas product innovation introduces technologically superior products or services to the firm's present market(s), product invention represents a two-dimensional change strategy. The firm is inventing a product that no firm has ever offered. The firm is also entering a market it has never served.

This strategy exemplifies the risk/return nature of entrepreneurship. The firm is halfway toward corpreneurship in its truest sense. The firm is introducing a first-generation product into an existing market. The firm is taking two risks: the risk associated with the uncertainty of whether the new product-service is in tune with the wants of prospective customers and the risk associated with entering a market with limited firsthand experience. Any time a firm introduces a radically different product-service it is taking a risk; to do it in a market that it has not operated in before reflects a corpreneurial approach to fostering business growth.

The rewards of offering a first-generation product-service will hopefully outweigh the risks. If the product is markedly better from a technological or convenience perspective and the market is searching for something clearly better than what is presently being provided by the firms already in the market, then the firm using the product invention growth strategy may be in an excellent position to harvest the market. This strategy will be particularly advantageous if the firm is able to secure a proprietary position.

A number of firms have become leaders by utilizing the product invention strategy. They provide products or services that are radically different from what the market has been offered by other firms. Merck and 3M have been cited by *Fortune* magazine as two of America's most admired firms for their introduction of new products. Merck recently introduced Proscar, which is formulated to shrink enlarged prostates and thereby minimize the need for surgery. Proscar provides a completely different alternative to prostate treatment. According to *U.S. News and World Report,* some four hundred thousand men who face surgery each year to remove an enlarged prostate can take a pill instead of undergoing surgery. This one-dollar-per-day drug represents a better alternative to the traditional operation that costs over $10,000.

3M demonstrates a similar propensity to utilize the product invention growth strategy. 3M has consistently ventured into different markets and developed new technology. 3M's bioelectronic ear, which helps restore hearing for people with inner ear damage, reflects the company's willingness to go where it has not gone before and to develop products that no firm has developed before. 3M's ability to bring varying levels of technology to market to meet established needs is the hallmark of the inventive organization.

Limmion Corporation and Bio-Energy International are two smaller companies that illustrate how whole new approaches can address existing problems that have become monumental concerns to our country. Both firms are positioned to capitalize on the inescapable need to deal with our country's pollution problems. Limmion Corporation has found a way to use plants to cleanse ponds of industrial waste and then collect the usable waste for recycling. Instead of using more chemicals to clean a pond, Limmion Corporation deploys these plants as underwater gardens. The plants' pods are regularly harvested to reclaim contaminants they have gathered. Bio-Energy International has obtained the rights to use a new microbe developed through gene-splicing that can turn garbage into alcohol. Bio-Energy International's first plant is expected to produce five million gallons of ethanol per year from organic waste such as wood, paper, and food garbage. Both firms demonstrate the entrepreneur's credo, "Within every problem there lies at least one disguised business opportunity."

Market Transfer Means Being "First to Market"

The market transfer growth strategy is designed to take the firm's existing product-service-technology mix into markets that are not being served by any firm. Firms using this strategy look for markets that are just emerging. This strategy is particularly appropriate for third-world or emerging countries.

Emerging countries may represent lucrative opportunities for firms that are willing to be the first to serve them. Yet, this strategy also has risks. The firm's success will be directly related to its ability to tailor its existing market mix to the uniqueness of the emerging target market. The risk associated with market transfer tends to be higher than that found in the market development strategy noted in the previous chapter. The newness of an emerging market means little data may be available and that the infrastructure for introducing and supporting the product-service offering may be limited or nonexistent.

Emerging countries may provide high levels of profit in the years to come for firms that are willing to take their products-services where no firm has gone before. As third-world and emerging countries improve their domestic productivity and increase their export activity, their disposable income and desire for a higher standard of living will also increase. Their people will be more interested and more capable of purchasing goods-services that are common in more developed countries.

As emerging countries develop an infrastructure capable of facilitating importing and currency exchange, firms operating in established and mature markets will attempt to transfer their marketing efforts to the emerging economies. Timing may be the key to success for firms using the market transfer growth strategy. If the firm waits until the infrastructure is established before it initiates its strategy, then it may be too late to harvest the opportunity. In a sense, this firm has failed to incorporate the Wayne Gretzky concept of being in the right place at the right time with the right capability.

Success in market transfer may be contingent on being positioned to enter the window of opportunity the moment it starts to open. If the firm waits until the window is fully open before it initiates the market transfer strategy, then it will likely encounter stiff competition from outside and possibly within that market. Bill Schroeder of Conner Peripherals captured the importance of speed to market when he stated, "The first guy into a market cleans up, the second guy does OK, the third guy barely breaks even. The fourth guy loses money."[5] Conner Peripherals, which makes computer disk drives, has the distinction of being the only company to go from start-up to $1 billion in sales in four years![6]

The market transfer strategy is already being used by numerous firms. There has been a noticeable increase in exporting by small U.S. firms into emerging countries. Smaller firms may be better prepared to enter emerging markets because larger firms tend to look for large markets and view emerging markets as not being worth their time and effort. Large firms also tend to stay away from markets that are fairly nebulous. Larger firms tend to do what stock brokerage houses do when there is limited information about a relatively new venture—they consider it to be "speculative." Yet the word "speculative" can be translated into an entrepreneurial opportunity for a firm positioned to take the first bite out of the apple. Bill Gates, founder of Microsoft Inc., suggests that growth companies have a major impact on the economy because "They are even more flexible than larger companies in terms of spawning new opportunities...Smaller companies make the most out of new markets. Even those that grow very big start out very small. A big company won't go into a small business."[7]

Ironically, many of the successful, more entrepreneurial firms that use market transfer strategy have received their funding from smaller, regional banks and investment companies. Larger banks are often reluctant to lend less than $1 million. The same may be true for larger businesses not being interested in emerging markets until they are big enough to harvest. This mentality is similar to the strategy, "Don't shoot until you see the white in their eyes!" used in combat. If a firm waits until the market is already established, then it may be too late. While there may be a higher probability of hitting the target at close range, success in business tends to come to firms that anticipate opportunities, harvest them before the market gets saturated, and get out in time to redeploy their resources to catch and ride successive waves of emerging markets.

The market transfer growth strategy may be appealing because it may require only a minimal initial capital outlay. The firm may test an emerging market by exporting its existing products-services with minor modification. If the emerging market responds with sufficient vigor, then the firm may consider additional modifications in its marketing mix to meet the emerging market's particular needs. Again, the issue of timing comes up. If the firm is first to market and there is penned-up demand, then prospective customers may be flexible in their expectations. As noted earlier, when you are the first firm to deliver pizza, it doesn't have to be great—it just needs to be warm and reasonably priced.

Market transfer permits the firm to test the temperature and depth of the water with its big toe rather than jumping in with both feet. If the level of interest is sufficient to warrant a higher level of commitment, then the firm may investigate the merit of establishing facilities or joint ventures in the emerging market. If the firm is technology-based, then it may consider licensing its technology. Licensing may be particularly beneficial because it requires minimal cash outlay.

One U.S. aquaculture firm provides a good example of the market transfer strategy. Management is looking into exporting its frozen fish fillets to an emerging country and entering into a joint venture with the government to build fish farms and processing facilities if their product is accepted and demonstrates economic viability. This firm sees this opportunity as almost too good to be true. Management had been trying to find a way of getting some revenue from the fillets that did not meet the company's high standards for U.S. restaurants and supermarkets. Exporting appears to have considerable merit because emerging foreign markets may not place the same standards on the color and size of the fillets. Ironically, many emerging markets seem to prefer frozen fish to fresh fish fillets because they will not spoil as quickly.

Market transfer strategy illustrates the saying that one person's bitter lemon can be the ingredients for another person's lemonade. One caution needs to be noted at this stage. Firms that attempt to use this strategy to merely dump their excess inventory are destined see market transfer fail. Market transfer strategy is not the same as throwing a handful of spaghetti at the wall to see if any of it sticks. Market transfer will work only to the extent the firm is committed to researching the emerging market and is prepared to tailor its marketing mix to that market's unique needs and features. Remember, a firm "invites" competition to the extent that it fails to meet the unique needs of that market.

William Golden has incorporated market transfer into his firm's growth strategy. He is taking American cleanup savvy to Indonesia and Malaysia. His company, International Environmental Associates, represents small U.S. environmental companies in Djakarta, where businesses are under pressure to stop polluting. Golden's firm is winning contracts because it did intensive research on Indonesian environmental laws—information not readily available in the United States. Golden also showed his interest in the market by sending his son to live for a time in Indonesia.

Growing environmental awareness also helped Lund's Fisheries of Cape May, New Jersey. Scandinavian governments are pushing fisherman to replace environmentally unsound drift net fishing with hooks.[8] Lund's Fisheries is selling its specialty squid by the boatload to the fishing industries of Scandinavia for use as bait.

A final point needs to be made about the market transfer growth strategy. Most of the preceding discussion has been directed toward exporting products-technology-services to emerging markets. Market transfer strategy may also be appropriate in the United States. While many markets are already saturated, new groups of customers with different needs emerge almost daily. The firm should be continually scanning immediate and distant horizons for groups of people who are developing a need for products-services the firm already offers. There was a popular Western on television around 1960. It was called *Have Gun, Will Travel*. Market transfer appears to be a modern "corpreneurial" version of that popular program.

Market Creation Is a Two-Dimensional Growth Strategy

Market creation represents a more entrepreneurial strategy than market transfer. Market transfer assumes the risk associated with entering an emerging market that is not being served by any firm. If the goods or services are being offered at all, they tend to be provided by local cottage-type microbusinesses that operate on a hand-to-mouth level or by consumers providing for themselves. Market transfer is primarily one-dimensional in nature because the firm already has experience with that product-service-technology mix. Market creation involves a two-dimensional risk. With this growth strategy, the firm is entering a virgin market, and it is getting involved in products-services in which it has little or no experience.

Market creation involves identifying an emerging market and developing products-services that are already offered by firms in established markets. While the firm may be involved in different products-services than it has experience in offering, it may not need to develop the products-services from scratch. If the firm does not have the desire, the time, or the ability to develop the products-services, then it may consider licensing rights from another firm that already has the experience. The firm may also consider a joint venture or even acquiring that firm to speed the process.

Perceptiveness and timing may be the key ingredients to market creation. Firms that already have the experience could enter the targeted emerging market using the market transfer strategy. Yet many firms practice "management by braille" and thereby fail to see opportunities around them. The ability to offer products-services is valuable only to the extent the firm is able to identify a market that values them. Firms that use market creation strategy are market-driven rather than product-driven. They spend their time looking for emerging markets. They figure that if they have sufficient lead time, then they can either develop the capability to serve the market or purchase the ability from a firm that did not see the opportunity.

A major hotel chain provides an example of the market creation growth strategy. Management is looking into establishing teleconferencing facilities in numerous emerging countries. They have recognized that emerging countries lack sophisticated means for linking themselves with other countries and companies.

The hotel chain has already established itself as one of the leaders in the hospitality field; now it is investigating the economic feasibility of securing telecommunications technology and licenses so it can build and operate facilities where people can have a hospitable environment for communicating with parties all over the world. Management of this firm recognized businesses will substitute teleconferencing for airline travel in the years ahead due to skyrocketing airfares and possible terrorism as well as the relative inaccessibility of some locations. This firm's strategy is based on the same concept as the fax machine. Businesses are now more accustomed to using their fax machines than air express. A similar situation may be the case with business travel.

Another example of the market creation growth strategy would be for a firm involved in pest control to broaden its product-service offering to include radon measurement and reduction. The growing concern about radon poisoning and the need for houses to meet acceptable radon levels before the title can be transferred has created a sizable business opportunity. It would make sense for a business that is already accustomed to making residential calls, inspection, and correction to expand into the emerging radon field by developing, licensing, or acquiring radon monitoring and elimination equipment. The same may also be true for lead paint eradication.

Pure Corpreneurship Is the Ultimate Challenge

This strategy combines market creation and product invention. Pure corpreneurship represents a bold strategy for positioning the venture to capitalize on the almost inevitable changes that will occur in the marketplace. With this strategy, management is committed to having the firm be the first to enter an emerging market with products-services-technology that did not previously exist for that or any other firm.

The question may be raised, "Which comes first, technological development or market surveillance?" Some firms are technology-driven while other firms are market-driven. Corpreneurship is neither a technology-driven nor an exclusively market-driven growth strategy. Corpreneurship in its purest form is an opportunity-driven growth strategy that fosters a synergistic effect by anticipating emerging needs with sufficient lead time to develop innovative solutions to them.

New ventures can learn from Jack Welch's crusade to transform General Electric into an opportunity-driven company. In the early 1980s, Welch sold various established businesses and then invested the firm's resources in emerging fields and industries. He recognized that General Electric could not be a cutting-edge firm if it used the more traditional strategy of trying to squeeze every last ounce of revenue from highly saturated, mature markets.

All the growth strategies profiled in the modified version of Ansoff's matrix place a premium on having a keen sense of timing. Timing is paramount in the pure corpreneurship growth strategy. Management must have the vision to anticipate the emergence of consumer or institutional needs before there are consumers. The firm must have sufficient lead time to invent the products-services to satisfy the needs as they manifest themselves. Pure corpreneurship may be the essence of the Gretzky approach to being in the right place at the right time with the right capabilities.

As the rate of change accelerates, it will be more difficult for firms to keep pace. Pure corpreneurship will force managers to think beyond present products, processes, services, and markets. The best way for the firm to establish itself in a leadership position is to be the first to enter the market and to have such a superior product-service offering that potential competitors look elsewhere.

Leadership means being more than a step ahead of the competition; it means being so far ahead that they choose not to enter the arena. Ironically, the desire to be ahead of the competition needs to be tempered with the realization that a firm could hit the market before the market is ready. This is a common problem for firms that are so technology-driven that they fail to recognize whether the market is ready to be harvested. Conversely, firms that are market-driven often ignore the importance of having a technological advantage. In their zeal to get something to meet unmet or emerging needs in the marketplace, many firms may fail to develop and offer superior products-services.

Some firms have experimented with the pure corpreneurship growth strategy as part of their overall strategy in their attempt to position their firms to capitalize on the changes the twenty-first century will bring. Airxchange Inc. illustrates pure corpreneurship in action. Its cofounder Donald Steele recognized that as Americans responded to the high cost of energy by insulating their homes, they were unknowingly creating a new problem. He knew that by tightening up their homes, indoor pollution was almost inevitable. He also knew that when a problem gets bad enough and is widespread, Congress almost certainly responds by enacting legislation. The 1987 Air Quality Act helped catapult Airxchange Inc.'s growth.

Airxchange anticipated the market for quite some time. According to Steele, "There's a market when the health and safety codes define one for you."[9] Airxchange has sold tens of thousands of units that are designed to remove harmful gasses and particles from the home.

Noise Cancellation Technologies Inc. also illustrates pure corpreneurship. This company recognized the growing interest in noise abatement and that few, if any, techniques were available for eliminating noise. Management also recognized that the elimination of noise would be an integral component in the quality-of-work-life movement that was destined to blossom in the years ahead.

Noise Cancellation Technologies developed a system that electronically analyzes noise sound waves and then produces precisely matching antinoise to eliminate the noise. All the conventional approaches merely tried to muffle the noise. Noise Cancellation Technologies offered noise elimination.

The irony of Airxchange's and Noise Cancellation Technologies' success is that both firms were dealing with what can be considered obvious rather than obscure opportunities. Moreover, management considered the opportunities and success to be almost inevitable. In their minds, they were not embarking on high-risk ventures.

Capitalizing on what entrepreneurs considered to be almost inevitable appears to be the rule rather than the exception. When Steven Jobs, the cofounder of Apple Computer, and Donald Burr, the founder of Federal Express, reflected on the success of their ventures, they claimed they did not consider them to be very risky. It is heartwarming to see that these men had the courage to go where no one had gone before. They changed the way we live and work.

Concluding Comments: The Firm May Use a Hybrid Growth Strategy

Firms that merely make minor changes in the present are destined to fail in periods of rapid change. Firms that are fixated on cost-cutting and fine-tuning operations will miss out on the myriad of opportunities that lie ahead. The traditional "incremental" approach to doing business will not provide high-growth opportunities. If the firm is to reach new heights, then management should consider adopting one or more of the corpreneurial growth strategies.

The marketplace is changing too rapidly for firms to operate from a reactive stance by responding only to today's needs and relying on today's technology. As Robert Reich, Secretary of Labor in the Clinton Administration noted in 1991, "The highest earnings in most worldwide industries are to be found in locations where specialized knowledge is brought to bear on problems whose solutions define new horizons of possibility."[10] He noted that "cutting-edge" businesses enjoy higher profit levels because their customers are willing to pay a premium for goods and services that exactly meet their needs. Reich also observed that knowledge-based firms have a distinct advantage because they cannot easily be duplicated by low-cost competitors elsewhere in the world.[11]

You must have the freedom to look beyond
what has been done before...I couldn't find
quite the car I dreamed of: so I decided to
build it myself.
                    PROFESSOR DR. ING. H.C. PORSCHE

CHIEF EXECUTIVE GUIDELINES

Name: Thomas V. Long II, Ph.D., Chairman and Chief Executive Officer
Company: Maricultura Inc.
Product/Service: Producer of Neutraceuticals
Awards/Distinctions:

1. Governor's "Entrepreneurship Award" for North Carolina in 1989, 1990, and 1991

2. Recipient of two Small Business Innovation Research Grants

General guidelines: When it comes to developing highly innovative products-services and entering new markets (corpreneurial strategies) as well as having the necessary lead time to be ahead of other firms, the E/ CEO should keep the following tips in mind:

1. Take the money and run: capital is *the* scarce commodity for a new venture. Therefore, accept capital investment at any reasonable valu-

ation when it is offered. But check out your potential investors' integrity and reputation as you would your potential wife—you're in bed with both for a long time.

2. Timing is everything. Pioneers are often the ones with arrows in their backs. Focus on opportunities where there is incipient demand and be prepared to shift focus rapidly.

3. Completely rethink your firm and its direction every two to three years—repackage.

4. Position your firm and technology so that it is attractive to very large (Fortune 100) firms as a strategic partner.

5. Search for niche markets that will evolve to major plays because of changing demographics or regulatory changes—positive effects of regulation, such as new formulation requirements.

Proceed with Caution Guidelines:

Have much more capital than you anticipate needing.

And I Would Be Particularly Careful Not *to:*

1. Be technology-driven. Demand-pull, not technology-push, is the only strategy for a new venture.

2. Let excuses or reasons given by venture capitalists or other investors for not investing influence decisions. There are a thousand reasons for declination and only one ("love that idea") for investing.

3. Locate more than an hour's drive from two or more major venture capital firms (those with funds of more than $50 million to invest). You will need a lead investor who can bring in other firms, and logistics dictate that he will need to be close geographically.

CHIEF EXECUTIVE GUIDELINES

Name: Donald H. Jones, President
Company: Automation News Network
Product/Service: Electronic Publishing and Database Marketing
Number of Employees: 100
Awards/Distinctions:

1. Founder of five highly successful new companies in the automation and electronic publishing fields

2. Profiled in *Success* magazine

3. Adjunct Professor of Entrepreneurship at Carnegie Mellon's Graduate School of Business

4. Tri-State "Entrepreneur of the Year" 1990 by *Inc.* magazine, Merrill-Lynch, and Ernst & Young

General guidelines: When it comes to developing highly innovative products/services and entering emerging markets (corpreneurial strategies) as well as having the necessary lead time to be ahead of other firms, the E/CEO should keep the following tips in mind:

1. Establish relationships with a few high-visibility potential customers prior to launching the development activity.

2. Keep in close touch with them throughout the development process.

3. Do not over promise either on features or time to complete.

4. Plan to spend more resources than initially planned (both in dollars and people).

5. If the product is of major significance to your strategy, stay close yourself—do not delegate the monitoring process.

Proceed with Caution Guidelines:

1. Limit the amount of new product innovations to a manageable few.

2. Do not get caught up in "what will be" but more in "how do we get it completed."

3. Only develop products that satisfy your current marketplace.

And I Would Be Particularly Careful Not *to:*

1. Expect quick results when you develop new products for new markets.

2. Underestimate the stress an organization experiences when developing new products.

9

Utilizing the Board of Directors

The board of directors is the Achilles heel of the American corporation...every time you find a business in trouble, you find a board of directors either unwilling or unable to fulfill its responsibilities.

KENNETH DAYTON,
FORMER CEO OF DAYTON HUDSON[1]

It is ironic that with all the commotion about what E/CEOs should do so their companies can be leading edge firms, the role that the firm's board of directors should play in improving their firm's performance has been overlooked. Organizations need a clear sense of direction in times of turbulence, challenge, opportunity, and change. This places a premium on having boards of directors that E/CEOs can look to for the wisdom, vision, perspective, and insights necessary to integrate financial and intangible factors into a logical framework for making the right decisions.

In theory, every corporation should operate under the guidance of its board of directors. In reality, few boards do what they are supposed to do. Leon Danco, founder of The Center for Family Business, notes, "Most business owners will automatically reject the idea of creating a working

---

Portions of this chapter appeared in the article "Corporate Directors: Visionaries or Back Seat Drivers?" by the author in *Business Insights,* Winter 1987, 26-29. Used with permission of The University of Southern Mississippi.

board of outside directors when it is first suggested. Their desire for power and flexibility is too strong."[2] If E/CEOs are serious about having the firm achieve its potential, then they must be committed to having a fully functioning board of directors. An emerging firm that does not have a fully functioning board of directors is like an eight-cylinder engine that has only six cylinders working—it will not be able to function to its potential because its rate of acceleration will be hindered. Ultimately, the engine, or in this case the emerging venture, will overheat and break down.

The attitude E/CEOs express about the role the board of directors should play in the direction of their firms reveals a lot about their approach to managing their firms. E/CEOs of emerging firms are frequently heard saying, "I can't afford it!", "I don't have the time!", "They will slow me down!", or "How could they help?...I built this business from the ground up!" Almost all the reasons for not having a board can be attributed to the E/CEO's ego. Either the E/CEO believes no benefits can be derived from having a group of professionals, or the E/CEO is unwilling to be put in a position where the board may see his or her weaknesses. Yet of all the types and sizes of firms, the emerging firm may need a fully functioning board the most. The emerging firm is the one that lacks management depth and breadth. E/CEOs who say they cannot afford a board need to recognize that a board is not a luxury or a burden; it is a managerial necessity.

E/CEOs often claim, "An organization is only as good as its people." E/CEOs should recognize that their firms will only be as good as the people who serve on their boards of directors! The people who are selected to serve on the board of directors and what they are expected to do reveals how serious the E/CEO and the firm's stockholders are about having a "professionally" managed firm.

The Board of Directors: A Managerial Paradox

Every corporation is required by law to have a board. Each board is expected to act in a fiduciary capacity for the firm's stockholders, employees, and society as a whole. The board is part of the check-and-balance system for corporate governance and performance. The board is responsible for clarifying the corporation's overall mission, establishing long-term objectives, approving financing for expansion, determining the distribution of earnings, deciding on major acquisitions and the sale of assets, as well as improving and reviewing corporate performance. This is a tall order for a group of individuals who may devote only a few days per year to their board functions.

Boards may represent a paradox. The board is supposed to provide direction, but it is not expected to be involved in daily operations. While the board is chartered to help clarify what type of firm the shareholders want that business to become, the firm's E/CEO is expected to follow the directions of the board.

The E/CEO is there to see that the firm's mission statement is fulfilled. The E/CEO is also responsible for formulating and implementing plans to achieve objectives set by the board. If the objectives are not met, the board is responsible for getting the firm back on track.[3] The board is also responsible for selecting, directing, reviewing, compensating and, if necessary, replacing the E/CEO.

From Phantom Boards to Professional Boards

State statutes may place certain stipulations on the minimum age for people serving on the firm's board of directors, but they rarely place requirements on the type of people who should serve on the board. This explains why boards can be so diverse. Emerging firms tend to have either phantom boards, good-old-boy boards, rubber-stamp boards, or professional boards.

Phantom boards are usually made up of family members with limited professional experience. Although they may meet legal requirements and even own stock in the firm, boards of "relatives" do little to improve corporate performance. They are boards in name only.

Rubber-stamp boards are usually made up of members of the firm's management team. While these people may have business experience and be familiar with the firm's operations and markets, rubber-stamp boards rarely add any value to the firm. People who report to the E/CEO also tend to be reluctant to challenge the E/CEO's ideas. The board is there to provide direction for the E/CEO. It is unlikely that people who report directly to the E/CEO five days of the week will be able to do a role reversal a few days each year.

A number of emerging firms have "good-old-boy" boards. While E/CEOs may proclaim to others that their firm has an "outside" board of directors, in most cases the outsiders are more window dressing than substance. These boards are usually made up of the firm's banker, attorney, and a handful of the E/CEO's friends who may have their own firms. On the surface, these boards appear to supplement the E/CEO's talents and skills. In reality, they tend be too close to the E/CEO (who almost always serves as the board's chairman) to be objective.

Good-old-boy boards also have the potential for a conflict of interest. Conflicts of interest may arise whenever the firm's banker, attorney, insurance representative, or any other person who is involved directly with the firm serves on the board. This is particularly true with bankers. Good-old-boy boards may meet regularly and approve recommendations made by the E/CEO, but they rarely add value to the firm. In a sense they tend to be an "external" rubber-stamp board of directors.

The fourth type of board is the professional board. These boards tend to be composed of a variety of professionals who truly fulfill the fiduciary role that should be played by the board of directors. It would be something if the majority of U.S. firms were governed by directors actively involved in providing direction and constructive criticism to the E/CEO. A study by Ahmad Tashakori and William Boulton, however, revealed that 90 percent of the boards in their sample took a relatively passive role in the corporation's strategic direction.[4] Recent studies of emerging firms indicate that less than half of them have an outside board. Fortunately, more firms are moving toward having professional boards. More E/CEOs are recognizing the need for a group of committed professionals on the board of directors who can assist them in charting the future direction of their firms.

Professional Boards: More than Window Dressing

Professional boards can add value by providing varied expertise; a breadth of business experience and philosophies; new contacts for customers, suppliers, and creditors; and leads when hiring key management and staff personnel. The professional board's greatest strength rests in its ability to ask the E/CEO questions that subordinates and close friends would never ask.

Professional boards are on the upswing because stockholders want to be sure their interests are being recognized and that top management is not self-serving. Professional boards can also ensure that top management is not allowed to look good by enhancing short-term performance while jeopardizing long-term corporate viability.

At Dayton Hudson, the board's position description states that the board's function as representatives of the shareholders is "to be the primary force pressing the corporation to the realization of its opportunities and the fulfillment of its obligations to its shareholders, customers, employees, and communities in which it operates."[5] With a professional board, there is a higher probability that the board and the E/CEO will represent the firm's stockholders rather than the firm's management.

Professional boards can also serve as a parachute or insurance policy in times of crisis. They can provide continuity when E/CEOs are unable to fulfill their responsibilities to the firm. If the E/CEO dies, becomes incapacitated, retires, is fired, or in any other way leaves office, then the board may be able to direct the operations of the firm while it conducts a search for the new CEO.

Who's on First?

The relationship between the E/CEO and the board should be a supportive one. The issue of who is really in charge, however, is frequently the subject of debate. The law is quite clear: the board's responsibility is "to monitor attentively and oversee the performance of the chief executive and the salaried team."[6]

The E/CEO is in a position to influence the extent to which the board has access to information about the firm. Even though the board provides direction, the E/CEO often directs the board. This is particularly true if the E/CEO serves as the chairman of the board of directors. Kenneth Dayton notes that in the overall direction of the firm "usually management is the primary force (or the only force), and the board is either a rubber stamp, a monitor, or just there in case of a crisis."[7]

Some people question whether it is in the firm's best interest to have the board be the primary force given the way most boards are structured and operate. A 1986 article in *Forbes* magazine asked: "It's all well and good to arouse boards of directors from their deep snoozes, but do we really want boards usurping the job of the CEO?...Would it be healthy for a board to interpose itself as a committee of part-time managers who meet once a month to second-guess the company's officers with endless kibitzing?"[8]

The relationship between the E/CEO and the board varies dramatically between small closely-held firms and larger publicly-held firms. Entrepreneurial CEOs tend to perceive the relationship with their boards in a different way than professional CEOs. The relationship is particularly interesting when the CEO is the founding entrepreneur and owns the largest block of stock. Because entrepreneurial CEOs are noted for their desire to be their own boss, they frequently put themselves at the top of the organizational charts. Professional CEOs, however, are hired by the board. They usually recognize that the board of directors appears at the top of the organization chart. They may not even be among the primary stockholders.

Inc. magazine has noted that boards are an inexpensive way to get hardheaded expert objective advice. This is particularly important for relatively new businesses that tend to be understaffed as they venture into uncharted waters. Rick Terrell, president of Microware Distributors Inc., holds ten meetings each year "not so much to discuss day-to-day operational stuff as to look at the strategic opportunities that are constantly presenting themselves."[9] George Clement, president of Clement Communications, Inc., relies on his outside directors to serve as a sounding board for future plans and to review the firm's performance. Clement says, "My board has made me a better CEO; CEOs who don't use outside advice run the risk of internalizing too much."[10] The reviewing role of the board has another potential benefit. By having top management present ideas, the board has the opportunity to observe other high-level managers who will require board approval for their next promotions and to see potential successors to the E/CEO when the time comes.[11]

Not all E/CEOs share the same feelings about the merit of having boards. Kenneth Hendricks, CEO of ABC Supply Company (the number one firm in the 1986 Inc. 500), asserts "The energy that goes into setting up a board and sitting down with them is a reduction of productivity...I'm a hands-on kind of guy, and the buck stops here."[12]

Thanks But No Thanks!

The question "Who's in charge?" is being raised today in courtrooms as well as boardrooms. The trend toward utilizing outside directors has encountered a major obstacle. Professionals have demonstrated a growing reluctance to serve on boards. When someone is now asked to serve on a board, the response is, "What kind of directors' and officers' [D&O] liability insurance coverage does your firm have?"

The Trans Union Corporation suit in 1985 sent shock waves though the corporate community. The directors were found individually answerable to the former shareholders for selling the company for too low a price to the Marmon Group. A Delaware court declared the board was too passive and failed to demonstrate a sufficient level of inquiry prior to making their decision on the merger.

Laws state that directors must exercise good judgment and due diligence in their activities. These areas, however, are rather nebulous. Boards, by their very nature, must make decisions affecting the future success of their respective companies. Directors are charged not only with the responsibility of making difficult decisions, they are expected to make the "right" decisions. These decisions, however, are usually made without the benefit of perfect information.

Our free enterprise system is based on the notion that profit is the reward for successfully taking a calculated risk. The catch-22 for today's boards is that they can be sued for taking too little risk by being too cautious or for taking too much risk by entering new markets, expanding facilities, and the like.

Americans seem to be crying out for our managers to be bold, to lead, to be innovative, and to go where no one has gone before. Richard Behar and Mark Clifford note that "Many of the greatest decisions of this century were gambles in which visionary chief executives either had the backing of their boards or rode roughshod over the opposition."[13] This brings up one of the major dilemmas faced by emerging firms that are committed to having professional boards. If the board is too businesslike and insists on checking everything twice, then it could rob the firm of the entrepreneurial spirit that is essential for sustained growth.

Behold: The Emergence of Advisory Committees

The increased risk of litigation by stockholders and other parties as well as the skyrocketing cost of D&O liability insurance coverage have prompted a number of firms to create advisory committees. If outside professionals are reluctant to accept the personal liability associated with serving on the board of directors, then they may be invited to serve on the E/CEO's advisory committee. The advisory committee may meet on a regular schedule or it may be convened by the E/CEO for special situations.

The firm will still be required to have a board of directors, but now it may be comprised of members of the management team and key stockholders who are willing to accept personal liability for their actions. This does not preclude the firm from creating an advisory committee made up of the same outside professionals who would have made up the professional board. With the advisory committee, however, these same professionals are no longer personally liable. They do not make decisions, therefore, they cannot be held liable for the outcomes of management's actions.

As with most things in life, advisory committees have their advantages and disadvantages. The primary advantage is that they provide a vehicle for a group of outside professionals to share their insights as well as express their concerns about plans or initiatives the E/CEO brings to them. Advisory committees are particularly beneficial in technology-based companies. The members of the advisory committee may be recruited for their expertise and industry contacts.

The major drawback of an advisory committee is the potential that proposals may not be reviewed thoroughly due to the limited liability associated with serving on an advisory committee rather than on the board of directors. As a director, one would be expected to be very thorough in reviewing the issues and diligent in making the decisions given the commensurate liability. The lack of personal liability as a member of the advisory committee may prompt committee members to just share their "first impressions" about the E/CEO's ideas.

It should be apparent that people who are asked to serve on the board of directors should be objective to the point that they will challenge the logic behind the E/CEO's proposals and be willing to provide candid and constructive criticism when appropriate. The advisory board can provide valuable assistance to the firm as a "sounding board" for the E/CEO's ideas. Nevertheless, it will be of value only to the extent that its members are willing to sound off when they believe the E/CEO is not pointing the firm in the right direction.

Fundamentals for the Professional Board

There are numerous issues that need to be addressed if the firm is to have a fully functioning, professional board of directors. The issues involve: when to form the professional board, who should serve on it, how often should it meet, and who should serve as its chairman. Too many firms wait too long to develop their professional board of directors. Banks may insist on outside directors before they will finance a major expansion. The stockholders may express their disenchantment with the E/CEO or the rubberstamp board by nominating a slate of professional outside directors. The E/CEO may even recommend adding outside professionals because he or she lacks the experience or expertise needed to address certain issues or challenges encountered in periods of growth or adversity.

In each of these instances, the board is destined to operate from a reactive mode. Boards of outside professionals need to be created before they are needed rather than when the firm is in the middle of a major challenge. It may take six months to a year for a board of outside professionals to develop collaborative group dynamics with each other and the E/CEO or chairman. It will take at least that amount of time to develop an understanding of the unique nature of the business, its markets, its competition, and the other factors that play an integral role during board deliberations.

All too often, professionals are added to the board when the firm is faced with a major crisis. Board action may be too late when radical surgery is needed. Professional boards should be created to help prevent crisis situations rather than to save a sinking ship. They are in a position to encourage the development of succession plans, to ensure that the pension plan is properly funded, to see that the E/CEO is making the changes recommended by the firm's auditors, and to make sure legal and ethical issues are incorporated in all policy-level decisions. The same rule of thumb that was used in forming the management team may be applied to creating the professional board—"Do it before you need it!"

It is unlikely that the E/CEO will form a professional board at the inception of the business. First, the business may be formed as a proprietorship or a partnership, which do not require a board of directors. Second, things move quickly in the formative months of a new venture. At this stage, the E/CEO is in a life-or-death dance with the elephants. A myriad of tactical decisions need to made on the spot. While it would be nice to have a professional board to provide advice, it would probably impede the E/CEO's entrepreneurial qualities that are essential at this stage.

If the E/CEO is committed to having a professional board, then he or she should create the board well before the business opens its doors. Having outside professionals serve on the board or as part of an advisory committee can bring a wealth of experience to the firm. They can increase the likelihood of the new venture's success even before it opens its doors.

A professional board can be beneficial as the initial business plan is being developed. The outside professionals may provide ideas, suggest sources of funding, and keep the E/CEO from being blindsided by identifying any fatal flaws that may have eluded his or her attention. The board should be able to identify the things that need to be done as the business is started. This way, the E/CEO will have a clear sense of direction when the dance with the elephants begins. Hopefully, the E/CEO will not need to stop and consult with the board whenever any issue comes up. Nevertheless, a business that has a professional board from the beginning, even if it is not used to its potential, is destined to be in a better position to meet the challenges that will arise later in its growth stage.

Staffing the Board

The question of who should serve on the board is not difficult to answer. It should be clear by now that if the firm does not have a professional board, then it really does not have a board of directors at all. Reality dictates that the firm's principal stockholders will probably insist on having a seat on the board. If these people have extensive business experience and are willing to do their homework in preparation for the key decisions that will need to be made, then their serving on the board may not be detrimental. If they lack the experience or are unable to commit the necessary time to thoroughly research the issues, then they should be open to having professional outsiders serve on the board who will represent the stockholders' best interests.

The board should be large enough to get expertise and diversity of views. Yet, the board should not be so large that it inhibits interaction or keeps its directors from feeling responsible for their actions. The size of the board may also need to reflect the number of stockholders who insist on having a seat on the board. Generally speaking, the more stockholders to serve, the larger the board should be so that it can have enough outside directors to make a difference. If there are one or two stockholders on the board, then the board could have as few as five members. If the firm's management team is thinly staffed or if the firm is about to go through a major growth stage, then it may need seven people on the board.

Ideally, the board should have people from outside the firm who have a wealth of experience as well as innovative ideas for moving the firm ahead. Particular attention should be given to attracting professionals who have expertise in the areas where the firm is moving such as international expansion, mergers and acquisitions, initial public offering, or even the sale of the firm. People with expertise in areas where the E/CEO and management team may be lacking such as strategic planning, financial analysis, and human resource management can be valuable. While it may be inappropriate to have someone from the same industry on the board, efforts should be made to attract at least one director who has experience in an industry that has experienced similar challenges. The board can be rounded out with one or two generalists who can provide broad-based perspectives.

In any event, people should be sought who have already experienced the types of challenges the firm is likely to encounter. These people may be in a position to identify ways to prevent certain problems as well as to identify opportunities beyond those that are presently being acted on that should be explored. One caveat, however, needs to be mentioned. Be sure the people who are asked to serve have an open mind. The phrase "This is how I did it" can be quite irritating. The issue is not how these outsiders did it, it is what this firm should do to thrive in the years ahead. What their firms did a few years ago or are doing today may be totally inappropriate for this particular emerging firm.

Ironically, the real value of the outside professionals does not rest in their ideas; it rests in their ability to ask the questions that will make the difference in whether the firm succeeds, stagnates, or fails. While the directors are not there to challenge everything the E/CEO or chairman proposes, they are there to be sure that the E/CEO's proposals and recommendations have been thought through. In instances when the E/CEO's proposals do not seem to be adequately supported by data or logic, then the outside directors need to be objective and have the courage to challenge the appropriateness of the proposal. In these instances, it may be appropriate for board members to play the devil's advocate. George Clement noted, "Sure there are times when you walk away [from a board meeting] unnerved and harassed...those are the times the board has earned its keep."[14] It is for this reason that the outside directors should not be the E/CEO's close friends. It will be difficult for them to be objective. They may also be reluctant to challenge the E/CEO when it is necessary.

It may be advisable to invite people to serve on the board who know the E/CEO professionally rather than personally. The real issue here is one of respect. The outsiders must have a track record that garners respect from the E/CEO. The professional directors' views must be welcomed by the E/CEO even though they may not always agree. The issue of objectivity is particularly important in instances where the E/CEO (even if he or she is a primary stockholder) has not performed up to expectations. In these circumstances, the people serving on the board must have the courage to replace the E/CEO. The question, "Will you be willing to support a recommendation to replace the E/CEO if he or she fails to perform up to the board's expectations?" should be asked of every prospective board member.

How Often Should the Board Meet?

The board should meet often enough to be able to address strategic issues and to review corporate performance. Yet it should not meet so often that it gets caught up in operating matters. Board meetings every two to three months seem to be about right. If the firm is in the middle of a major transition, then it may be advisable to meet every two months. If things are going fairly smoothly and management is primarily involved in implementing the approved business plan, then quarterly meetings may suffice.

The members of the board should be mailed a copy of the monthly financial statements. The chief financial officer should attach a brief summary of any major variances and indicate if any corrective action has been taken. The E/CEO should also attach a brief cover letter that highlights key developments. If goals, budgets, and timetables are part of a business plan that has been approved by the board, then the board can operate on a "management by exception" basis throughout the year.

The board should also receive an agenda in advance of the board meeting that indicates issues to be discussed and decisions that may need to be made. Supplementary information may also be provided so the board members are well versed on the issues to be addressed at the upcoming meeting. Board members should be encouraged to contact the chairman if they would like to have a report on certain matters or if they would like to add "new business" to the agenda. The minutes from the last meeting should also be included in each board member's packet.

The board may also have a number of committees to deal with various matters. The most common committees are the executive committee, the compensation committee, and the audit committee. These committees may meet more frequently than the regular board meetings. The executive committee will be particularly important if the board is fairly large and if the full board is scheduled to meet only a couple of times each year. The compensation committee may meet only a few times a year to review the E/CEO's salary and possibly the other top executives' salaries. This committee could play a very important role in reviewing the E/CEO's performance. This would be critical if the E/CEO also serves as chairman of the board. The audit committee may serve as a "watchdog" by reviewing the auditor's report and monitoring the extent to which recommendations are implemented.

One caveat needs to be mentioned. The board needs to focus its attention on strategic and entrepreneurial issues. The board is there to ensure that the E/CEO and management team are not insulated from the outside world—that they are not overlooking major trends and emerging opportunities. The board is not there to do the E/CEO's job or that of any other member of the management team. It should not get involved in personnel issues or discussions about what type of microcomputers to buy. Operational issues can be like quicksand to a board. The professional board members may have experience in the same operational matters, but they should avoid getting sucked into them.

The board meetings have another benefit. If the E/CEO serves as the chairman of the board, then the directors have the opportunity to see a sample of his or her approach to managing the firm. The board will be in a position to see if the E/CEO is open to ideas, uses the appropriate data in decision processes, delegates important operating issues to the management team, and has the strategic orientation that is essential for leading today's emerging firms.

Who Should Serve as Chairman of the Board?

The issue of whether the E/CEO should serve as chairman of the board or even be on the board is the subject of debate. According to Kenneth Dayton, "The board or the executive committee cannot really be independent if the CEO is chairman."[15] At Dayton Hudson, the board provides the CEO with an annual written review and evaluation so that he knows exactly where he stands. Dayton also notes, "Every CEO deserves such a review. Unfortunately, few want it and fewer still ever get it."[16]

While it may be best in theory and work well in a few large firms to have someone other than the CEO serve as chairman of the board of directors, in most smaller organizations the E/CEO is likely to serve as chairman of the board. In instances where the E/CEO serves as the chairman, it is even more important that the board be comprised of outside directors. Without objective outside directors, the firm may function as an extension of the management team or as a good-old-boy board. There is little likelihood that management's assumptions or courses of action will be questioned. Even though one of the major strengths of smaller businesses is their ability to quickly change what they are doing, without an objective professional board to encourage the E/CEO to "look before he or she leaps," the firm could be courting disaster.

If the firm is to have a professional board, then it needs to be independent of the E/CEO. The E/CEO would probably benefit most from having a chairman and board who are supportive but not reluctant to ask questions and deal with sensitive issues. An outside board can add value by keeping the firm pointed in the right direction and out of trouble. E/CEOs need to remember John Gardner's words from his book *No Easy Victories*, "I would lay it down as a basic principle of human organizations that the individuals who hold the reins of power in any enterprise cannot trust themselves to be adequately self-critical."[17]

How Much Should the Directors Be Paid?

The saying "You get what you pay for" does not need to be the case when it comes to having professionals serve on the firm's board of directors. Few emerging firms are in a position to pay the kind of directors' fees provided by large firms. *Fortune* magazine estimates directors for the largest firms receive about $34,000 per year.[18] Fortunately, emerging firms may be able to attract quality directors for $2,000 to $4,000 per year. This usually comes out to $200 to $400 per meeting. The overall amount depends on whether the directors also serve on one or more committees.

Each director's per meeting fee is more an honorarium than an attempt to pay them what they are really worth on an hourly or daily basis. It is interesting to note that the more you pay the directors, the less likely they may be to fulfill their fiduciary duties. If directors are paid a considerable amount of money, then they may be reluctant to challenge the E/CEO, chairman, or the other members of the board when a critical issue arises. If they depend on their fees to make ends meet, then they may be reluctant to risk them by raising their concerns.

It is surprising how many professionals are willing to serve on a board of directors if they can be covered by director's liability insurance or allowed to serve on the advisory committee. A number of professionals see serving on a board as something that brings variety to their lives. Serving on the board of an emerging firm can be viewed as a form of vicarious "parenting." While professional directors can periodically share their views, they do not have to put their blood, sweat, and tears into the business on a daily basis!

How Long Should the Directors' Terms Be?

As noted earlier, it will take at least six months for a board member to develop an understanding of the unique nature of the business. It is for this reason that the corporate bylaws should provide directors with two- or three-year terms. While it may take some time for new directors to become familiar with the firm's situation, certain safeguards should be in place to keep directorships from being like supreme court judgeships where people may serve for life. Most directors lose their drive to probe and to challenge.

Having outside directors may bring a fresh perspective to the firm. Most directors, however, lose their "freshness" by the fourth, fifth, or sixth year. Directors' terms should be limited to no more than six years. The only people who should be allowed to serve longer are primary stockholders who are in a position to insist on it. Effort should also be made to stagger the terms of the directors so they do not come and go as a block.

There should also be a provision for the review of each member of the board. The chairman should solicit input from the E/CEO and the board members on the relative contribution or "value added" by each board member. This should not be viewed as a popularity contest. Instead, each board member should be reviewed according to whether he or she has been diligent and acted in good faith. If a board member has not fulfilled his or her responsibilities, then he or she should be encouraged to resign.

Concluding Comments: Where Do We Go from Here?

The problems and accelerating expenses associated with getting D&O liability insurance coverage will continue to plague the corporate community until the free market and legal systems respond to fill the void. Until that time, directors should approach their jobs in a manner that will reduce their risk without shirking their responsibility to move firms ahead. The rules for responsible directorship have been the same for years. Today's environment merely accentuates the need for directors to do what they have been charged with doing all along.

Directors need to take their jobs seriously, commit the time and attention the stockholders deserve, be diligent and prudent by requesting all relevant information, set performance objectives that justify the stockholders' investment in the firm, challenge management's assumptions and recommendations when in doubt, seek legal counsel on sensitive issues, make sure accurate minutes are kept so the board's actions are documented in the event its actions are challenged, operate in line with the corporation's bylaws, act in good faith, and last but not least be willing to exercise the judgment they were elected to the board to use. The board must also be bold enough to remove the E/CEO if he or she: (1) does not provide it with the information it needs, (2) fails to provide the opportunity to challenge recommendations, or (3) is unwilling to follow its direction.

Directors should remember the immortal words of Thomas Watson Jr. who as CEO of IBM in the 1960s said, "There never has been any future in the status quo...the status quo means inevitable failure."[19] Boards are there to ensure that their firms will be in a position to thrive in the twenty-first century. This will happen only if boards as well as their respective management teams have the vision, judgment, and courage to accept the risks associated with finding new ways to do things and new things to do.

Too often, boards serve as figureheads once did on clipper ships. They looked good, but they contributed nothing to the vessel's ability to negotiate rough waters.
                                    STEPHEN C. HARPER

CHIEF EXECUTIVE GUIDELINES

Name: Fred Eshelman, Phar.D., Chief Executive Officer
Company: Pharmaceutical Product Development, Inc.
Product/Service: Contract Pharmaceutical Development Services
Number of Employees: 300

General guidelines: When it comes to the role the board of directors should play in the direction of the firm, the E/CEO should keep the following tips in mind:

1. The board is foremost a resource to be drawn upon in the execution of the company's vision and long-term strategy.
2. The board is responsible to the shareholders for assuring that the company will be operated in a competent and legally proper manner.
3. The board can be used to diffuse problems among major shareholders as the firm grows.
4. The board members should contribute new ideas while at the same time enabling the CEO to effect the agreed-upon business plan.

Proceed with Caution Guidelines:

1. Develop a strong board very early in the firm's existence.
2. Draw from multiple disciplines.
3. Draw high-visibility players from the company's industry to aid in attracting capital, going public, and so on.
4. Be sure that the board forces discipline into the planning for the company.

And I Would Be Particularly Careful Not *to:*

1. "Stack" the board to assure certain lines of thinking in every situation.
2. Form a board that cannot or will not work with the CEO.
3. Appoint inexperienced individuals.
4. Let the board lead the CEO rather than the other way around.

CHIEF EXECUTIVE GUIDELINES

Name: Salim A. L. Bhatia, Chief Executive Officer
Company: BroadBand Technologies, Inc.
Product/Service: Telecommunications Equipment
Number of Employees: 220
Awards/Distinctions:

1. Profiled in *Fortune* magazine
2. "Award of Excellence" Council for Entrepreneurial Development
3. 1991 ComForum Award, BroadBand Technologies, Inc. Fiber Loop Access FLX System

General guidelines: When it comes to the role that the board of directors should play in the direction of the firm, the E/CEO should keep the following tips in mind:

1. The board and the CEO should operate as partners. The CEO should not view the board as his or her boss. The board and the CEO must share a common vision for the partnership to work.
2. It is important for the board to help the CEO by understanding and calibrating the vision, goals, objectives, and strategies. The board can

help the CEO achieve a balance between "stretch" objectives and "provincial" objectives.

3. The board will be more objective than the CEO and management team will ever be. While the CEO and management team know much more about the business, the right board will know more about similar issues in other companies and industries. The board can add value by bringing different insights, perspectives, and objectivity when the CEO presents his or her ideas.

4. You want the board to give the CEO input and to be objective. You also want to be sure the board knows enough about the business.

5. When you are as close to the business as the CEO, it is easy to lose perspective, to get caught up in daily operations, and to be affected by setbacks. The board is there to put things in perspective and to look for emerging trends. They can help the CEO be realistic. Our board meets every other month. They have the distance to see things evolving and to see trends.

6. The board can serve as an excellent sounding board for the CEO. The process of explaining to other "smart" people is an excellent way for the CEO to develop a clear understanding of what he or she is thinking and doing.

7. The board can help develop contacts. It can also help in recruiting and screening executive-level talent. The board can give feedback on their perceptions of management prospects. The board can also add stature to the company. When the board interviews prospective executives or managers, the company is sending a message that it is serious about its management and its future.

8. Different board compositions make sense at different stages of the life cycle of the company. In the early stages when financing is so important, a board with strong financial experience can be invaluable.

Proceed with Caution Guidelines:

1. Remember, the final responsibility rests with the CEO. The board may provide a lot of ideas and input into the firm's overall direction. The CEO's job is to make sure that he or she is open to and using the input that is being offered. In the end, however, the CEO does not have the opportunity to say, "But you told me to do this."

2. The board is there to ensure the CEO is getting the job done for the shareholders. If the CEO is not getting the job done, then it is up to the board to deal with the CEO.

3. "Veteran" CEOs can get complacent. A professional board can keep them on their toes. If you have a board that is filled with investors, they will expect financial performance to justify the firm's existence.

4. The board needs to have a vested interest in the firm's success. Without a vested interest, it is easy for board members to function as consultants who just throw out ideas. If board members have a vested interest, then they are more likely to view their roles with passion.

10

Developing the Unified Strategic Vision

Where there is no vision, the people perish.
PROVERBS 29:18

Lewis Carroll's *Alice's Adventures in Wonderland* captures the dilemma faced by many emerging firms. When Alice asks the Cheshire cat which path to take, the cat asks her where she wants to go. When Alice indicates she does not really know where, the cat states, "When you don't know where you're going, any road will take you there...no where!" While emerging ventures may be experiencing a high level of growth, many lack the focus needed to succeed in later years. Like adolescents, they may not have an answer when asked, "What do you want to be when you grow up?" In their success, some firms may also be sowing the seeds of their own destruction. John Gardner advises "Self-congratulation should be taken in small doses. It is habit-forming, and most human institutions are far gone in addiction."[1]

Self-congratulation can also cause a blindness wherein management's attention is directed only to what is happening at the moment. This "management by braille" can have a devastating effect on a relatively new firm.

Portions of this chapter appeared in the article "Strategic Thinking: Backwards from the Future" by the author in *The American Business Review,* June 1991, pp. 1-9. Reprinted with permission of the School of Business, The University of New Haven.

123

Managers who only deal with what is immediately within their reach are prone to merely "fine-tune" present products and practices. This can have a considerable opportunity cost because it keeps managers from identifying, cultivating, and capitalizing on emerging opportunities. Firms that are preoccupied with meeting their present customers' interests will devote little attention to identifying who their future customers should be and what it will take to satisfy them.

Chapter 6 stressed the need to plan at least "one market" ahead. While the firm is harvesting its present market opportunities with today's breadwinners, management must also be committing resources to the markets, products, services, and processes that will be tomorrow's breadwinners. Companies that are not in tune with changing market conditions are destined to fall by the wayside. In the dance with the elephants, firms that are perceptive and quick on their feet have a chance, those that manage by braille will be trampled to death!

Management's concern with the present—no matter how successful the firm may be—must be complemented with a vision of what the firm should be seven to ten years from now. The twenty-first century will offer a myriad of opportunities. Companies will grow and prosper only to the extent they are led by executives who have the vision to see the opportunities and the ability to strategically position their firms to harvest them.

The importance of having a vision was illustrated in the movie, *The Carpetbaggers*. The film profiled the life of a Howard Hughes-type of entrepreneur and adventurer. In one scene, the entrepreneur and his partner secure a government contract to deliver the mail between two cities. When the partner, who is a pilot, asks the entrepreneur what they should name their new business, the entrepreneur responds, "Trans International Airlines." The partner exclaims, "Trans International...we aren't even crossing the state line!" The visionary entrepreneur then replies "I'm naming it for what it will be, not what it is."

This chapter emphasizes two essential points. First, the E/CEO must adopt a "strategic" perspective. Managers who have an extended time horizon are less likely to "manage by braille." Second, the firm needs to be driven by a "unified corporate vision" rather than whatever is the "flavor of the week." Firms that lack a vision are destined to either drift and thereby drain their limited resources or be seduced by short-term opportunities or fads that offer no lasting value.

Strategic Management Helps Prevent the Here Today, Gone Tomorrow Syndrome

Most E/CEOs spend their time in three areas. First, they direct some of their attention to their firm's present customers, territories, technology, products, services, and personnel. Second, some of their time is spent reacting to unexpected circumstances, situations, and threats. Third, they oversee operational matters. E/CEOs of new ventures rarely spend enough time on strategic issues. Quite a few E/CEOs exclaim "I don't have time to think about the future" or "things are changing so quickly...there's no point in planning any more...all I can do is see what is happening and try to respond to it."

Life would be fairly predictable if times were stable and conditions certain. There would be little need for planning, risk taking, or innovation. But as Alvin Toffler indicates in his book *Future Shock,* while change has always been with us, the rate of change is accelerating! Managers now have less time to anticipate, prepare for, and initiate change. Craig Hickman and Michael Silva note in their book *Creating Excellence* "Technical innovations, global communications, and fierce competition can bring change overnight that once took decades or even centuries to manifest themselves."[2]

E/CEOs of relatively new ventures need to extend their vision beyond today. For that matter, they need to extend their mental horizon beyond tomorrow. E/CEOs need to be concerned with tomorrow's tomorrow. The higher the position in the organization, the more the job involves conceptual rather than technical matters, a long-term rather than a short-term time horizon, and issues concerning the type of business the company should be rather than how the company should do business.

Dealing with unexpected problems and operational matters can be like quicksand for the E/CEO. Without a strategic perspective, E/CEOs are destined to live a perpetual "fire fighting" existence. It's time for a reality check. If E/CEOs don't concern themselves with the firm's future, then who will? As someone once noted, "The firm that does not prepare for the future will have no future!"

It would be easy to say, "Wait a minute...if we don't take care of business today...we won't be in business tomorrow!" Operational tasks must be performed—and they need to be done well. Firms that fail to control costs, assure deliveries are made on schedule, and monitor accounts receivable, quickly lose efficiency, lose customers, and lose money.

Lasting success will come only to firms that have managers who practice "bifocal" management. They focus their attention on strategic issues and operational matters. A sports analogy illustrates bifocal management. Golfers frequently stand on the tee of a par three hole dreaming what it would be like to get a hole in one. The best golfers take the wind, exact distance, and the slope of the green into consideration when they select a club. As they position their feet, they "envision" the flight of the ball and where it needs to land to roll into the cup. The best golfers do one other thing with the same precision—they keep their heads down so they don't "whiff"!

The best golfers demonstrate bifocal vision when they "mentally" aim for the pin while keeping their eyes on the ball. They know the importance of distance and direction. They also know the importance of execution. Some golfers hit the long ball, but their games suffer because: (1) they can't play the "short" game, (2) they are penalized for going out of bounds, or (3) they "spray" the ball in a zigzag fashion all over the course. Other golfers are very deliberate in their approach to the game. They practice all the time so they make few mistakes. Unfortunately, their preoccupation with not making mistakes keeps them from wanting to play truly challenging golf courses. The prospect of losing a ball or getting a double bogey is frightening.

Michel Robert's book, *The Strategist CEO*, presents a "strategy/operations" matrix that classifies firms according to the extent their executives direct their attention to strategic issues and operational matters (see Figure 10-1). Robert defines the "strategy" dimension as the extent management concerns itself with "what" the firm should be like in the future. The "operational" dimension deals with the extent management is concerned with "how" things are to be done.[3] The plus on the vertical axis indicates the firm manages operational matters well. The plus on the horizontal axis indicates management has a clear vision for the future of the firm.

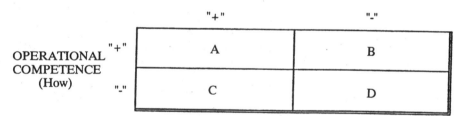

STRATEGIC VISION (What)

		"+"	"-"
OPERATIONAL COMPETENCE (How)	"+"	A	B
	"-"	C	D

Figure 10-1. Robert's Vision/Operations Matrix.[3]

According to Robert, firms can be classified according to their degrees of effectiveness on these two all-important dimensions. In the A quadrant, firms tend to do well because everyone involved has a clear vision of what the firm is striving to become. The business is also managed very well on an ongoing basis. In quadrant B, the firms may be "operationally competent," but people do not have a clear vision for the firm. A number of new ventures fall into this category. They die an early death because they spread themselves too thin. They tend to pursue almost anything that comes along.

Quadrant C is the flip side of quadrant B. These firms have a clear vision, but they lack the operational guidelines that must be addressed for the firm's vision to become reality. In quadrant C, the E/CEOs may have exciting ideas about what their firms can become, but operational incompetence is destined to cause their firm's demise. This is frequently the case with firms that expand too fast. Too many things fall through the cracks. Firms that operate in quadrant D don't last very long. Their lack of focus and lack of attention to operational matters cause a quick death.

Developing a Unified Corporate Strategic Vision

When George Bush was president of the United States, he used to refer to the "vision thing." It was apparent that either he did not understand the importance of having a clearly articulated vision or he did have a clear vision for the future of the United States but couldn't describe it. Jimmy Carter also had difficulty with the "vision thing." While President Carter was considered to be a very intelligent person, his staff indicated that his views about the future were like the back side of a tapestry—you could see a general outline but the figures were not very crisp. Unfortunately, too many new ventures also operate without a clearly articulated vision of what they are striving to be.

It may be helpful to start the discussion on developing a unified corporate vision by indicating what a vision is not. First of all, it should not be confused with a firm's "mission" statement. For years, consultants have encouraged CEOs to develop mission statements for their firms. While mission statements have merit and every firm should have one, they also tend to be like the back side of a tapestry. They may be colorful and may even inspire a few people to strive to new heights, but they tend to be too general to provide a clear sense of direction.

Most mission statements are nothing more than a string of platitudes. Nearly every mission statement sounds like a corporate version of the national anthem whereby the firm expresses its commitment to providing the highest level of quality and service, to being innovative, to being a conscientious employer, and to being a responsible corporate citizen. Let's face it, mission statements are so generic that they provide little direction. You might as well say the company's mission is "To be the best that it can be!"

The unified corporate vision should not be confused with the firm's corporate strategy or its long-range plan. The unified corporate vision represents the desired future "position" for the firm. In a sense, the vision represents the firm's desired future destination with a date of arrival. Corporate strategy indicates "how" the firm plans to get there. The firm's long-term plan can be viewed as the road map to be used for navigating the firm as it travels from where it is to where it wants to be at a specified date in the future.

While a firm's mission statement may indicate the type of business the firm is striving to be, the unified corporate vision is intended to serve as the front side of the tapestry. It should clearly identify what the firm should be like at a specific time in the next seven to ten years. John F. Kennedy illustrated the difference between a mission statement and a unified vision. After the Soviets launched *Sputnik* in 1957, NASA was created so the United States could be "The world's leader in space." This mission statement was nice and appealed to our patriotism, but it wasn't until Kennedy's presidency that a true vision was articulated. Kennedy's vision, "To land a man on the moon and return him safely to Earth before the end of the decade," provided a sense of direction. Because it provided a benchmark by which to measure progress, it created a sense of urgency and a bias for action.

The unified corporate vision should spell out what markets the firm is expected to be in, its anticipated size in terms of employees and assets, and whether it will be a domestic or global enterprise. It should also indicate whether the firm will be publicly traded and whether it will have acquired other firms. Developing the unified corporate vision doesn't replace long-term planning, but it does facilitate the planning process.

The unified corporate vision serves as the North Star in every decision to be made by every manager at every level every day. Anytime any issue comes up, the question can be raised, "Will this action move us toward the fulfillment of our unified corporate vision?" All too often, when people are asked what the firm wants to be, no one can articulate the vision, or there is a wide range of responses. In either case, the future of the firm is in jeopardy. When the vision is stated as a specific destination with a specific date of arrival, decision making becomes a lot easier for everyone in the firm.

Strategic Management Is Essential in Times of Accelerating Change

The process to be used for developing a unified corporate vision is deeply rooted in what is now known as "strategic management." Strategic management consists of a nine-step process that starts on a very conceptual level and gets narrower with each step, as shown on the next page.

Step One: Accepting the Need for Strategic Thinking

Strategic thinking can be characterized as the process whereby executives are encouraged to extend their time horizons beyond the typical three- to

---

The Strategic Management Process

Step One: Accepting the Need for Strategic Thinking
Step Two: Undertaking Strategic "Inquiries"
Step Three: Developing Contingency Scenarios
Step Four: Gaining Strategic Insights
Step Five: Clarifying Strategic Opportunities and Threats
Step Six: Identifying Possible Strategic Positions
Step Seven: Creating a Unified Corporate Vision
Step Eight: Selecting the Target Strategic Position
Step Nine: Identifying Strategic Initiatives

---

five-year planning cycle. Through strategic thinking, executives contemplate the world at least twice as far into the future as in their long-range plan. James Adams notes, "Strategic thinking is not automatic. It is a divergence from business as usual and not easy since it causes us to confront the large uncertainties associated with the future."[4] According to Adams, "Strategic thinking means dealing more with intangible rather than tangible factors as well as qualitative rather than quantitative variables. It will require a broad, fresh data base."[5] Craig Hickman and Michael Silva note that vision can be viewed as "a mental journey from the known to the unknown, creating the future from a montage of current facts, hopes, dreams, and opportunities."[6]

Strategic thinking encourages executives to rip off the blinders that have limited their perceptual fields to their firms, industry, country, training, and experiences. Executives need to adopt a "kaleidoscopic" perspective whereby they do a "mental" pirouette. This will enable them to see the world from a 360-degree perspective rather than the usual 150- to 180-degree perspective.

The liberally educated and broadly experienced executive is best suited for strategic thinking. Technical training and operational knowledge of one industry may have helped the firm get started, but narrowness of perspective and background undermine one's propensity to think strategically. Rosabeth Moss Kanter observes, "Purely technical experts are often unable to put all the pieces together to manage a business in a demanding, rapidly changing environment."[7] The ability to distill tangible and intangible factors as well as see the forest without getting lost in the trees are marks of the visionary leader.

The more executives think about the future, the more comfortable they feel about it and the challenges it will bring. After a while, strategic thinking becomes second nature. The future becomes something one welcomes rather than something ominous that evokes anxiety. Firms that are run by people who practice "ostrich management" by burying their heads in the sand in response to the accelerating rate of change are destined to falter as they get left behind in the marketplace.

Step Two: Undertaking Strategic "Inquiries"

Extending one's time horizon and broadening one's perceptual field are essential components of strategic thinking. Even though strategic thinking may not provide a clear picture of what the future may hold, it will provide a foundation for making "strategic inquiries." Undertaking strategic inquiries encourages executives to investigate what the future may hold. In periods of rapid change, extending one's time horizon encourages executives to contemplate what may be beyond the horizon. The authors of the article, "Management and the Year 2000" note, "While no one can foresee the future with complete accuracy, the seeds of future change already have been planted and broad estimates of the direction and extent of change—and recommendations for the future—can be made."[8]

Undertaking strategic inquiries means pondering what life may be like in ten to twenty years. Attention is directed to changes in demographics, population movement, shifting values, changing lifestyles, emerging consumer interests, technological breakthroughs, changing government regulation, and the like. Environmental scanning plays a key role in undertaking strategic inquiries. Environmental scanning serves as a form of organizational radar. It is a deliberate effort to get a reading for what may be over the horizon. R. M. Narchal, K. Kittappa, and P. Bhattacharya indicated an environmental scanning system can be viewed as "a set of radars to monitor important events in the environment that may create opportunities or threats for the organization. These events tend to be visible in the environment in the form of weak signals and generate early warnings for organizations."[9]

Undertaking strategic inquiries means executives conduct an "environmental audit" to identify major factors and forces that may affect the overall environment in the future. These factors may be sociological, economic, technological, legal, international, political, and/or competitive in nature. The Quick Environmental Scanning Technique, known as "QUEST," offers a systematic way for executives to identify and contemplate future environmental factors that may have critical implications for the strategic positioning of the firm.

QUEST is a multistep process that enables executives to gain insights into what the future may hold. Each step is discussed in varying degrees of depth in this chapter. A more detailed description of QUEST can be found in the book, *Leaders: The Strategies for Taking Charge,* by Warren Bennis and Burt Nanus.[10] With QUEST, the firm's executives:

1. Put aside day-to-day operations so they can think about the future.
2. Share their views about external environments that have critical implications for the future of the firm.
3. Do environmental scanning to identify factors and forces that have the potential to shape the world in general, the future of the industry, and the company.
4. Identify the firm's key stakeholders.
5. Analyze the stakeholders' expectations and their potential impact on the firm.
6. Identify key events or trends that could be opportunities or threats to the firm.
7. Construct scenarios that reflect potential sequences and time frames of events.
8. Estimate the probability the major events and scenarios could occur.
9. Construct a "cross-impact" matrix that indicates how important developments can affect one another as well as their impact on the performance of the firm if it does not change what it is presently doing.
10. Identify the factors and forces with the highest priority that must receive management's undivided attention in developing the unified corporate vision.
11. Generate a list of possible strategic positions for the firm.
12. Evaluate each of the strategic positions in terms of risk, resource requirements, lead time, opportunity for competitive advantage, financial return, and so on.
13. Choose the best course of action for gaining the firm's target strategic position.

Environmental scanning and key factor monitoring are essential if the firm is to be aware of emerging opportunities and threats at the earliest possible moment. The importance of timing, especially having lead time over present and future competitors, cannot be overemphasized. As noted in the Wayne Gretzky example in Chapter 2, the ability to be at the right place at the right time with the right capabilities can give the firm a formidable competitive advantage. Executives who have the vision to see things others don't see, who can think thoughts others can't think, and who can do things others can't even dream of doing are destined to lead their firms "where no firms have gone before!"

Step Three: Developing Contingency Scenarios

Strategic management encourages executives to run various scenarios about what the future may hold. Strategic management relies more on scenario building than traditional forecasting techniques. Forecasts often have limited value because they tend to be extrapolations from the past. As Peter Drucker notes, "In turbulent times, managers cannot assume that tomorrow will be an extension of today."[11]

Most forecasts concentrate on quantitative data. According to Pierre Wack, "Sooner or later forecasts will fail where they are needed the most: in anticipating major shifts in the business environment that make whole strategies obsolete."[12] Scenarios try to identify factors that are new and different as well as qualitative in nature. Scenarios are particularly useful in times of ambiguity and discontinuity. By running "What if?" scenarios, executives may become aware of a whole range of possibilities.

Scenario building is a key component of visionary leadership. Most executives consider their jobs to be "coming up with the answers" to various questions. Visionary leaders operate from an anticipatory stance. They go two steps beyond coming up with the answers. Visionary leaders recognize they need to be able to identify the questions that will need to be answered in the years ahead. They also know that success comes to those who have the answers before anyone else is even aware of the questions.

Scenario building enables executives to identify various situations that could occur. It also encourages executives to think the unthinkable and to prepare for the unexpected. Scenario building may put the firm in a position to harvest lucrative opportunities that are not visible to the untrained eye. It may also keep the firm from being blindsided.

Burt Nanus illustrates in his book *Visionary Leadership* how a firm that makes pet food can use environmental scanning to identify "key factors" that have the potential to have a significant impact on the firm's future. Nanus then shows how scenarios can be run to identify possible situations or sequences of events that could have a significant positive or negative impact on the firm. Nanus's example also indicates the need to pay particular attention to the firm's key stakeholders.

QUEST incorporates potential changes in the needs and expectations of suppliers, pet owners, competitors, distributors, veterinarians, breeders, government agencies, and the public as a whole. QUEST also considers possible changes in economic, political, technological, legal, and other relevant external conditions. Nanus's pet food company example outlines numerous possible changes including:

1. The rising population of show animals, such as pedigree dogs, increases demand for special foods and "gourmet" items

2. A breakthrough in pet longevity

3. An increased reliance on veterinarians as sources of advice and perhaps as suppliers of pet foods

4. The demand for "treats" such as dog biscuits and snacks increases faster than any other pet food category

5. An increased demand for convenience and self-feeding in pet foods

6. The discovery that pets may be harmful to human health

7. An increased demand for pet foods that more closely resemble human foods

8. An increased concern with pet health and nutrition, including special diet foods[13]

While most of these changes may not occur overnight, all of them could happen within a few years.

Once the list of key factors or trends has been generated, then scenarios can be constructed to reflect a string of events that could unfold over a period of time. One scenario could involve a major economic downturn. This trend would have significant implications on pet ownership, the size of pets owned, the market's sensitivity to pricing, how much space retailers would be willing to provide, package sizing, and ingredients to be used.

Another scenario could involve the reduced desire by adults to have children. This trend may increase pet ownership and the amount of money people would be willing to pay to feed their pets. The scenario in which medical findings indicate pets carry a virus that is life threatening to humans would have major implications for a pet food company. Other scenarios may include the entrance of foreign competitors, major government regulation, competitors merging, and a breakthrough in the development of synthetic foods.

Retail and service firms can also benefit from running scenarios involving changing economic conditions, the entrance of a major chain or franchise in one's geographic area, and the enactment of stiff government regulation. For example, a jewelry business should run scenarios involving the imposition of a 20 percent luxury tax, a shift in values away from conspicuous consumption, and a period of sustained economic growth.

Step Four: Gaining Strategic "Insights"

By asking "What if?" questions and formulating a list of possible scenarios, executives may gain insights into what may be over the horizon. In many cases, executives will recognize certain events are no longer in the "whether or not" category. Certain events or situations are almost inevitable as you extend your time horizon and consider the possibilities. If such scenarios arise, executives need to focus their attention on: (1) when they are likely to happen, (2) what the leading indicators will be that will precede the corresponding situation, and (3) how they can position their firms to benefit from the situations. The following examples illustrate how running scenarios may provide insights into what the future may hold:

Example No. 1: One day, the managing partner of a one-hundred-person engineering firm became concerned about the diminishing number of projects that were coming up for bid. He scheduled a retreat for top management to discuss his observation. A consultant served as the facilitator to assist them in breaking away from the present and thinking about the future.

The management team looked at the trends in their industry and concluded it was going to wane sooner than they originally thought it would. The firm had been very successful in designing a specific type of structure for governments throughout the world. Management now realized that within five years, few governments would need any more of these structures built. This "insight" prompted management to realize that if it didn't change what it was doing, then it would be out of business in just a few years.

The insight that their very profitable business was about to die was like being hit by a truck. However, it served as the "awareness" stage that must precede change. Fortunately, management recognized its precarious position early enough to do something about it. It spent the next six months reviewing the firm's strengths and competencies as well as emerging opportunities. Management identified one particular opportunity that had the potential within the decade to be as lucrative as its present market had been—if the firm could position itself to meet the emerging market's needs.

This lead time gave the firm a head start over other engineering firms that had not recognized the emerging opportunity. Within three years, everyone in the firm had gone through a major training program so that they would possess the answers to the questions their "new" clients would need. As noted earlier, when you have the answers before any one else even knows the questions, you are destined to be ahead of your competition. This brings up another line from the movie, *The Carpetbaggers*. When the young pilot asks his entrepreneur partner "How can we get into plastics when we don't know anything about plastics?", the entrepreneur responds, "You're right, but I'm flying to Germany to learn as much about plastics as I can. When I return, I will know more about plastics than anyone else in the United States!"

Example No. 2: A young sales manager for a firm that had a number of retail outlets in the Southeast was very concerned about how the CEO and vice president of marketing had been taking the market for granted. He believed the market was becoming saturated with competition and that predatory price wars would soon follow. He was frustrated because the marketing VP felt everything was fine. The VP noted that the firm had record sales and profits. The young sales manager sought the advice of a friend who was a consultant. The consultant advised his friend to stop wasting his time trying to convince his boss of the need to change. The consultant cited the words of Louis Armstrong, the famous trumpet player: "There are people who don't know and you just can't tell them."

The consultant suggested a different strategy. He encouraged his friend to spend his evenings analyzing the profit potential, distribution sites, and capital requirements for other geographic markets. The consultant told his friend to be patient; if his friend's prognosis was correct, then there would come a time when his homework would pay off. A year later, the CEO frantically called a meeting to inform everyone that while the firm's sales had dropped by only 20 percent, its profits had disappeared as a result of price competition. The CEO looked around the room and asked if anyone had any idea how to turn the situation around. The sales manager followed the consultant's advice and did not automatically volunteer his advice. When it was clear that no one—especially the vice president of marketing—had any ideas, the sales manager stated, "If I could have five minutes of your time, I would like to brief you on..." The sales manager then distributed copies of his proposal to enter three different geographic markets that had the potential to restore the firm's profitability. After the meeting, he became the new vice president of marketing.

Example No. 3: An MBA student asked one of his professors about the prospects of going into teaching as a career. The student wanted to know if it would be worthwhile spending four more years to earn a doctorate so he could teach on the college level. The professor indicated that teaching was a tough profession because of the "publish or perish" mentality that existed at most universities. The professor also told the student about the economic problems that were expected to continue to affect universities and how video-enhanced computer technology was changing how courses could be taught.

The professor ran a scenario aloud about what the future might bring. At that moment, he realized two major developments could transform the whole educational environment within the next ten years. First, tight budgets would force legislators to explore drastic methods to reduce funding for education at the college level. Second, interactive technology would make it possible for one professor to teach a class at twenty different universities at the same time. With this insight, the professor not only discouraged the student from going into teaching, he forced himself to contemplate what he would do for his "second" career since he was only 45 years old. What he had thought would be a career for a lifetime, now appeared to be less certain.

The professor indicated that with interactive video students wouldn't even need to go to the university to attend classes. They could take classes from their homes on visually interactive personal computers. When the student asked, "What will we do with all the classroom buildings and dormitories?", the professor responded, "I guess we'll turn them into prisons as the government did with some of its military bases after the Soviet Union fell."

The realization that certain situations may be inevitable and the development of new insights are significant steps in the strategic management of the firm. Running scenarios is like figuring the odds that one birth control technique or device will work. If the probability of it not doing the job is just one in a hundred, then you may go ahead with it. But if you look at the odds associated with doing something over an extended period of time, then the odds may not be sufficient to justify the risk. Statistics 101 tells us that the odds of something failing the first time are the same as it failing the hundredth time. Sooner or later, someone will get pregnant. This insight can change the way people approach moments of intimacy. The same reasoning may also apply to the prevention of sexually transmitted diseases.

With a better understanding of what the future may hold, executives can shift their attention to identifying ways the firm may be able to capitalize on the challenges that lie ahead. They will also be in a position to minimize the likelihood they will trampled to death by a herd of roaming elephants. The sooner you realize or accept that something is inevitable, the sooner you can prepare yourself to deal constructively with it. As soon as you recognize that "never" will happen and that "someday" could be tomorrow, the sooner you will stop putting off to tomorrow what should be done today!

Step Five: Clarifying Strategic Opportunities and Threats

Executives with a long-term horizon and mental dexterity are able to develop different perceptions of the future. Scenario building may not provide them with a crystal clear picture of what the future may bring, but it will alert them to various possibilities. Executives may also gain insights into potential opportunities and threats. For example, by thinking on a global basis rather than just about one's domestic markets, executives may identify emerging markets that will offer greater price margins, candidates for joint ventures or licensing arrangements, and funding assistance from the respective governments.

Being aware of these problems and opportunities enables executives to operate from an entrepreneurial stance. As someone once said, "Within every problem, there lies at least one disguised business opportunity." The existence of a dynamic global marketplace means consumers and institutions throughout the world will be looking for new ways to do things and new things to do. There will be millions of consumers in search of businesses with the technological and managerial capabilities to meet their evolving needs.

When the prospects of entering foreign markets or utilizing a radically different technology to serve markets are raised, managers of most new ventures exclaim, "But I don't know anything about doing business abroad" or "I know very little about that technology!" This is the value of having a strategic orientation and running scenarios. If you identify an emerging opportunity early enough, you have a head start on everyone else. You have the time to study potential foreign markets and to learn the "ropes" about selling products in those markets. With lead time, you won't be rushed into anything. This reduces uncertainty and takes a lot of the anxiety out of doing something that you have never done before. Additional lead time also gives you a chance to get the bugs out and develop a high level of proficiency before competition enters the scene.

Step Six: Identifying Possible Strategic Positions

The visionary executive recognizes that the future will offer an almost unlimited number of opportunities. No firm, no matter how large, has the capability to meet all the needs of the global marketplace. In the years ahead, the name of the game will be "nichemanship." The firms that thrive in the years ahead will be the ones that identify emerging markets early and develop the ability to meet the market segment's needs to the point no other firm will even consider entering that market.

At this point, executives need to develop a list of possible strategic positions for the firm. Executives at the helms of most new ventures have limited understanding of the concept of strategic positioning. They utilize a "short-term forward" or "incremental" approach to managing their firms. Even if they are able to identify where they want their firms to be in three years, their targets tend to be an extrapolation of the last few years' growth rate. At the end of this year, they will simply add another year to their three-year plan. These executives also tend to have no more than a three-year time horizon. Instead of "managing by braille," they are practicing "white cane" management. They may have extended their reach, but they are still destined to operate from a reactive rather than a strategic and entrepreneurial mode.

In times of rapid change, having a three-year time horizon is far better than having a one-year time horizon. Nevertheless, firms with short time horizons are destined to be preoccupied with operational matters and to live a hand-to-mouth existence. They try to squeeze what they can from existing markets rather than capitalize on emerging opportunities. Visionary firms position themselves to get the "first bite of the apple." Short-term time horizon firms are relegated to the futile existence of trying to sustain life from the apple's core after the visionary firms have discarded it.

Strategic management encourages executives to adopt a "long-term backwards" perspective. This approach is quite different from the short-term forward approach. When visionary executives are asked the question "How do you climb a mountain?", they respond, "from the top down." They know that by mentally envisioning what it would be like to stand on the summit, they can see the best path for climbing the mountain. If they were to climb the mountain from where they presently stand, it would limit them to the path immediately in front of them.

Visionary executives realize that there may be many paths to the summit and that the best path may not be the easiest, shortest, or even the one they are presently on. With the long-term backwards approach, executives identify where they want the firm to be in seven to ten years. Then they work backwards from that date by asking, "If we want to be there in the year 20XY, where will we need to be in the year 20XY–1?" The process of identifying each of the preceding year's prerequisite positions is calculated until it is brought back to the present.

The long-term backwards approach has two major advantages. First, it recognizes that seven to ten years of an incremental approach may lead to a completely different and probably less advantageous position. It takes time to identify, cultivate, and capitalize on emerging opportunities. The short-term forward incremental approach may miss them altogether. Second, when executives use the long-term backwards approach, they often realize they are already at least two years behind schedule. Their timetable may indicate a twelve-year "critical path" to achieving the desired ten-year strategic position. This fosters a sense of urgency and a bias for action to initiate action plans that might otherwise be postponed or never implemented. This perspective also unleashes people's minds throughout the firm to find innovative ways to compress the critical path to meet the firm's desired date of arrival.

Fred DeLuca started Subway in 1965 at the age of seventeen to finance his college education. His business plan projected thirty-two stores within ten years. When he and his partner realized they would not be able to finance their expansion, they redirected their efforts to franchising their business. In 1988, DeLuca's vision for Subway was to have five thousand franchise outlets by 1994. This meant developing between two and three locations per day! This ambitious vision became a driving force for Subway. It had established over five thousand units by the end of 1990 and by the end of 1992 it had over seven thousand units. DeLuca's vision and the wherewithal to make it a reality have put Subway in a position to become the largest fast-food franchise in the world.

The whole issue of strategic thinking raises the question of what the difference is between short term and long term? Short-term means basically dealing with the here and now—almost everything is given. Few things can be changed. This means getting the most out of the products, processes, personnel, customers, suppliers, technology, capital, and equipment you presently have available. Short-term in one industry may be long-term in another. For example, in the software industry, three years may be a long-term time horizon. Software packages may become out-of-date in just six months. In the biotechnology field, long-term may be a five-to-seven-year time horizon given the time it takes to get FDA approval.

Medium-term means certain resources can be substituted (such as machines for labor), products can be modified, and new "ways" of doing things you have been doing can be initiated. Long-term opens the door to all sorts of possibilities. Everything can be changed. The firm can change its products, locations, and processes. It can find all new things to do including moving into emerging industries.

Strategic thinking fosters a whole new mentality. If you were to ask your staff to develop a whole new product or a revolutionary way to provide a service—and to have it ready within the next thirty days—they would say it can't be done. However, if you encourage them to find a way to meet the needs of an emerging market that the firm may enter three years from now—their response might be far more enthusiastic. They may even indicate they can have it ready before then!

When people recognize there is limited value in continuing the status quo by utilizing an incremental approach for the next seven to ten years, they are more willing to direct their attention to envisioning what the firm should become rather than what it is. The long-term backwards approach means almost anything is possible. Emerging opportunities can be harvested and formidable obstacles can be overcome.

Step Seven: Creating a Unified Corporate Vision

The first six steps of the strategic management process are prerequisites for creating a unified corporate vision. Management should now be in a position to clarify what the firm should strive to be. The vision not only clarifies what the firm is trying to become, it also states what the firm is trying "not" to become. The unified corporate vision serves as the basis for saying "yes" and for saying "no" when managers are confronted with the myriad of decisions that come with changing times.

When Robert Townsend took over Avis Corporation years ago, he found himself at the helm of a firm that was involved in numerous endeavors. Like most firms in the same predicament, Avis was not positioned to capitalize on the changes that were on the horizon. Townsend and his executive team engaged in some serious soul-searching to determine what type of firm Avis should strive to be. After six months of extensive analysis of evolving market conditions and introspection, it was determined that Avis should strive to become "The fastest growing company with the highest profit margins in the business of renting and leasing vehicles without drivers."[14] With this new vision statement, everyone in the firm had a North Star to navigate by. Whenever any question came up, the Avis team would ask, "Will this action move us one step closer to being the leader?" This statement also provided the impetus needed to sell those endeavors that would not contribute to the actualization of Avis's unified corporate vision.

The "focus" elicited by a vision of what is possible, even if it hasn't been done before, can have an incredible effect on the people involved. The ability to see the big picture and the opportunities less insightful executives did not see in the marketplace may explain why Steven Jobs believed everyday people would buy Apple personal computers, why Fred Smith was so sure the concept of Federal Express was destined to succeed, and why Fred DeLuca believed Subway could succeed in a world composed of hamburger franchises. These visionaries and others who have been able to transform their visions into reality have changed the way we eat, work, and live.

Step Eight: Selecting the Target Strategic Position

The formulation of the unified corporate vision is an effort to identify what the business should become. Attention now needs to be directed to what type of business the firm should be in. The vision provides a basis for navigating the seas of change. It also serves as the basis for selecting the firm's target strategic position—also known as the firm's desired future destination.

The target strategic position will serve as the measure of whether the firm is fulfilling its destiny. The target strategic position identifies the markets to be served, the technological expertise it will need to develop or acquire, the resources it will need to have at its disposal, and the comparative advantages it must have over its competition. It will also indicate the size the firm will need to be in terms of the number of people, assets, and facilities.

Selecting the target strategic position is a deliberate effort to identify the industries or markets the firm will be in, where it expects to be in each market life cycle, the geographic territories it will operate in, and the configuration of the firm in financial and structural terms. This may explain why General Electric sold off its small appliance business. Jack Welch, as CEO of General Electric, believed his company's future would be in medical technology. He used the proceeds of the sale of the appliance division to finance the development of medical technology products that would be major breadwinners for G.E. in the years to come.

Too many executives wait until their markets are saturated and industries in decline before they start looking for ways to keep their firms afloat. They tend to adopt one of two approaches for dealing with their predicament. They may take the "wishful thinking" approach in which they rationalize away recent sales declines and resulting losses as nothing more than temporary consequences of a cyclical economy. Other executives tend to take the "throw more resources at it" approach. They increase advertising budgets, engage in price wars, and make minor modifications in product design or packaging to reduce the slide. Neither of these approaches has lasting value. When executives operate with a short-term time horizon, they are not likely to see the need for major repositioning until it is too late.

Step Nine: Identifying Strategic "Initiatives"

The targeted strategic position clarifies where those at the helm want their firm to be seven to ten years into the future. Once the "where" has been targeted, attention can be directed to "how" to get to the desired destination. If the firm plans to initiate a major repositioning effort, it should be apparent that fine-tuning existing products and processes will not be enough.

Executives who want to transform their firms need to recognize that strategic initiatives must be identified and implemented for nearly every dimension of the firm. Life in the firm will be anything but "business as usual." New markets will need to be researched, new prototypes will need to be created and tested, new technologies will need to be developed or adopted, new production and distribution capabilities will need to be developed, and new skills will have to be learned. Financial reserves will have to be set aside because the firm may experience a lean period as it makes the transition.

The firm's management system will also have to be changed to make sure everyone's attention is directed to doing the things that will move the firm to its targeted strategic position. Goals must be set for new product development, incentives must be established to reward people for being innovative, and performance reviews must focus on the extent each person has moved the firm closer to its target strategic position. The firm's unified corporate vision is essential because it integrates the firm's corporate culture and its corporate strategy. The importance of carefully orchestrating the firm's strategy and corporate culture will be discussed in the next chapters.

Concluding Comments: Strategic Thinking Must Be an Ongoing Process

Strategic positioning does not have to mean that you throw the baby out with the bathwater. It means management must take an objective look at where the best opportunities may be for the firm in the years to come. It also means management must make a deliberate effort to lead the firm in such a way that every person, every resource, and every moment in time are directed to moving the firm to its target strategic position. Rosabeth Moss Kanter notes, "The skill of corporate leaders, the ultimate change masters, lies in their ability to envision a new reality and aid in its translation into concrete terms."[15]

Warren Bennis's study of fifty outstanding CEOs identified certain characteristics. According to Bennis, the successful CEO:

1. Develops a compelling vision of the firm's future.

2. Translates the vision into reality by concentrating on the keys to success.

3. Remains deeply involved at the very heart of things, spurring the action necessary to carry out the vision.

4. Motivates employees to embrace the vision.

5. Constantly articulates the vision so that it permeates all organizational levels and functions, taking the firm where it has never been before.[16]

If management adopts a strategic orientation and can demonstrate the qualities associated with visionary leadership, then it should be able to chart an evolutionary course rather than resort to a radical line of action. As in surgery, the more radical the procedure, the higher the probability the patient will not survive the operation.

Identifying the strategic position of the firm is not something that is done every seven to ten years. It is an ongoing process whereby management regularly ponders what may be over the horizon, identifies and monitors key factors, conducts environmental scanning sessions, runs various scenarios, and does all the other activities to remain in tune with what is possible. Only then will management be able to capitalize on the opportunities that lie ahead.

Executives with clear vision invent excellent
futures for their firms; those who lack it set
their companies adrift in dangerous waters.[17]
        CRAIG HICKMAN AND MICHAEL SILVA

CHIEF EXECUTIVE GUIDELINES

Name: Michael W. Creed, P.E., President
Company: McKim & Creed Engineers, P.A.
Product/Service: Engineering
Sales: $12,000,000   Number of Employees: 180
Awards/Distinctions:

1. "Award of Excellence" from the Professional Services Management Association

2. Five "Engineering Excellence Awards" from The Consulting Engineers Council of North Carolina

General guidelines: When it comes to adopting a strategic perspective and developing the firm's vision, the E/CEO should keep the following tips in mind:

The CEO of a small, rapidly growing business must beware of "missing the forest for the trees." We get so busy doing the work that originally made us successful that we are in danger of failing to see our own changes and our market changes. After ten years of business we hired a marketing/communications consultant to help us with a new corporate identity program.

Lois Boemer, president of Boemer Associates in Boston, came into our office and listened to a small group of our leaders talk about who we were, what we did, and how we perceived ourselves. She accurately observed that our actions did not match our words regarding one of our market sectors. We were spending nearly 50 percent of our man-hours serving a market sector we "said" was undesirable. Conversely, we were spending only about 10 percent of our time in a market sector we said was our most important. As a result of Boemer's observations, we were able to "focus" our rapidly growing company in the more desirable market.

My recommendations for the founding partner or CEO who originates a company that is growing rapidly include:

1. Hire an outside consultant to critically evaluate your "alignment," i.e., what you do versus what you say.

2. Make sure you have a specific vision of your own role in your company in ten years.

3. Quit "doing" and start teaching, coaching, and facilitating.

4. Prepare a written Mission Statement that is both inspiring for your employees and differentiating for your customers (P.S.: Involve lots of people).

5. Prepare a comparison statement that we call our "Vision." This should be a picture of your ideal destination.

6. Develop a statement involving values or "guiding principles." These capture the corporate integrity.

7. After the last three things are written, recognize that every action or inaction you perform will be compared against what you have written (moral: walk your talk).

8. Develop a written long-range plan whose "planning horizon" is at least ten years.

9. Verbally promote and sell your long-range plan to everyone in the staff.

10. Include a schedule for replanning every two or three years and involve everyone in the organization.

CHIEF EXECUTIVE GUIDELINES

Name: Fred Sancilio, Ph.D., President
Company: Applied Analytical Industries
Product/Service: Pharmaceutical Product Development
Number of Employees: 360

General guidelines: When it comes to adopting a strategic perspective and developing the firm's vision, the E/CEO should keep the following tips in mind:

1. Make sure that the vision *can* be clearly communicated. That is, ideas tend to be clear to the visionary but words that are used to communicate a thought are not necessarily of equal clarity. So plan on far more difficulty in "passing on" the vision to associates, partners, financial institutions, and customers.

2. Keep the overall "business" (vision) simple. Too many great ideas tend to dilute both resources and focus. So your conceptualization of a business should be kept simple.

3. Don't crowd your plans with "escape" side businesses that will "save" the venture if the primary opportunity doesn't materialize.

4. Plan on the vision you see in the conceptualization stage of the business to change. Some people have a hard time accepting that they are fallible and that change *is* growth in an entrepreneurial business.

5. It always "takes longer," "is harder," and "costs more" than you think! Consequently, plan on having all these elements noted above in substantial excess, i.e., more time, more help, and more money!

6. As a result of the above, plan for total involvement in your vision. You *must* devote all of your energy to success. The only difference between successful implementation and failure is effort and tenacity. Don't give up when the going gets tough, that's the starting point of success.

Proceed with Caution Guidelines:

1. Include the best people, not the most available, in the initial operation of the company.

2. Learn to interview and select a candidate only after five have been talked to even if the first meets all your criteria.

3. Focus your energy in one opportunity (it doesn't really matter which) and don't divert.

4. Understand exit strategies better than I did and work that into the vision. For example, do you plan on keeping your business forever? If so, what happens to it when you're too old to run it...?

And I Would Be Particularly Careful Not *to:*

Underestimate the amount of work, attention, and money implementation will take.

11

Formulating a Winning Competitive Strategy

If we can know where we are and something
about how we got there, then we might see
where we are trending—and if the outcomes
which lie naturally in our course are
unacceptable, to make timely change.

ABRAHAM LINCOLN

Corporate strategy plays an integral role in the firm's success. While the unified corporate vision may indicate "where" the firm wants to be at some point in the future, corporate strategy represents "how" management plans to transform the vision into reality. In World War II, the Allied forces' vision may have been "to achieve the unconditional surrender of all Axis forces by the summer of 1945." The Allied forces then had to determine the best strategy for "winning the war." Their strategy represented their overall game plan for gaining the unconditional surrender.

The Allies had to decide whether they would rely more on air power, ground troops, or naval forces. Decisions also had to made about whether they would focus their attention on northern Europe or the Mediterranean. Questions about how to deal with Russia, the weather, financial matters, and political considerations also had to be answered. Many of the decisions that were made about the Allies' strategy affect our lives today. The development of nuclear weapons has changed the way we view our world. And while the Cold War with the Soviet Union may be officially over, the boundary disputes continue. It is apparent that "how" the Allies tried to win the war and the deals that were struck to provide peace had long-term implications. The same may apply to the development and implementation of a firm's competitive strategy.

The firm's strategy indicates what industries it will be in, the market segments it will serve, and the areas where the firm will try to gain and sustain a competitive advantage. Corporate strategy represents how the firm tries to create and maintain customers for a profit. The firm's strategy can be viewed as a long-term scenario of actions that will enable the firm to achieve the target strategic position and fulfill its unified corporate vision. Chapter 10 discussed the step-by-step procedure for identifying the firm's unified corporate vision. This chapter will describe the step-by-step process for formulating the firm's competitive strategy.

A number of factors need to be identified and analyzed before the firm can determine the most appropriate strategy to follow. Strategy can be viewed as a three-stage process. First, management must do a "situation analysis" to identify the factors outside and within the firm that can affect the firm's ability to develop competitive advantages. Second, management must evaluate the various possible strategies to determine which one has the highest probability of fulfilling the vision. Third, management must make a deliberate effort to ensure the strategy is properly implemented. Without diligent implementation, even the simplest strategy is destined to flounder. Implementation will be discussed at the end of this chapter. It will also be addressed in Chapter 12 on managing corporate culture and Chapter 13 on developing the long-term business plan.

Conducting the Situation Analysis

One of management's greatest responsibilities is to answer the question "What business are we in?" Yet the real question should be "What business should we be in?" While most managers can answer the first question, few managers can answer the second one. The firm's unified corporate vision may have been the product of strategic thinking, QUEST, and the consideration of general trends and other relatively intangible factors. The development of the firm's strategy requires more in-depth analysis of the firm's present situation and future possibilities.

When entrepreneurs are thinking about starting new ventures, they usually start by identifying the industry that has the best potential for success since they are creating a new venture from scratch. They are in a position to ask, "What business should I be in?" Their "broad" perceptual field permits them to consider various opportunities. Those at the helms of relatively new ventures tend to have narrower perspectives. They tend to direct their attention to improving the business they are already in. As noted in the last chapter, executives need to break away from this "short-term forward" mentality and direct their attention to what business their business should be in.

There are two very simple yet effective models for coming to grips with whether the firm is properly positioned to fulfill its vision. The "strategic planning gap" model in Figure 11-1 asks three questions.[1]

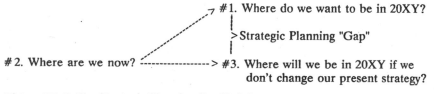

Figure 11-1 The Strategic Planning Gap Model.

The unified corporate vision should answer the first question. Hopefully, the firm has a management information system that provides a specific answer to the second question. The third question can be viewed as a strategic management "gut check." If the firm's present strategy is almost certain to fulfill the firm's vision, then there is no strategic planning "gap." When most firms take an objective look at their present strategy, they realize they are not on the best path for fulfilling their vision. Some firms are not even pointed in the right direction! Too often, management finds that it is merely continuing to do the things it has been doing rather than doing what will need to be done to properly position their firms for the years ahead. The greater the gap between what needs to be done and what is presently being done, the greater the magnitude of the change that will need to be made in the firm's strategy.

Years ago, General Electric's top management realized the firm was spread out in so many industries, markets, territories, products, and services that the firm was losing its competitive edge and missing out on a number of emerging opportunities. General Electric and McKinsey & Company developed what is known as the "stoplight" model[2] (see Figure 11-2). This model helped management put all of the firm's efforts in perspective. Management evaluates each corporate endeavor in terms of how favorable the industry it is in and the extent to which the firm is operating from a position of competitive strength. The 3×3 matrix indicates the nine possible situations a product, service, or business can be in. The industry under review can have: (1) high attractiveness, (2) medium attractiveness, or (3) low attractiveness in terms of present and future growth and profits. This model may apply to market segments within an industry as well as the overall industry. On the other dimension, the firm can either operate with: (1) significant competitive advantage, (2) competitive parity with some strengths and weaknesses, or (3) no real advantage with a number of weaknesses.

THE FIRM'S COMPETITIVE POSITION

		HIGH	MEDIUM	LOW
INDUSTRY ATTRACTIVENESS	HIGH	GREEN #1	GREEN #3	YELLOW #3
	MEDIUM	GREEN #2	YELLOW #2	RED #2
	LOW	YELLOW #1	RED #1	RED #3

Figure 11-2 The G.E./McKinsey "Stoplight" Strategy Matrix. This model is reproduced with permission of *Business Week* magazine.[2]

The stoplight model encourages management to identify the endeavors that should get attention and resources as well as those that should be phased out. The "Green #1" position is obviously the position every firm would like to be in. The industry is very healthy and the firm has a significant competitive advantage. If the marketplace is viewed as a pie, then the pie is growing. The firm's share of the pie is also growing. Management needs to make sure the firm's strategy continues to capitalize on this opportunity. Resources will need to be allocated to this endeavor so the firm can maintain its competitive strength. Without sufficient resources, the firm may slip into a medium competitive strength position. Management must also keep a vigil for the almost inevitable slowdown in the market whereby the industry's attractiveness goes from high to medium. While it may still be in a green cell, its future may be less lucrative.

Each of the other eight cells indicates the need for a different strategy. If the firm is in Green #2, then it needs to harvest what it can while trying not to lose its competitive strength. A firm can enjoy a very lucrative existence if it positions itself in market segments that will grow at a much higher rate. Certain segments may experience a high level of growth in medium- and low-growth industries. The size of the overall pie may not be growing much, but if the firm has competitive strength then it should be in a position to continue growing by attracting customers from other firms.

In Green #2, as is the case with almost all the other cells, management must also make every effort to ensure that it does not lose its present customers. Too many firms exhibit a complacent, if not arrogant, attitude toward their customers. Most firms take their present customers for granted while courting new customers. Competitive strategy, as in sports and war, needs to have offensive and defensive dimensions. While trying to win new customers, you need to make sure you are not losing the ones you already have.

Green #3 also represents a favorable position for the firm. While the industry may be very attractive, the firm maintains its share of the expanding pie by maintaining competitive parity. Management needs to determine if the firm will be able to develop its competitive strength to move into Green #1. Management also needs to determine whether the expected financial returns will justify the additional investment. In any event, management must be alert to the prospect that the market may slow to medium attractiveness. Management must also be sure that the firm does not lose its competitive parity. In either case, the firm would be slipping into a yellow zone.

The yellow zones mean "proceed with extreme caution." Yellow #1 is a tenuous situation. While the firm may have a strong competitive position, the industry is not attractive. Management must carefully analyze the industry's situation to determine if there is potential for growth and if market segments exist that still offer a reasonable return. In any event, the firm should resist investing its scarce resources in an industry that offers limited gains. The firm also has to determine if it can maintain its competitive strength. Yellow #1 represents a marginal existence in which the firm hopes the industry will have a second wind. In most cases, management needs to have the guts to either sell this part of the firm or phase out its assets so they can be invested in more promising endeavors.

Yellow #2 represents a two-dimensional situation. The firm is in a lukewarm competitive position and the industry is moderately attractive. Management needs to determine if the industry will become more attractive or if the firm can improve its competitive position. If either or both of these happen, then the firm will occupy one of the three green cells.

Yellow #3 represents another tentative situation. If the industry begins to slow, then the firm falls into a red zone. Management must decide whether it is worth the effort and resources to move to competitive parity by reducing the firm's competitive weaknesses or if it should sell or phase out its investment in that endeavor. When the firm is in any of the yellow zones, management needs to change the firm's strategy to move the firm into a green zone or to get out of that endeavor altogether.

All three red zones indicate the firm must discontinue those endeavors. In Red #1, the industry is low in attractiveness. The industry would have to improve and the firm would have to gain competitive advantage before it would occupy a green cell. Red #2 also represents a discouraging situation. The firm would have to go from a position of competitive weakness to one of competitive advantage to occupy a green cell. The only other reason for staying would be if the industry became very attractive and the firm gained competitive parity. Red #3 represents the worst of all situations. The industry is weak and the firm's competitive position is also weak. Managers whose firms are in this cell should be taken out and shot.

The G.E.-McKinsey model is very helpful in providing a framework for analyzing the firm's present situation. As the slogan goes, "Awareness precedes change." Two points, however, need to be made about this model. First, it tends to focus on the present. Management needs to look at it with the future in mind. Attention needs to be directed to whether the industry is trending up, how much it will grow or decline, and how long the trend or current level of industry attractiveness will continue. Management also needs to consider potential strategies of present and future competitors. The amount of time, money, risk, and expected gain for maintaining or changing one's competitive strategy must also be factored into the equation.

Smaller firms need to recognize that because they have limited ability to change the attractiveness of an industry, they should focus their attention on areas where they can improve their competitive strength. The horse and jockey analogy presented earlier in this book may apply here as well. The jockey can be viewed as the firm's competitive position. The horse can be viewed as the industry's attractiveness. Smaller firms need to remember, no jockey has ever won a race by carrying his or her horse across the finish line! While a resourceful firm may be able to generate a modest profit from a lackluster industry or market segment, the same level of resourcefulness will usually provide a much higher return in a more favorable industry or market segment.

The Structure and Maturity of the Industry Must Be Considered

The G.E.-McKinsey model illustrates the need for competitive strategy to reflect the dynamics of the industry in which it will be implemented. Numerous factors must be considered when doing a situation analysis of an industry. Factors affecting the industry include: (1) the degree of industry maturity, (2) whether a few firms dominate it, (3) the extent and speed of technological change, (4) how sensitive it is to economic conditions, (5) how susceptible it is to government regulation, (6) the nature of competition, (7) the ease of entry, and (8) the relative strength of suppliers and customers. These and other factors can have a significant impact on industry attractiveness and long-term profitability.

Industry maturity plays a major role in competitive strategy. Most industries and market segments go through the following six stages:

Conception ⇑Emergence ⇑Growth ⇑Maturity ⇑Decline ⇑Death

Few firms are involved in the conception stage that precedes the creation of an industry. These firms are the pathfinders. They identify a need that is not being addressed at all. They invest considerable time and resources in the creation of a whole new industry. In a sense, these firms are the ones who plant the apple tree so they can take the first bite of the apple when the market emerges.

In the emergence stage, one or two firms usually have the "emerging" market to themselves. At this stage, corporate strategy usually involves letting the market know that such a product or service is available and getting it to the first wave of potential customers. Price competition tends to be minimal. These firms are trying to generate sales and cash.

Things get pretty lively in the growth stage. If the market shows even a moderate level of demand, then new competitors enter the market with what is known as the "second bite of the apple" competitive strategy. These firms may not be as innovative or venturesome as the firms that started the industry or market, but they tend to have a real proficiency for quickly imitating the first firms. They may also introduce a variety of models to meet the needs of particular segments that may be worth specific attention. Competition may take place in terms of distribution outlets, brands and models, promotional programs, as well as quality and service. Market demand tends to exceed or match the supply of products and services so price competition does not tend to play a major role in competitive strategy at this time. Producing, promoting, and supplying products and services is the name of the game in the growth stage.

Firms operating in the growth stage of the industry or market life cycle need to position themselves for the maturity stage before it arrives. They should incorporate nichemanship and the "value-added" concept in their corporate strategies. Nichemanship recognizes no industry is totally homogeneous—different customers have different desires and expectations.

Nichemanship involves identifying the various segments of the market and determining each segment's relative attractiveness. A firm is far more likely to create and maintain customers for a profit if management focuses its attention on one segment of the market rather than trying to be all things to all people. The same applies to creating and maintaining a competitive advantage. If the firm merely provides the marketplace with the same offering as other firms, why should consumers go out of their way to give that business their money? Firms will succeed in attracting and keeping their customers only to the extent they offer them what they want, how they want it, when they want it, where they want it, and at a price they consider to be reasonable.

Nichemanship provides focus that increases the firm's ability to develop lasting competitive advantages. Most firms' competitive strategies are too general. They are like archers who aim for the target and try to pierce it with as many arrows as they can. Smaller businesses are like master archers: they focus their attention on the bull's-eye and make sure each arrow hits the mark. If you focus your attention on a specific segment and tailor your firm's market offering to that specific segment's needs, then you are more likely to know what those consumers want and to provide them with a higher level of satisfaction than firms that fail to differentiate the overall market. Competitive strategy is not about being better than your competitors. It is about being so much better that no firm even tries to compete in that market segment.

Nichemanship has a second major benefit. When your market offering is tailored to a particular segment, consumers tend not to be as sensitive to the price of your products and services. This gives the firm some latitude in its pricing strategy. Nichemanship should thereby enhance the firm's profitability as long as the firm's prices are within reason.

The maturity stage represents the beginning of intense competition among the firms. The "pie" has stopped growing, so firms that want to continue growing must take customers away from other firms. Some firms continue differentiating their product-service offerings so they will have special appeal to customers and not be viewed as commodities. Price competition, however, tends to be the name of the game for a significant number of firms. Firms that overestimated the growth stage now have excess capacity. This situation is compounded by the entrance of new firms who also want to get a piece of the apple or action. Many firms also lower prices due to the existence or expectation of declining sales.

Nichemanship becomes the battle cry for most firms in the late stages of maturity. This is particularly true for smaller firms. Smaller firms tend to be better off if their competitive strategies avoid going head to head in price competition with larger firms that may have economies of scale. They increase their chances for success when they recognize the benefit of focusing their attention on market segments that may not be served as well or at all by other, especially larger, competitors. One way to keep from being trampled to death by a herd of elephants is to avoid dancing with them altogether!

Hopefully, management will have prepared the firm for the market's or industry's eventual decline. While the maturity stage can last for years, management should be looking for the early warning signals of late maturity and early decline. Management should carefully position the firm where it can serve market segments that may continue to produce a reasonable return on investment. The late maturity and decline stages can serve as a source of positive cash flow if management resists the temptation of trying to keep a product, territory, or service alive beyond its useful life.

The firm must have an exit strategy before it enters the decline stage. Without objectivity and quantified parameters, the firm is almost certain to stay too long in a futile effort to prolong the life of a product that should have been put to rest much earlier. Procrastination will drain the firm of valuable resources that could have been invested in earlier stages of more promising products. A point that was emphasized in Chapter 6 should be repeated here. The best firms carefully monitor a product's performance at each stage of the life cycle. Their managers constantly look for early indicators of a turn in the market in order to adjust their strategies so their firms are positioned for what lies ahead rather than what has already happened. The best firms play "one or two markets" ahead.

The "Competitive Matrix" Helps Identify Areas for Competitive Advantage

Firms looking for market opportunities and areas for establishing a competitive advantage should utilize the mental framework associated with the competitive matrix. The competitive matrix is developed using the following seven-step process:

Step 1. Management identifies the various segments that comprise the overall market or industry.

Step 2. Management does an initial screening of the segments to identify the ones that are attractive and may have lasting profit potential.

Step 3. Management constructs a competitive matrix for each of the segments that appear to have the greatest potential. Management needs to be careful about how it defines "greatest potential." The largest segments may already be saturated. Saturated markets are susceptible to severe price cutting. While the segment's overall sales level may be tempting, profits may be fleeting. Management's attention should be directed to segments that have the potential to experience sustained growth for at least the next three to five years. Segments with only a few firms serving them, especially segments with no dominant firms, warrant particular attention.

Step 4.   Management compares the competitive matrices to identify the market segments that are not being served well.

Step 5.   Management evaluates its ability to develop a sustainable competitive position in each segment that represents an opportunity.

Step 6.   Management evaluates the time and capital requirements as well as the risks and returns associated with each opportunity.

Step 7.   Management selects the most attractive segment and begins modifying its present strategy to meet the expectations of that segment. If the firm decides to direct its attention and resources to more than one segment, then a specific strategy will need to be developed that is tailored to each segment.

By developing a competitive matrix for each of the more promising market segments, management is able to identify segments that are not being served well. The competitive matrix also identifies areas where the firm should develop a competitive advantage. The competitive matrix is constructed by listing all the businesses vying for a particular segment of customers in a particular geographic area (see Figure 11-3). Management then identifies the competitive factors that are relevant to that market segment. Market research is conducted to determine the relative importance of each competitive factor of the marketing mix for that segment. The relative importance is listed in the upper right-hand corner for the row of the matrix that corresponds with that factor. Each segment of the market may place a different value or priority on the various dimensions of the marketing mix. For example, a market segment comprising upper-income, double-wage-earning couples without children may be interested in an exclusive brand, knowledgeable salespeople, delivery services, evening hours, and the opportunity to place phone orders.

Each firm serving that market is then rated on each factor. Each firm's rating is indicated in the lower left-hand corner of the corresponding cell. The matrix then indicates each firm's score in that dimension for that segment. If the segment considers quality to be a major factor (a weight of five) and that particular firm is rated as a four, then the firm gets a score of 20.

A firm is competitive to the extent its offering meets or exceeds that particular segment's expectations. If the market segment places a weight of five on a particular factor and that particular firm only rates a three on that factor, then that firm is not competitive on that dimension. With this data, management can determine if gaps exist between what consumers in that segment desire and what existing businesses offer. Gaps represent opportunities. They represent customers in search of a business. If the segment places a premium on service (a score of four or five) and no firm has a rating higher than a three on service, then a firm that is trying to appeal to this segment could develop a competitive advantage by providing a high level

Competitive factor	Business #1	Business #2	Business #3	Business #4	Business #5
Price	[3] 3 x 3 = 9	* [3] 1 x 3 = 3	* [3] 2 x 3 = 6	[3] 4 x 3 = 12	[3] 3 x 3 = 9
Quality	* [5] 3 x 5 = 15	* [5] 3 x 5 = 15	* [5] 2 x 5 = 10	* [5] 3 x 5 = 15	* [5] 2 x 5 = 10
Selection	[3] 4 x 3 = 12	[3] 4 x 3 = 12	[3] 3 x 3 = 9	[3] 3 x 3 = 9	[3] 4 x 3 = 12
Promotion	[2] 3 x 2 = 6	[2] 4 x 2 = 8	[2] 2 x 2 = 4	[2] 4 x 2 = 8	[2] 2 x 2 = 4
Services	* [5] 4 x 5 = 20	[5] 5 x 5 = 25	* [5] 2 x 5 = 10	* [5] 3 x 5 = 15	* [5] 4 x 5 = 20
Customer service/ sales personnel	* [5] 3 x 5 = 15	* [5] 3 x 5 = 15	* [5] 1 x 5 = 5	* [5] 3 x 5 = 15	* [5] 3 x 5 = 15
Facilities/ atmosphere	* [4] 3 x 4 = 12	[4] 5 x 4 = 20	* [4] 2 x 4 = 8	* [4] 2 x 4 = 8	* [4] 3 x 4 = 12
Location	[2] 3 x 2 = 6	[2] 4 x 2 = 8	[2] 2 x 2 = 4	[2] 2 x 2 = 4	[2] 3 x 2 = 6
Relative strength for this segment	95	106	56	86	88

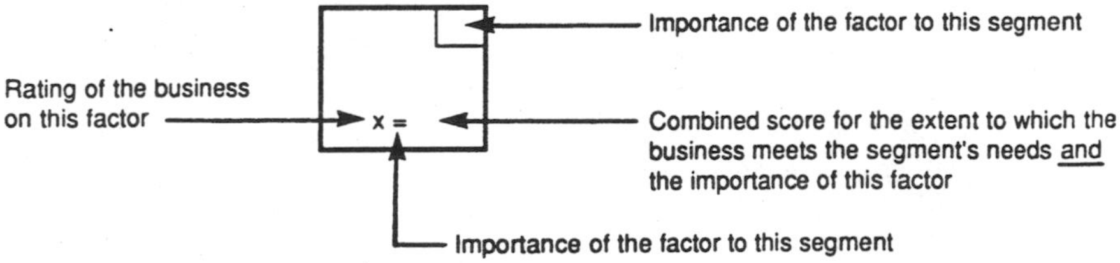

Importance of the factor to this segment

Rating of the business on this factor ——→ x = ←——— Combined score for the extent to which the business meets the segment's needs <u>and</u> the importance of this factor

Importance of the factor to this segment

* Indicates that a "gap" exists between what this business offers and what this segment wants.

Figure 11-3 The Competitive Matrix.

of service. This applies to firms already serving the market as well as firms considering the prospect of entering that market segment.

LaQuinta Motor Inns analyzed the hotel market and found that business travelers with midlevel income were not having their needs met. Market research indicated there was a large segment of business travelers who visited the same city many times during the year. Market research also revealed this segment of travelers were very price-sensitive and did not want all the amenities offered by full-service hotels. They did not want transportation services, meeting rooms, or a pool. They just wanted a nice room at a reasonable rate. LaQuinta found that if it targeted this segment, it could offer quality accommodations for less than half the rate charged by full-service hotels. LaQuinta also reduced its construction cost by not having a restaurant. Instead, it located its inns next door to restaurants that were open around the clock. This positioning strategy paid off. LaQuinta's revenues nearly quadrupled in the last 10 years.[3]

Each competitive matrix should be updated on a regular basis. Additional firms may enter the segment while other firms are making their exit. Existing firms are almost certain to alter their strategies to create strengths and reduce their weaknesses. The consumers' expectations may also change over a period of time. Each segment's relative attractiveness will also vary with time.

In the short run, the firm may focus its attention on improving its competitive position within its present market(s). In the intermediate term, the firm may move into more promising segments of the same industry. In the long run, the firm can reposition itself to capitalize on emerging opportunities in other industries as well. The firm is far more likely to be successful if it uses a long-term backwards approach and the concept of planning at least one market ahead.

It should be apparent that the firm will need to have the ability to make "tactical" changes in its strategy on an ongoing basis. Tactical changes are needed to fine-tune the firm's strategy. Some tactical changes will be offensive in nature to "seize the moment" when some unexpected opportunity arises in the firm's target market. Defensive tactical changes may need to be made when a competitor initiates a media blitz or offers a special discount. A long-term time horizon, however, is essential if the firm is to be able to analyze various markets and industries, to garner the right resources, to develop competitive advantages, and to properly position itself to capitalize on the opportunities that lie ahead.

Strategy Formulation Must Incorporate the Firm's Culture

One additional factor needs to be incorporated into the strategy formulation process. This chapter has already noted the need to have a future-orientation, to monitor changing consumer needs, to consider the resources the firm has at its disposal, and to ponder what present and potential competitors might do. The strategy "equation" also needs to include the firm's present "culture." Every corporation has a distinct culture. Its culture reflects the firm's values and attitudes about change, technology, risk, and a whole set of other factors. The firm's culture also affects what decisions are made, how they are made, and how well they are implemented.

The strategy development process must include an analysis of the firm's present culture. Most firms will only consider strategies that are consistent with their respective culture. Firms with a more venturesome culture tend to be very adaptive. These firms prefer to be pacesetters and to roll the dice on almost everything they do. By formulating innovative corporate strategies that explore emerging markets and develop alliances with suppliers and customers, they play at least one market ahead. Their managers are in tune with the dynamics of the environment and the work force takes pride in being at the leading edge. These firms have cultures that recognize the need for continuous change and innovation. They go after the first bite of the apple!

Management needs to recognize that the greater the strategic planning gap, the greater the magnitude of change in the way things will need to be done in the firm. A firm's present culture not only influences which strategies management is willing to consider, it also affects how well the strategy will be implemented. Whenever corporate strategy changes, there will need to be corresponding changes in the corporation's structure and work processes.

In visionary firms, people at all levels are accustomed to doing things they have never done before. They take pride in their ability to rise to the occasion. Some firms have a culture that has an aversion to taking risks. Their strategies are more incremental than entrepreneurial. These firms tend to go for the third or fourth bite of the apple rather than break new ground. Their managers try to maintain a substantial reserve of working capital as an insurance policy against adversity. Other firms have cultures that are even more reactive. It usually takes a major crisis, opportunity, or change in ownership or leadership for them to reevaluate and change their strategies.

Unfortunately, some firms have such a death grip on maintaining the status quo that only when they are on the brink of bankruptcy will their people even consider changing how they do business. These firms will not survive the dance with the elephants. Firms that dwell in the past are less likely to have a future. The need to have a favorable corporate culture is discussed in depth in the next chapter.

Pitfalls to Avoid
When Formulating
and Implementing
Corporate Strategy

It should be apparent that a multitude of factors need to be considered when developing the firm's competitive strategy. Michael Porter identified the following five mistakes in corporate strategy:[4]

Mistake 1:   Misreading Industry Attractiveness

Mistake 2:   Possessing No True Competitive Advantage

Mistake 3:   Possessing a Competitive Advantage that Is Not Sustainable

Mistake 4:   Compromising a Strategy to Grow Faster

Mistake 5:   Not Making Your Strategy Explicit and Not Communicating It to Your People

It is very easy for management to be infatuated with an industry or market that may be experiencing an exponential increase in sales. Too often, management is seduced by the sales figures to the point that it fails to investigate the investment requirements and profit potential. Markets that are experiencing high rates of growth can be like roses; they may look great but their thorns can produce nasty cuts if they are not handled carefully.

Management should heed two cautions before committing the firm's resources to a "growth" market. First, there is no such thing as a permanent growth market. All markets mature. Technological innovations have the ability to make popular products obsolete almost overnight. The Pony Express that started with such fanfare in 1860 closed its operations for good in 1861. Management needs to make sure the market will be around long enough for the firm to get a return on the firm's investment. Remember, "All that glitters may not be gold." Second, growth markets attract other firms as well. Be sure your cost-volume-profit projections and corporate strategy include additional competitors and the likelihood of price competition. If management is considering entering a growth market, it should consider nichemanship to reduce the likelihood of destructive price competition. Management should also have an exit strategy prepared before it is needed.

The second type of mistake gets to the heart of corporate strategy. Businesses are formed to "create and maintain customers for a profit." To do this, the firm must be markedly better than its competitors. And to be better than its competitors, it has to be different! Yet, the key to success is not just being different and better—the firm has to be different and better on the factors that really matter to your target market.

Management should incorporate the 80:20 rule as it formulates the firm's corporate strategy. Management needs to find out what the target segment values and make sure the firm is superior in its offering on those dimensions. Firms that use imitative strategies must offer lower prices to attract customers. In a world where discounters use 1-800 numbers, it will be difficult for most firms to offer the lowest price. Value-added marketing is the name of the game.

The third type of mistake is quite common with relatively new firms. According to Michael Porter "A lot of companies succeed initially because they discover some hot new product or service...But they are so busy getting off the ground and finding people to buy their product that they forget what will happen if they succeed."[5] They get so enthralled in their new product that they lose sight of what the market desires and what their competitors may be doing. Firms need to stay in tune with the changes that are constantly taking place in the marketplace. The ability to sense changes and to modify one's offering will be essential in the years ahead. Donna Vinton notes, "In today's economy, the company that survives will be the one that can develop, produce, and deliver products and services to customers faster than its competitors."[6]

The firm should avoid being too preoccupied with what its competitors are up to. The best firms compete against themselves! They don't wait around to see what their competitors do next. They focus on what their target market wants. When a firm focuses its attention on its competitors, it is destined to operate from a reactive stance. When the firm competes against itself, it is constantly trying to improve its ability to satisfy its customers. Firms with strategies that focus on "beating" their competitors' prices, advertising budgets, and the like run the risk of losing sight of what customers really value. Firms with strategies that focus on meeting their customers' needs rarely take their eyes off the target.

The fourth type of mistake occurs too frequently. Most firms that are experiencing a high rate of demand do not have the ability to say "no." They will do almost anything to get the next sale. They experience uncontrolled growth. Sales personnel continue making calls and taking orders without checking credit ratings or whether the firm will even be able to provide the goods as promised. These firms often buy or lease additional capacity. Accounts receivable quickly get out of hand, and they start losing customers because they are not able to meet delivery commitments. All of a sudden, customer goodwill vanishes, the firms have excess capacity, and they have no cash to meet weekly operating requirements.

The firm's strategy should be flexible so that it can deal with changes that take place. Without adherence to the strategy, however, the firm moves from method in its madness to pure madness. When everyone is "doing their own thing," chaos is certain to follow.

The fifth type of mistake can happen in even the smallest firms. Most people expect communications problems in large firms. All too often, managers in smaller firms fail to communicate what the firm is trying to achieve and its strategy for making its vision a reality. The vision statement and corporate strategy need to be understood by everyone in the organization. The best way for employees to understand and accept the firm's corporate strategy is to have them involved in its development. If the firm's employees are coarchitects of the firm's strategy, then they will be more committed to implementing it. This is very important. Without effective execution, even the simplest strategy is destined to fail.

Robert Allio emphasizes another key point about implementation in his book *The Practical Strategist*. According to Allio, "Eloquent statements of strategy will have little value if they are not implemented. Managers need to put in place the programs necessary to assure timely implementation—and they must define responsibility and accountability for each program."[7] If management systems that define who will be responsible for what equipment, funds, and results are not in place then the firm is destined to waste valuable resources and lose its competitive edge. Allio notes that while Steven Jobs conceived a brilliant strategy for Apple, only when John Sculley arrived to give attention to implementation did Jobs's strategy begin to produce good results.[8]

Concluding Comments: Remember the Three "Cs"

No firm can operate in a vacuum. The formulation of the firm's corporate strategy needs to incorporate the three Cs: customers, competition, and competencies. If the firm is to create and maintain customers for a profit, then it will have to create and maintain competitive advantages that provide a level of satisfaction for its target market that cannot be matched by any other firm.

When all is said and done, the strategy formulation process should indicate where the firm is headed and how it plans to get there. A well-developed strategy will address:

1. which of the firm's present products, services, and territories will get more, less, or the same level of attention.

2. which products, services, and territories will be developed.

3. which current customers will receive more, less, or the same level of attention.

4. which new types of customers to court and emerging markets to explore.

5. which geographic areas will be served.

6. which technology will need to be developed or acquired.

7. the size, composition, and competencies of the firm's work force.

8. which facilities will need to be built, enlarged, phased out, or sold.

9. the timetables to be followed.

10. whether the organization's structure will need to be changed.

11. the alliances to be formed with suppliers, customers, competitors, or governments.

12. the contingency plans to address changes in competition, technology, and economic conditions.

Competitive strategy thereby represents the firm's overall game plan for creating, cultivating, and capitalizing on present and future opportunities. It also helps position the firm to reduce the likelihood of being blindsided by challenges that would otherwise keep it from fulfilling its vision.

The people who get on in this world are the people who get up and look for the circumstances they want, and if they can't find them, make them.
                                GEORGE BERNARD SHAW

CHIEF EXECUTIVE GUIDELINES

Name: Chris Sullivan, Chief Executive Officer
Company: Outback Steakhouse Inc.
Product/Service: Casual Dining
Sales: $360,000,000   *Number of Employees:* 7500
Awards/Distinctions:

1. One of "America's 100 Fastest Growers," *Fortune* magazine, 1993

2. "Entrepreneur of the Year" Award for Florida, *Inc.* magazine, 1992

3. "Golden Chain Award" *Nation's Restaurant News*

General Guidelines: When it comes to developing a strategy that will give the firm an edge over its competitors, the E/CEO should keep the following tips in mind:

1. You must have focus, consistency, and patience. This is part of leadership.

2. You have to understand what drives your business. In most cases, there are three or four critical issues that are important for gaining a competitive edge and being successful. You need to develop a strategy that develops these areas. Then you need to constantly focus on improving them.

3. You have to try to identify ways to be different and better, yet at the same time you need to provide a good image. Consumers need to feel that they can count on the business to provide what they want, but they also want "newness."

4. Once you have developed your strengths in these areas, then you need to look for ways to make them even better. Usually this is more a matter of fine-tuning what you are doing than making major changes.

5. You also need to monitor what is going on in the market and make the appropriate changes.

Proceed with Caution Guidelines:

1. Watch what people do. When you have an idea or a strategy, you've got to go out and validate it by observing people's behavior. Market research is helpful, but watching how people behave may be better than asking them.

2. Identify key personnel needs soon enough so they can understand what is going on to implement the strategy.

3. Have sufficient capital. You can't go forward unless you have the funds.

4. Try to anticipate what you need to do rather than react to what needs to be done.

CHIEF EXECUTIVE GUIDELINES

Name: John McConnell, Chairman and President
Company: Labconco Corporation
Product/Service: Laboratory Equipment
Awards/Distinctions: Profiled in *Inc.* magazine

General Guidelines: When it comes to developing a strategy that will give the firm an edge over its competitors, the E/CEO should keep the following tips in mind:

1. The firm needs to have a "strategic" orientation. All the managers, especially the top managers, need to have a sense of where the company and industry will be in the long haul.

2. Everyone needs to agree on how the firm is going to be different and better.

3. Everyone needs to be fully cognizant of the opportunities and challenges that will arise in the long term.

4. You need to know the stage of "primary" (end-user) demand in the long and short term.

5. You need to understand and emphasize what *really* (product portfolio, competencies, etc.) makes money for the firm.

6. You need to know what the key elements of product differentiation are.

7. You need to know if your business can sustain its technological advantage.

8. You need to know how the customer's mind must attractively be positioned.

9. You need to create a system whereby people are committed to the firm's future—the days when you have done your job just by showing up are over. Every person at every level of the firm will need to be "committed" if the firm is to be competitive.

10. Emphasize the importance and impact of building a quality organization.

11. Reinvest, reinvest, and reinvest again in differentiating everything.

Proceed with Caution Guidelines:

1. Do whatever it takes to avoid managers who have short-term mentality and a short-term time horizon. Make sure your goals, incentives,

and compensation packages do not encourage your managers to manage for the short term.

2. Make sure your business can sustain the objectives, technologically, financially, etc.

3. Maintain a conservative financial posture at all times. No "ranch betting."

4. Put people in key positions who appreciate and understand the ongoing relationship with *"The Customer."*

And I Would Be Particularly Careful Not *to:*

1. Get overextended financially.

2. Get carried away with unique technology that customers won't buy.

3. Think that the United States is the only market. We are in a world-wide economy.

12

Developing a High-Performance Corporate Culture

The changes businesses are being forced to make merely to remain competitive—improving quality, increasing speed, adopting a customer orientation—are so fundamental that they must take root in a company's very essence, which means in its culture.[1]

BRIAN DUMAINE

When most executives are asked, "What does it take to succeed in business today?" they talk about having a superior product or service, efficient operations, sufficient working capital, a good information system, and other "tangible" things. It is becoming clear, however, that the "human" side of the enterprise may be the most important ingredient in the formula for success. After all, the firm's products, processes, patents, and profits come from its people. Lasting success is contingent on the extent to which the firm's employees are committed to the firm's vision and to creating and maintaining a competitive advantage.

The "people" side of managing is a source of frustration for most E/ CEOs of relatively new ventures. Most E/CEOs are idea people. They take pride in having created something from nothing. Their background may have been in sales, finance, or engineering. How many E/CEOs say they have a background in people? This may explain why so many firms fail altogether or fail to grow to their potential.

The E/CEO may be able to identify a lucrative market opportunity. The E/CEO may even be able to develop a well-crafted strategy for positioning the firm to capitalize on that opportunity. The firm may even have sufficient resources to support the strategy. Yet, when it is time to implement the strategy, nothing happens. The firm resembles a high-performance automobile—but there is no spark to start the engine.

The people side of the firm represents the spark that makes the firm come alive. If people throughout the firm are committed to fulfilling the vision, then great things are possible. If they view the firm merely as a place where they happen to spend eight hours a day, then the firm will slip into mediocrity.

Two significant changes have taken place regarding the people side of the enterprise in the last few years. First, more E/CEOs are beginning to recognize the crucial role that people can play in the success of their respective firms. Some E/CEOs genuinely feel their people are their firm's most significant competitive advantage. Second, a better level of understanding now exists of the set of factors that constitute the people side of the firm.

Each firm, no matter how small, how new, or what technology it uses, has its own distinct "corporate culture." The firm's culture serves as the basis for the way most people behave while at work. Just as individuals have a personality that serves as a basis for their behavior, each firm has a culture that influences how employees feel about change, risk, time, and other factors that affect their decisions, their behavior, and their performance.

Corporate Culture's Influence Should Not Be Underestimated

There was a time when managers viewed the whole issue of corporate culture in the same manner most golfers view spending their country club's funds. Some golfers have been known to say, "If you can't putt on it, then don't spend any money on it." Because corporate culture did not appear as a line item on the firm's income statement or balance sheet, most managers did not give it much thought. Fortunately, yesterday's ignorance may be giving way to a more holistic perspective. A *Fortune* magazine article notes, "Smart executives are as concerned about their organization's culture as they are about next quarter's earnings. The reason is simple: they realize it affects the bottom line."[2]

Corporate culture can be so pervasive that it can affect the firm's performance for years to come. Heinz Weihrich notes, "Culture is the general pattern of behavior, shared beliefs, and values that members have in common...an organization's culture is fairly stable and does not change quickly."[3] According to Weihrich, "We like to think of a value as a fairly permanent belief about what is appropriate and what is not that guides the actions and behavior of employees in fulfilling the organization's aims."[4] Daniel Dennison states "These values, beliefs, and principles serve as the foundation for the firm's management system."[5]

The firm's management system affects managerial practices that, in turn, affect how people behave. Managers who scoff at the notion that values and beliefs could have such a tangible effect on the firm should review Dennison's empirical research. It indicates a close relationship between the culture of an organization, its management practices, and its future performance.[6] It seems that even the financial community that has traditionally relied on spreadsheets, pro formas, and industry ratios to analyze businesses recognizes the role corporate culture may play in a firm's performance. John Kotter and James Heskett asked 75 industry analysts whether corporate culture had any effect on the performance of the firms they followed. Only one analyst thought the culture of one of the firms being followed had little or no impact on its performance.[7]

Corporate Culture and Corporate Strategy Must Be Compatible

The role that corporate culture plays in the performance of the firm is similar to the role that the mind plays for people who run marathons. The best marathon runners make sure their bodies are prepared to go the distance. They also know their minds must relish the challenge and be free from distraction. For centuries, Zen masters and philosophers have suggested that one can attain greatness only when one's mind and body operate harmoniously.[8] In the corporate world, strategy represents the body, and culture represents the mind. Corporate performance is based on the formula:

$$\text{Performance} = f(\text{Strategy \& Implementation})$$

Corporate culture affects management's attitudes toward customers, employees, stockholders, and competitors. These attitudes then affect the types of strategies the firm is willing to consider. Corporate culture also affects the extent people in the firm are committed to implementing the strategy that is selected. For the firm to succeed, it will need to be have a strategy that is in tune with external realities and a culture that expedites the implementation of that strategy. A brilliant strategy is destined to fail if the firm does not have a healthy culture. Conversely, a healthy culture cannot implement an impossible strategy.

Management also needs to recognize that strategy and culture must be properly aligned. According to Robert Allio, "Strategies that violate organizational norms fail to muster organizational commitment and are difficult to implement."[9] Clashes between newly formulated strategies and existing cultures are common today. For example, a firm that has placed considerable emphasis on face-to-face customer relations may find its employees reluctant to embrace the introduction of technology that minimizes personalized attention. A firm that has operated with centralized decision making may have difficulty getting employees to make decisions in the field. A firm that has been fairly conservative and risk averse may encounter difficulty if it tries to initiate a strategy that encourages people to be more entrepreneurial.

The importance of formulating a corporate strategy that is in tune with external realities was noted in the last chapter. The markets the firm targets to serve will influence how the firm will do business. Each industry has its own unique set of factors that affect the firms in it. The computer industry changes each day. Firms that make or distribute computer-related products must be very adaptive to keep pace. Technological innovations can make hardware and software obsolete overnight. Retailers and other businesses in the distribution chain can be bypassed altogether by any firm with a 1-800 number and overnight delivery. To succeed, the firm must have a culture where people are constantly seeking ways to strengthen their competitive advantage. Firms with cultures that dwell on the good old days are not likely to develop exciting new ideas, attract new talent, or identify emerging opportunities. They get out of step and go out of business.

Atari, Apple, Intel, and IBM demonstrate varying approaches to doing business. Each firm had its own distinct culture that enhanced its growth in its formative years. In their prime, Atari and Apple had corporate cultures that were free and open. Nolan Bushnell built a culture at Atari that placed a premium on innovation and fun. Creative, fun-loving engineers set the pace, management allowed employees to come to work in T-shirts at any hour, and workers throughout the firm engaged in marathon brainstorming sessions on a regular basis.[10] The "Mac" team at Apple flew a flag with the skull and crossbones on it over their building to symbolize their commitment to operating outside the boundaries of conventional thinking.

Intel's founder, Andrew Grove, epitomizes his firm's commitment to open communication. He doesn't even have an office. Like everyone else, his desk is out in the open where he can be seen and approached. Intel's culture is a far cry from what can be found today at IBM.

At one time, IBM had a culture that encouraged initiative and other proactive qualities. There is a story about a young manager who was called into Thomas Watson Jr.'s office at the end of a project that was a real disaster. Watson, who was IBM's CEO at the time, asked the young man if he knew why he had been summoned. The young man responded, "Sure, I'm about to be fired." Supposedly, Watson reared back in his chair and said, "Fired?...You've got to be kidding, we've just given you a ten million dollar education...we're going to keep you around to see what you've learned!" That attitude toward trying new approaches was part of a culture that produced a line of new products and a level of customer service that was unparalleled in the computer industry.

Unfortunately, IBM's strategy and culture failed to keep pace with the dynamics of a rapidly changing global marketplace. Its strategy failed to position IBM to capitalize on emerging opportunities. IBM's culture lost its ability to come up with state of the art ideas and to bring them to market before anyone else.

The same types of changes are taking place in retailing and service fields. There are a number of high-growth firms that are in tune with their ever changing environment. They are constantly experimenting with new things to do and new ways to do things. There also seem to be a number of firms that are out of touch with external realities and that have cultures that just don't seem to provide any spark. Ironically, some of the reactive firms, like IBM, once were "cutting edge" firms.

It may be worth noting at this point that firms that have enjoyed sustained growth have had corporate cultures that supported their growth. 3M is one of those rare firms that has been able to maintain an enviable rate of growth since its inception. 3M's management takes pride in the fact that its culture continues to be the spark for new ideas like Post-it pads. Management not only encourages its employees to cross departmental lines to come up with new ideas, it expects 25 percent of each division's sales five years from now to be from products that don't exist today.

It is ironic that so many large firms are now trying to act like emerging firms. It wasn't that long ago that emerging firms wanted to operate like Fortune 500 firms. More and more Fortune 500 firms are trying to adopt "corporate entrepreneurship" in their strategies and cultures so they can be more agile and opportunistic. The moral to the story seems to be, "If you have the right culture, keep it. If you've lost that entrepreneurial feeling, see if you can get it back."

The Formula for Success: Have a Strong and Adaptive Culture

Managers need to recognize that before they can manage their firm's culture, they must first understand it. This situation is similar to the strategic planning gap that was discussed in the last chapter. First, management must determine the type of culture the firm needs to have to implement the firm's strategy. Then management analyzes the firm's present culture. The greater the gap, the greater the need to change the culture.

A firm's culture can be described on two dimensions. A firm's culture can be classified in terms of its strength and adaptability. A firm is considered to have a strong culture if its values are shared by people throughout the firm. If the firm does not have a distinct set of values, beliefs, and principles, then it has a weak culture. If management espouses a set of beliefs but most people fail to internalize them and have them serve as the basis for every decision they make and every action they take, then the firm does not have a strong culture. Management and employees may "talk the talk," but if they don't "walk the talk" then the firm has a weak culture.

Strong cultures are characterized by commitment and consistency of action. Weak cultures are characterized by people who lack conviction and where there is no method to the madness. The difference between commitment and just going through the motions can be illustrated in a high-cholesterol breakfast of ham and eggs. The chicken may have "participated" in the meal, but the pig was "committed" to it. The days of going through the motions are gone. In the dance with the elephants, only firms with visions, strategies, and cultures that foster commitment are likely to succeed.

In strong cultures, people know what the firm values, what its priorities are, what is rewarded, and what is not tolerated. Firms with strong cultures don't need to rely on policy manuals or management's directive—everyone knows what to do and how to do it. For example, if the firm's culture places a premium on customer service, then everyone knows they should do whatever it takes to satisfy the customer. People Express provided a good example of an emerging firm that had a strong culture. People Express was an upstart airline that became a major carrier in a very short time. It was a fascinating blend of low prices and customer service. While it marketed itself as a "no frills" airline, the firm was committed to serving its customers. As a David in a world of Goliaths, its management knew that it would need a level of commitment from its people to enable the firm to offer low prices. At People Express, your fare was for a seat on the plane. If you wanted a meal, you could buy it. If you wanted to check a bag, you paid an extra charge. Customers only paid for the services they wanted.

Every employee had the title of "customer service representative." If a customer needed assistance with a piece of baggage, then anyone who worked for People Express was expected to help out. Every employee had the opportunity to buy stock in the new airline. This helped foster a commitment to customer service. People Express developed a truly unique culture for an airline. Unfortunately, People Express self-destructed when Donald Burr, its CEO, initiated an acquisition strategy that was too ambitious for the firm's management and resources.

In weak cultures, people operate in a fog. They are reluctant to make decisions and to act because there is no clear sense of direction. In the absence of a clear set of values and priorities, everyone waits for management to tell them what to do and how to do it. This inhibits initiative because people are reluctant to go out on a limb. Weak cultures are particularly punishing to professionals who take pride in doing things well and operating without much supervision. They don't know what will be rewarded and what will be punished. Weak cultures also hurt newly hired people who need direction. Weak cultures are usually the result of the absence of leadership at the top.

Weak cultures may have one redeeming feature. They may be easier to change than strong cultures. The strength of a firm's culture is measured by how much its values are internalized. If the firm's values are inappropriate for what the firm needs to do to create and maintain a competitive advantage, then management will need to either change its strategy or change the firm's culture. The stronger the culture, the more difficult it will be to change it.

The Lewin Change Model Provides a Framework for Managing Change

Kurt Lewin suggested that change is a three-step process. Before you initiate change, you first need to "unfreeze" present behavior. The internalization of strong cultures makes it more difficult to change them. People will be reluctant to discontinue what they have been doing because the culture has been a way of life for them. Management will need to demonstrate that if people continue their present practices, the firm will lose its edge. Weak cultures are easier to unfreeze.

Lewin Change Model

Step One: ⟶ Step Two:"Introducing ⟶ Step Three:
"Unfreezing"   the Change"   "Refreezing"

The second step in the change process involves introducing a new set of values and priorities as well as a new way to do things. Management needs to recognize that this can be a time-consuming process. The final step in the process is called "refreezing." Lewin noted that even though the new values, priorities, and behavior may appear to management to be far superior to past practices, people will need to have the opportunity to try the new ways without fear of being reprimanded.

Learning takes time and usually involves making mistakes. Management must encourage, support, and reward the new values, priorities, and behavior. If management does not do a good job refreezing the desired values and behavior, then people in the firm may regress to their older, more comfortable, and inappropriate ways.

Having a strong culture does not necessarily mean that the firm has an appropriate culture. The firm's culture must be aligned with the firm's strategy if the strategy is to have any chance of being implemented well. The second major dimension of corporate culture involves the extent to which the culture is adaptive. As noted earlier, management may need to alter the firm's strategy so that it is more consonant with changes that are occurring or are expected to occur in the firm's external environment. Changes in strategy may necessitate changes in the structure of the firm, its management system, and its culture. The lack of adaptiveness of the firm's culture to evolve or change to meet new external realities could jeopardize the firm's existence.

If the firm's culture is strong and not adaptive, then it is even less likely to change. Adaptiveness does not mean that the firm has to discard its present culture and replace it with an entirely different culture. In many cases, the firm's present value system may still be appropriate. People may simply need to change the way they approach certain situations. Evolutionary change is usually far more effective than radical crisis-driven change.

The ideal situation would be for the firm to have a strong culture that supports the implementation of the firm's strategy and a culture that is highly adaptive so that it can evolve to meet changing conditions. If change is going to be a fact of life, then it would be helpful if the firm has a culture where adaptability is a way of life. Management would be wise to instill the value of adaptiveness in the firm's culture. In times of change, what we refreeze today may need to be unfrozen tomorrow!

If management did a good job formulating the corporate strategy, then it should have a fairly good idea about the type of behavior needed to carry it out. If the firm is merely going to continue to do what it is doing today, then all management needs to do is make sure that today's culture supports that strategy. If the strategy calls for modifying some of the firm's existing products, improving efficiency, and adopting the next generation of technology, then management needs to be sure the firm's management system encourages experimentation, constructive criticism, and occasional mistakes.

If the firm's strategy involves bold initiatives in terms of product innovation, expanding into emerging foreign markets, and having cutting edge technology, then management will need to be sure it encourages and rewards unconventional thinking, cross-cultural analysis, and developing alliances with other firms. If the firm already has this type of culture, then there is no corporate culture gap. If the gap is wide, then management will need to step back and determine if the culture is adaptive enough to implement the strategy.

Factors That Influence Corporate Culture

Management needs to play an active role in the creation and evolution of the firm's culture. Since culture can play such a major role in the performance and overall success of the firm, management cannot afford to leave the formation of its values, beliefs, and priorities to chance. Management needs to recognize that everything it does influences the firm's culture.

The firm's culture started to take shape the moment the firm's founder got the twinkle in his or her eye to start the venture. The E/CEO's original vision was based on certain values, beliefs, and priorities. The industry and markets the firm was established to serve affected the firm's culture. The firm's choice of location and even its first facility affected its culture. The first people to be hired also affected the firm's culture.

There are three major "stakeholders" in business. They are the firm's employees, customers, and stockholders. The firm's culture will reflect the relative priority given to each type of stakeholder. While it may be natural to place the stockholders' interests at the top of the list, recent thinking puts this notion in an interesting light. Leading strategists believe the firm needs to focus its attention more on satisfying the firm's customers and employees. This is called the "field of dreams" perspective. According to this line of reasoning, if management does what it needs to do to meet the customers' desires and the employees' needs—then profits will come. If the firm focuses its attention primarily on profits, management may cut corners with the firm's customers and employees. If this happens, there will be no profits.

How the firm was financed also affects the firm's culture. If the founder is the only stockholder, then there would be less influence by outsiders. If the E/CEO permitted some of the people joining the firm as part of the management team to buy stock in the firm, then their values would influence the firm more than if they were merely employees. If every employee is given the opportunity to buy stock in the firm, then the firm could develop a markedly different culture. If people outside the firm put up the money, then their expectations about risk, time, and dividends could affect the formulation of the firm's strategy. If the stockholders are looking for rapid growth, then they may support product development, geographic expansion, and the acquisition of other firms. If they are looking for a steady flow of dividends, then the firm would have to consider different strategies.

Cultures Reflect the Firm's People and Their Values

The people who make up the firm have the greatest influence on the formation and evolution of the firm's culture. The E/CEO's vision, personality, background, and priorities can have a profound effect on the firm's culture. If E/CEOs are visionary, enthralled with the latest technology, and prepared to boldly go where no one has gone before, then they will probably try to attract people who also want to do exciting things. If the E/CEO's background is in finance, accounting, or law, then the firm may develop a more conservative culture.

Firms with strong cultures tend to attract the types of people who share those values. People who "fit in" tend to be hired and rewarded. Those who go against the grain usually do not fare well. People who thrive at Apple may be shunned at Microsoft. Management needs to be aware of the "goodness of fit" dimension of corporate culture. Strong cultures tend to arise where people share similar values.

The firm may be vulnerable if all the employees look like they were cloned. Management needs to be sure there is some heterogeneity in the people who are hired. It may be easier to manage and interact with people similar to oneself, but it may not be the best situation for the firm. Adaptiveness usually requires an openness to new ideas and new approaches. Different people provide different ideas. If everyone thinks alike, then the firm runs the risk of having tunnel vision. According to Robert Allio, "Cultural change [adaptiveness] requires an openness to new ways of perceiving the world and responding to it."[11]

When management goes about hiring people, it should look for people who are committed to the vision, who have an open mind, and who are prepared to learn whatever has to be learned.

Most E/CEOs do not put enough thought into the emergence of the culture as they start their businesses because the dance with the elephants has begun. Their main concern is to find enough customers to generate enough sales to cover cash obligations. They don't see the need to take the time to think about the type of culture they need, or they won't take the time to deal with it. In a sense, the E/CEOs are the people side of their businesses. People are usually hired one at a time on an "as needed" basis. Two other factors also affect the type of people hired. First, the people hired usually serve as "extra hands." They are there to do things so the E/CEO has more time to manage the business. Second, the firm is usually strapped for cash so the E/CEO usually tries to save money by hiring people at the lower end of the pay scale.

The first few people hired may indicate a lot about the people side of the business in the future. If the E/CEO hires inexperienced people at the lowest pay rate, then the E/CEO will still have to make every decision and closely supervise their actions. Two sayings illustrate this point. First, "If all you offer your people is peanuts, then don't be surprised when they act like a bunch of monkeys." Second, "You get what you pay for!"

Low pay also reduces the level of commitment to the firm. If another employer offers a little more money, then they will leave. If E/CEOs are committed to creating a culture that supports the firm's growth, then they need to offer an attractive enough pay package so people will help make the vision a reality.

People are likely to leave if the E/CEO doesn't have any method in his or her madness. The first few years for most businesses tend to be filled with mistakes. Some people will leave just because they prefer a certain level of predictability in their day and their paycheck.

The first people hired and those who follow serve as the foundation for the firm's culture. If E/CEOs invest in good people and treat them right from the beginning, then they will be able to delegate more decisions to them. Too many E/CEOs hire people just for the job that needs to be filled. They need to hire people who will also be able to grow with the business. If the firm is to grow in a dynamic environment, then it will need people who can learn quickly and who don't require much supervision.

The type of people hired in the first year or two has a lot to do with the management systems that are set up and the extent to which the E/CEO is involved in day-to-day operational matters versus more strategic issues. The E/CEO's support of the people will, in turn, affect the employees' level of commitment and productivity. It will also affect employee turnover and the business's reputation with people who are thinking about applying for a position. Hiring good people and not cutting corners with them can provide dividends later.

Delegation can enhance performance by increasing commitment. When the business grows to the point that it needs to have a first-line supervisor to coordinate the people already hired, then there may be at least one good prospect for that position among the people already hired. Selection of someone from within who is qualified for the position sends a message to everyone that they are valued and that opportunities exist for them to grow with the business. If the E/CEO hires the first-line supervisor from outside, then employees quickly learn that they are just hired hands. The E/CEO's approach will be like a pebble thrown into a pond. It will send ripples out to all employees in the business. The ripples the E/CEO makes at the beginning of the venture are particularly noteworthy because they will have a lasting impact on the development of the firm's culture.

The dance with the elephants has another interesting effect on the people side of the firm. In the frenzy to hire people, E/CEOs usually fail to provide them with an orientation to the overall nature of the firm. Instead, employees are told what their job is and how to do it. New employees are either closely supervised or told to see the E/CEO if they have any questions. As the firm grows and first-line supervisory positions are created, the E/CEO usually plays a smaller part in the hiring and supervision process. The E/CEO also plays a lesser role in the "question and answer" loop.

E/CEOs need to take the time to provide an orientation session for employees as soon as they are hired. Actually, a miniorientation should take place in the hiring process so prospective employees can determine if there is a good "fit" between what the business expects and provides and what the employee expects and values.

The orientation of new personnel does not need to be very formal nor does it need to be time-consuming. The orientation session gives the E/CEO a chance to welcome that person to the firm, to share with that person the E/CEO's vision for the business, and to indicate how everyone will benefit if they are committed to making the vision a reality. If the E/CEO is not willing to take the time or is unable to put the vision and its relevance into words for each person, then the level of employee commitment will reflect it.

Management Needs to Direct the Firm's Culture

Everything management does influences the firm's culture. Some things have a significant and immediate effect on the development and evolution of the firm's culture. Other decisions and actions may be more subtle. The firm's facilities can affect the people and their attitudes. If management leases the cheapest place, then employees may have to contend with cramped space and frustrating working conditions. If the E/CEO has a plan for growth, then most people will be willing to put up with the craziness that comes with rapid growth. If the E/CEO shows little concern for the working conditions, however, the culture will reflect it too. The physical side of the firm makes a statement about what the firm values. If management values the people who work for the firm, then the location, size, layout, and decoration of the facilities should reflect that commitment.

Management's values will be reflected in the firm's choice of a long-versus short-term time horizon, an entrepreneurial versus an incremental approach to growth, and its willingness to place a premium on its employees, customers, and/or owners. The E/CEO needs to recognize that the management systems that are developed to operationalize the vision and strategy also affect the culture. Management systems affect how goals are set, how plans are made, what incentives are offered, what fringe benefits are provided, how performance is reviewed, and how people are supervised. Management needs to give a lot of thought to the type of culture the firm should have as it develops these systems.

These systems need to be environmentally consonant and internally consistent. Management needs to be sure the systems reflect external realities and support the implementation of the firm's competitive strategy. If the firm is in a market that is experiencing dramatic change, then decisions also need to be made quickly. The firm will need an information system that provides its people with the most current information available. The firm will also need to be able to initiate changes to keep pace. If management fails to provide sufficient hardware and software, then people will not be able to make the right decisions. Yet providing an information system may not be enough. If management fails to give people at the appropriate level the authority and resources to decide and implement a new course of action, then the level of commitment will suffer. If the firm develops bureaucratic practices and does not support its people, then a culture of apathy and cynicism will emerge.

The firm's management systems also need to be internally consistent. Each system must support every other system. If the firm's planning system sets goals for new product development, then the firm's performance review and incentive systems must monitor and reward innovation. If management emphasizes promotion opportunities when recruiting people, then management must be willing to delegate key decisions and provide the funds and time off for people to get additional training.

Most emerging firms have major inconsistencies in their management systems. This is common because in the beginning the E/CEO makes all the decisions. The E/CEO serves as the firm's management systems. With the passage of time, certain approaches become standard operating procedures. The firm's management systems are far more likely to be internally consistent if the E/CEO gives them more attention from day one.

One of this book's guiding points is that management needs to anticipate when change needs to be initiated—and do it early! This applies to the development of management systems. Management shouldn't wait for employees to wonder what they are supposed to do. Management needs to establish goals, timetables, performance review processes and criteria, and incentive systems early. If the firm's management systems are logical, environmentally consonant, internally consistent, and clearly understood by people throughout the firm, then the firm's culture is likely to be supportive of these endeavors.

Corporate Culture Can Be Viewed As the Firm's Social Architecture

The formulation of the firm's corporate strategy and development of its management systems represent the engineering side of the firm. They are part of a "master" blueprint for directing people's behavior toward the realization of the firm's objectives. Management should recognize that corporate culture is also influenced by other factors. While management influences the firm's vision, strategy, systems, and working conditions, management also needs to be aware of social factors that affect corporate culture.

There is a social architecture dimension to corporate culture. Every firm develops an "atmosphere." Some firms are very formal. Meetings follow rigid guidelines, management's offices are away from where the work is done, and everything is structured. In these firms there is a place for everything, and everything is in its place. Other firms have a different atmosphere. They are very informal. Everyone is on a first-name basis: Anyone can talk to anybody about anything at any time. There are times when it may not be clear to an outsider who are the managers and who are the workers. Ideas flow freely, and constructive criticism is frequently aired. While the more formal firms may be run like banks, the more informal firms often resemble circuses! Neither type of culture is right or wrong. Instead, the question is whether the culture supports the implementation of the firm's strategy.

Different cultures attract, support, and reward different types of people. If the firm places a premium on its people, then it needs to create an atmosphere that makes the firm the best possible employer to the people it wants to attract and keep. It should be apparent that if the firm wants to gain the highest level of commitment from its people, then management will need to pay attention to the firm's social architecture.

The degree of informality, openness, individual latitude, and overall pace can have a profound effect on the level of commitment and other aspects of the firm's culture. Firms may not need to go as far as some Silicon Valley firms that provide Friday afternoon beer busts, Nautilus machines, and aerobic centers. Management should consider, however, how flextime, job sharing, child care, and other types of benefits can affect the atmosphere at work.

Most successful high-growth new ventures place a premium on celebrating their successes and milestones. They have developed "rituals" that reflect key values and recognize people who have made major contributions to the firm's success. These firms frequently have three other common features. They enhance organizational communication through regular meetings, have some form of a company newsletter, and sponsor social-recreational events to bring people together.

Managers of these firms bring all the employees together on a regular basis to talk about what is going on as well as what is on the horizon. These sessions tend to be very interactive. People are free to ask questions, and management is candid in its responses. These firms also use written or electronic avenues for keeping people informed about what is going on. These firms also recognize the need to focus everyone's attention on the firm's vision and strategy. Newsletters serve as an excellent vehicle for reinforcing key values. Newsletters can also be used to recognize employees who reflect the values the firm desires for all its people.

The more enlightened firms also find ways to get the employees' families to be supportive of the business. These firms sponsor family picnics, dinners, and sports teams, and support various charities. E/CEOs of most firms consider these activities to be luxuries because they drain valuable cash and reduce profitability. Many E/CEOs of high-growth firms see these activities as integral components of the firm's social architecture and essential to the health of their firms. For example, Quad/Graphics, located in Pewaukee, Wisconsin, sponsors a Christmas gala each year. Most of the firm's employees rehearse for months on their own time for this event. Harry Quadracci and his wife know that the more people enjoy being part of the firm, the more they will be committed to it. They also know that such activities help attract people to the firm, provide goodwill to the community, and get favorable press coverage.

Concluding Comments: Everything Management Does Affects Corporate Culture

Every firm develops its own distinct culture. Management's job is to foster the development of a culture that helps the firm implement its strategy. Management also needs to ensure that the culture is adaptive enough to meet changing conditions. Management must recognize that every action it takes, no matter how small, will affect how people think and act in the firm. E/CEOs need to be particularly aware of their impact on corporate culture.

When they created their ventures, they were planting the seeds for its culture. With each passing day, they need to set the example for others to follow. Their values, beliefs, priorities, and behavior will either contribute to or subvert the firm's culture and resulting performance.

The people who built the companies for which America is famous all worked obsessively to create strong cultures within their organizations.[12]

TERRANCE DEAL AND ALLAN KENNEDY

CHIEF EXECUTIVE GUIDELINES

Name: Douglas J. Burgum, President and Chief Executive Officer
Company: Great Plains Software
Product/Service: Accounting Software
Number of Employees: 600
Awards/Distinctions:

1. Identified as one of the 36 best "Employers of the Year" by *Inc.* magazine, 1993

2. Chosen as one of "The One-Hundred Best Companies to Work for in America" by Robert Levering and Milton Moskowitz (Doubleday Publishing), 1993

3. North Dakota "Business Innovator of the Year" by the Greater North Dakota Association

General Guidelines: When it comes to developing a corporate culture that fosters innovation, customer satisfaction, and employee motivation, the E/CEO should keep the following tips in mind:

1. Build mission statements that focus on customer satisfaction, quality, innovation, and continuous learning.

2. Hire people who are motivated by the satisfaction and fulfillment that comes from contributing to a company mission that is focused on helping customers.

3. Immerse your employees in customer feedback.

4. Deliver personal, visible leadership in response to customer concerns. You are a role model—your team will emulate your response.

5. Celebrate individual and team achievements in a sincere and timely manner to foster repeat performances.

6. Live the three "Cs"—

Caring: For your customers and employees.

Commitment: To innovation, to quality; set expectations clearly and strive toward them.

Courage: (1) To do what is right, even if it is not "profitable" in the short term, (2) To see your own shortcomings as a leader-entrepreneur, and (3) To create products and services that have never existed before.

Proceed with Caution Guidelines:

1. Ask more questions.

2. Listen to employees and customers even more.

3. Create more small teams with clear goals.

4. Have more fun and encourage others to do the same.

And I Would Be Particularly Careful Not *to:*

1. Accept the first explanation for why things are the way they are.

2. Allow the fear of change, retribution, failure, or trying new ideas to repress enthusiasm and/or restrict innovation.

3. Underestimate the potential in each person in the firm.

Great Plains Software Mission Statement

"To improve the life and business success of partners and customers by providing superior accounting software, services and tools."

Great Plains Software Shared Values

We must foster a close relationship with our partners and customers that will result in a better understanding of what they are experiencing.

We must encourage innovation, independent action, team spirit, and personal growth in all employees.

We must be sure everything we do reflects exceptional levels of quality.

We must show high integrity in all business relationships.

CHIEF EXECUTIVE GUIDELINES

Name: Margie Tingley, President and Chief Executive Officer
Company: Tingley Systems, Inc.
Product/Service: Managed Health Care Software Developers
Awards/Distinctions: Profiled in *Business Week, USA Today, Nation's Business,* and on CNN

General Guidelines: When it comes to developing a corporate culture that fosters innovation, customer satisfaction, and employee motivation, the E/CEO should keep the following tips in mind:

1. Creativity often clashes with tradition.

2. As the coach, the CEO must always remember that the game is won as a direct result of the participation of the players, and each employee needs to understand he or she is a part of the game and that his or her contribution will impact the outcome of the game.

3. Freedom to explore one's own idea is often the best teacher and, with guidance, may be the fastest way to bring someone to your own conclusion.

4. Creative thinkers need a leader to introduce thought-provoking challenges that enhance and innovate the process while providing guidelines to keep them focused.

5. The work environment needs to be structured in such a way that it meets the requirements of the employee in order to encourage pride and personal ownership of their workplace and their product.

6. A clearly defined corporate culture must be sold over and over again to all employees.

7. Loyalty, dedication, honesty, and personal integrity can never be overemphasized.

Proceed with Caution Guidelines:

1. Listen to your intuition without reservation or hesitation.

2. Produce a clearly defined written description of corporate expectations for each employee.

3. Clearly emphasize the importance of each employee's contribution.

And I Would Be Particularly Careful Not to:

Hesitate to dismiss an employee who did not buy into the corporate culture or function as a team player.

13

Formulating the Long-Term Business Plan

We work day after day, not to finish things,
but to make the future better...because we will
spend the rest of our lives there.
CHARLES KETTERING

Many entrepreneurs like to see themselves as the masters of their destiny. They started their ventures so they could "be their own boss." They liked the prospect of making decisions on the spot and not having to submit plans to someone else for approval. For the emerging business to enjoy sustained growth, however, the way the business is managed must change. The greatest change may take place in how the E/CEO approaches planning for the firm's future.

While most E/CEOs say they started their businesses with a plan, a closer look usually reveals they started with an idea and a "to do" list that seemed to grow with each passing day. E/CEOs whose firms survived the start-up stage now look back with pride at how "fast they were on their feet" in their first dances with the elephants. As the firm adds more people and equipment, expands its territory, and makes even greater commitments to various stakeholders, management must be able to choreograph the firm's operations.

When the firm was small, the elephants may not have been aware of its existence. As the firm grows, however, the elephants begin to notice it has been taking some of their customers. Larger firms that once may have considered the emerging firm to be a nuisance now make it a target. Emerging firms may also become a target for other emerging firms. If the firm does not do a superior job serving its target markets, then other firms, even new ventures, may enter the scene.

Planning Is the Essence of Professional Management

The firm can no longer afford to be run by the seat of the E/CEO's pants. Managing growth is like trying to traverse a minefield. You have a much better chance of surviving if you approach it systematically. Planning increases the likelihood the firm will sustain a healthy rate of growth.

Planning is the first step the E/CEO must take in moving toward a professionally managed firm. Management may have enjoyed the environmental scanning activities and introspection associated with developing the firm's vision and identifying the strategy to make it possible. Now it's time for management to get down to the specifics of what needs to be done, by whom, by when, and with what resources. Robert Allio notes "Eloquent statements of strategy will have little value if they are not implemented."[1] Allio raises an interesting point. The purpose of planning is not to develop plans. It is to develop plans that when implemented—achieve objectives! Plans that are not implemented are either dreams or exercises in futility for those who helped draft them.

The business may have been run by the E/CEO until now, but the time has arrived for the business to be run by a plan. The firm's long-term plan needs to be based on thorough analysis, and it must be put in writing. Growth can be seen as a journey from simplicity to complexity. Thousands of decisions will need to be made. Every turn in the road brings a new decision junction. The plan serves as the firm's road map. It lets people know before they get to the junction whether they will need to go straight or turn left. It also identifies key milestones so people throughout the firm can gauge whether they are on schedule and operating within their budgets. The planning process thereby helps identify the questions that will need to be answered.

Planning gives management additional lead time so it can gather the necessary information to make the right decisions. For example, if management can project when the firm will need the infusion of additional funds to increase production capacity, add more retail outlets, or acquire another firm, then it may have the time to look into refinancing, doing a private stock offering or even to consider an initial public offering. The additional lead time often makes the difference between doing something well, which enhances a firm's competitive advantage, or being thrust into a decision junction where there is no clear path to follow. In the dance with the elephants, firms that see the herd coming are less likely to be trampled to death.

Planning Puts Things in Perspective

Without a commitment to planning, the E/CEO is destined to have a short-term time horizon and to get caught up in operational matters. Planning reduces the tendency for E/CEOs to manage by braille. It forces managers to think about the future and to distinguish between the things that are truly important and the things that are just urgent.

Planning helps identify initiatives that will take considerable time so they can be started early. Too many E/CEOs live in a world full of "somedays." They say "Someday, we need to look into foreign channels of distribution" or "Someday, we need to develop additional products so the firm's future won't be tied to just one product." Planning reduces management's use of the word "someday." Long-term plans put everything that is important on a time line that indicates when things are to be started and when they are to be completed. Planning represents one of the best ways to reduce the tendency to procrastinate and postpone things when the rate of growth accelerates.

It is easy for E/CEOs to get so wrapped up in getting through the day that they are unwilling to take the time to prepare for tomorrow. They say "If we don't take care of business today, then we'll have no tomorrow." There may be some truth in this perspective, but if management doesn't prepare for the future, then it is destined to spend all its time putting out fires that could have been prevented with some foresight and resourcefulness.

Managers who live only in the present are guilty of the "yellow banana syndrome." This term comes from a town's alderman so fixated on present issues that he would not discuss any issue that did not have to be addressed at that meeting. Rumor has it that he never purchased a green banana. Apparently, he did not have the faith or patience to wait for a green banana to ripen and turn yellow. Planning keeps firms from operating on a hand-to-mouth basis.

Planning Identifies Key Priorities

There is a story of a homeowner who kept a blackboard on the kitchen wall that indicated when things might need to be replaced. The list, which covered a ten-year time span, included replacing the roof, the furnace, the cars, and all major appliances. He also kept a sheet of paper that indicated the anticipated replacement cost (taking into account the projected rate of inflation) and how each asset would be financed. He developed a special sinking fund for those assets so there would be enough funds available when they needed to be replaced.

The E/CEO needs to approach planning for the firm's future in the same fashion. Planning for the firm's future is one of the E/CEO's primary responsibilities. If the firm is to grow, then the E/CEO must serve as the firm's chief *executive* officer. If E/CEOs spend time on day-to-day and operational matters, then they are serving as the firm's chief *operating* officer rather than its chief *executive* officer. If this happens, the firm has no one to provide it with direction.

Planning helps identify what needs to be done, when it needs to be done, who will be responsible for doing it, what resources will be required, and how the resources will be funded. In business, the "what is to be done" involves identifying the opportunities the firm wants to capitalize on, the products and services it will have to offer, the timetable to be followed, who will oversee those initiatives, and what resources will need to be provided.

Planning helps management focus on emerging opportunities and prevent potential threats. Planning also helps reduce the likelihood of being seduced by short-term fads. There are times when the life of the E/CEO is like that of Odysseus in Homer's *Odyssey*. When Odysseus encountered the twin Sirens' enticing voices, his commitment to fulfilling his quest gave him the discipline to have his men tie him to his ship's mast so he would not be lured to his death as had so many others who preceded him. Without a plan and the discipline to implement it, many E/CEOs follow short-lived paths that drain valuable resources and destroy their firms.

The need to carefully plan the firm's journey served as the basis for a firm in Ohio to establish an interesting award. One day the president of the firm approached a manager with a plaque that had "The Christopher Columbus Award" engraved on it. The manager was thrilled that he was finally being recognized for his contribution to the firm. When the manager asked why the award had that name on it, the president responded, "You see, Columbus didn't have any idea of where he was going when he left port, and he didn't know where he was when he arrived in the West Indies...You were selected to be the first recipient of this award because your approach to managing most resembles Columbus's approach." When planning is done right, everyone has a crystal clear idea of where the firm is heading, when it plans to get there, the course it is to follow, and the role each person is expected to play in making it a successful voyage.

Few things reflect the quality of management and the culture of a firm more than the priority given to planning and how planning is conducted. Some firms do not have long-term business plans. Their managers operate from a totally reactive stance. These firms don't last long in the dance with the elephants. They will zig one too many times when they should zag. Other firms hire consultants to develop sophisticated plans. Without the support and understanding of the E/CEO, plans quickly become "drawer liners" rather than tools that actually shape the way people at all levels approach their work.[2] Cypress Semiconductor Corporation, on the other hand, is a firm that eats, drinks, and breathes by its planning process. As CEO, T. J. Rogers oversees a computer-based planning system that tracks the goals of every employee. With the touch of a few keys, Rogers can call up any one of the forty-five hundred goals of his hundreds of employees.[3]

Planning Is a State of Mind

If the E/CEO is willing to play a major role in the development and execution of the firm's plans, then the firm will be one step closer to gaining a competitive edge. If the E/CEO avoids the planning process like a vampire avoids sunlight, then it's all over but the funeral. The old sayings "Businesses that fail to plan for the future will have no future" and "Businesses that fail to plan are planning to fail" apply even more today. It is the E/CEO's job to ensure that tomorrow is better than today. There seems to be no limit, however, to how some E/CEOs rationalize their lack of involvement in planning. Here are a few of the excuses E/CEOs frequently use:

Excuse 1: "I don't have time to plan!" What could be more important than identifying where the firm should be and developing a path for getting there? As the saying goes, "Lead, follow, or get out of the way!" If E/CEOs are not spending at least 20 percent of each week on issues that will affect the firm two to three years out, then they need to start doing it or hire someone else to lead the firm.

Excuse 2: "Things are changing so quickly that it's impossible to plan!" If the world didn't change, then people would not need to plan. Everything would be known and predictable. The world isn't that way. Nicholas Murray Butler noted, "The world is comprised of three kinds of people: those who make things happen, those who watch what happens, and those who wonder what happened." Management's job in growth-oriented firms is to identify emerging opportunities and to develop innovative ways to capitalize on them. You can't drive at 65 miles per hour while looking through the rearview mirror! E/CEOs need to do environmental scanning, run scenarios, develop action plans, and take their best shots. If things don't go as planned, then contingency plans should be activated to get the firm back on course. Change tends to wreak havoc with plans. Nevertheless, it is usually easier to activate a contingency plan than it is to have no idea of what can be done. Anyone who expects a plan to predict and deal with every possible situation is a fool. One day, a young E/CEO told a veteran CEO about how his firm had just made a mistake with one of its new accounts. The young E/CEO was extremely frustrated that the firm had made such a mistake. The CEO laughed and said, "Everyone makes mistakes...the question is how long did it take to fix it?" Things will go wrong...and when they do, the difference between success and failure may be tied to how quickly and how well you respond. This is particularly true for emerging businesses that are trying to earn a reputation for doing first-class work. As the firm grows, customers, creditors, and suppliers tend to be less forgiving. Plans that include indicators for measuring progress will provide an early warning system so management can initiate the changes that will generate goodwill and keep the firm out in front. Awareness is prerequisite to change!

Excuse 3: "I started this business without a plan so why do I need one now?" You also started the firm by yourself. Unless you hire people with ESP, no one will have any idea of what needs to be done. The larger the business gets, the more its stakeholders will want to know what management plans to do. Why should an engineer want to quit her job to join an emerging firm that is run by someone who says, "Trust me...I know what I'm doing." Suppliers, creditors, and customers may also want to know what the plan encompasses before they will do business with the firm. For example, one of the largest retailers in the U.S. asked to review a small manufacturer's five-year marketing plan before it would place its next order. The manufacturer didn't have a five-year plan. It didn't even have a one-year plan! The manufacturer had to scramble to develop a document that indicated it planned to continue producing that line and that it would have the capacity available to increase production on short notice to keep pace with demand. The lack of a plan jeopardized an account that represented 40 percent of sales and all of the small manufacturer's profits!

Excuse 4: "Plans are like straitjackets...they keep me from being flexible." Plans don't restrict flexibility. Instead, the planning process should identify different ways of doing things and different things to do. Planning should broaden management's perceptual field so it can see new opportunities. Planning also provides additional lead time so the firm doesn't have to change everything it is doing every moment of the day because it is in a fire fighting, reactive mode.

Excuse 5: "My time is too valuable...planning can be delegated." This usually means the E/CEO doesn't know how to lead the firm's planning process. Again, the E/CEO needs to lead, follow (the lead of the management team, if there is one), or get out of the way! Delegation and participative management are very important processes and they should be practiced as much as possible. The E/CEO needs to remember, however, that while decisions can be delegated, responsibility cannot. To paraphrase Harry Truman, "The buck stops with the CEO."

Excuse 6: "We'll cross that bridge when we get to it." Planning is not something you wait to do. It is an ongoing process. A CEO of a small firm called a consultant for assistance in drafting the business's five-year plan. The consultant was surprised at the request because she knew the firm had been using a plan for the last few years. When the consultant asked the CEO why he needed assistance, he responded, "The last thing I had to do in the young executive program offered by the university was to develop a five-year plan. Well, that was five years ago, so I need to develop another five-year plan." Plans need to be updated on a regular basis. When the first year of the five-year plan is completed, then the firm needs to identify what will need to be done in what is the "new" fifth year to move the firm closer to fulfilling the firm's vision.

Excuse 7: "It is too hard to set goals...there are too many external factors that can affect whether we achieve them." This is the ultimate cop-out. The E/CEO is trying to avoid being accountable for performance. When a city manager was asked by a real estate developer when the city planned to have various infrastructure projects completed, the city manager stated, "I learned a long time ago that if you set dates for the completion of things, then you run the risk of being late....If you don't set goals, you can't be held accountable for poor performance." E/CEOs who demonstrate this "municipal mentality" should be taken out and shot.

Planning: What It Is and What It Isn't

Planning is a multidimensional process. Most E/CEOs have misperceptions about what it is and what it is supposed to do. Peter Drucker helps clarify the nature of planning. According to Drucker, "Planning is not a box of tricks, a bundle of techniques. It is analytical thinking and commitment of resources to action."[4] Planning needs to be viewed as a way of thinking. Management needs to start the process by asking the three questions posed in Chapter 11 that identify the firm's strategic planning gap:

Question 1: What should our business be?

Question 2:   What is our business?

Question 3:   What will it be if we don't change what we are presently doing?[5]

The difference between where (or what) the business wants to be at a specific time in the future and where it will be if it doesn't change represents the firm's "strategic planning gap." Once these questions have been answered, management needs to ask three more questions:

Question 4:   What do we have to do now to attain our objectives?[6] The long-range plan identifies how the gap will be bridged. Two additional questions play a critical role in the planning process. Drucker notes that in order to prepare for the future, management must be willing to "slough off" the past. This is important for two reasons. First, what the firm has been doing may not necessarily be what it should be doing. Second, no firm has unlimited resources.

Question 5:   If we were not committed to this today, would we go into it?[7] If the answer is no, then the firm needs to figure a way to get out of it. Resources will need to be pruned from low-yield products and activities so they can be invested in future products and processes.

Question 6:   What new and different things do we need to do and when?[8] Planning involves taking the initiative. The firm may need to develop new things to do and new ways to do the things it should continue doing. This is especially true with developing new products, offering new services, entering new territories, expanding facilities, and hiring and training new employees.

Planning Should Not Be Done in an "Incremental" Fashion

Most E/CEOs approach planning in the wrong fashion. They do "short-term" forward planning. Their long-term plans are merely five one-year plans strung together. They figure where they want to be a year from now. This is the first-year's plan. Then they figure where they want to be a year after that. This becomes the second-year's plan. They follow this process for three more years. This becomes their five-year plan.

The "long-term backwards" five-year plan tends to be quite different from the "short-term forward" five-year plan. The short-term forward approach is similar to the writer who starts a novel by writing the first page. At the end of the first page, the writer then decides what the second page will contain. Successful writers figure out where they want the book to end and then write the book to create the desired effect.

Long-term planning needs to be done with the firm's vision in mind. If management laid the foundation for planning by identifying a corporate strategy for fulfilling the vision as described in Chapter 10, then it should be in a position to work its way backwards from the desired strategic position to the present. For example, the vision may involve becoming a firm that in 10 years will provide a $400,000 profit after taxes. If the firm's overall strategy includes developing an innovative line of products to generate a sales level of $12 million, then the firm will target market segments that will yield at least a 60 percent gross margin and a 3.33 percent profit margin after taxes. Management then works its way backwards on a year-to-year basis to determine the level of sales and profit the firm will need nine years from now, eight years from now—all the way back to the coming year.

	Year 10	Year 8	Year 6	Year 4	Year 2	Year 1
Sales	$12,000,000	$9,566,200	$7,626,200	$6,079,600	$4,846,400	$3,863,600
Profit A.T.	400,000	318,870	254,206	202,653	161,546	128,800

The long-term backwards approach quickly identifies whether there is a strategic planning gap. In this example, if management projects the coming year's sales to be $3,794,600 with an after-tax profit of $113,800, then it will realize it is already behind schedule for fulfilling the firm's ten-year vision. With the short-term forward approach, a projected profit of $113,800 may seem fine when compared with the past year's profit of $103,400. The 10 percent increase in sales and profits over the past year may be better than what other firms have done. Yet the real issue remains—if the firm is to achieve its ten-year vision, then sales will have to grow 12 percent per year rather than 10 percent. Profit after taxes will need to average 3.33 percent rather than 3 percent. If the firm continues its short-term forward approach by continuing for nine years what it projects for the coming year, then the firm will miss its profit vision by $131,600. Profit will be $268,400 on sales of $8,947,400. The long-term backwards approach thereby indicates a strategic planning gap exists and that management will need to initiate action plans that will increase sales and profit margins.

The long-term backwards approach gives management the incentive to slough off products, processes, and services that will not help bridge the gap for the coming year as well as for the years that follow. Management is also in a position to look at: (1) where each product is in the product life cycle, (2) when various assets will need to be replaced, (3) the number of people who will need to be hired, (4) when it may need to borrow money to finance expansion of the firm's facilities, and (5) whether it will need to acquire other firms to fulfill the ten-year vision.

In some firms, management may find that it will need to change nearly everything it is doing if it is to fulfill the vision. Management may also find that it will need to improve what it offers prospective employees. More firms are considering child care vouchers and flextime in their efforts to be competitive in attracting and keeping good people.

Management may find that it needs to establish innovation goals to increase new product development. As noted earlier, 3M expects 25 percent of sales five years from now will come from products that don't exist today.

The five-year plan will need to be drafted in such a way that the firm will be halfway to fulfilling its ten-year vision. The first five years will need to serve as the foundation for the five years that follow them. From a project management perspective, the first five years can be viewed as the first five steps in a ten-year critical path.

Planning needs to be approached in the same fashion one should approach financing one's retirement. Instead of just saving what is left at the end of each month, one should figure the type of lifestyle one would like to have during retirement and the amount of money needed to provide the appropriate level of annual income to support it. When people do the long-term backwards approach to planning for their retirement, they usually find they will need to increase their contributions to their 401(k) programs and adopt a more aggressive investment strategy. Most people find they also have a strategic planning gap when it comes to their physical well-being. Again, awareness precedes change. They need to put themselves on a "wellness" program so they will be around to enjoy their retirement.

Guidelines for Effective Planning

While numerous techniques like PERT (Program Evaluation Review Technique), capital budgeting, and the Delphi method are available to assist managers with the various aspects of planning, the fact remains that planning is not a panacea nor is it an exact science. Planning is primarily a systematic process for incorporating the multitude of ideas, factors, and forces in decision processes that will affect the future success of the firm. The following ideas should be helpful when formulating the firm's long-term plan:

1. *Don't Try to Do It on a "Time Available" Basis.*   Planning is not something that can be added to someone's agenda. It needs to be the agenda. Too

many E/CEOs try to squeeze planning between operational issues at their regular meetings. Planning takes time and it takes preparation. Most planning issues warrant serious discussion. The E/CEO and the management team should take a planning retreat away from the firm each year to extend their time horizons and to begin the process of updating the long-term plan. The E/CEO should then schedule quarterly half day sessions to monitor major trends and to discuss emerging issues. A cautionary note should be made here. Don't have the planning retreat at a location that sends a message to everyone else who was not invited that management is really taking a vacation. The location will indicate the extent management is committed to the planning function.

2. *Select the Appropriate Time Horizon.* The time horizon for the firm's long-term plan will vary from industry to industry. Robert Allio notes, "A planning horizon that is too short invariably exaggerates the importance of short-term profit, and few investments are made to secure the long-term viability of the firm."[6] Management should realize that as it extends the time horizon, the plans will need to be more general in nature. While the first year of a ten-year plan may indicate weekly or monthly sales projections, the eighth year may target sales on an annual basis.

3. *Differentiate between Objectives, Strategies, and Plans.* Objectives serve as targets. Strategies represent the overall game plan for achieving the objectives. Plans represent the step-by-step process management expects to follow using the strategy to hit the targets. While the firm can set ten-year targets and develop an overall strategy to achieve them, plans should be fairly specific. They need to include budgets, timetables, resource requirements, and contingency plans. These issues can be addressed without much difficulty with a one-year horizon. With long-term planning, management makes a deliberate effort to identify the key parameters for at least the next three to five years.

4. *Identify Key Assumptions.* The E/CEO started the business with the assumption that customers wanted the product or service, that he or she had the ability to offer it at a reasonable price, and that the firm would generate a sufficient level of sales to cover debt obligations. The long-term plan will be based on assumptions about the rate of inflation, repeat purchases, government regulation, what competition will do, the cost of capital, and the firm's ability to develop new products and services by a certain point in time. Management needs to realize its plan is based on assumptions and not facts. Management needs to list the key assumptions and periodically check to see if the assumptions are holding up. If the assumptions do not reflect reality, then the plan will not be able to transform the vision into reality.

5. *Take Uncertainty into Account.* If the firm is embarking on a journey where little is certain, then it may be advisable to run three different scenarios when making projections. Project managers frequently use a technique called PERT when they attempt something that hasn't been done before. This technique addresses potential time and cost variations by having optimistic, pessimistic, and "most likely" time and cost estimates for every major activity or event. Project management software helps managers identify and manage critical activities. Management can also use spreadsheet software packages to run various cost-volume-profit scenarios.

6. *View the Plan as a Pyramid of Objectives and Actions.* The long-term plan can be viewed as a pyramid of objectives that goes from the long term to the present. It also extends from the firm as a whole down to the specific departments. The long-term plan starts with a statement of the firm's overall objective(s). Then it identifies objectives for areas like marketing and finance that will need to be achieved for the firm to achieve its overall objective(s). The plan thereby indicates how each unit's goals and corresponding plans serve as building blocks.

7. *Keep It as Simple as Possible.* Some people say that it isn't possible to have a simple long-term plan. They say, "If it's simple, then it isn't a plan. To be a plan, it needs to address everything." Here again, the amount of detail is what differentiates the long-term plan from the annual operational plan. The long-term plan identifies key objectives and how they will be achieved in fairly general terms. Long-term plans serve as the basis for annual and quarterly operational plans that provide specific guidelines, timelines, budgets, and performance parameters. Robert Allio notes, "The curse of the planning process is the three-pound plan....The best plan fits on one page, and any manager who cannot meet this standard should be given another job."[7] Cin-Made demonstrates that brevity may be a virtue. Bob Frey, Cin-Made's CEO, has distilled the essence of his business's five-year game plan into a one-page summary. The sheet shows what products Cin-Made is committed to harvesting, growing, or developing as well as how those aims can be achieved. Cin-Made's plan has been written so that everybody from the members of the board all the way down to the machine operators can use it when deciding how to put the firm's resources to use.[8]

8. *Don't Forget about the Importance of Implementation.* Two consultants were known for constantly debating which was more important: the quality of the idea or the quality of execution. One consultant stated that if you come up with a really good idea, it will almost implement itself. The other consultant stated that almost any idea can produce outstanding results if it is implemented well. Which is better? The answer is: "both." The firm will have a competitive advantage only if it is more perceptive, more innovative, and more thorough in the development and execution of its plans. When plans are

developed, they should indicate who is to be doing what, when, and with what resources. Plans should also monitor performance on a periodic basis to ensure the firm's performance is meeting expectations.

9. *Incorporate "Management by Exception."* When management drafts the firm's plan it is also establishing the firm's control system. By having specific targets, management has the basis for monitoring performance to be sure things are going as planned. Management needs to identify an acceptable level of variance for key performance areas. While computer technology may be available for monitoring every dimension of the firm's operations, managers and employees don't have the time to stop what they are doing every time something is off standard. The best firms practice "management by exception." Management by exception establishes variance limits. As long as performance is within limits, no corrective action needs to be taken. For example, if a target of $300,000 in sales is set for the coming month, as long as the actual sales are within plus or minus 5 percent, management will not modify the firm's plan.

Above $315,000="*red*" *zone*=exceptional variance

$315,000 (upper 5 percent limit of "yellow zone")
yellow zone=proceed with caution

$309,000 (upper 3 percent limit of "green" zone)
green zone=sales level is OK

Goal=$300,000

green zone=sales level is OK
$291,000 (lower 3 percent limit of green zone)

yellow zone=proceed with caution
$285,000 (lower 5 percent limit of yellow zone)

Below $285,000=*red zone*=exceptional variance

Management may use a stoplight system for indicating the extent of the variance. The green zone indicates sales are right on target. This range could be plus or minus 3 percent of the sales target. The yellow zone indicates the sales are close to the target and that the plan seems to be working. The yellow zones indicate management should carefully monitor sales during the following period. Management may not need to modify the plan if sales are in the yellow zone for one month. Two consecutive yellow zone months in the same yellow zone, however, usually indicates the need to modify the plan.

Management almost always needs to modify the plan when performance enters a red zone. While the sales manager may be jubilant if sales exceed $315,000 in one month, he or she needs to recognize sales are out of synch with the overall plan. The firm runs the risk of having a stock-out. Management will have to see if it can extend the delivery schedule or increase production by using overtime. Either of these options will cost the firm money or goodwill. If sales comes in at less than $285,000, then management will have to look into the variance to determine whether the firm needs to lower prices, increase advertising, or modify its distribution channels. Generally speaking, the greater the volatility, the greater the consequences, and the longer it will take to correct it; the narrower the acceptable range should be, the more closely it should be monitored, and the greater the need to prepare contingency plans in advance.

10. *Make Planning an Integral Part of Performance Reviews and Rewards.* People go in the direction that they are encouraged, reviewed, and rewarded. If they are to be committed to the plan, then the extent they achieve its goals must be an integral part of the firm's performance review process and its reward structure. Management can stress the importance of achieving corporate goals every day of the week, but people will not be committed to the firm's objectives unless their bonus, raise, or promotion is directly tied to the extent they achieve them. This also applies to the E/CEO.

The board is there to establish the vision of what the firm should be, to deal with major policy issues, and to review the E/CEO's performance. The E/CEO is there to develop a strategy and a comprehensive long-term plan to fulfill the board's vision. The board of directors needs to be sure the E/CEO is rewarded to the extent the firm is moved one year closer to achieving the firm's long-term objectives. The board will not be in a position to do this unless the firm has a long-term plan that includes quantitative performance indicators. When E/CEOs are not held responsible for developing a long-term plan and are not held accountable for their contribution to the firm's performance, then the board has not fulfilled its fiduciary responsibility.

Concluding Comments: Getting from Point "A" to Point "B" Can Be a Challenge

Planning is not a science. It requires finesse. The E/CEO must: (1) balance innovation with risk, (2) use quantitative information yet recognize certain qualitative factors also need to be considered, (3) focus on the future while not losing sight of the present, and (4) be committed to the plan yet still be perceptive enough to recognize when it needs to be modified. Planning also requires a keen sense of timing and a balanced perspective. The plan needs to identify and address the opportunities and threats. It also needs to take into consideration the firm's strengths, weaknesses, resources, and corporate culture. If the firm is to operate from a proactive stance, then management will need to be committed to the planning process and resist the temptation to put off tomorrow what needs to be done today.

It is not the ship so much as the skillful
sailing that assures the prosperous voyage.[9]
GEORGE WILLIAM CURTIS

CHIEF EXECUTIVE GUIDELINES

Name: Gregg L. Foster, Chief Executive Officer
Company: Elyria Foundry
Product/Service: Iron Castings
Sales: $30,000,000   *Number of Employees:* 310
Awards/Distinctions:

1. "Turnaround Entrepreneur of the Year" *Inc.* magazine, 1992

2. Weatherhead 100 Fastest-Growing Ohio Company, 1989-91

General Guidelines: When it comes to developing a long-term business plan, the E/CEO should keep the following tips in mind:

1. The purpose of planning is to cause your physical and financial resources, your technical and production capabilities, and your customers' needs to converge at the same time and place. In other words, your company is a conduit between your customers' needs and the skills of your people. Equip them with the resources to sell their most profitable skills.

2. Frame your business plan in rock solid principles and values that will never become obsolete with changes and fluctuations in the economy or markets that you serve.

3. Don't make capital-facility plans beyond the visible horizon of your customers or markets. If you lead your markets by too much, you can equip a facility for business you can only access by price selling.

4. Communicate your business plan in terms of goals and objectives to your people. Everyone must understand where you are going. Business plans are often written on a level that is not meaningful to the people who add value to your products. Try to detail a list of business goals that will indicate the achievement of your business plan. Tell your people what you must do to actualize the plan, not just what the plan is.

5. Determine which customers are your long-term "keepers." Get to know their top management. Own some of their stock if they are a public company. Get newsletters. Know where they are going and get there first.

Proceed with Caution Guidelines:

1. Focus on the six-to-twelve month period in front of you. Long-term planning can cause a sense of patience that can make your organization lethargic. Most people need interim finish lines to be satisfied.

2. Involve all top management in the process.

3. Validate your "direction" with your customers.

And I Would Be Particularly Careful Not to:

Hang on to a bad or obsolete plan too long. Scrap the plan the minute the horizon changes.

CHIEF EXECUTIVE GUIDELINES

Name: Dr. Robert P. Freeze, President
Company: Alphatronix, Inc.
Product/Service: Data Management Solutions for Network Storage
Sales: $12,000,000   *Number of Employees:* 60
Awards/Distinctions:

1. National Winner, "Blue Chip Enterprise Award" from the U.S. Chamber of Commerce (recognizing exemplary small businesses across America), 1992

2. "One of the Best Small Businesses to Work for in the U.S." *Inc.* magazine, 1993

3. "U.S. Distinguished Inventors of the Year Award" presented to the firm's founders in Washington, D.C., for their invention of the optical disk, 1989

4. National Runner-Up, "Entrepreneur of the Year Award," *Inc.* magazine, 1992

General Guidelines: When it comes to developing a strategic plan, the E/CEO should keep the following tips in mind:

1. Don't consider starting or taking over a business without a strategic plan any more than you would consider driving a car blindfolded...You need to know where you want to be in the long term before embarking on plans to implement the shorter term.

2. Set aside two or three days each year at the same time to rethink, modify, or revalidate your strategic plan. Ideally, senior management should hold an off-site meeting away from phones and daily issues to openly discuss and review strategic directions for your company. The formal review each year will help enable you to remove yourself temporarily from day-to-day issues and force the discipline to plan strategically every year. The off-site meeting will encourage open and free discussions away from pressing daily issues. Most importantly, planning with the key members of your management team will provide a variety of new, different, and fresh perspectives to strengthen and improve your strategic plan. Others will also appreciate the opportunity to help direct the long-term goals of their organization, thereby building a longer-term, stronger, and more cohesive team.

3. Strategic and tactical planning are often confused. Both can be likened to a trip. You first need to strategize about where you want to go and why you want to get there. Tactical planning involves how to get there, how long it will take, what resources will be needed, what routes to take, and what turns to avoid.

4. Every time an idea or project is proposed, stop and double-check the idea against your strategic goals. If the idea takes you away from your strategic objective, you need to either veto the suggestion or rethink your strategic plan.

5. Don't be too concerned with the length or wordiness of your strategic plan. It is most important to identify your long-term objectives. Some of the best plans use a few key outlined points on one or two pages.

6. I believe that strategic plans that look five years out are optimal for most businesses. Plans of less than five years will, by their nature, be

too short-term in nature, while ten-year plans are too far removed from today and look more like dreams.

Proceed with Caution Guidelines:

1. Early on, while you are starting your business and dealing with daily emergencies that threaten the survivability of your business, it is easy to overlook the need for strategic planning as an unnecessary luxury. In hindsight, the strategic plan is an investment necessity that takes only a relatively few hours to complete. It is a necessity that pays itself back quickly because by determining and setting your goals, you will avoid making unnecessary and expensive mistakes implementing plans that don't lead you to your ultimate goal. In hindsight, I should have implemented a strategic planning process earlier and forced the discipline to do it every year from the beginning.

2. I would specifically involve more people than just myself at the early stage when the company is in the process of incorporation. Every new entrepreneur thinking of founding a business dreams of the future. One must be careful not to mistake a dream of the future for a strategic plan! One way to avoid this mistake is to involve others at a very early stage so the group can determine the strategic goal together.

14

Capitalizing on the Firm's Human Resources

In entrepreneurial companies, people know what's at stake; they are part of the destiny of the enterprise...it's the old story that the most efficient bilge pump in the world is the sailor with a bucket and water up to his knees.[1]

STEVEN BRANDT

When entrepreneurs start their ventures, they worry about whether they will be able to attract and maintain sufficient funds to keep their firms afloat. They also worry about whether they can attract and maintain enough customers to make a profit. Most entrepreneurs overlook the fact that for their firms to grow and succeed, they will also need to be able to attract and maintain capable and committed employees. Some entrepreneurs believe they can be all-knowing and ever present. Growth quickly brings them down to reality. Firms will grow only to the extent that they have the right number of people in the right place at the right time with the right capabilities.

E/CEOs frequently underestimate the role their employees play in the success of their firms. The firm's products, processes, patents, and profits come from the people who work there. Too often, E/CEOs are rudely awakened by the fact that their inspiring visions, bold strategies, and wonderful product-service ideas will become a reality only to the extent people throughout the firm are committed to the firm. The emerging firm's future is contingent on how management treats the firm's employees today.

Service firms are particularly vulnerable to the consequences of short-changing the people side of the firm. In a service business, the firm's employees are its products—if the firm doesn't have the right number and types of employees, then the firm runs the risk of having a stock-out! Customers are hard enough to find today. To lose a sale and possibly the customer altogether because the firm does not have its people "act" to-gether is a sin. The people side of the business may be just as important in every other type of business. If the firm doesn't have a qualified person to make a decision, to answer the phone, or to order a part, then things quickly fall through the cracks.

Employees are frequently the weakest link in the firm's chain of priorities. It is ironic that so many firms spend so much time developing strategies to attract and satisfy customers that their managers fail to see the relation-ship between employee relations and customer relations. According to Steven Brandt, the author of *The Ten Commandments of Building a Growth Company*, "Customers can't be number one if employees are number five."[2]

Growth stretches the firm's resources thin. The best-managed firms get more return per advertising dollar, per square foot of space, and per customer. They also seem to get more return per employee. They consider their people to be resources that need to be valued as much as their capital and their customers. They recognize early on that without good people, there would be no customers and no capital.

Enlightened E/CEOs recognize two other important things about the people side of the firm. First, they will not be able to afford the number of people they need. Second, they will not be able to hire the best people in the world. While these two points seem to be a bit cynical, they are merely based on reality. Instead of wishful thinking, E/CEOs of growth firms should adopt Mae West's view about people. Years ago, West was playing the part in a movie of a madam who ran a saloon. When West was asked by a lady from back east about her philosophy about men, she responded, "Honey, it's not how many men you have in your life that counts...it's how much life you have in your men that counts!" West's comment might raise a few eyebrows today, but it does capture the essence of managing the firm's human resources. Instead of hoping for more and better people, E/CEOs and managers throughout the firm should focus their attention on creating and maintaining an environment that "brings out the best" in the people already in the firm. As someone once said, "The best indicator of leadership is when ordinary people do extraordinary things."

This chapter addresses the various factors and processes management should consider when creating an environment that will make the firm's human resources one of its competitive advantages. If the firm's people are able to come up with better ideas and demonstrate a higher level of commitment than the firm's competitors, then the firm should have an edge.

Human Resource Planning Is Essential

E/CEOs of emerging firms frequently state that their firms are too small to have a "personnel" specialist to oversee the people side of the firm. They may be right. Years ago, Robert Townsend, then CEO for Avis, stated that every firm would be better off if the whole personnel department was eliminated.[3] Townsend was trying to make the point that if firms didn't have personnel departments, then each manager would have to be responsible for the management of the firm's human resources. Townsend's comment may be extreme, but it does tell E/CEOs that there is no point in postponing the deliberate management of the firm's human resources until the firm is large enough to hire a human resource manager. That time may come, but until then the E/CEO will need to recognize the multidimensional nature of managing the firm's human resources.

Human resource management is not just a sophisticated name for what used to be called personnel management. Personnel management usually was a single-dimension process. When a position needed to be filled, the personnel department was expected to fill it with someone who had a pulse. As more and more E/CEOs recognize the crucial role played by people in their firms, they have adopted the ideas associated with human resource management.

Human resource management involves attracting, orienting, training, motivating, reviewing, and compensating people at all levels of the firm. This chapter addresses the first three areas. The following two chapters will cover the other three areas.

Human resource management begins with human resource planning. It utilizes a long-term perspective and is closely tied to the firm's corporate strategy. Management needs to take a look at where the firm should be in the next three to five years. The markets the firm plans to serve and the products-services the firm plans to offer will affect the types of skills people will need in the next few years. The firm's strategy will also indicate the projected structure of the firm. The structure will identify the number and nature of positions as well as whether the firm will need more managers.

If the firm presently has 30 employees and the strategy calls for a total of 48 employees in three years, then the firm will need to have a game plan for filling new positions and the vacancies that will arise via attrition. Some of the firm's present employees will quit and others may be let go. If the firm has a turnover rate of 15 percent, then it will need to hire at least 33 people in the next three years. Eighteen of the people will be hired for growth, and 15 people will be hired as replacements due to attrition. This hiring "goal" demonstrates the impact of growth and attrition. It also indicates two other things. First, if the firm can reduce the number of people who leave the firm for greener pastures by offering them a competitive employment package, then it will not need to hire as many people. Second, only 15 of the 48 people to be employed by the firm are presently in the firm. At least 70 percent of the employees who will work for the firm three years from now will have to be oriented to the firm's vision, strategy, and culture.

The firm's human resource forecast helps identify the "gap" that will need to be filled in terms of the number and nature of people to be hired. As noted earlier, emerging firms need to hire people who can grow with the firm. There is a rule of thumb that says, "Half the people you hire should be for that job. They should be the type of people who will enjoy doing that job for years. The other half should be the type of people who will be able to grow to do more challenging jobs later on." If you hire people who can only do the job they are hired for, then those people will be of little value when their jobs change. You will also need to hire most of your managers from outside the firm. Few people will have the talent to rise above their hourly positions.

High-growth ventures need to go beyond the 50:50 guideline. As these firms grow, nearly every job will change. New jobs will be created, and the original jobs may be deleted. It is preferable whenever possible to promote from within. The firm should place a premium on hiring people who will be able to perform their initial job well but who also have the ability and desire to grow with the firm. When Lou Grubb, one of the leading auto dealers in the country, was asked what qualities he looked for in the people he hired, he stated, "Judgement and self-motivation...everything else can be taught."

Becoming the "Employer of Choice"

If the firm wants its people to be one of its major competitive advantages, then management needs to place a premium on "attracting" the type of people who will make it possible rather than just "hiring" people to fill vacancies. Management needs to approach the process of attracting talent in the same way it attracts customers. Management should strive to be the "employer of choice"—the most preferred employer for its prospective and present employees. Management can begin this effort by constructing a "recruiting matrix." The recruiting matrix follows a process that is very similar to what was involved in developing the competitive matrix.

The recruiting matrix can be constructed by using the following four-step process. First, management identifies the type of person it is seeking. Second, management tries to find out what they want from employers. The matrix lists the salary levels, advancement opportunities, and availability of flexible working hours. The matrix also includes health insurance, educational assistance, day care, and other fringe benefits. Certain types of people place a premium on certain dimensions of the employment package. If prospective employees are seeking day care, flexible schedules, dental programs, and educational assistance programs, then these dimensions will receive a score of four or five on a five-point scale. Third, management determines what other firms are offering prospective employees. Their offerings are rated on each of the employment dimensions in the matrix on a five-point scale. Fourth, management steps back and objectively asks the question, "What does our firm offer prospective employees?"

This process indicates gaps between what the firm offers and what prospective employees are looking for. It also indicates where the firm has competitive disadvantages in attracting talent and areas where the firm may be offering things that have little appeal to prospective employees. The matrix thereby highlights areas where the firm may be able to improve what it offers prospective employees to give it a competitive advantage in attracting talent. This process can also give management considerable insight into the extent to which the firm is providing its present employees with a competitive employment package. Progressive firms periodically analyze their present employees' needs, what they are offering them, and what other firms are offering to attract talent. They recognize that the less the firm provides its present employees with what they want, the less they will be committed to the firm. The greater the gap, the more they will look elsewhere to have their needs met.

The Search for Talent
Should Not Be Left
to Chance

Numerous firms have developed resourceful ways to be more competitive in attracting talent. The first step in this process is to make sure the firm has a competitive advantage. Management needs to find a way to let the targeted people know the firm offers what they value. E/CEOs of emerging firms believe that they are at a disadvantage because they cannot match the salaries offered by more established firms. This may be the case if their firms offer compensation packages far below what other firms offer.

Management needs to do a "gut check" to see if the firm is really committed to attracting quality talent. If the firm is prepared to pay a competitive wage or salary, then it may have a chance to attract good people. The recruiting matrix may indicate prospective employees who are looking for flexible working schedules, part-time jobs, certain fringe benefits, profit-sharing programs, opportunities to buy stock in the firm, advancement opportunities, or even the chance to try out one's own ideas without a lot of red tape.

Some firms take a very active role in attracting talent. While they may still use personnel agencies and classified ads to find people, they enlist the help of their employees in the process. This makes sense because present employees know the firm's culture. They are in a position to know whether a prospective employee will be an asset to the firm. There appears to be a trend for firms to offer incentives to employees who attract prospective employees. Nonfinancial incentives range from getting two days off with pay for each person the firm hires to being recognized as "recruiter of the year." A few firms offer financial incentives. One recruiting incentive system gives employees a poker chip with their name on it for each employee they help attract to the firm that year. The employee whose poker chip is drawn from the mason jar at the end of the year gets a check. The amount of money and the number of chips drawn can be varied given the number of people employed.

If the firm is looking for talent that is in high demand, then the firm may up the ante. Cunningham Communication Inc., a 60-person public relations firm located in Santa Clara, California, pays its employees $1,000 if a person they recommend is hired.[4] This was considered a bargain when it was compared with what the firm had been paying a headhunter before the incentive system was established. Other firms offer an amount that is a percentage of the newly hired person's first year's salary. This can be a real incentive to network with professionals outside the firm. One caution, however, needs to be raised. If the firm offers incentives, then it should stipulate that employees will be eligible only if the new person stays for a certain period of time. The period may range from six to twelve months.

Tapping the New "Part-Time" Employees

Emerging firms may not be at a disadvantage when it comes to attracting talent. The soft economy has actually helped emerging firms. Layoffs and downsizing efforts by larger firms have put a lot of good people on the streets. These people have gone through a period of attitude adjustment when it comes to drawing large paychecks and lasting job security. The growing number of people who are looking for part-time employment also adds to the pool of prospective employees. People who took early retirement and parents of young children can provide valuable assistance on a part-time basis. Their job expectations may differ from people who are primarily driven by paychecks and advancement opportunities.

Many firms have experimented with temporary employees as an alternative to hiring people altogether. Temporary employees may be beneficial if the firm's work flow fluctuates. They may also be useful as substitutes for people who will return to work in the near future. Firms looking for ongoing employees who may be flexible in the number of hours they are able to work should look into hiring permanent yet part-time employees.

Many E/CEOs are reluctant to hire people on a part-time basis because they believe they will not be as committed as regular employees and may leave after they have been trained to do their jobs. This doesn't need to be the case. If management treats the part-time people as valued members of the firm, then they may provide value to the firm. If management treats them as second-class employees, then it is natural for them to lack commitment. Commitment must begin with management. The firm must make an effort to attract the right type of person, to learn what they want from the firm, and be flexible in what it offers them so their needs are met.

Quill Corporation and Starbucks Coffee Company demonstrate how firms can take a more constructive approach to attracting and keeping part-time employees. Quill is an office supply company based in Lincolnshire, Illinois. Jack Miller, president of Quill, notes that massive layoffs by other employers and the emphasis on family life have created a huge pool of talent eager for part-time jobs. According to Miller, "We have found people with PR experience, bookkeeping experience, CPAs, and all kinds of different skills."[5] While Quill's work flow varies, management promises each part-time employee at least 10 hours of work a week. This program has saved the company hundreds of thousands of dollars since it was started in 1990.[6]

Starbucks is based in Seattle. It manufactures and retails coffee. Howard Schultz, who transformed the firm from a local coffee manufacturer into a national retailer, is quick to attribute the firm's 80 percent annual growth rate to the quality of its work force. He views Starbucks's people as the firm's only sustainable competitive advantage. Starbucks offers a comprehensive employee benefits package that includes health care, stock options, training programs, and product discounts to all the full-time and part-time employees. Schultz feels strongly about the need to provide a generous employment package. He states, "To scrimp on these essentials helps reinforce the mediocrity that seeps into many companies. Without them, people don't feel financially or spiritually tied to their jobs....We can't achieve our strategic objectives without a work force of people who are immersed in the same commitment as management."[7]

Part-time workers make up more than half of Starbucks's retail sales force. Starbucks's compensation package is firmly rooted in the belief that how a firm treats its people is directly related to product quality and the way customers are treated. Schultz is convinced people work smarter and harder because they have a stake in Starbucks's stock option program. He also attributes the firm's low pilferage and turnover rates to the employment package and corporate culture.[8] It should be apparent that for the firm to be a leader, it must be committed to creating and maintaining an attractive employment package. Only then will it be "the employer of choice."

The Firm's Orientation Program Should Not Rely on Osmosis

Most firms either fail to provide new employees with any formal orientation, or they just race through a list of guidelines employees are expected to follow. If the firm is serious about its people, then management must take the orientation process seriously. Steven Brandt notes, "The best companies do a helluva job in their orientation programs, devoting a lot of resources and perhaps 20 to 30 hours to every new employee from the senior executive to the janitor."[9] The best orientation programs go well beyond discussions of fringe benefits, vacation schedules, and payroll dates. Moreover, training doesn't count as orientation.

When orientation is done right, new employees sense the unique nature of the firm and what makes it tick. Emphasis is placed on the firm's vision, strategy, history, and culture. The orientation is not just designed to have new employees understand the firm, it is to have new employees mentally "buy" into the firm. Roger Fritz, president of Organization Development Consultants, indicates that getting employees to think and act like owners is the greatest single factor in a company's long-term success. According to Fritz, "When employees think like owners, their whole outlook changes. They put more into their work. They quibble less about hours and working conditions. They become more concerned about the company's future."[10] He further states, "Helping employees develop an ownership attitude involves two steps: (1) management knowing the employee's goals and (2) employees knowing the firm's goals. If your employees believe you truly care about their objectives, they will care about yours."[11]

This mutually beneficial employer-employee relationship is called "alignment." It would be nearly impossible for the firm's objectives to be identical to each employee's personal needs and interests. Alignment exists when what the firm wants its people to do also enables the employees to satisfy their own needs. The term "alignment" is appropriate. If a car's front wheels are not properly aligned, then they will wobble, the tires will wear out more quickly, and fuel efficiency will decrease. The same applies to the firm's employees.

The more the firm's orientation program demonstrates employer-employee alignment, the greater the level of employee commitment.

A firm based in Oklahoma has a program where management "blue-prints" the employee's expected career progression with the firm. The employee's blueprint indicates the positions the employee should be eligible for as well as the training and experience requirements that are prerequisite to each position. The blueprint also includes a projected timeline. The firm does one other thing that separates it from other firms. It makes a commitment to employees that their salary will be at least twice the present salary within five years if the employee follows the blueprint. This commitment is noteworthy because most people borrow money to finance cars and homes. This gives them some idea of what is down the road.

The orientation process should foster mutual understanding. If it is done right, new employees will see the relevance in what management expects and management will know what employees expect. The ultimate goal is to gain a high level of commitment to the enterprise from the first day. If new employees see they have a major stake in the future of the business, then they should be willing to go the extra mile, to learn new ways to do things, and to strengthen the firm's competitive edge.

Training Is Essential for Maintaining an Edge

There is a saying that success in retailing is based on three things: location, location, and location. When asked what it takes to have the firm's human resources be one of the firm's competitive advantages, the answer may be, "It takes twenty things." Training is one of the twenty things.

This may be a good time for another reality check. If you can't hire the most people or the best people, then you've got to get the best from the people that you have. This comes down to placing people in positions that use their talents, improving their talents, motivating them to do their best, and rewarding them for their contribution to the firm. If the firm is to be better than its competitors, then its people will need to make better decisions, create better products, provide better quality, offer better services, and be better at finding ways to be more productive and efficient. Working "harder" used to be management's human resource strategy for beating competition. In the dance with the elephants, only those who can work smarter and adjust quicker will survive.

In the rapidly changing, highly competitive marketplace, what worked well yesterday will be less effective today, inappropriate tomorrow, and obsolete the day after that. Training is one of the firm's ways of maintaining an edge. Few emerging firms do a sufficient amount of training. They are growing so fast that managers say they can't stop what they are doing to take the time to train their people. Someone once said, "If you don't have the time to do it right the first time, then you may not have the chance to do it a second time." If quality and customer service are important, then training must be a high priority. If training is a priority, then it will be given the time, attention, and funding it deserves. Training will also require a continuous commitment. It must not be seen as something that is undertaken on a "time and funds available" basis.

It is ironic that most people look forward to their favorite software being updated. They anxiously wait for a new generation that is quicker, more convenient, and has added capabilities. Even with tight budgets, funds are found somehow to acquire the latest technology. When it comes to upgrading the firm's human resources, however, most emerging firms put training on hold. Steven Brandt states, "I would guess that the average outlay for training programs is less than $100 per person per year in most companies....this formula will create nothing but trouble in the years to come."[12]

Actually, every firm does have a training program; it is called "on-the-job" training! This form of training has merit, but it tends to be more of a trial-and-error process. Employees also tend to learn how the job has been done rather than how it should be done. If training is done right, then employees will have a chance to learn and apply cutting edge ideas and techniques. This goes beyond on-the-job training. For example, Starbucks has each employee go through 25 hours of training before they start work behind the retail counter. Starbucks's management trainees spend eight to twelve weeks in classes that include Coffee Knowledge 101.[13] The Tattered Cover Bookstore in Denver places such an emphasis on customer service that all its employees go through two weeks of training that includes body language and the best phrasing to use when answering customer questions.[14]

Training Should Go beyond One's Present Job

Training needs to be done on an ongoing basis for all managers and employees. Most training is done to improve performance in one's present position. Training should also be conducted to prepare for future positions and situations. Training that focuses on areas beyond the present job is called "development." Development frequently involves cross-training people so they can do various jobs. This is particularly important for emerging firms. They usually do not have a number of people doing the same thing. The firm's people represent human inventory. If someone fails to show up for work, quits, or dies, then the firm risks being in a stock-out situation. This can be expensive. If people are cross-trained, then the firm is less vulnerable to absenteeism and attrition. As stated earlier, management needs to do a risk assessment for the whole firm and have contingency plans ready for situations that could jeopardize the firm's performance and future. This includes the people side of the firm. People should be cross-trained as a contingency plan for the most critical jobs.

The same principle applies to management succession. Every manager should make a deliberate effort to train at least one person in his or her area as a potential successor. Some of this training may involve management techniques. Additional training can involve delegation of various decisions. An Ohio-based firm is so serious about successor training that it has the policy, "Any manager who does not have at least one employee who is able to serve in the manager's absence...will be fired." Managers know that it is in their best interests to delegate and develop their people. At that firm, managers are promotable only to the extent they are expendable in their present positions.

A few firms include "skills training" in their pay scales. While most firms pay people for the position they occupy, other firms pay people according to their repertoire of skills. In most companies, your raise may be based on performance. In the other companies, your raise is tied to performance and the skills you developed during the year. Eaton Corporation in Cleveland has reorganized its work flow so people work in teams. Instead of paying them for the quantity of work they do, their pay is based on their skills. Employees are expected to learn how to perform other team members' tasks. They are paid according to the number of tasks they can do. This system has made the employees more self-directed, and it has given them greater job security. Management has also found that employees are more flexible because they can see the work environment from various perspectives.[15]

Training and development should be an integral part of the business. Cunningham Communication Inc. has its own "university" where it holds off-site seminars that are run by the firm's key executives. It also allots $1,000 for every employee to attend a professional or industry conference.[16] A high-tech firm in North Carolina establishes training and development goals for each employee at the beginning of the year. Each employee is expected to have at least 40 hours of formal training during the year. Managers are expected to do an additional week of off-site development. The time for training is built into the annual calendar, and the funds are budgeted for these endeavors each year. This firm is different in another way as well—nothing is allowed to preempt training.

There are other resourceful ways emerging firms can enhance their training and development programs. Firms with limited funds may consider monthly training sessions where a specialist is brought in. One of the firm's top performers may also be invited to share tips and approaches to a certain situation. The firm can also send one of its employees to a seminar and have that employee lead one of the monthly sessions on that topic. The firm may consider forming a cooperative association with other firms that have similar training needs. The association can bring in a speaker to discuss a "hot" topic. The association may even be able to negotiate the right to videotape the presentation for use by its members. This can save a lot of money. The firm may also consider establishing its own library of books, magazines, audio tapes, and videotapes on various topics. The audio tapes are particularly user-friendly. They are inexpensive and can be played during commute and other travel times.

Concluding Comments: Going through the Motions Will Not Cut It

Getting the right number and types of people can be a never ending challenge. Once you've hired them, you still need to gain their commitment. Anything less than a total commitment by management will jeopardize the firm's competitive advantage. Remember the saying about eggs (participation) and bacon (commitment) from Chapter 12. Going through the motions will not cut it. For the firm to succeed, management will have to be committed to creating an environment that attracts and improves the firm's human resources.

Our greatest resource is the human resource. Unlike others, its quality is infinite and expandable.
        THOMAS R. HORTON, AS PRESIDENT OF THE
        AMERICAN MANAGEMENT ASSOCIATION

CHIEF EXECUTIVE GUIDELINES

Name: Stephen H. Braccini, President & Chief Executive Officer
Company: Pro Fasteners
Product/Service: Electronic Hardware and Components
Sales: $13,000,000   *Number of Employees:* 75
Awards/Distinctions:

1. Profiled in *Inc.* magazine and *Distribution* magazine

2. "Vendor of the Year" by numerous electronics manufacturers
3. Speaker at the "Inc. 500" Conference on Quality

General Guidelines: When it comes to attracting, selecting, orienting, and training employees, E/CEOs should keep the following tips in mind:

1. Define the position. How can we hire the right person if we don't know all the duties and responsibilities of the position? Define the position to the smallest detail. Unless new employees know exactly what their duties are, they will never meet your expectations.

2. Hire slowly. We often hire the first person that appears to fit the job—don't. Develop a thorough and comprehensive job application that works for you rather than a "canned" form. Learn to read and analyze résumés. Take the time to interview all the candidates. Ask for and speak to their references. Check out their employment history. Hone your interviewing skills by preparing a script and then following it, asking leading questions without giving the answers, thereby improving your listening skills.

3. Use the "buddy system." New employees need time to become acclimated to a new environment. Assign a knowledgeable, positive employee from the same department as a "buddy." They can show where everything is, who's who, and what the routine is around the office. This process will help cultivate a sense of teamwork, communication, and goodwill.

4. Train, train, train. At a minimum, one hour per week per employee should be devoted to training. We care about our employees, and we want to see them improve their skills and knowledge. Whether the training is in job skills, personal development, or a specific task or motivation, the dividends returned will more than offset the expense.

5. Review regularly. Communicate with the employees on a constant basis about their development and progress in the position. Don't wait for the "annual review"—make it a weekly occurrence. It is less time consuming and much more constructive to have constant feedback and communication with the employee.

6. Fire fast. Why do we wait so long to fire someone? We know if a person isn't working out and they know it as well—so do it! It is less painful for the employee and you to terminate the relationship quickly instead of allowing it to drag on and on.

Proceed with Caution Guidelines:

1. Delegate new responsibilities as employees reach higher personal and skill levels. It's important to continue the education and motiva-

tion of employees. Added responsibilities show trust and confidence and serve as well as a reward for perseverance and hard work.

2. Hire for traits and abilities. You can always provide the training and education to create a productive employee. Experience is great, but you can create your own experience through training. You can't teach a cheerful disposition or true concern for people, and these particular traits are indispensable when dealing with clients.

3. In sports you draft the best available athlete—in business always be on the lookout for talent. When you see or hear about a particular person, look them up and see if they fit your organization. Maybe you don't need them now, but at least you will know about them when you do need someone.

4. Establish a forum to allow constant communication between management, departments, and employees in the organization. Empowerment of the individual is only possible through communication. Without it we all lose invaluable sources of motivation, ideas, and improvements.

5. Encourage company-wide participation of all employees in the managing of the business. Whether it is self-directed work teams or employee advisory groups, management needs the resources of all its employees to best sustain the company's competitive advantages. This management style will only work if employees believe they have a voice and management truly listens. Upper management must continually commit themselves—the rewards are substantial.

6. Develop, maintain, and follow company policies. Every organization requires structure; some more than others. Draft an employee handbook that includes not only policies but also guidelines concerning procedures and benefits such as time off, health care, and employer-employee rights. This important step can save you not only from small in-office hassles but also from expensive employee lawsuits.

I Would Be Particularly Careful Not to:

1. Promote employees above or outside their skill or ability level. We have all heard the story about the company's best salesperson being promoted into the sales manager's role and then being terminated because of poor managerial skills. Recognize their limitations first and then begin work on improvements. In the long run, both you and the employee will win.

2. Make promises you can't or are not sure you can keep. Employees have a long memory, and if you make promises that you don't or

can't keep they will remember. Your credibility is at stake, and there is nothing more demoralizing than working for someone you can't trust or believe in.

3. Change directions often or quickly. Your employees want a sense of continuity, of planned successes. Changing your mind, trying new ideas every other day, is unnerving to the employees. They understand that you want continuous improvement; what they don't understand is why don't you have a plan to achieve it. That's what your job is—to develop and present the plan, measure the plan's progress against goals, and fine-tune the plan to ensure success. The constant and continuous commitment from management must be maintained. If it teeters or fails, it can cause instant uncertainty and chaos at lower levels.

4. Reward every success with a raise in pay. Give bonuses based on performance instead. They don't interfere with wage scales and salary budgets, and are not expected or scheduled and therefore have a greater impact. Increasing salaries every time something good happens quickly prices your employees out of their own jobs—maybe not with you but certainly in your industry and local job market. It is our responsibility to be fiscally responsible not only to our companies but our employees as well. We can reward them; we just shouldn't penalize them later for our generosity.

5. Try to be friends with your employees. Being a "good" boss is not based on your popularity. Socializing with employees is not the proper way to cultivate employer-employee relationships. There will come a day when you must handle unpleasant duties and friendships will make it that much more difficult. Mutual respect and trust are not exclusive to personal friendship.

CHIEF EXECUTIVE GUIDELINES

Name: Palmer A. Reynolds, President
Company: Phoenix Textile Corporation
Product/Service: Distributor of Institution Textiles
Sales: $46,000,000   *Number of Employees:* 92
Awards/Distinctions:

1. *Inc.* magazine, "Employer of the Year," (one of twenty-five such companies in the U.S.), 1993

2. "Entrepreneur of the Year," 1992

3. St. Louis Small Business Award Winner, 1989

4. *Inc.* magazine "500 Fastest Growing Private Companies," 1988

General Guidelines: When it comes to attracting, selecting, orienting, and training employees, E/CEOs should keep the following tips in mind:

1. Enthusiasm about your company is essential in a salesperson. Make your employees true believers!

2. Create realistic expectations for new hires.

3. Always be training a replacement for your best performer.

4. Don't be afraid to transfer employees into new disciplines.

5. Model integrity in every aspect of your business dealings to attract the best.

6. Overdo personal attention and recognition.

Proceed with Caution Guidelines:

1. Admit people mistakes quickly and move on.

2. Treat all employees equally rather than fairly. Exceptions create dissension.

3. Rely on intuition in addition to the facts rather than instead of the facts.

4. Maintain personal relationships with key employees despite rapid growth.

5. Renew employees' vision regularly.

And I Would Be Particularly Careful Not *to:*

1. Be over impressed with experience.

2. Tolerate petty dishonesty.

3. Allow management to shield favorites.

4. Allow employees to see personal discouragement.

15

Creating an Environment Conducive to Performance

*Nothing serves an organization
better—especially during times of agonizing
doubts and uncertainties—than leadership
that knows what it wants, communicates
those intentions, positions itself correctly, and
empowers its work force.*[1]

WARREN BENNIS AND BURT NANUS

As they say in the tire business "This is where the rubber meets the road." Considerable effort may have been devoted to developing a master strategy, to drafting a logical plan for fulfilling the vision, and to attracting good people, yet it could all be for naught if the firm's people lack commitment. Management's job at this stage can be seen as "creating an environment that is conducive to performance." If the environment is there, then anything is possible. If it isn't, nothing is possible.

Interesting similarities exist between the management of people and the management of crops. Just as there are people who appear to have "green thumbs," there are E/CEOs who have the ability to develop people to their potential. To achieve a high yield, agriculturists must satisfy three conditions. First, they must have a definite idea of what they want to have at the end of the season. Second, they must identify the types of seeds that need to be planted to produce the desired end result. Third, they must plan and develop the right environment so the seeds can grow to their potential.

The E/CEO needs to do the same three things for the firm to be successful. First, the E/CEO and everyone else in the firm must have a clear understanding of what is to be accomplished in the coming period. The need for a clearly articulated plan was discussed in Chapter 13. This chapter will discuss the need to utilize a "management by objectives" system for directing employee behavior. Second, the firm needs to have the right number of people with the right capabilities to achieve the objectives. The preceding chapter discussed this area. Third, the E/CEO and other managers need to create the right environment or working conditions for the firm's human resources to contribute to the firm's objectives. This chapter is directed at creating an environment that is conducive to performance. Chapter 16 is devoted to creating a high-commitment environment that enhances employee motivation.

It should be clear by now that a business will only be as good as its people. Yet the extent to which people are committed to the firm is directly related to the quality of its management. While there are no experts when it comes to managing people, a few things are clear. First, as with crops, there is more to managing people than just hiring good people or planting the seeds. Managing is an active and continuous process. Gardeners who stand around and expect the seeds to grow by themselves are as naive as managers who expect high levels of performance by "telling" their people to work. The wrong type of management can stymie good people and transform a healthy enterprise into an ailing and wilted organization.

Managers Need to Apply the "Rule of Finger"

Managers need to accept the responsibility for creating an environment that is conducive to performance. If people in the firm are not stretching to their potential, then management needs to step back and take an objective look at the way people are being managed. Most managers are quick to blame poor performance on their employees' lack of motivation. Japanese managers adopt a different perspective when performance falls below their expectations. In Japan, there is no such thing as a "people" problem—there are only "management" problems!

An agricultural example may demonstrate this point. Farmers would look pretty silly if they spent their time jumping up and down yelling at the crops for not growing. Why is it that managers spend most of their time blaming their employees for not doing what they are supposed to do? This brings up what is called the "rule of finger." This may be the most important principle of management. According to the rule of finger, "Whenever things don't go well and managers try to point the finger of blame at their employees, managers need to look at their own hands. They will see that while one finger may be pointing at their employees, their hands will also have three fingers pointing back at them." When things go wrong, managers need to ask, "What did I do that contributed to poor performance?" or "What could I have done differently to enhance performance?" The rule of finger can also provide interesting insights when it is applied to customer and supplier relations.

The rule of finger demonstrates the cause-and-effect nature of management. The role that management plays in business success is depicted in the following model:

Creating the Right → Gaining Employee → Outstanding
Environment   Commitment   Performance

The rule of finger illustrates that if management wants high levels of performance, it will need to create an environment that fosters the level of commitment that will give the firm a competitive edge in the marketplace.

This chapter pays particular attention to the need to set the example for others to follow, to identify performance goals, to keep people informed, to solicit employee ideas, and to review their performance in a constructive manner. Chapter 16 will focus on removing barriers that impede performance, making jobs more challenging, developing incentive plans, and whether fringe benefits have any motivational value.

Managers Need to "Lead by Example"

If the firm is to be ahead of its competition, then it will need managers who can lead the way. No factor is more important than leadership when it comes to creating an environment that is conducive to performance. Being a manager, or even the firm's E/CEO, does not automatically make that person a leader. Leadership is not a position; it is a relationship that may or may not develop between those who interact with the manager. Leadership is not automatic; it has to be developed. Leadership is like goodwill. It develops over a period of time, not just by words but also by actions. It does not require charisma, but it does necessitate being able to provide a sense of direction and a commitment to setting the example for others to follow.

When things go wrong, the rule of finger almost always points back to the firm's managers. Managers either lead by example or manage by hypocrisy. For the firm to be highly productive, every manager needs to set the right example. Leadership by example simply means that managers should not ask or expect others in the firm to do what they are not able or willing to do themselves.

The following example illustrates the difference between leading by example and managing by hypocrisy. The E/CEO of a 30-person service business asked a consultant to advise him on how to handle a particular problem. The E/CEO was extremely frustrated because (1) the employees no longer took their jobs seriously, (2) the firm had lost some of its major customers, and (3) what was once a profitable business was now running in the red. When asked to provide some specific examples of what he meant by "not taking work seriously," the E/CEO said, "they come in late, leave early, spend too much time socializing, take more than an hour for lunch, and spend too much of the business's time on personal matters." He summed up his comments with, "They just don't work as hard or as well as they used to. Somehow, they have changed."

The consultant agreed to spend a couple of days observing operations and interviewing the employees. An hour into the first morning, the E/CEO came in the front door, welcomed the consultant, and asked if the consultant had any early observations or conclusions. The consultant indicated that while it might be too soon to draw any conclusions, there might be one underlying factor that prompted the visit. The consultant, however, said it would take a little more time to confirm his suspicions. The E/CEO responded, "Great, the sooner we turn things around, the better." The E/CEO then asked the consultant if he would like to join him for lunch at about 11:30 to share his thoughts. As soon as the two sat down at one of the city's most expensive restaurants, the E/CEO said, "I've just finished reviewing last month's P&L and things look like they are getting worse." He added, "The time has come to get rid of the people who are not pulling their load." The E/CEO then asked the consultant who he needed to fire.

A good consultant, like an umpire, has to be objective and tell it like it is. The consultant started by stating that the E/CEO did not have an "employee" problem. The E/CEO quickly responded, "Then tell me which of my two supervisors is not doing his job?" The consultant's response was simple and to the point—he was the manager who was not doing his job; he was not setting the example he expected others to follow. If the E/CEO expected them to come to work on time, then he would have to be there before them. If he expected them to take their work seriously, then he would have to take it more seriously than anyone else. If he didn't want them to spend time on personal matters, then he would have to devote all his time at the office to being the firm's full-time chief executive.

The consultant indicated the employees naturally concluded that the business was merely a vehicle for providing the E/CEO with the money to play golf, pursue various hobbies, and participate in various civic activities. "Why should your people take work seriously—you don't!" The E/CEO exclaimed, "I own this business—I can do as I like—isn't that the prerogative of being your own boss?" The consultant acknowledged that from a legal point of view the E/CEO was right. The consultant then stated that a manager's behavior affects people far more than the number of shares of stock he or she owns. He may have been the owner, but he surely was not setting the type of example that constitutes being a leader.

The remainder of the discussion at lunch was devoted to how to lead by example. The consultant noted that instead of trying to change the way his people behaved, he needed to concentrate on changing his own behavior to serve as the example for others to follow. The E/CEO had been setting an example all along, but it had been the wrong example.[2]

Leadership Requires Perceptiveness and Flexibility

Leadership by example consists of four basic steps. First, the manager identifies the objectives to be achieved. There needs to be a clear understanding of what is to be accomplished, when it is to be accomplished, and why it must be accomplished. Second, the manager identifies the type of behavior the employees will need to exhibit to achieve the objectives. This is essential because management is defined as "achieving results through others." Third, the manager identifies the type of behavior he or she needs to exhibit to serve as the proper example to facilitate and reinforce the desired behavior from the employees. Fourth, the manager needs to follow through on step three.

Leadership by example is not the way most managers operate. They typically expect their employees to modify their behavior to achieve the firm's objectives. Leadership by example asserts that managers must be the prime mover; they must serve as the stimulus that produces the desired response from their people. To be a leader, managers must be able to modify their behavior to fit the circumstances and the people involved.

Most managers are relatively inflexible. They expect their people to change their ways. These managers are characterized by a "Don't do as I do, do as I tell you to do" approach to managing people. This brings up another example. A research project was undertaken a few years ago exploring the impact of chief executive behavior on the character of organizations. The E/CEO for an 80-employee manufacturing firm was asked if he would be available for an interview. The E/CEO responded, "I'm not sure that I can spare the time—if I'm not meeting with a customer or a supplier, then I might be in the plant sweeping the floor!" While some may argue that the E/CEO should not be out in the plant sweeping the floor, he realized that even the few minutes he spent doing it each month had significance. The E/CEO claimed it (1) gave him a way to interact with the people in the plant, (2) demonstrated the importance of keeping a clean facility, and (3) showed that he was not above doing the tasks that others were expected to do. He also noted, "When I get tired of sweeping, who can I give the broom to?" He chuckled when he said, "Anyone—no one, not even the general manager can say—that's not my job!"

This example demonstrates that managers need to plan their actions. They need to recognize that every word they speak and every action they take will convey certain values and priorities. This is particularly true for the E/CEO. If management is committed to having state-of-the-art technology, then the E/CEO must be computer proficient. If management is committed to reducing costs, then the E/CEO cannot afford to fly first-class. Finally, if management is committed to having its human resources be one of the firm's competitive advantages, then the E/CEO and every other manager must be committed to soliciting the employees' ideas and delegating decisions to the lowest possible level in the firm. Only then will the people throughout the firm be truly committed to its success.

Performance Goals Need to Be Established

Every manager and every employee is hired for one purpose. They are there to help the firm achieve its objectives. Firms develop business plans to guide the managers in their decision processes and in the allocation of resources. Unfortunately, management seldom brings the firm's goals down to each manager's and employee's level. This causes two problems. First, employees who have little idea of what they are supposed to accomplish will accomplish very little. They don't have a target to shoot for. Second, employees usually do not see how the firm's performance will have a direct impact on their personal well-being. Managers say their employees are apathetic when the real issue is one of relevance. If employees see a direct link between how well they do (and how the firm does) and how well they will be rewarded, then they are more likely to be committed to the firm.

Management needs to make sure everyone knows what the firm's objectives are and how the firm's success will be beneficial to those who help make it possible. The firm's goals represent targets. Every employee needs to have a goal that represents the bull's-eye for that "performance" target.

Management needs to recognize that the better job it does in identifying the target, the easier it will be for each employee to concentrate on hitting his or her respective bull's-eye.

George Odiorne, who was one of the founding fathers of management by objectives, noted that if you can't put your goals into numerical form, then you probably don't know what you are talking about and should forget it as an objective.[3] Too often, managers talk about increasing profits, improving customer service, and reducing costs. These aren't goals, they are directions.

Goals need to be stated as destinations with a desired date of arrival. Goals need to be quantified in terms of quantity, quality, time, and cost dimensions. If the E/CEO wants to improve customer service, then specific performance goals will need to be set for the firm, for each manager, and for each employee. Performance goals could include the percentage or number of repeat purchases, returns, and referrals as well as shorter waiting times.

Goals need to be set for every factor that affects performance. The relative importance of each factor also needs to be known. If the employee can't do it all, then he or she will be able to concentrate on the factors that will make the greatest contribution to performance.

Setting specific objectives represents the first of four steps in "managing by objectives." The second step involves developing "action plans." Action plans indicate how the objectives are to be accomplished. They also identify timelines and resource requirements. The third step involves conducting "periodic reviews." As the action plans are implemented, they need to be checked to see if they are within the quality, quantity, time, and cost dimensions. If there are significant variations, then contingency plans will need to be activated to get the action plans back on target. Annual performance reviews represent the final step in managing by objectives. Annual performance reviews indicate the extent to which each manager and each employee achieved the goals that were set for them at the beginning of the year.

If everyone in the firm has a clear idea of what is to be accomplished, how it is to be accomplished, by when, and with what resources, then they will be in a better position to manage themselves. The firm's overall objectives serve as the foundation for everything in the firm. If the objectives are not appropriate and not specific, then the firm will be operating on very shaky footing.

Performance Reviews Need to Focus on Performance

There is still too much "Do your best" and "I'll let you know if it isn't right" going around in today's firms. The quantification of goals pierces the fog that inhibits employee contribution. Specific goals enable the manager and employee to monitor the employee's progress in achieving the objectives. The rule of finger states, "If you cannot specifically define the desired type and level of performance, then you have no right to expect your employees to achieve it."

Managers also need to concentrate on what constitutes varying levels of performance. Setting specific performance goals is not enough. Managers need to indicate what they consider to be excellent, very good, good, fair, and poor levels of performance. If management cannot describe specifically what constitutes excellent performance, then how can employees shoot for it?

A quality control example may illustrate this point. If a goal of 3 percent rejects is set for the coming period, then the manager may set the following criteria: excellent=a reject rate of less than 1 percent; very good=a reject rate between 1 and 2 percent; good=between 2 and 3 percent; fair=between 3 and 4 percent; and poor=a reject rate greater than 4 percent. The same performance criteria can be set for overtime, accidents, quantity, new accounts, or almost any other performance dimension. There are too many occasions when employees go into a performance review session expecting an excellent review only to learn that management considers their performance to be good or average. Firms that set specific objectives are less likely to leave their employees in the dark.

Managers also need to relate performance levels to individual rewards. Employees should know at the beginning of the period what levels of rewards will come with specific levels of performance. If management is able to show that an excellent rating will result in a 15 percent raise or a 10 percent bonus, then employees will see the relevance of contributing to the firm's objectives.

Two more points need to be made about the goal-setting process. First, management needs to be sure that each employee is in a position to influence the level of performance in the dimensions that are identified. Few things are more frustrating than being held accountable for performance over which one has little or no control. Expecting results outside one's area of influence, such as economic conditions or government regulations, makes as much sense as evaluating salespeople according to the prime rate or criticizing them for losing an account when a major customer goes bankrupt or has a wildcat strike. Second, management should make every effort to permit employees to participate in the goal-setting process. People are more likely to accept goals if they participate in setting them. They are also more committed to implementing plans they helped establish.

AVX Corporation, which makes electronic parts, serves as a good example of the merits of employee participation. The AVX plant in Myrtle

Beach, South Carolina, had been plagued by high turnover for years. Hourly employees would quit and work for area hotels during the tourist season. The hotel and restaurant jobs did not necessarily pay higher wages, but they did offer some variety compared to the daily routine at AVX. AVX's management recognized the situation and initiated a quality circle program. The turnover rate dropped dramatically. As one employee put it, "We want to stick around and see our ideas at work." The reduction in turnover is particularly noteworthy because there was no financial incentive system tied to the quality circle program.

Do Not Practice "Mushroom" Management

Management needs to create an environment in which employees can participate in setting goals, developing action plans, and suggesting their own ideas for improving the firm's performance and working conditions. A recent *Fortune* magazine article notes, "You've never needed every employee's two bits so much, yet many companies don't even try to listen."[4]

Too many managers of emerging firms are guilty of practicing "mushroom management." Mushrooms are grown in the dark in manure. When they grow to a certain size, their heads are cut off—then they are canned! Mushroom management even exists in firms where there are few levels between the E/CEO and the lowest level worker.

All too often, when employees are asked a question by a customer or supplier, they respond, "How should I know?...I just work here." When management fails to keep employees informed, it is like slapping them in the face. A number of firms now refer to their employees as "associates" or "partners." This is supposed to convey the message that they are considered full-fledged members of the firm rather than hourly employees. If management is serious about treating them as valued members of the firm, then managers must stop keeping them in the dark. Managers will also need to solicit their ideas on how the firm's performance can be improved.

As CEO of Texas Instruments, Mark Shepherd noted, "We need to view every employee as a source of ideas, not just a pair of hands."[5] Emerging firms have too few people to begin with. They cannot afford not to capitalize on the full potential of each employee. One employee at AVX Corporation exclaimed, "If you would let us experiment with all our ideas, then the firm wouldn't need those industrial engineers on the payroll to find ways to improve productivity and quality."

The AVX work force also reinforced the benefits of training. When people recognize the personal relevance of maintaining the firm's competitive edge and are given the opportunity to develop critical job skills, they usually rise to the occasion. While most college students balk at the need to take a course in statistics, many of AVX's hourly employees, who did not even finish high school, volunteer to take a class in statistics on their own time at a local community college. They know that without good quantitative skills, they will not be able to diagnose and correct performance problems. They also know that in Japan every child starts studying statistics in the second grade!

Managers Need to Solicit the Employees' Ideas

If the firm is going to pay people to come to work, then it might as well solicit their ideas—it won't cost any more money. Managers need to recognize that they don't have a monopoly on wisdom. There is no way that they can know the "one best way" for every aspect of the firm's operations. AVX is just one example of what can happen when employees are given the opportunity to analyze operations, upgrade their skills, and share their thoughts.

While the best way to get employees to share their thoughts may be to ask them and to ask them often, a few firms have developed some innovative ways to increase employee input. J. W. Kisling, CEO of Multiplex Inc., has instituted a "breakfast with the boss" program in which he gets together regularly with line employees.[6] J. W. Kisling also uses a formal survey to get a feel for what is going on and for how well the firm is being managed. Cunningham Communication Inc. holds "town meetings" every month where its "associates" can describe a problem to a group of employees and collect their ideas.[7]

Management at Peak Electronics expects each of its 125 employees to contribute at least one idea per month to the firm's suggestion plan. Management doesn't expect earthshaking suggestions. Instead, employees are encouraged to come up with ways they could improve their jobs by changing something within two arms' lengths of their work spot. When they have exhausted those possibilities, they can broaden their views to anything in their respective departments.[8]

United Electric has also benefited from its effort to open the firm's lines of communication. At least 90 percent of the employees at the firm's headquarters have responded to management's plea for new ideas. The employees have consistently demonstrated their ability to come up with good ideas. Nearly two-thirds of their ideas are implemented each year. Management has indicated that the employees have transformed an otherwise drab and tedious work environment into one full of devices the workers invented themselves to do their work faster and better.[9]

By the way they solicit employee ideas, some firms even demonstrate what is either a rich sense of humor or a considerable insight into human nature. Peak Electronics and The Body Shop (a retailer) use employee bathrooms to solicit ideas. Peak installed suggestion boxes in its rest rooms so employees can make anonymous suggestions without fear of reprisals from their managers.[10] The Body Shop goes so far as to invite workers to write suggestions on bathroom walls. The Body Shop's founder, Anita Roddick, notes that this system occasionally produces a "gem of an idea."[11]

Concluding Comments: We're All in the Same Boat

Goals, open communication, and performance reviews can go a long way toward providing a sense of direction. There is no substitute, however, for management that has a genuine concern for the well-being of the people who work for the firm. Management must set the example for everyone to follow. If the firm is striving to be out in front of its competition, then it will need to create an environment that capitalizes on every employee's ideas and gives them a chance to be coarchitects in creating an environment that is conducive to performance. Remember Mae West: "It's not how many men you have in your life that counts, it's..."

In recent years, most organizations have come to recognize that their continued vitality depends on aggressive recruitment of talent. But the still untapped source of human vitality, the unmined load of talent, is in those people already hired but thereafter neglected.[12]
JOHN W. GARDNER

CHIEF EXECUTIVE GUIDELINES

Name: Pamela L. Coker, Ph.D., President
Company: Acucobol Inc.
Product/Service: Acucobol-85, A Computer Programming Language
Sales: $8,000,000   *Number of Employees:* 60
Awards/Distinctions:

1. U.S. Small Business Administration "Exporter of the Year," 1993 (Southwest Region)

2. Profiled in *Nation's Business,* 1992

3. Member of the Software Advisory Council to IBM, 1990-1992

4. Member of the Software Advisory Council to NCR, 1992-present

General Guidelines: When it comes to developing an environment that encourages and rewards employees for their ideas and setting the example for others to follow, the E/CEO should keep the following tips in mind:

1. Have a "can-do" attitude.

2. Love to overcome challenges.

3. Exhibit a high level of energy.

4. View mistakes and failures as a necessary part of growth and learning.

5. Everyone in the firm must view learning as a lifelong occupation and preoccupation.

6. Constantly relate new information to the big picture.

7. In a fast-growing company with few written guidelines, new situations appear daily that require good basic judgment. This ability appears to be independent of age and experience. Hire people who are bright, who have the ability to learn quickly, and who have basic common sense.

8. Care about your employees as unique individuals. Care about their career goals, their health, and their families.

9. Encourage your employees to join professional associations and to be involved in their community.

10. Give your employees the tools to be productive.

11. Help your employees grow, excel, and prosper. Be committed to helping every employee attain his or her dreams. They in turn will put their energy and ideas back into your company.

12. Make sure everyone is having fun. If they are having fun, then they are more likely to be committed to the firm's goals.

Proceed with Caution Guidelines:

Don't let your personnel staff get too big. When this happens, managers lose touch with employees. Don't delegate the personnel function to a department. Dealing with people is the essence of management—it is everybody's job.

CHIEF EXECUTIVE GUIDELINES

Name: Robert Davies, President
Company: SBT Accounting Systems
Product/Service: Modifiable Accounting Software
Sales: $11,000,000   *Number of Employees:* 100
Awards/Distinctions:

1. Number One Software Vendor—*VAR Business* magazine, 1993

2. Best Database Accounting Software, 1993, Sixth Consecutive Award—*Data Based Advisor* magazine

3. Number One Accounting System, 1993, Fourth Year, *DBMS* magazine

General Guidelines: When it comes to developing an environment that encourages and rewards employees for their ideas and setting the example for others to follow, the E/CEO should keep the following tips in mind:

1. Recognition is the most cost- and time-effective motivator.

2. The CEO must proactively and personally solicit ideas from employees.

3. The CEO must make him or herself accessible and open to employees.

4. There must be a mechanism to allow anonymous feedback from employees.

5. The CEO should ask for "Ideas you could be fired for suggesting."

Proceed with Caution Guidelines:

1. Give more responsibility and authority sooner to subordinates.

2. Give greater profit-sharing sooner to more employees.

3. Provide more frequent recognition to more employees.

4. Discharge employees earlier with poor attitudes or performance.

And I Would Be Particularly Careful Not *to:*

1. Criticize.

2. Embarrass.

16

Developing a High-Commitment Environment

If you are going to manage a growing
company, you have to concentrate on
managing people, not ignoring them. When
people are highly motivated, it is easy to
accomplish the impossible. And when they're
not, it's impossible to accomplish the easy.[1]

BOB COLLINGS,
AS CEO OF DATA TERMINAL SYSTEMS

Motivation is a multidimensional proposition. While there are no experts when it comes to human behavior at work, a few basic guidelines can go a long way toward enhancing performance and providing worker satisfaction. Two points should be made right away. First, managers need to remember what a wise manager said when asked, "How do you motivate a group of people?" She responded, "One person at a time." Managers make a big mistake when they treat a group of people as a group. When they do this, they treat their employees the same way. People are not alike. They are unique in their interests, their aspirations, their capabilities, their strengths, their weaknesses, and what they want from their jobs. If managers want to bring out the best in their people, they need to start by not treating them alike.

Second, managers need to recognize that they probably cannot motivate people. Motivating another person is like trying to push an employee up a ladder. The employee may eventually be pushed to the top, but the manager will need to take a break to catch his or her breath. Moreover, if every employee needs to be pushed every inch of the way, then the firm certainly will be at a competitive disadvantage. The best employees are the ones who are motivated from within and who take pride in what they are doing.

Most managers make the mistake of assuming they know what their employees want from their work. They also tend to believe they know what is best for their workers. Managers don't have ESP nor are they all-knowing. E/CEOs frequently rely on the Golden Rule when they put together worker compensation packages. The time of "doing unto others as you would want them to do unto you" is over. It is time for managers to adopt the "Platinum Rule," which says, "do unto others as they would like." What managers offer as a reward is motivating only to the extent that it is valued by that employee.

Just as beauty is in the eyes of the beholder, what is a reward to one person may be of little value to the second person, and a punishment to a third. One employee may prefer tuition assistance over a raise. Another employee would relish the opportunity to be an assistant manager in charge of store promotions while another employee would hate to be put in the position of having additional responsibility.

Managers also need to recognize that each employee's needs and interests may change over a period of time. An employee may appear to have been reasonably content with her salary. Then she may seek a promotion, a chance to work overtime, or any other opportunity to improve her financial situation. It is amazing how an unexpected bill or a high credit card balance can transform a mild-mannered employee into a money-hungry fanatic.

Managers should also be aware of how rewarding one particular employee can affect other employees. Many employees are part of the "me" generation. They may want the reward even though they may not have earned it or even value it. Managers need to recognize that each employee has different needs and expectations. They need to make sure that differing levels of performance provide differing types and levels of rewards. When managers fail to reward those who contribute more than other people, the firm has begun its slide into mediocrity.

Managers should sit down with each employee on a regular basis to learn what he or she wants from work. Management then needs to design the work environment so that workers will be rewarded to the extent they contribute to the firm's objectives. Only then will there be "alignment" between what is needed for the achievement of the firm's objectives and the satisfaction of each employee's needs and expectations.

Tapping "Discretionary" Motivation

The remaining pages of this chapter assert that it is the manager's job to create an environment that fosters motivation from within. This chapter also incorporates Mae West's emphasis on productivity—for getting the most from the people you have rather than asking for more people.

We don't know what people are truly capable of doing. Work environments that are supposed to facilitate employee growth and contribution frequently do the exact opposite. Too many firms have managers and work environments that inhibit growth and minimize "alignment." At a time when firms need the best from their people, the Public Agenda Foundation reports that 44 percent of the people in their study admit they "exert no effort over the minimum."[2] The report found that only 23 percent of the workers surveyed work to their maximum.

Management's job can be seen as: (1) finding ways to get the 44 percent to do better, (2) getting the 33 percent who are doing more than their minimum but less than their maximum to do their best, and (3) developing ways to support and reward the other 23 percent who are already doing their best to continue doing their best. The Public Agenda Foundation's research paints a dreary picture of the ability of most managers to create environments that foster employee commitment.

There may be some good news, however, in the Foundation's study. It shows there is plenty of room for improvement. It demonstrates that the lack of employee motivation may reflect the lack of incentives. When there is little incentive, there will be little commitment; people will do just enough to keep from being punished. The study does not suggest that people don't want to do a good job. Rather, it indicates that people will do better if they believe that it will be worthwhile.

The key to motivating people may be finding constructive ways to capture the level of "discretionary" motivation that separates doing just "enough" from stretching to one's limits. If the firm is to succeed in the marketplace, then its managers will need to find ways for the majority of the firm's employees to demonstrate a higher level of commitment than its competitors' employees.

Eliminating the Red Lights

Studies conducted over the last few decades indicate that motivational programs work best when they operate in a two-step fashion. The first step involves reducing or eliminating organizational barriers that slow people down. The second step involves providing factors that enable people to do their best. This is similar to the fitness training process prize-fighters go through. First, they try to lose the weight that slows them down. Then they work on enhancing their speed and punching ability. If they tried to do both at once or trained in reverse order, they would not fare well.

Management needs to identify factors in the work environment that serve as "red lights" that slow people down. The best way to do this is to ask each employee, "What are the things that make it difficult for you to do a good job?" Managers need to ask each employee because different factors may affect different employees. The factors may include physical working conditions (humidity, heat, cold, noise, unsafe factors, and so on), lack of training, uncooperative fellow employees, "mushroom management," bureaucratic policies, and/or out-of-date equipment. The lack of competitive wages and fringe benefits may also keep people from doing a good job.

A study conducted a few years ago asked people what they looked forward to most in their jobs. A significant number of employees responded "5 p.m.!" If managers want to change their employees' response to "8 a.m.!" then they will need first to deal with the red lights that keep people from doing a good job. Red light factors are what make work seem like work. If management is serious about being competitive, then out-of-date equipment will need to be replaced by state-of-the-art equipment. If wages and fringe benefits are out of line, then they will have to be brought into line. If employees are bogged down in red tape, then processes will need to be streamlined.

Management should remember four things as it embarks on its journey to learn about and address the red lights. First, the employees may generate a list of red lights that is quite formidable. If this occurs, management should work closely with the employees to identify the corresponding cost and time requirements. Effort should be made to eliminate or reduce the red lights that will make the greatest difference in the shortest period of time. Management should also develop a timeline that indicates when changes will be made. Employees may exhibit some patience if they see there is some light at the end of the tunnel. If they sense that management is not interested in their views or is not committed to making the necessary changes, then employees will either leave the firm or join the ranks of the people cited by the Public Agenda Foundation who just go through the motions.

Second, management should make every effort to have the employees be coarchitects in the process of removing the red lights. As noted earlier, people will be more committed to change things when they have participated in identifying ways to fix them. Third, management should not expect every employee to freely share his or her thoughts on what the red lights are. If the employees' views have not been encouraged in the past, then they may be hesitant to share their thoughts. This will be particularly true if management has reprimanded, ridiculed, or ignored the employees' ideas or constructive criticism in the past.

Management needs to recognize that the rule of finger applies to the list of red lights. Managers frequently are the number one red light. Few employees, however, feel secure enough to bring this up. It is for this reason that a number of firms use surveys to get a better idea of what the red lights may be. Fourth, if the employees do not identify any red lights, then either management is halfway to creating a high-commitment environment or it has intimidated the employees to the point that they are reluctant to do anything that could jeopardize their jobs.

A small bottling company provides an excellent example of how management can improve motivation by reducing red lights. When the company was bought out, the new CEO met with the employees who were involved in delivering the beverages. The "route salespeople" indicated that their trucks broke down so often they were unable to make their sales calls and meet their delivery schedules. Management eliminated this red light by hiring a mechanic to work in the evenings to repair and tune the trucks. Management also made a commitment to having one of the two replacement trucks it purchased be available so the route salesperson could still meet that day's sales, delivery, and commission targets.

The new CEO also asked the people working in the bottling operation what kept them from meeting production goals. They indicated that the previous owner had not purchased any new bottles for quite some time. Old bottles frequently broke while on the line. This meant that the line had to be stopped. Breakage made work very frustrating and reduced efficiency. It also sent a message to the workers that the owners were not committed to having a first-class operation. One worker captured the feeling of most of the workers when he stated, "If the original owner wasn't willing to give us the best equipment, then why should we have given him our best effort?" The new CEO immediately replaced half of the old glass and made a commitment to the workers to replace the remaining "tired" glass within six months as funds became available.

Management may find there are situations when it may not be feasible, practical, or economical to remove certain red lights. This is particularly true in mundane jobs. Automation has been able to eliminate the need for people to do some jobs that are very repetitive. Yet some jobs still need to be done by people. Management has four options for dealing with jobs that are boring, mundane, or demeaning. First, it can subcontract out the work to firms that specialize in those jobs. Many firms contract with service firms to do their cleaning and maintenance. Second, management can pay very high wages for those jobs. Firms have traditionally paid higher wages to the people who work the late shifts, especially the "graveyard" shift. The same principle could apply to boring or dangerous work. The second option should be the last resort because it increases costs without increasing productivity.

Third, the firm can hire people who look forward to having those jobs. This is not an endorsement for hiring illegal aliens. Instead, management should consider hiring the mentally or physically disadvantaged. If management is not able to redesign the job to be free of the red lights, then it should consider hiring people who do not consider those factors to be red lights.

Two examples illustrate the value of hiring people who are suited for "aligned" jobs. When a consultant visited a small manufacturing facility he complimented the CEO on the firm's beautiful grounds. The grass looked like a green carpet and the shrubs were manicured. The CEO indicated that he had tried for years to find a person who would do a good job on the grounds. The people who had been hired said it was boring and too hot. The CEO talked to a friend who suggested hiring a man who was mentally disadvantaged. The CEO hired the man, and the rest is history. The man continues to be excited about coming to work every day. The job gives him dignity, and he has pride in his work. He told the CEO that he views his work to be that of a sculptor. The man comes to work on time, never complains about the pay, and wears the uniform that has his name on it with pride.

Another CEO used this approach when he was faced with a similar challenge. His firm's manufacturing operation was extremely noisy. He could not afford machines that were a lot quieter, so his employees had to wear bulky, sound-blocking earmuffs. The employees complained about the discomfort caused by the earmuffs and their inability to talk to each other while on the job. Apparently, the work environment did not permit them to satisfy their "social" needs. Their supervisor also expressed frustration due to the difficulty he encountered whenever he tried to give them instructions on the plant floor.

The CEO realized that if you can't change the work to fit the people, then you should change the people to fit the work. Through attrition, he replaced the production crew with hearing-impaired people. After a few months, the whole production line was staffed with the hearing-impaired. This change produced numerous benefits. The new employees did not complain about the noise nor did they complain about the bulky earmuffs—they didn't have to wear them. They did not complain about the inability to socialize—they were able to communicate through sign language. The supervisor found that productivity went up, turnover went down, and accidents disappeared.

The fourth approach involves making the best of a bad situation. Management should create an incentive system that rewards people for doing less than desirable tasks. The employees may not like the work, but they may like the incentives. Wendy's has a contest called the "Sparkle" program in which its restaurants are rated by unannounced inspectors in terms of the cleanliness of its floors, windows, and bathrooms. People who earn top honors in the contest win cash, vacations, and even cars. Dave Thomas, CEO of Wendy's, notes, "You can hold contests for anything and everything."[3] The use of various incentives and mystery customers will be discussed later in this chapter.

Providing the Green Lights

The preceding example demonstrates that most people are willing to do good work if they are provided with an environment that permits them to do it. For the firm to be truly competitive, however, it will need more than "good" performance. To be the best, the firm will need to have employees who are committed to doing their best.

Removing red lights from the work environment may improve the situation, but management will need to do more to foster high levels of motivation and performance. When management makes an unsafe environment safe, offers good fringe benefits like a pension program, and provides a competitive wage, then the frustrations and propensity to look for greener pastures may be reduced. The removal of red lights, however, needs to be followed with the provision of green lights that will bring out the best.

The red light/green light motivation process gets its name from a situation motorists may experience. The presence of a stop sign obviously impedes forward progress. If the stop sign is removed, motorists will proceed, but they will proceed with caution. Motorists will still look to both sides to make sure they are not about to be hit from the side. If a traffic light is installed that signals a green light, then the motorist can focus on the road ahead and drive at the fastest allowable speed. Management's job is to remove the stop signs that impede performance and to provide the green lights that will encourage people to contribute to the firm in such a way that it can be far ahead of its competition.

Factors that represent green lights tend to be quite different from the factors that constitute red lights. Red lights tend to be related to the environment surrounding the job. Green lights tend to be related to the job itself. For example, the firm could have a Nobel Prize chemist on its staff. Removing unsafe laboratory equipment and providing a fully paid pension program may be nice, but these factors will not bring out the chemist's best. As the red light factors are addressed so employees are able to do a good job, management needs to ask each employee, "What do you need to do a truly outstanding job?" The chemist might say she would like to have: (1) the opportunity to try some of her ideas, (2) more authority to make decisions, and (3) some release time to meet with other chemists in Washington, D.C., to brainstorm ways to deal with pollution issues. Few emerging firms have Nobel Prize chemists. This process, however, can be applied to almost any type of firm and any type or level of employee.

Managers usually underestimate the importance of these factors to most workers, especially hourly employees. While wage rates, raises, and bonuses may be very important to nearly everyone, managers should not assume people are only motivated by their paychecks. In a recent study, managers were asked what they thought employees wanted most from their jobs. The managers rated "money" as the factor they thought their employees valued most. When the rank-and-file employees were asked what they valued most, they indicated "interesting work"—money ranked fifth out of ten work-related items.[4]

Research has consistently shown that when people are asked what they need to do an outstanding job, they say: interesting and challenging work, recognition, the opportunity to manage oneself, the opportunity to participate in corporate decision-making processes, the opportunity to advance in the firm, and the opportunity to grow. Employees can exhibit incredible levels of motivation, resourcefulness, and creativity if they are given the opportunity and resources to suggest and implement their own ideas. For example, when retail employees are given the opportunity to suggest ways to promote, display, and price the firm's products, they frequently come up with innovative ways to increase sales and improve customer satisfaction.

Money as a Motivator: "How" May Be as Important as "How Much"

Money can be a green light factor if it is used to recognize the employee's contribution. The bottling company cited earlier provides a good example of how money, other tangible rewards, and recognition can produce high levels of motivation. The new CEO was committed to creating an environment where the present sales force would leave its competition in the dust. Management determined the sales potential for each route salesperson's territory. Each salesperson was then evaluated according to what was possible for his or her territory. This system was considered to be better than rating salespeople according to total revenue.

The route salesperson who had the highest percentage of projected market potential for that month was given the use of a fully equipped luxury sedan leased by the company for the following month. The salesperson was also given the best parking place in the firm's lot as well as unlimited gasoline for the car. The salesperson also received a $500 voucher to be used at a resort during that month. While this monthly amount was substantial compared with similar firms, the firm didn't stop there. Billboards were leased in the salesperson's territory, near his or her home, and at the entrance to the firm to salute the "salesperson of the month." A smaller sign was attached to the back of the salesperson's truck. That sign said, "You are following John Smith, salesperson of the month." This obviously provided an extra incentive for that salesperson to pass the competitions' trucks! The firm also bought a number of radio spots to salute the salesperson of the month.

Management did one other thing that made the incentive system an outstanding success. It wanted to make sure every salesperson was motivated even if he or she did not earn "salesperson of the month" status. At the end of the year, the firm recognized the salesperson who had the best overall percentage. It was possible to be the "salesperson of the year" without being the best for any month. A person could win if he or she had the second- or third-highest percentage for most of the months. The salesperson of the year received an award worth $10,000! This was in addition to his or her commission.

Every incentive system has advantages and shortcomings. This firm's incentive plan produced the second-highest market share for its beverages for any territory in the United States. Only the territory surrounding its franchisor's headquarters had a higher market share. Management, however, did not provide a high-incentive environment for the employees who worked in the bottling operation. Management should have developed a gain sharing system for them. For example, Grand Rapids Steel and Wire offers a bonus based on profitability and quality. The size of the bonus pool is based on profits, scrap, returns, and rework. Management believes the system works because "It's the continual improvements in the factory that ultimately sell customers on Grand Rapids."[5]

Guidelines for an Effective Incentive System

Incentive plans work only to the extent they fit the specific nature of the work environment. Six particular points should be kept in mind when designing a system.

1. *Relevance:*   The rewards must appeal to the employees.
2. *Valence:*   The rewards must be large enough to get employees to exert additional time and effort. This is similar to when a firm reduces the

price of a product. A 5 percent discount may not change anyone's behavior. For incentive plans to work, they need to make a difference in one's paycheck, lifestyle, or feeling of self-worth.

3. *Influence:*   Employees must be able to affect the performance factors. This is why cost-reduction sharing systems usually work better than profit-sharing systems. Economic conditions and the actions of competitors can have a significant impact on the firm's level of sales. If sales and profits drop because of "external" conditions, workers may not continue to support the system. In cost-reduction systems, the employees get a bonus for their performance even if the firm does not earn a profit.

4. *Simplicity:*   The system should be simple to understand. The employee with the least experience and education should be able to understand it.

5. *Participation:*   The employees should be coarchitects of the plan. If they help design it, then they will be more likely to support it.

6. *Fair:*   The incentive system needs to be able to differentiate and reward varying levels of individual or group contribution. Performance deteriorates when everyone is given the same level of reward.

For the incentive system to work, each employee has to believe that it is in his or her best interest to do the best possible job. When this happens, people look forward to 8 a.m. on Monday rather than hanging around waiting for 5 p.m. on Friday!

Two more examples illustrate how incentive systems can make a difference. The first example involves a bottling company that is located in a "hunter's paradise." For years, management had been faced with the dilemma of what to do on the first day of deer hunting season. Worker absenteeism on that day had grown to the point that the plant could barely operate. For years, management had threatened to punish those who failed to show up. The situation deteriorated to the point that management even contemplated firing people who did not show up that day—and replacing them with people who did not hunt. Management dropped that alternative when it became clear that the workers' desire to hunt may have been stronger than their desire to work. Management also recognized nearly everyone in that community was an avid hunter.

Management finally realized it usually is far more constructive to swim with the current than against it. Management worked with a group of employees to develop a system where every employee who exceeds a month's performance target receives a voucher for a half day off with pay. The performance targets were fairly challenging, but they could be accomplished if the employees raised their level of effort. The only provision was that the employee would have to give a week's notice before using one or more vouchers so production and sales would not be hurt.

The system was an outstanding success. Instead of threatening people with the loss of their jobs, management was able to declare the first day of hunting season a corporate holiday. The provision for one week's notice before using one's voucher(s) permitted the firm to bottle and distribute enough soft drinks that the firm did not have to be open on that day.

Incentives are not restricted to sales and production operations. Retail and service businesses can also develop ways to encourage employees to perform at a higher level on a daily basis. The most popular program for employees who deal with the public involves the use of "mystery customers." Management selects a set of customers to note instances when they are given exceptional service. The mystery customer gives a special chip to note the service to either the employee or the employee's manager. The employee's manager then gives the employee a modest cash bonus or a gift certificate from a local business. Some firms offer discount coupons for their products or services.

A few firms provide a little twist on the mystery customer incentive system. Employees who earn chips sign their names on the chips and place them in a mason jar. Each quarter, one or more chips are drawn. The winners get a more substantial cash bonus. This appeals to employees who like to gamble. The first approach is nice because it is immediate, and the employee gets something near the time the service is provided. The second system has appeal because it may serve as a basis for bringing the employees together for a company-wide event. The five or so people who earn the most chips can also be recognized at this event. The mystery customer incentive system can also be used for employees who interact with the public by phone. A select group of customers merely calls a special number where someone records the employee's name when his or her behavior warrants recognition.

The mystery customer system also seems to work well for "internal" customers. A number of employees in the firm are selected to be the mystery customers. Any time they receive or observe exceptional service by someone else employed by the firm, they notify a specially designated individual who records the name and documents the type of service. The employee's manager then receives a copy of the report and a chip with the employee's name on it.

If the firm does not want to use internal or external mystery customers, it can provide managers with a discretionary account that can be used to reward employees on the occasions when they do something that is particularly noteworthy. Managers can give the employee a gift certificate to the movies or something else the employee can share with his or her spouse, friends, or kids.

Stock Options as a Motivator: Proceed with Caution!

Numerous firms offer stock options to increase employee motivation. Stock options represent a way for employees to feel like owners of the business. If the firm does well, then the employees may be able to build their personal balance sheets. Dennis Flynn, who heads Heritage Asset Management, has the philosophy, "I'm not going to get rich alone—we're all going to get rich together. If we don't, then we'll all go out of business together."[6] A number of the people who worked for Wal-Mart and Food Lion in the early years will go to their graves regretting they did not buy stock in those firms. Some hourly employees who bought stock in those firms are now millionaires. Randy Fowler, president of Identrix Inc., uses stock options for another reason. He offers stock to help keep the firm's software developers and other technologists from going to other firms.[7]

Stock option plans obviously involve tax factors, extensive record keeping, and possibly close scrutiny by the Securities and Exchange Commission. Some firms use "phantom" stock instead of actually issuing shares. This way, each employee has an account where a record of equivalent shares is recorded. Employees do not actually purchase shares of stock. When they leave the firm or want to "cash in," the firm simply pays them for what the net proceeds would be if actual shares had been purchased and sold. Phantom stock plans can be tricky so management needs to be sure the firm complies with all regulations.

Stock option plans may also represent a vehicle for raising funds for the business. Employee stock ownership plans (ESOPs) represent the ultimate avenue for gaining commitment to the firm. These plans may also provide an avenue for the founder to get his or her cash out of the business. ESOPs represent a way for employees to gain an ownership position in the firm. While ESOPs may sound good in theory, they are not without their drawbacks. The Labor Department has placed numerous restrictions on how the firm can be governed. The firm may need ESOP plan administrators and trustees in addition to its board of directors. ESOP experts also note that even the most carefully drafted plan may not boost productivity, jump-start morale, or rescue a failing company from unfavorable market trends.[8]

Management should keep three things in mind whenever the issue of providing stock options comes up. First, any time you deal with stock you are adding to the complexity of managing the firm. Second, stock prices are not immune to gravity. What goes up can also go down. It is bad enough for people to lose their income if the business fails. It is even worse if they also lose their balance sheets. Third, check out other avenues for motivating people first!

Fringe Benefits Usually Don't Increase Productivity

Most fringe benefits come with the job. Employee health insurance, pension contribution, and family leave benefits usually are not based on whether the employee performed particularly well in the last quarter. While fringe benefits play an important role in attracting and keeping employees, they usually do not boost productivity. Management needs to remember there is a difference between providing benefits that make work more satisfying and providing incentives that enhance performance. For example, Pride In Graphics pays its employees time and a half when they are on vacation. John Ekizian, who owns the Chicago-based printer, believes he keeps valuable workers happier by putting some extra money in their pockets at vacation time.[9] There is little doubt that this benefit may attract people and increase morale. It may even keep people from leaving. But management needs to recognize that this and other benefits may not increase performance for the other 50 weeks of the year.

Fringe benefits may affect employee performance in four particular situations. First, employees may be more motivated to do better if they will be promoted and thereby qualify for an additional or higher level of benefit. Executive dining rooms, preferred parking, and fancier offices fall into this category. Ironically, these "status" distinctions have fallen into disfavor recently. They go against the egalitarian concept that places a premium on having the firm operate as a community of peers rather than a managerial hierarchy.

The other three situations are more subtle. More firms are experimenting with flextime, child care facilities or programs, and the opportunity to work at home. Flextime seems to have merit because it gives workers the opportunity to adjust part of their workday to their personal lifestyles. Employees with children may be able to drop them off at school and take them to the doctors. Flextime also gives people the opportunity to do their shopping or exercising at times that are more convenient and less crowded. At first glance, flextime does not appear to enhance productivity. A closer look, however, indicates that it reduces lateness, absenteeism, and short-term "disappearances." Flextime thereby increases the time people are at work as well as profits.

Some firms have experimented with four-day, forty-hour workweeks. This is not the same as flextime. Compressed schedules have had mixed reviews. Some people prefer this system and are able to maintain their level of performance. Other people find it not to be worthwhile. The compressed workweek plan accentuates some of the challenges that accompany flextime. There may be times when the full staff may not be present to provide assistance to customers and other people in the firm. The fact that a number of employees might like to leave work at 3:30 in the afternoon or have Fridays off does not mean the firm's customers will want to adjust their schedules accordingly.

Child care has become an issue for some firms. A growing number of young employees consider this to be a major factor in deciding between employers. There are a variety of ways to address the child care issue. Some firms simply pay people more so they can deal with it themselves. Other firms provide vouchers that help subsidize child care expenses.

A few firms provide an on-site facility. In these instances, there is some indication that productivity may go up. If the parent is worried about the child, then he or she may use a break to see the child. If the child is being cared for at some offsite facility, then the parent may spend the day worrying about the child or take an "extended" break. The mental and/or physical "drift" associated with offsite care can have an adverse effect on performance.

On-site facilities also have their drawbacks. First of all, they require funds to be built, maintained, and staffed. Second, if children are close by, employees may take frequent breaks to visit them. Third, because the facility is on-site, employees may expect it to be free. Fourth, there are various schools of thought on child care—the firm may be putting itself into a no-win situation. Fifth, employees who don't have children may feel they are short-changed. They may seek equitable consideration in lieu of child care.

The opportunity to work at home appears to be gaining momentum. This concept has many facets. First, the electronic-information revolution has made it possible for people to do their work at home. The "information highway" has considerable appeal when compared to the congested "asphalt" highway. Some employees work at home for at least one day per week. A growing number of employees work at home all week. They may "go to work" once in a while for meetings, to meet with customers or suppliers, or to just see if the building is still there.

There seems to be a real trend toward working at home. Employees like it because it reduces the time they spend commuting. Given that the average commute to work in many cities is 45 minutes each way, this has merit in terms of time, cost, and sanity. The firm also benefits because it may not need as much space. This can have a major impact on capital requirements, overhead, and profitability. The firm could become a business without walls if the electronic highway is taken to the extreme. Electronic commuting may have two additional benefits. Employees will need to become more proficient with computer technology. It will also reduce the need for clerical workers. This will further reduce payroll and space needs.

Management should keep two things in mind when it thinks about fringe benefits. First, while they may have limited motivational value beyond attracting and keeping talented people, they can be very helpful in removing red lights. If people are worried about getting sick and going bankrupt, then they probably won't stay with a firm that offers minimal health insurance coverage. The same reasoning applies to pension programs. Jeff Daggett, who heads W&H Pacific, indicates that his firm has made a deliberate effort to "create an environment in which employees don't have to worry about those things."[10] It offers a 401(k) plan, an employee assistance plan, and an aggressive health-care plan.

Management also needs to remember that employees do not have the same needs and expectations. Moreover, their needs and expectations are likely to change with the passage of time. If the firm offers a benefit that does not fit that employee's needs, then the firm will get no return on its investment. Management can do two things to improve this situation. First, it can survey employees on a regular basis to find out what they value. Second, management can move toward a cafeteria-based fringe benefit program.

Cafeteria-based fringe benefit programs give employees a menu of benefits to choose from. When it comes to benefits, "one benefit does not fit all." The more employees are able to tailor the benefits to fit their particular needs, the more the firm will be the employee's "employer of choice." The employer also benefits because it will get more "bang for the benefits buck." It wasn't that long ago that smaller firms could not even consider offering competitive fringe benefits like health insurance and pension programs. The prospect for offering cafeteria-based plans was even bleaker. Today, computerization has reduced the cost of administering these benefits and created a more level playing field in pursuing employees.[11]

Concluding Comments:
Work Should Be More than
Just a Paycheck

If the firm is to have a competitive advantage, then it will need to have people who take pride in their work rather than merely go through the motions. There is no law that says managers cannot trust employees and treat them with respect. Trust and respect go both ways. Roger Fritz notes, "If your employees trust you, they will give you the benefit of the doubt when you want to make changes in production services and schedules."[12]

Some firms have even made an effort to make work fun and collegial. Cunningham Communication Inc. uses teams to build esprit de corps. It even has a "fun" committee that gives out free concert tickets and finds other ways to make work seem less like work.[13] Other firms hold victory celebrations whenever they complete a major project. Ben and Jerry's has a party whenever it introduces a new flavor.

There are only two limits to what a firm can do to create a high-incentive environment. The first limit is management's commitment to the people who work there. If management considers itself to be better than its employees, then the workers will probably exhibit a "Thank God it's Friday" mentality. If this happens, management needs to remember the "rule of finger" when it looks for an explanation for the low level of employee commitment. The other limit is simply management's imagination in coming up with innovative ways to make work more rewarding. In this case, management should solicit the employees' ideas and have them be coarchitects of the high-incentive environment.

Within us all there are wells of thought and dynamics of energy which are not suspected until emergencies arise. Then, oftentimes we find that it is comparatively simple to double or triple former capacities and to amaze ourselves by the results achieved.
THOMAS WATSON, JR.

CHIEF EXECUTIVE GUIDELINES

Name: Peter D. Behrendt, Chairman and Chief Executive Officer
Company: Exabyte Corporation
Product/Service: High Capacity Tape Drives and Libraries For Computers
Sales: $287,000,000   *Number of Employees:* 1100
Awards/Distinctions:

1. One of "America's Fastest Growers" *Fortune* magazine, 1991, 1992, and 1993

2. Profiled as #12 of "America's 100 Fastest-Growing Small Public Companies," *Inc.* magazine, 1992

3. "Business Person of the Year," 1992, Colorado Chamber of Commerce

General Guidelines: When it comes to motivating managers and employees with financial and psychological incentives, the E/CEO should keep the following tips in mind:

1. Create a sense of "ownership" among all employees. This is particularly important in periods of stress.

2. Offer 100 percent of your employees rights to stock options in the firm's stock.

3. Offer profit sharing to 100 percent of your employees.

4. Provide every employee with a business card as a representative of the company in the community.

5. Create a sense of excitement, especially if the company is doing something that has not been done before.

6. Create few rules and keep bureaucracy to a minimum. If people approach doing business with the "What is right for the customer?" attitude, then you won't need a lot of rules. They will know what to do.

7. Delegate decision-making authority to your people. People on the line must be free to stop it if customer problems come up. They need to be empowered to do whatever it takes to make the customer happy. This is great for business because things get resolved quickly.

8. Don't second-guess your people's decisions—otherwise they won't make decisions.

9. Have quarterly "all-employee" meetings. Use this time to update them on financial results, product status, and other key issues. Bring "customer executives" in to talk to the group so they learn what happens in the real world when they screw up. Provide at least one half hour per meeting for a "question-and-answer" session.

10. Have regular small group meetings with top management for sharing ideas and views.

11. Have a "rumor control" system.

12. Make sure your employees feel they are important enough to be communicated to.

13. Try to make the work environment fun and enjoyable.

Proceed with Caution Guidelines:

1. If you are to treat your employees like owners, then you've got to communicate with them like they are the owners. Owners need to be informed.

2. It's great when you have widespread stock ownership if the stock goes up. When you have unsophisticated employees, however, they may not understand the dynamics of the stock market—especially when it goes down. Make sure your employees realize the volatility of the stock market and that "external" factors can influence the price of your firm's stock.

CHIEF EXECUTIVE GUIDELINES

Name: Ed Rogan II, President and Owner
Company: Rogan Corporation
Product/Service: Decorative Plastic-Molded Control Hardware
Sales: $9,600,000   *Number of Employees:* 107
Awards/Distinctions: One of "The Best Small Companies to Work for in America" *Inc.* magazine, 1993

General Guidelines: When it comes to motivating managers and employees with financial and psychological incentives, the E/CEO should keep the following tips in mind:

1. You've got to be honest and open.

2. You've got to be trusted: no games.

3. Everyone must be on the same page seeking the same goal.

4. Weekly reporting of results is essential, and the results must be current.

Proceed with Caution Guidelines:

1. Set up a gain sharing compensation plan as soon as it would be feasible. (We are starting a new company doing this.)

2. Never ever give rewards that weren't earned.

3. Don't dwell on failed bonus programs—move on.

4. Keep time segments firm—no extensions to complete goals.

And I Would Be Particularly Careful Not *to:*

1. Give unstructured bonuses.

2. Give automatic annual raises.

3. Make excuses—stick with facts.

4. Allow persons or departments to manipulate the results.

17

Providing First-Class Customer Service

*It is clear that organizations not totally
customer-focused will be surpassed by those
who are*

LARRY T. HORNER,
CHAIRMAN OF KPMG PEAT MARWICK

A management professor started the first day of class with the true or false question, "Businesses are in business to sell products and provide services." The students responded, "True!" The professor informed them they were all wrong. He stated that businesses are in the business of providing "satisfaction." Products and services are merely the means to the end—customer satisfaction. Disney reminds all its employees that Disney World is not in the business of providing rides, meals, and lodging—it is there to "make people happy!" As president of Revlon, Charles Revson may have captured the essence of business when he stated, "In our factories we may make cosmetics, but through our products we offer 'hope'!"

Management's job may be to develop a strategy that creates and maintains customers for a profit, but the firm will succeed only to the extent that it is able to provide customer satisfaction. Stanley Marcus, chairman emeritus of Neiman Marcus, put it simply, "You achieve customer satisfaction when you sell merchandise that doesn't come back to a customer who does." The average business loses 20 percent of its customers each year. A considerable portion of each firm's marketing effort is directed to regaining customers who have taken their business elsewhere. Firms that want to maintain a healthy rate of growth need to do an excellent job of attracting new customers as well as keeping their present customers.

There is a story about another college professor who was overheard mumbling to himself, "You know, this job wouldn't be so bad if there weren't any students!" His job might have been easier if he didn't have any students, but he also wouldn't have had a job. It is amazing how so many firms fail to demonstrate a total commitment to creating and maintaining customers. The saying "If only the walls could talk!" is particularly true when it comes to a firm's customer orientation. The walls would reveal that most employees talk about the firm's customers as if they were distractions or inconveniences. Most employees seem to have forgotten (if they even realized it in the first place) that while the firm's name may be at the top of their paycheck customers actually provide the payroll!

Customer Service: The Height of Ignorance, Arrogance, and Complacency

The lack of commitment to customer satisfaction is particularly evident in the area of customer service. The United States learned the hard way in the 1970s about its dependence on foreign oil. In the 1980s, American manufacturing firms realized that they were not competitive in the global arena when it came to providing consistently high levels of product quality. It is apparent that in their recent efforts to improve efficiency and product quality, management has failed to recognize that customer service may be the firm's best competitive weapon. Even with all the changes in the marketplace, the issue of paramount importance remains, "Is the firm providing what the market values?"

Management should not confuse making a sale with providing satisfaction. A purchase is a moment in time. Satisfaction is what keeps the customer coming back. Satisfaction is what prompts the customer to be the firm's best salesperson when he or she promotes your business to other people. A customer's testimonial to a colleague will beat the efforts of the firm's best salesperson every time.

A number of managers claim their firms have a 90 percent customer retention rate. Managers frequently confuse repeat purchases with customer satisfaction. They believe 90 percent of their customers are satisfied. The 90 percent retention rate can be misleading. Does it mean that 90 percent of the firm's present customers are 100 percent satisfied? It may mean that 10 percent of last year's customers found another firm that was in a better position to satisfy their needs and that the 90 percent who have continued buying from the firm are actively looking for an alternative. Retention should not be confused with loyalty.

Managers need to recognize that competitors don't "steal" customers. In most cases, the firm either failed to offer what the customer really wanted or it did something that prompted the customer to look elsewhere. It is very easy for people in high-growth firms to take their present customers for granted. The firm's efforts to attract and serve new customers often overshadow the need to provide first-class service to existing customers. The following cry for attention written years ago still captures how some of the firm's "silent customers" feel today:

Remember Me?

v I'm the fellow who goes into a restaurant, sits down, and patiently waits while the waitresses finish their visiting before taking my order.

v I'm the fellow who goes into a department store and stands quietly while the clerks finish their little chitchat.

v I'm the guy who drives into a service station and never blows his horn but lets the attendant take his time.

v You might say I'm the good guy. But do you know who else I am?

v I'm the fellow who never comes back.

v It amuses me to see businesses spending so much money every year to get me back—when I was there in the first place.

v And all they needed to do was give me some service and extend a little courtesy.

The author of this sad yet accurate commentary may be unknown, but each day a portion of each firm's customers shares this frustration. The days of "service" stations may be a thing of the past but similar frustrations continue today. A newer version may read:

Remember Me?

v I'm the person who goes to the computer store and stands quietly while waiting ten minutes for someone to take my money.

v I'm the person who flies coast to coast only to be told my hotel room isn't ready yet because "It has been a busy day for the hotel staff."

v I'm the person who has to drop off my car at the dealership at 7 a.m. for the whole day because the manufacturer that advertises "Quality Is Job

One!" didn't get it right the first time, and the dealer's service department keeps banker's hours.

ᵥ I used to be a good guy. But do you know who else I am?

ᵥ I'm one of a growing number of people who are fed up with businesses that claim to provide service but who have no concept of what true customer service is.

ᵥ I'm the person who encourages people to start a business to compete against you because of your complacency.

ᵥ I'm the new business's first customer, and I'm part of their corps of "volunteers" who tell your customers there is a new business in town that truly values its customers.

The "Rule of Finger" Also Applies to Customer Satisfaction

Managers frequently rationalize the loss of customers on the "soft" economy or predatory pricing practices by their competitors. It usually turns out that even in a "soft" economy, customers continue buying; they just happen to be buying from someone else. When a former customer indicates she changed to a competitor because the other firm offered a lower price, this may be nothing more than a socially acceptable "smoke screen" to avoid having to say, "Your firm's lack of service drove me away."

It turns out that price may play a secondary role in the purchasing decision for many products and services. The Strategic Planning Institute's Profit Impact of Market Strategy (PIMS) database shows that firms that provide higher levels of quality and service rather than the lowest prices have higher returns on investment.[1] The PIMS database also reveals customers are willing to pay more for quality. The data indicate firms that provided better service charged about 9 percent more for their products. Yet they grew twice as fast as firms that offered lower levels of service and lower prices. Firms that were rated in the top half of their markets for service enjoyed a 12 percent return on sales compared to a 1 percent return for the rest.[2]

Price may get a prospect's attention and even the sale, but lasting business relationships tend to be based on quality, service, honesty, dependability, and responsiveness. Firms that focus on price quickly lose sight of the customer. There will always be some firm out there that will offer lower prices. This does not mean that the firm has to position itself to serve only market segments that aren't price-sensitive. Lucrative business opportunities exist in various price segments. Yet customers still enter into business relationships with certain expectations. Someone once said, "When you buy a $1.25 side salad, you may not expect artichoke hearts, but you do expect the lettuce to be crisp!" Customer satisfaction exists only when what the business offers meets, or exceeds, the customer's expectations.

The hospitality industry provides some interesting examples of how firms can drive their true "employers" away. Few hotels are truly "hospitable." Most hotels represent a virtual minefield for their customers. At times, it looks as if they are actually trying to discourage patronage, eliminate return visits, and elicit an unfavorable word-of-mouth reputation. Let's start with the 1-800 phone reservation system. First, you are put on hold. When you ask about special rates, the "customer service representative" tells you that you need to call that hotel directly—which is not an 800 number. When you do that, you are put back on hold for what seems like an eternity. You are then told to call back during "business hours." After you make your reservation—which seems like a more rigorous process than applying for a working capital loan—you are informed that check-in time is 3 p.m. You are then told that if you plan to arrive after six o'clock, you need to guarantee payment with your credit card. By the way, does the hotel guarantee it will pay for your room somewhere else if they don't have a room for you when you show up on time?

When you finally arrive at the hotel and try to register, you find a line that appears to be a half mile long. A quick time and motion study reveals that at the pace they are going, the two registration people will probably handle your check-in just before your 11 a.m. checkout time the next day! The irony of the situations just described is that the "best" hotels are not much better at providing customer service than mid- and lower-priced motels.

Cruise lines are even worse. Somehow their managers believe people take vacations to stand in line. You stand in line to catch the shuttle from the airport to the pier. You stand in line at the dock. You stand in line for your room. You stand in line to get a "debit" card for charging activities and drinks. Then you stand in line to get your off-ship activity packages. You also have to wait for your baggage because no one told you it would be at least three hours before your baggage would get to your room—if it gets there at all. And just as your cruise is about to end and you are bracing yourself for the line to get through customs, you have to stand in another line to pay your debit card balance. It doesn't take a cost accountant to figure what you pay per hour to go on a cruise. Either this figure has eluded the cruise lines or they figure once you're on board, they have your money—why should they concern themselves with whether you will travel on their line again or worry about what you say to your friends and associates when they ask you about their line?

The irony of this almost comical situation is that most of what the cruise lines refer to as "minor inconveniences" could be eliminated with a state-of-the-art reservation and information system. A brief promotional video could be mailed out in advance to highlight various options and brief customers on what they can do to make the cruise more enjoyable. The 1-800 customer service rep could handle reservations and billing for most of the "extras" before the trip even begins. The cruise line would even get the use of the money that was charged to the customer's credit card in advance. The cruise line would also find that their customers might actually spend more money while on board because they would have already paid for a number of things months earlier. The managers of cruise lines should take a good look at what they are offering their customers. If things continue going the way they have been, cruise lines will be known more for their "lines" than their "cruises"!

Putting the Customer First

Most businesses have mentally reversed the role that customers should play with the role employees should play in the theater of business. Most businesses operate in such a way that they expect customers to make it easier for the employees rather than the other way around. Stew Leonard is known for his ability to put customer service in perspective. He constantly reminds his staff that customers don't enter the store saying, "What can I do for Stew Leonard today?" They ask, "What can Stew Leonard do for me?" Ross Perot gained considerable support when he reminded the public that the people in Washington are supposed to be "public servants." Every employee in every job at every level of the firm needs to recognize that it doesn't matter whether their firm is a manufacturer, wholesaler, or retailer—every business is in the service business and each person is a "customer service representative"!

Most people have seen the sign titled, "What Is a Customer?" While the author may not be known, a few excerpts may be appropriate here:

What Is a Customer?

∨ A customer is not dependent on us. We are dependent on him.

∨ A customer is not an interruption of our work. He is the purpose of it.

∨ A customer does us a favor when he comes in. We aren't doing him a favor by waiting on him.

∨ A customer is not someone to argue or match wits with. Nobody ever won an argument with a customer.

ᵥ A customer is not just money in the cash register. He is a human being with feelings and deserves to be treated with respect.

The last point is particularly important. The preceding chapters stressed the need for employees to be viewed as partners or associates rather than as hired hands. The "What Is a Customer?" sign emphasizes the need to view customers in a more favorable light as well. Disney employees, for example, are not only oriented to view customers as "guests," they are expected to treat them as if their jobs depended on it—because they do!

Each Point of Customer Contact Is a "Moment of Truth"

As CEO of SAS (Scandinavian Airlines), Jan Carlzon coined the term "moments of truth." According to Carlzon, the first 15-second encounter between a passenger and the frontline people, from ticket agent to flight attendant, sets the tone of the entire company in the mind of the customer.[3]

Carlzon notes that each of SAS's 10 million customers each year comes into contact with five SAS employees for an average of 15 seconds each time. He stresses the point that SAS is "created" 50 million times a year, 15 seconds at a time. Carlzon believes these 50 million "moments of truth" are the moments that will ultimately determine if SAS succeeds or fails.[4] Carlzon realized that SAS should not be viewed as a collection of assets on a balance sheet. Instead, he believed SAS needed to be viewed as the quality of contact between an individual and SAS employees who serve the company directly.

Every point of contact with potential and existing customers needs to be viewed as a situation in which the customer is at a "buy" or "do not buy" decision junction. These moments of truth begin with the phone call to find out when the business opens, when the customer drives in the parking lot, when the customer enters the building, and when the customer is greeted.

There is a story of a CEO who decided to stop by one of the firm's field offices for a brief and unannounced visit while on vacation. When he entered the outer office he was not given the time of day by the receptionist. When he returned from his vacation he called the manager of that field office to tell him to fire the receptionist. The manager responded, "The receptionist didn't know who you were—if we had known you were coming, we would have rolled out the red carpet for you!" The CEO then said, "You've missed the whole point. I don't want her fired because of the way she treated me—she should be fired because no one should be ignored when he or she walks into our office." The CEO closed his sermon with "Everyone should get red carpet service."

Moments of truth continue after the sale when the product is delivered and when the customer wants service assistance. Nature's Best, which distributes natural foods, even trains its truck drivers how to make a good impression. Randy Lindberg, president of Nature's Best, states, "We recognized our truck drivers spend more time with our customers than even our sales reps do. Customers could base their entire opinion of us on how our drivers treat them."[5] A number of companies send all their employees to Dale Carnegie customer service programs.

Jan Carlzon's concept seems to be built on the premises, "You never get a second chance to make a first impression" and "Opportunity doesn't knock twice." Everyone in the firm needs to recognize that every customer should be treated as the firm's first customer was treated. Most E/CEOs forget how delighted they were to make the first sale. They forget they approached the first customer as a lover is courted before marriage. Too often, firms treat their customers like someone they just divorced. They aren't the slightest bit cordial, don't return their calls, and harass them for money.

Some customers leave out of neglect. A few leave in a fit of rage. Ninety percent of dissatisfied customers never let their dissatisfaction be known to the firm. A study by Technical Research Assistance Programs indicated that over 95 percent of the customers who have a bad experience with a business do not voice their complaints to that business. Frustrated and dissatisfied customers vote with their feet. They just don't come back.

The study also revealed that the few people who do complain to that business don't come back because their complaints were handled in such a negative fashion. The irony of the situation is that 82 to 95 percent of the customers who are dissatisfied would have continued their relationship with the firm if their complaints had been handled in a timely and thoughtful manner.[6]

Jan Carlzon recognized the need to provide customer service and the need to address problems the moment they occur. Carlzon noted, "If we are truly dedicated to orienting our company toward each customer's needs, then we cannot rely on rule books and instructions from distant corporate offices. We have to place responsibility for ideas, decisions, and actions with the people who are SAS during those 15 seconds."[7]

If management is committed to customer service, then people on the front line need to be given the authority and the resources to do whatever it takes to make sure customers value their relationship with the firm. Stew Leonard has two simple rules for guiding his employees in their relations with customers. Rule number one is: The customer is always right. Rule number two is: If the customer is ever wrong—remember rule number one!

What Is the Cost of Losing a Customer?

The fact that firms in the "hospitality" industry cited earlier miss the mark in providing customer service by such a wide margin is evidence of the sad state of customer service in other industries as well. It seems there are lines for lines and waiting rooms for waiting rooms. There are phone numbers that are never answered. In the unlikely event they are answered, you are on hold so long that by the time someone answers the phone, you have forgotten who you called! A number of firms rationalize their lack of customer service with, "We have to keep our costs down to remain competitive." They fail to recognize that after a few instances, people stop standing in line, they stop waiting, and they hang up the phone. The lack of service also has a cost—it is called bankruptcy. An *Inc.* magazine flyer for its customer service seminar noted that improving the company's retention rate can have the same effect on profit as decreasing cost by 10 percent. Viewed in this light, first-class customer service should not be considered a luxury that only the biggest firms can afford. If it is done right, first-class customer service is free.

We live in a time where software programs try to model the real world. These programs work only to the extent that they reflect reality. American auto manufacturers got in serious trouble years ago when their "optimization" models indicated they should strive for 93 percent product quality. The formulas indicated that it would have been cost prohibitive to provide a higher level of quality. Toyota and Honda also used optimization formulas, but they placed a higher cost on customer dissatisfaction.

American auto manufacturers made two mistakes in their calculations. They looked at the purchase of an auto as a onetime event. They also assumed that when a new car had problems, the consumer could just take it back to the dealer and have it fixed under the warranty. Honda viewed the purchase of a car as one event in a series of lifelong car purchases. Honda wanted the customer to be satisfied to the point that when the consumer went to buy the next car, he or she would automatically buy a Honda. This level of satisfaction can be contagious. In a world of product uncertainty, people will quickly buy products that are the subject of customer testimonials. When a customer buys a product, the firm has made a sale—when the customer is delighted, the firm has gained an "apostle." This will only happen when the firm "delights" each customer.

The first step in fostering a customer service orientation may be to show that customer satisfaction has a major impact on the bottom line. Management needs to recognize that it takes fives times more money to find a new customer than it takes to keep a present customer. Repeat customers save the firm money in many ways. The firm does not need as many salespeople because repeat customers are already "sold." Ordering time is also quicker because repeat customers are already familiar with the process.

Management also needs to recognize the consequences that customer dissatisfaction can have on potential customers. The Technical Assistance Research Programs study revealed that customers who have had a bad experience with a firm usually tell at least nine colleagues about the experience. The study also indicated that 13 percent of the people who were dissatisfied told at least 20 people about their experience.[8]

Management needs to compute the cost of a lost customer rather than just the cost of a lost sale. If the average customer buys one item a month for $150, then the firm loses more than the $150; it runs the risk of losing the customer altogether. The opportunity loss could be figured over the life of the customer or just the next 10 years. If 10 years is used as the base, then one bad service incident could cost the firm $18,000 in sales over the next 10 years. This loss may be compounded if the person tells prospective customers about the incident. The lack of customer service could cost the firm $180,000! This may be an extreme estimate, but it should reduce the tendency for people in the firm to have a cavalier attitude and say, "Oh, she's just one customer." People tend to pay more attention to customer service when they realize each moment of truth could cost the firm $180,000.

Firms that focus their attention on the financial side of the firm tend to lose sight of the role that individual customers have on long-term growth and profitability. A firm striving to achieve a target return on investment that requires sales of $50 million may indicate that it needs to find ten thousand customers to buy its $500 product. When top management is asked to identify who these customers are, the response usually is, "It doesn't matter who they are—just find ten thousand people who will buy the product!" When people are treated as numbers, they tend to be processed in the quickest possible way. Instead of trying to develop a lifelong relationship with them by satisfying their individual needs, people in the firm merely say, "next!" Before long, there is no one in line to yell "next" to.

Customers show little mercy to firms that treat them as interchangeable parts. Firms that value customer satisfaction know that you create your customer base "one customer at a time." Each customer has a name. Each customer has specific needs. Each customer can go elsewhere. No customer is forced to do business with you.

Growth Begins with Customer Retention

Tom Peters and Bob Waterman stressed the need for firms to be "close to their customers" in their book *In Search of Excellence.* This "closeness" can take many forms. First, management needs to place a premium on establishing a favorable "relationship" with the firm's customers. The word "relationship" is important because it implies respect for one another and two-way interaction. If the firm will retain customers only to the extent their needs are fully met, then management needs to make every effort to find out what the firm's customers value and whether their needs are being met.

Many managers make the mistake of assuming their customers are satisfied. They are like managers who have "open-door" policies for their employees. If their employees do not come in to express their concerns, they assume everything is just fine. In medical terms, there is a big difference between not being sick and being well. The absence of disease does not mean the person is healthy. The same applies to customer goodwill. The absence of customer complaints does not mean customers are totally satisfied. Managers need to view the firm's customers as partners. They need to make a deliberate effort to learn what customers want and the extent to which the firm is providing total satisfaction.

Firms that are totally committed to serving their customers don't wait for their customers to take their business elsewhere before they see the light. They take a proactive stance and try to prevent the loss of customers by developing a responsive, ongoing relationship with them. Responsiveness begins by creating various avenues for soliciting customers' views. Just as the best salespeople sell with their ears, customer responsiveness begins with listening to their views. Some firms use focus groups to solicit their customers' views. Focus groups are a very effective way to gain insight into how customers perceive the firm. They can also be an excellent source of ideas for new products and services.

When the CEO of a bank in California realized the boardroom was being used only once a month, he decided to invite different groups of customers to it for a catered lunch each week. Management used these luncheons to solicit the customers' ideas about what the bank does well and what management can do to improve their banking partnership. Some firms have even established "Customer Advisory Boards." These boards meet regularly so management can see things from the customers' perspective.

A few firms go well beyond the typical suggestion system and customer service phone numbers in their quest for unparalleled customer satisfaction. Great Plains Software actively solicits its customers' and distributors' ideas. At any one time, the company has 10,000 to 15,000 suggestions that it tries to fit into a "feature list" for its software. In 1991, Great Plains introduced its Version 6 that included 100 new features that were distilled from 2000 suggestions.[9] Intuit also offers some interesting approaches to learning from its customers. While some firms invite their customers to participate in focus groups, Intuit has focus groups comprised of people who buy their competitors' products.

Most computer users have grown leery of software company claims that their programs are "user-friendly." The owner of a small retail business recently followed up on an ad that boasted how easy the firm's accounting program was to use. When the caller asked about the instruction manual, the software maker's customer service representative said that the revised edition has been reduced to "only" 400 pages! Will there ever be a time when software manuals will be only five pages long and be comprehensible by someone with less than a Ph.D.? Somewhere along the line, software companies lost sight of the fact that their products are supposed to make life easier. If this country ever bans capital punishment, then nearly every software package will be banned. While most software companies are proud of how far they have come, when most consumers try using their programs they frequently mumble to themselves where they would like the software programmers, manual writers, and salespeople to go.

Intuit appears to be a firm that is committed to making its new software truly user-friendly. On one occasion, Intuit invited a group of Junior League–style novices in to run its software. Intuit monitored their eye movements to see where they hesitated and where they had quizzical looks. The staff at Intuit recognizes that every glitch and momentary hesitation reflects a fault in their software. Intuit even has a "follow me home" program where customers are asked if an Intuit representative can go home with them to observe them as they use their Quicken software the very first time.[10]

Some firms have "tiger teams" of customers test and evaluate new products and services before they are offered to the public. They are encouraged to use and even abuse the firm's products-services. These firms recognize management is too ego-involved to be objective and that R&D labs cannot simulate all the nuances found in the marketplace. For example, before a dish is put on the menu at one of Jack Williams's restaurants in California, it has been tried by about 3,000 customers.[11]

If management is really serious about learning if the new product is ready for the real world, then it should consider having it tested by Japanese consumers. Paul Hawken notes the Japanese are the most demanding customers in the world. According to Hawken, "If a Japanese company can survive and prosper in its marketplace, when it comes to our marketplace, it's a cakewalk, because American businesses have done quite the opposite. Our businesses have tried to make us stupid. In Japan, they say, Is it good? In America, we say, Is it good enough?"[12]

Customer Responsiveness Requires a Good Database

Information technology has played an integral role in enhancing customer responsiveness. John Deighton of the University of Chicago's Graduate School of Business states, "The person who owns the data owns the relationship with the customer." Waldenbooks has a customer database of four million names. The database is used for selling to particular segments and building customer loyalty. For example, it can compile a list of all members who have bought mysteries and mail them a special Agatha Christie two-for-one offer. Waldenbooks' Preferred Reader program offers customers the opportunity to buy by mail or through an 800 number in addition to their retail stores.[13]

Vipont Pharmaceutical Inc. also demonstrates the value of having an excellent customer database. Its database enabled the firm to go from $13,000 in sales of its oral hygiene products to over $37 million in just eight years. Computer technology reduced the cost of storing and accessing a single customer name from over $7 to less than one cent.[14]

A number of firms regularly survey prospective and present customers. Granite Rock Company even puts together an annual report card from its customers. It uses survey data to compare its performance with each of its competitors. The surveys indicate what customers value and where the company is vulnerable to its competitors.[15] Intuit uses surveys as a source for future ideas. It conducts new customer surveys each year. Intuit's 20-minute, 14-page survey of a cross section of new customers is used to forecast what customers may need in the next five years.[16] A word of caution may be appropriate here. If the firm solicits its customers' views, then management must be prepared to make appropriate changes—and to make them quickly!

Some firms use less sophisticated techniques to measure the quality of customer service. Steamboat Ski Corporation takes pride in its friendly, family-oriented environment. Customers selected at random are given envelopes containing a gift certificate that can be redeemed for $10. Whenever a customer receives exceptional service, he or she can give the certificate to that employee.[17] This system not only identifies staff who are providing exceptional service; it also indicates those who need to improve.

Au Bon Pain Company has a more elaborate mystery customer program. Thirty anonymous non-company-affiliated customers are paid to buy a meal at one of the company's restaurants. They then complete a four-page questionnaire to determine if the company's quality and service standards are being met. The corporate office tracks trends and long-term performance for each of its units. The data is used to recognize and reward employees who have provided high levels of service. It also indicates areas that warrant improvement. Ron Shaich, Au Bon Pain's co-chief executive, notes that the results of the program are as important as the profit-and-loss statement for tracking the health of the company. Shaich states, "If you've got customers, you ought to be looking at what you do through a customer's eyes."[18]

The notion of looking at the business through the customers' eyes seems like a "no-brainer." Yet too few managers and employees place themselves in the role of their customers. For example, hotel registration and front desk staff should sleep in various locations of the hotel to get a better feel for varying noise levels produced by ice machines and people waiting for elevators. They will also find out if there is enough hot water to take a shower at seven o'clock in the morning and if room service is prompt. The firm's effort to see its operations through the customers' eyes can even be as elementary as calling the company's regular number to see how many times it rings before it is answered, how the caller is greeted, if the caller is put on hold, and how long it actually takes to be connected with someone.

Management should also call the firm's customer service number on a random basis to ask typical service questions to see how long it takes to get an answer. Management should be particularly cognizant of whether customer service spends its time making excuses for product-service problems or if it has a genuine concern for solving the caller's problems. It is ironic that customer surveys reveal that service departments and customer service phone lines are frequently cited as sources of poor service.

Transforming Customer Complaints into Customer Goodwill

Growth involves keeping present customers and attracting new ones. Management needs to recognize that the loss of a customer usually is an indication that the firm was not meeting the customer's expectations. Instead of rationalizing the loss of a customer on factors outside the firm, management needs to take the initiative to learn what the firm did that prompted the customer to go elsewhere.

The loss of a customer is usually just the tip of the customer dissatisfaction iceberg. There may be dozens of customers who have similar frustrations who are on the verge of switching to another firm. L. L. Bean recognized the importance of customer retention years ago. In 1912, he put out a circular that read, "Should the person reading this notice know of anyone who is not satisfied with our goods, I will consider it a favor to be notified." It is not surprising that L. L. Bean today has a 24-hour-a-day, 365-day-a-year toll-free sales and customer service number.[19]

One of today's great mysteries involves how firms handle their mistakes. If a firm was developing a prototype for a new product and an engineer found a problem that had eluded the product's design team, then he or she would be commended for finding it before the product was available to the public. Why is it then that when customers find faults in the way the firm conducts its business they are ignored or harassed?

Customer complaints need to be solicited and rewarded. Every complaint should be viewed as a suggestion for how the firm can improve its competitive position rather than as an attack on the firm. Why pay for consultants to identify areas where the firm can be improved when the firm's customer suggestions and complaints often identify the same areas?

Management needs to view every customer complaint as a learning experience. In addition to addressing each customer's concerns, management needs to analyze the situation that prompted the complaint. George Walther, who serves as a sales consultant, indicates that a firm is wasting its time trying to attract new customers when there is some "bump" in the business process that is driving its present customers away. He notes that if management is unaware of or unwilling to deal with a product defect, a badly designed service policy, or a problem employee, then all the efforts to attract new customers will be wasted.[20]

The firm needs to do more than just listen to customer complaints. The person fielding the complaint should apologize for the difficulty and ask enough questions to make sure the situation is clearly understood. The customer should then be told when to expect action and how it will be forthcoming—by phone, by letter, or even in person.[21] Tom Peters not only agrees with the study cited earlier that found you can get 82 to 95 percent of your customers back if you can resolve the complaint in a timely and thoughtful fashion; he believes that a well-handled problem can generate more loyalty for your business than existed before the negative incident.[22]

Proactive firms don't wait for complaints to surface. They call their customers on a regular basis to make sure the firm is meeting their expectations. George Walther encourages businesses to fax customers newspaper clippings on subjects that may be of interest to them and to provide them with ideas that can help their businesses. He states, "If you keep the relationship so full of benefits, the customer won't want to relinquish it."[23] This is what relationship management is all about.

Forging Customer Partnerships

Management needs to view the whole firm as a "customer problem solver." If management embraces this concept, then it will pursue every opportunity to establish partnership relationships with its present and prospective customers. The ultimate level of customer service is demonstrated when firms start relationships with their customers well in advance of the purchase of products-services. These partnerships may be as simple as selecting a person within the firm to be the "liaison" or customer service representative for that customer. Service tends to be better when a person is designated as the customer's representative. The liaison should have direct access to the customer's database as well as sufficient authority and resources to deal with the customer's needs. DuPont's "adopt-a-customer" program takes this one step further. Blue-collar workers are encouraged to visit a customer, learn the customer's needs, and be that customer's representative on the factory floor. When quality or delivery problems occur, the worker is more likely to see them from the customer's point of view and help make a decision that will keep the "adopted" child happy.[24]

Awareness and concern for each customer's specific needs are prerequisites for providing first-class customer service. Even if the firm does not designate a specific individual on the shop floor, it is advantageous to have the people who are involved in any aspect of making the product or handling the orders visit the customer so they can meet the customer. It is easier to cut corners when customers are known only as multidigit account numbers. Relationships work best when both parties know one another as individuals.

Some partnerships use electronic linkages between the firms so orders can be made at any time of the day. A few firms have such a strong partnership that the supplier is authorized to make the product and ship it without an order even being placed by the customer. Procter and Gamble has this type of relationship with Wal-Mart. Anyone could provide diapers to Wal-Mart, but P&G adds value to the diapers it supplies by performing the inventory management process.[25] P&G thereby relieves Wal-Mart of its ordering process, its inventory management expenses, and most of its inventory carrying costs.

Supplier-customer partnerships can go beyond addressing immediate needs and problems. Milliken has established "customer-action teams" to find new market opportunities in partnership with existing customers. A team is created when a customer agrees to work with Milliken representatives in seeking solutions to better serve existing markets and to create new ones.[26] A firm that prefers to remain anonymous went one step further. It canvassed the marketplace for a potential customer that had a significant market position but had not introduced any new models for a number of years. The firm developed a whole new model and then approached the firm to see if it wanted to use it!

The R&D firm was taking a considerable risk by committing its funds to the project without contacting the potential customer. Its proactive approach to establishing a mutually beneficial relationship with the other firm, however, indicates that the boundaries that used to separate suppliers and customers are quickly coming down. It is amazing what can happen when leading providers and leading users form alliances to expedite the flow of products and information.

While a few of the preceding examples describe how customer service is handled by larger firms, company size is not the key—commitment to customer satisfaction is the driving force. Even the neighborhood seafood store can use customer service to differentiate itself from all the other retailers who sell fish. Most seafood stores emphasize freshness, price, and selection. One very successful retailer's first "moment of truth" with the customer starts with the question "How do you plan to serve the fish?" The retailer recognizes that certain fish may be better for certain occasions. Every other seafood store can carry the same fish. This store differentiates itself by its ability to provide advice that will make the fish easier to prepare and better tasting. The store also carries vegetables and other items that can be prepared with the fish so customers do not have to go elsewhere for them.

The seafood store's database includes each customer's seafood preferences as well as the days of the week the customer buys seafood. This store's employees frequently call customers to see if they would like to have a couple of pounds of fish or shrimp prepared and wrapped for them so they will not have to wait when they come in that day. While the other seafood stores try to sell fish, this store is committed to providing a pleasurable dining experience! Firms that offer this type of service tend to have "cradle-to-grave" relationships with their customers.

Concluding Comments:
Customer Service Reflects
the Firm's Integrity

Customer service involves more than having service goals, catchy slogans, and toll-free numbers. First-class service will only be possible if it is part of the firm's very soul. In too many instances, catchy slogans like, "You asked for it, you got it" (Toyota), "Have it your way" (Burger King), and "We know what you're looking for" (J. C. Penney's) are not matched by first-class service. The "moments of truth" tend to leave the customers asking, "Where's the beef?" (Wendy's).

Customer responsiveness begins with a commitment to establishing a lifelong relationship with each customer. Firms with long-term time horizons are less likely to cut corners or grow complacent. As president of Piedmont Airlines, William Howard demonstrated a commitment to customer service before that firm merged with USAir. When Howard was asked to identify the things he thought contributed to Piedmont's growth and success, he indicated the use of the hub-and-spoke system, the addition of transatlantic routes, and the transition to wide-body jets, but he also noted that he thought Piedmont's practice of providing the customers who flew coach class with the whole 12-ounce soft drink could also make a difference! He noted that if you value your customers, then you don't treat the 90 percent of your customers who fly coach like second-class citizens by "rationing" their beverages. The practice of providing the whole can also meant that the flight attendants could spend more of their time on other aspects of customer service and less time running around filling up glasses.

The most successful firms recognize that there is a direct relationship between customer relations and employee relations. If management cuts corners with the firm's employees, then employees will cut corners when it comes to customer service. If the firm is committed to providing first-class customer service, then the firm must be a first-class employer. Firms that hire part-time employees and/or pay marginal wages will not be in a position to provide first-class service. The same applies to orientation, training, performance appraisal, and rewards. In the best firms, management emphasizes the importance of customer service in every aspect of the firm's operations. People are constantly trained and cross-trained so that there is always someone in the firm who can provide customer assistance. Performance reviews also include a measure of customer responsiveness. Some firms even solicit their customers' views when they review employees who deal directly with the public. Finally, if you want high levels of customer service, then you need to reward it. If the firm is committed to customer service, then management must make sure that the reward structure encourages and rewards it. Firms that offer careers rather than jobs are also more likely to provide first-class customer service.

Firms that are committed to first-class customer service also recognize that their advertisements and salespeople should only make claims that the firm can honor. The whole issue of integrity is centered around whether the firm actually provides a consistent level of quality and delivers the goods-services on time. Relationships are built on trust. Any breach of that trust may cause a multiplier effect whereby the firm not only loses that customer, it may lose other customers as well.

The issue of integrity was particularly evident a few years ago when customers started to complain about the lack of "on time" arrivals by the airlines. Instead of trying to improve their operations, some airlines merely lengthened their flight times so they appeared to arrive on time! IBM Credit took a more constructive approach when its customers and staff became concerned about the length of time it took to prepare and process a financing package. IBM looked at every step in the process and completely reengineered it. What used to take seven days now takes four hours! Moreover, IBM Credit improved its turnaround time without adding to its staff.[27] IBM Credit recognized customer service involves knocking down the barriers as well as creating avenues for expediting the process.

Trust is particularly evident when it comes to guarantees and customer service after the sale. If the firm is committed to providing first-class service, then it needs to have a 100 percent satisfaction guarantee. Nordstrom and Toys-R-Us attribute some of their success to their "no questions asked" guarantees. Conditional warranties mean that the firm is unwilling to stand behind its products and its services. Oakley Millwork Inc. is so committed to meeting its customers' needs that it established a 100 percent in stock guarantee—any item that has to be backordered is free. Glen Johnson, who heads Oakley Millwork, attributes the firm's 20 percent increase in sales to the guarantee.[28] He recognizes stock-outs drive customers to competitors.

Intuit has very strong feelings about service after the sale. While most software firms charge for service assistance, Intuit believes something is wrong when your customers have to pay a fee because something does not work as well as it should. Scott Cook, Intuit's president, notes, "We're not going to charge. If our customers have problems, we pay. That makes us get the product right the first time."[29] Intuit even installed a $500,000 state-of-the-art phone system so customers would not have to wait very long for assistance. Cook refers to his commitment to total customer responsiveness as "operating without a net." When you know you don't have a net to break your fall, you make every effort to get it right the first time, every time. Cook recognizes that the dance with the elephants is like operating without a net—one wrong move and you are history.

A customer orientation has a limited value unless it's embedded in the very fiber of the enterprise—at all levels, and at every place that directly and indirectly impacts the customer.

FROM A UNISYS CORPORATION AD

CHIEF EXECUTIVE GUIDELINES

Name: Katherine B. Moore, President
Company: Eastern Delivery Service Inc.
Product/Service: Trucking
Sales: $800,000   *Number of Employees:* 14
Awards/Distinctions:

1. "Entrepreneur of the Year" for North Carolina, *Entrepreneur* magazine, 1992

2. "Blue Chip Enterprise Award," U.S. Chamber of Commerce, 1991

3. Avon "Woman of Enterprise" Award, 1990

General Guidelines: When it comes to providing first-class customer service, the E/CEO should keep the following tips in mind:

1. It may sound corny but "The customer is always right."

2. Chief executives should handle as many complaints as possible.

3. Abusive customers should be referred to the chief executive.

4. A representative should *never* respond disrespectfully.

5. Always return customer service calls immediately.

6. Be willing to refund the money when the customer is not satisfied.

Proceed with Caution Guidelines:

1. Avoid being on the defensive when responding to complaints.

2. When making an effort to please, be cautious about making outrageous commitments that can be costly.

3. Be cautious in pricing and bidding. You must make money on a venture in order to survive. However, do not expect to make money on *every* single job. But cut losses.

And I Would Be Particularly Careful Not to:

1. Have friends and family work in your business. This is the most dangerous thing in any business. None have ever worked out for me.

2. Hire friends and family of employees. Beware!

3. Share company financial information with clients and employees. Never do it!

CHIEF EXECUTIVE GUIDELINES

Name: Steven Agnoff, President
Company: Efson Inc.
Product/Service: Plastic Power Transmission Components
Sales: $10,000,000   *Number of Employees:* 80

General Guidelines: When it comes to providing first-class customer service, the E/CEO should keep the following tips in mind:

1. The customer is king. Everything you do in your business should be focused on making it easier for your customers to do business with you.

2. Be reactive! Better to follow up too much than not at all. Quote new projects as soon as possible, and many times you will have an order while the competition is still getting their numbers together.

3. Communicate the bad news as well as the good. If you are going to be late on a delivery, let your customer have time to plan around it.

4. Strive to constantly improve your product and service. "Knock off" yourself before someone else does.

5. Ultimately all products are commodities. Excellent customer service is what keeps your customers from going to the competition.

Proceed with Caution Guidelines:

1. Make sure the infrastructure is in place to support your growth. You cannot provide customer service if you cannot keep your promises.

2. Make sure everyone in the company maintains a customer focus that is consistent with your customer service philosophy. It is hard to preach partnership with your customer when accounting will not release shipments because of credit problems.

3. Have key customers make presentations at plant meetings to reinforce how important your products are to their success and to put a face on the order the production people see.

4. Conduct customer surveys to find what areas need to be improved.

5. Make sure outside sales reps responsible for accounts are well-informed on projects at the home office. Keeping them out of the loop undermines their credibility with the customer.

And I Would Be Particularly Careful Not to:

1. Make commitments to customers that are beyond your capabilities. Many customers have been lost due to good intentions.

2. Take jobs that do not meet corporate profit goals. Adjusting prices after the initial order causes bad feelings.

3. Alienate major accounts. As your company grows and there are more demands on your time, you don't want major customers to perceive that you are "handing them down" to lower-level employees.

4. Pay outside sales reps primarily on a commission basis. This does not reward sales reps for providing excellent customer service to smaller accounts.

5. Get so caught up in day-to-day problems that you completely delegate customer contact and get out of touch with the marketplace.

18

Adopting Total Quality Management

*We can only achieve quantum steps of
improvement if we get the organization
looking at the issues in totally new ways.*[1]
GERHARD SCHULMEYER,
CEO OF ASEA BROWN BOVERI INC.

It would be impossible to discuss every dimension of total quality management (TQM) in a single chapter. The subject is too comprehensive, and it continues to evolve each day. This chapter is intended to stress why TQM is essential, highlight the components that may be the most important to an emerging firm, and note some of the cautions management needs to heed as it embarks on the endless journey toward excellence.

Let's set the record straight; TQM is not a "technique." It is much more than that. It is a way to run the entire business enterprise. TQM needs to be an integral part of the firm's culture and strategy. It must be the very pulse of the firm. TQM is not something that can be added to the firm's bag of managerial tricks. It cannot be learned in a couple of hours at some slick seminar nor can it be implemented in a few days.

TQM takes patience and persistence. It requires a willingness to take an objective look at everything the firm is doing and how it is doing those things. There can be no sacred cows—and no rationalizations. TQM is not for the squeamish. It constitutes a continuous effort to turn the business inside out. TQM not only looks at the big things; it also probes every nook and cranny. In its purest form, TQM resembles a shrew that must eat more than its body weight each day to survive. TQM starts its never ending meal by devouring complacency, arrogance, and ignorance. Then it shifts its attention to organizational practices that represent barriers (or red lights) that keep the firm from being competitive. Finally, it directs its attention toward providing facilitative processes (green lights) to foster world-class excellence.

The term "TQM" may not even be used in a few years because another term (possibly reengineering) may be coined that better reflects the never ending quest for excellence. This is already the case in Japan. Managers in the United States and other countries have jumped on the TQM bandwagon. Japanese managers don't have a bandwagon to jump on because their commitment to quality is part of the very fabric in which business is conducted. They do not see quality as something that now needs to be emphasized; pride in quality has been a part of their culture for centuries. The Japanese have always exhibited pride in their craftsmanship.

Western firms did not pay much attention to world-class quality until it was almost too late. In many instances, American managers accused Japanese firms of unfair trade practices. By the end of the 1970s, however, a few American firms began to recognize their firms were totally out of synch with changes taking place in the global marketplace. In 1979, Xerox received a "wake up call" when Canon introduced a midsize copier for less than what it cost Xerox to make a similar machine. In 1985, Motorola toured Japan and found calculators and computers being made with defect rates up to 1000 times better than U.S. manufacturers.[2]

As long as managers view quality as a "dimension" that is separate from the other dimensions they oversee like cost reduction and asset turnover, they will miss the whole point. Quality is so intertwined with the whole business process that it cannot be seen as a dimension of a business—it is how the business is defined.

Total Quality Management Reflects the Very Nature of the Firm's Management

Managers tend to approach TQM from one of six perspectives. The first group of managers say, "Oh, it's just a passing fad." These managers may acknowledge TQM, but they fail to recognize it is becoming one of the facts of business life. The second group of managers say, "Oh, we're already into quality." Executives of firms that are known for their years of commitment to quality openly admit they are just beginning to develop a true understanding of the complexity and magnitude of TQM.

Managers in the third group say, "Only Fortune 500 firms need to be concerned about TQM." Managers in most small firms believe only firms that are competing in the global arena need to adopt TQM. The same people believe smaller firms don't have the funds, staff, or time to adopt TQM. Their assumptions may be their downfall because more companies expect their suppliers to have TQM processes in place. A growing number of firms are now requiring "ISO 9000" certification of their suppliers. ISO 9000 is a certificate awarded by independent auditors who indicate the firm has met quality management requirements set by the International Organization for Standardization. ISO 9000 is quickly becoming the standard for doing business abroad as well as for larger firms within the United States.[3] The ISO 9000 standards are available from the American National Standards Institute in New York.

Smaller firms are learning the hard way that their competitors don't just live down the street—they are crossing state and national boundaries in their search for new customers. It turns out that it may actually be easier for smaller firms to adopt TQM. Smaller firms tend to: (1) be closer to their customers, (2) have fewer levels of management that often serve as barriers to worker suggestions, and (3) be newer so they are easier to change.

The fourth group of naysayers is comprised of managers who view TQM as the latest "flavor of the month." They decide to dabble with bits and pieces of TQM. They resemble children who have to eat their vegetables—they may put a piece in their mouth but they are reluctant to swallow it. They may rally around TQM's slogans but they fail to sink their teeth into it.

Managers in the fifth group claim, "We can have TQM up and running within a week." A number of firms that enlist in the quality "crusade" quickly lose faith and interest when they realize it requires a total and continuous commitment. When their managers realize TQM is like boot camp and the quality war is not going to be won by Christmas, their commitment fizzles—and they return to business as usual. These are the firms that say TQM just doesn't work.

Many firms have rallied around the flag, but few are going the distance. Their managers fail to recognize that good ideas work only to the extent they have good implementation. Some firms just don't have the type of culture, infrastructure, or time horizon that is needed to support TQM.

A few firms, however, are in the sixth group. They are going the distance. Their managers and employees have made TQM a way of life. They are the ones that serve as the "benchmarks." They are setting new standards in quality, efficiency, timeliness, responsiveness, and profitability. The irony with these firms is that even though they have made great strides, their managers and employees see the glass as being only half full. Firms that have totally embraced TQM can be distinguished from lesser firms because they recognize achieving excellence is not a destination—it is a never ending quest.

Embracing the Total Quality Management Challenge

TQM is so multifaceted that when managers try to adopt it they resemble the six blind men who encounter an elephant. The first blind man feels the tail and thinks the beast must be snake. The second blind man grabs an ear and concludes it must be the wing of a gigantic bird. Each of the other four blind men touch a different part of the elephant and believe it to be something else. The moral to the story is firms that go blindly into the dance with the elephants are likely to be trampled to death.

The same situation frequently occurs with TQM. Most managers see TQM through their "eyes of experience." People with an engineering and manufacturing background tend to see TQM as a way to get the rest of the people in the firm to finally use statistical quality control and other quantitative techniques. People in marketing see TQM as the messiah who will lead the firm toward a "total" customer orientation. The saying, "If you give a child a hammer, he or she will find everything needs to be hammered" applies to how TQM is perceived in many firms. If TQM is viewed as a marketing hammer or a manufacturing hammer, then TQM is destined to die an early death. TQM must be seen as an integrated "business" hammer.

If TQM is to work, then numerous prerequisite conditions must be met. First, TQM must be viewed as a "comprehensive" way to run the business. TQM affects every dimension of the business and every decision that will be made. Second, everyone in the firm must accept the need to adopt TQM. Third, everyone must be committed to changing whatever needs to be changed to make TQM work. This is particularly true for the E/CEO and the management team. Michael Barrier of *Nation's Business* notes, "If there is one vital ingredient for a successful TQM effort in small firms, it is the CEO's visible and unreserved commitment to TQM. Without it, other managers will hang back."[4]

Management must realize that TQM is rapidly becoming a "do-or-die" proposition. E/CEOs are now at a decision junction where there are only two paths. If they are unwilling to embrace TQM, then they should sell their firms while there is something left to sell. Firms that make the quantum TQM leap today will be in a position to reap its benefits in the years ahead. Firms that fail to operationalize TQM in the next few years are not likely to last another 10 years. Naysayers and footdraggers will not have the responsiveness customers will expect, the consistently high levels of quality their customers will demand, and the economies that will enable them to offer competitive prices.

Operationalizing TQM Is a Multistep Process

Managers of firms that accept the need for TQM and demonstrate the commitment to operationalizing it frequently are left with the question, "Where do we go from here?" The awareness and commitment stages need to be followed by the "learning" stage. While numerous road maps may be available for operationalizing TQM's journey, the following steps capture the basic milestones:

Awareness>Commitment>Learning>Choosing
Targets>Implementation>Measurement

The learning stage begins the continuous improvement cycle associated with TQM. Management needs to recognize that everyone in the firm must develop a holistic understanding of TQM. Training will take a considerable amount of time. Every manager and every employee will need to go through formal training during the first year. TQM training cannot be done on a "time available" basis. TQM training must be considered as important as meeting this week's production deadlines. If management hedges on the importance of training, then the firm should forget about TQM altogether.

Training not only requires people to be away from their jobs (even with in-house programs), it also requires a major financial commitment. Funds will need to be budgeted for training materials, for people to attend seminars, and possibly for a TQM consultant to help management operationalize it. When the expenses associated with operationalizing TQM are added up, many E/CEOs blow the whistle and call a time-out. Firms that are already stretched for cash are tempted to postpone operationalizing TQM until they have the funds. This is circular reasoning. If the firm does not fund TQM today, it will not have the competitive edge to provide the funds at some later date.

When E/CEOs are faced with funding TQM, they should view TQM as the essential investment that it is rather than as an expense that drains the firm's cash. G. Christian Lantzch, vice chairman of Mellon Bank, notes, "Every time we examined a quality issue, we found a way to reduce costs. A lot of people think quality costs money. The exact opposite is true; poor quality costs a lot."[5] E/CEOs of emerging firms should remember Arden Sims's experience with TQM. His firm, Global Metallurgical

Inc., was the first small company to win the Malcolm Baldrige National Quality Award. He estimated his firm's investment in quality has produced a 40 to 1 return.[6]

Once management and the other employees have immersed themselves in learning TQM concepts and processes, they can direct their attention to operationalizing it. TQM's comprehensiveness makes it impossible for any firm to implement all of its components overnight. Smaller firms with limited resources need to heed the words of the sergeant who, seeing that his troops were running low on ammunition, said, "Choose your targets carefully and don't fire until you see the whites of their eyes!" Smaller firms will be more successful in operationalizing their TQM efforts if they choose their targets carefully.

Managers may find the salami technique and Pareto 80:20 rule to be useful concepts at this stage. The salami technique is commonly used in time management. When a person buys a "log" of salami, he or she usually cuts it into bite-size pieces. The same applies to operationalizing TQM. Management should break it into identifiable and manageable parts. Firms that have tried to implement TQM in too short a time are frequently overwhelmed by the amount and magnitude of change that may be necessary. This is not to say that the firm should just pick pieces it likes and forget about the dimensions that will require considerable time, funds, and change. Clare Crawford-Mason, coauthor of *Quality or Else,* notes, "It's not like a Chinese restaurant menu. You can't take a little from column A and a little from column B. You have to do the whole thing or it doesn't work."[7] The salami technique helps managers operationalize TQM by having them see it as a "set" of interrelated pieces.

The Pareto 80:20 rule encourages managers to identify the pieces they should focus their attention on first. If you cannot do it all at once, then you should focus your attention on the parts that will make the biggest difference. The 80:20 rule is based on the premise that in most situations, 80 percent of the total potential gain usually comes from 20 percent of the factors. This applies to employee accidents, customer profit contribution, inventory turnover, and most of the other aspects of business.

As management develops the blueprint for building TQM, it should identify the components that should be the initial targets of its attention. Management should look for the areas of the firm's operations that will make a significant difference, that can be addressed in a short period of time, and that will require the least resources. Management can use these early successes as the lead dominos that are so important in sustaining the firm's commitment to TQM. Experience has shown that firms embarking on the TQM journey should focus their "80:20" attention on benchmarking, reducing cycle time, enhancing employee empowerment, and creating a culture that fosters continuous improvement.

Benchmarking Demonstrates a Whole New Level of Performance Is Possible

Most people view completing the 26-mile marathon as some superhuman feat—the physical limit to how far a human being can run. Yet there is a tribe of Indians in Mexico that regularly runs 70 miles at a time! People in most firms get lulled into the belief that it isn't possible to make substantial improvements in efficiency, customer service, quality, and cycle times. When firms embark on the TQM journey it seems like most employees are from Missouri, the "show-me" state. Benchmarking helps people see that truly extraordinary levels of performance are not only possible, it shows them there are a number of firms that have been doing the impossible for quite a while.

Benchmarking involves comparing the firm's level of performance in key value-added areas against the levels of performance in those dimensions by the leading firms in their industry and other industries. Benchmarking helps remove the mental blinders that keep people from seeing what is possible. It also represents a way for managers to deal constructively with the naysayers who claim, "There's no way we can reduce our error rate to less than 2 percent." When they learn that L. L. Bean correctly filled 99.9 percent of their customers' orders for the year, they begin to realize that a whole new plane of performance may be possible. This figure is particularly impressive because it includes L. L. Bean's Christmas shipments that average 134,000 packages a day! It is difficult to say no firm can operate at the 99.9 percent level when Manchester Stamping Company had only seven defective parts out of the 540,000 it shipped to Honda. Solectron Corporation also provides an excellent example of what is possible. Its TQM efforts have helped chop defects from 100 parts per million to two parts per million.[8]

It is ironic that the "six sigma" concept that people scoffed at a decade ago is becoming the common denominator in benchmarking. The six sigma concept measures quality in terms of errors per million. This concept requires a whole new mindset for managers and employees who have thought about quality in terms of errors per 100 units! To measure quality in errors per million implies there will not be errors per 100 batch or even per thousand batch!

American firms have looked at quality the same way that American consumers have looked at their car's odometer. American car odometers have traditionally gone up to 99,999 miles. Most foreign cars have odometers that go up to 999,999 miles before they have to rotate over. American car odometers defined the end of the auto's life to be 100,000 miles. This "100,000-mile" mindset is similar to the mindset people had about the edge of the world until Columbus decided to test the maps and assumptions that defined the limits of what could be accomplished.

Benchmarking creates the awareness that will serve as the basis for change in how the firm does business. When people see what is possible, they usually want to learn how the other firms have made the impossible possible. When managers and employees tour and study benchmark firms, a number of them exclaim, "There's no way we can do that in our firm." At this point, management needs to qualify their skepticism with, "You're right, we can't achieve that level of performance—if we continue doing things the way we have always done them." Ford Motor Company experienced this type of situation. Management thought that it had set an ambitious goal of trimming its accounts payable staff by 20 percent. When Ford studied Mazda's accounts payable function, it was amazed to find that Mazda was able to do a comparable level of work with 80 percent fewer people than Ford![9]

Research indicates that most benchmarking firms didn't achieve their levels of performance by fine-tuning their past practices. They achieved exceptional levels of performance by looking at the total operation and developing better ways to provide quality, service, and efficiency.

Four points need to be made about benchmarking. First, while it may be exciting to try to emulate world-class firms, it may be more advisable to set the firm's sights on being the best in its present market(s). As the firm develops its proficiency, then it can shoot for world-class performance. Second, management should be selective. It should focus its attention on areas the marketplace values. Third, management needs to be sure the culture and infrastructure are prepared to support the initiatives that will be required. The firm must be mentally and physically prepared to make the changes. Joshua Hammond of the American Quality Foundation notes that if a company doesn't have a quality-oriented infrastructure in place and hasn't trained its employees in quality principles, trying to be the best will just disrupt operations.[10] Fourth, take the time to learn from the best. The International Benchmarking Clearinghouse, which is part of the American Productivity & Quality Center in Houston, maintains a database of firms that are willing to share information.

Reducing Cycle Time May Provide New Insights

Most people believe that to improve quality you need to work at a slower, more deliberate pace. Many firms that have embraced TQM have found the exact opposite to be true. Their efforts to reduce the time it takes to go through the complete cycle of a process from start to finish also yielded interesting insights into improving quality and reducing costs. James Swallow, vice president of A. T. Kearney Inc., notes, "If you go after cycle time, you lower the water level in your lake, and suddenly all the rocks stick out."[11]

As CEO of Iomega Corporation, Fred Wenninger may be the leading advocate of the role cycle time may play in a firm's TQM efforts. In 1989, it took Iomega 28 days to make a disk drive. By 1992, Iomega's production cycle was trimmed to 1.5 days. Wenninger notes, "Find your main bottleneck and attack it relentlessly." Removing bottlenecks in the process is what TQM is all about. It is a continuous effort to identify and eliminate any aspect of cycle time that slows the process. This is called the Deming Circle. As the firm removes one roadblock that slowed the overall cycle time, another factor in the cycle becomes the focus of attention. This process continues until all the roadblocks are minimized or eliminated.

Efforts to remove factors, practices, and processes that have an adverse effect on speed, quality, costs, and customer responsiveness are far more constructive than the traditional "after-the-fact" approach to fixing something once the cycle is completed. For example, Iomega spent close to $20 million a year to find and repair defective disk drives.[12] With TQM, Iomega's people redirected their attention to "mistake-proofing" the whole production process.

Some TQM changes may be as simple as clustering machines next to one another. The realignment of equipment and people not only reduces the movement of goods, it may also reduce the need for inventories along the way. TQM has traditionally been seen as an effort to fine-tune existing processes. The Japanese term *kaizen* means continuous incremental improvement. In other cases, however, radical surgery may be necessary to change the whole process.

Michael Hammer and James Champy encourage managers to throw the existing processes out so the whole process can be "reengineered" from start to finish. Their effort to go beyond TQM's traditional "incremental" approach has considerable merit. According to Hammer and Champy, "Reengineering isn't about fixing anything—the heart of business reengineering lies in the notion of discontinuous thinking—identifying and abandoning the outdated rules and fundamental assumptions that underlie current operations."[13] They also note, "Unless companies change these rules, any superficial reorganizations they perform will be no more effective than dusting the furniture in Pompeii."[14]

Efforts to reduce cycle time can also be applied to customer service, new product development, and various other processes. When Ford Motor Company realized that only half of its customers could get through to Ford's customer service representatives with its regional service numbers, management decided to scrap the whole system and replace it with a national toll-free number. Most firms would have simply increased the number of lines and customer service representatives. Ford realized that improving the existing system would not assure them of the highest quality customer service; a whole new approach needed to be developed. Ford reengineered its system so complaints are electronically forwarded to dealers who are expected to contact disgruntled customers. The local dealer is expected to initiate efforts within 24 hours to resolve the situation. Each customer's concern is also forwarded to marketing research and engineering so overall changes can be made.[15]

Whether the firm uses TQM's incremental approach or the more radical reengineering approach, it is clear that quantum improvements can be made in its competitive position. Solectron Corporation received the Baldrige Award in 1991 because it reduced its cycle time by 80 percent.[16] Bell Atlantic reengineered its process for providing high-speed digital circuits for business customers. Service is now installed in three days rather than thirty days. The new process also generates fewer errors.[17]

Cycle time may play an even greater role in the future. Firms that are able to quickly meet customer needs in a rapidly changing marketplace are more likely to be leaders in their industries. This is particularly encouraging for emerging businesses. When the marketplace was price-sensitive, larger firms could capitalize on their economies of scale. In the years ahead, speed to market may be far more important than a few price points. Smaller firms have the potential to move more quickly than their larger competitors. Steven Hronec of Arthur Anderson & Company notes that if your competitors deliver something in 20 weeks and you're all by yourself with a six-week schedule, your firm has a lot more flexibility with pricing. Arthur Anderson has a rule of thumb that says firms which offer one-third the cycle time can earn three times the profits and grow three times as fast.[18]

Employee Empowerment Is the Lifeblood of TQM

TQM represents a major reversal in the role people play in the management of most firms. In the past, managers tried to improve performance by motivating their employees to work harder. Managers frequently blamed organizational ills on the lack of employee motivation. TQM does not dwell on motivational techniques. TQM is based on the premise that employees already recognize they have a vested interest in the firm's performance and that they will help improve the firm's performance if they are given the opportunity to do so.

TQM is rewriting the rule book regarding the role managers should play in making decisions and interacting with workers. TQM encourages employees to work in problem-solving teams. It also empowers employees to correct the things that impede high levels of performance. With TQM, managers are viewed as facilitators and resource providers rather than as bosses and controllers.

More firms are moving toward self-directed work teams that operate without a formal manager. The emphasis on teams rather than individuals has had a profound effect on firms that have adopted TQM. Performance review and reward systems are focusing more on team performance than individual contribution. Managers of conventional firms usually balk at the notion of having teams of workers identify and solve organizational problems. This is to be expected for firms that have failed to provide their employees with a sufficient level of training and information about their jobs. This is why training is so important in TQM's initial stages. Training in statistical analysis and problem-solving techniques must precede employee empowerment. Without training, employees are destined to look like a bunch of fools.

The time spent training employees in problem-solving techniques and other aspects of TQM is only the tip of the iceberg. TQM constitutes an about-face from the way most people are accustomed to working. Raymond Marlow, CEO of Marlow Industries, notes management must have patience with managers and employees as they learn TQM's way of doing business. He believes it takes a couple of years before employees work smoothly in problem-solving teams. He also believes top management must display a consistent commitment to the process to keep things moving in the right direction.[19]

While a lot of the concepts in TQM seem to have a Japanese origin, there may be some major differences in how they should be approached with American workers. A study by the American Quality Foundation revealed Americans aren't as interested as the Japanese in making small incremental improvements. Americans are more interested in achieving breakthroughs. In this situation, managers adopting TQM should not dwell exclusively on fine-tuning operations. Employees should be given a longer leash. The study also indicated that while Japanese workers tend to be more methodical, American workers need to feel they have a personal stake in achieving things.[20]

Research also indicates that American workers aren't motivated when management emphasizes the importance of earnings, dividends, and market share. American workers seem to be influenced more by opportunities to do things that make a difference, things they can be proud of—quality is one of those things. If managers want the firm's employees to embrace TQM, then they will need to show how it is relevant to them and their personal well-being. If management presents TQM as the latest flavor of the month, then it should not be surprised when employees just go through the motions. If employees realize TQM is a "do-or-die" proposition, then they may enlist in the effort. TQM is like most things in life; it is never a matter of apathy—it is a matter of relevance.

The plant manager for a high-tech firm experienced one of the usual frustrations associated with implementing TQM. His efforts to get his employees to take quality seriously had fallen on deaf ears. After a couple of years of frustrating efforts to get employees to embrace the quality movement, he realized that his attention had been directed toward demonstrating why providing world-class quality was so important to the firm. He realized the employees had not seen how the failure to provide first-class quality would have a direct and immediate impact on their lives. When the workers realized that the plant would be shut down within 24 months if they could not achieve and maintain a significant quality edge, they realized they could either join the plant manager in the quality procession or join him in the unemployment line. When the workers saw a direct relationship between the quality of the firm's products and the quality of their marriages and mortgages, they joined the TQM procession!

Management Must Create a Culture that Fosters Continuous Improvement

Total quality management is based on a set of values. TQM will succeed only if the firm is totally committed to serving its customers and providing an environment that supports employee contribution. TQM is not for the faint-hearted or those who are looking for a quick fix. TQM is not like a hobby or going on a diet. TQM must be the pulse of the firm rather than something that can be done during one's spare time or sampled like an hors d'oeuvre.

TQM works best in firms that value employee input, innovation, and experimentation. It relies on collaborative efforts where people from various areas of the firm are free to identify ways to improve quality and customer service. TQM stresses the need for employees in the firm to view fellow employees and departments as "internal customers." TQM also means traditional boundaries will be torn down that have separated the firm from its suppliers as well as its customers. With TQM, the firm develops alliances with its suppliers and customers so all new levels of quality and service can be reached.

TQM is based on the philosophy that whatever the firm strives to do, it will do it the best way—the first time, every time. It eliminates the need for "inspection after the fact." Instead, TQM tries to develop what the Japanese call *poka-yoke* procedures and processes. With *poka-yoke* procedures and processes, it is nearly impossible for people in the firm to do something in any way other than the best way. Quality is thereby built into every product, service, and process from the beginning.

TQM is a never ending process. Unfortunately, most firms have adopted the attitude, "If it ain't broke, don't fix it." Firms that embrace TQM and the concepts associated with "reengineering" are not complacent. They operate with the attitude, "If it ain't broke, fix it anyway." These firms don't wait for things to break. They don't wait for their customers to complain about the lack of service or quality. They don't wait to see what their competition is doing before they try to find better ways to do things and better things to do. They leave no stone unturned in their quest for excellence. No operation is too small to be taken for granted and no customer need is too insignificant to be ignored.

In a sense, TQM firms don't compete with their competitors. They compete against themselves in their ability to fit their customers' needs like a second skin. They know that when you focus your attention on what your competitors are doing, you run the risk of losing track of what your customers really value. TQM keeps the firm from getting too wrapped up in product or service features because management knows that it is the customer—not the firm or its competition—who defines what quality and service should be.

Emerging firms should strive to meet their customers' needs to the point that the customers do not even think about doing business with any other firm. This will be possible only if the firm has a culture that is built on pride in quality, that has contempt for the status quo, that rewards continuous improvement, and that is committed to delighting the firm's customers.

TQM will be more successful in firms that demonstrate a sense of urgency and have a bias for action. It is easy for management to get so wrapped up in studying the various dimensions of TQM that employees may be hesitant to initiate it because they are afraid of making a mistake. In these instances, it may take top management's direct involvement to get TQM up and running. TQM efforts should start with parts of the firm that lend themselves to continuous improvement and provide tangible value to the customer. Initial successes will provide the momentum needed for TQM to be operationalized in other areas of the firm.

Concluding Comments: Let the Journey Begin but Be Sure It Is the Right Journey

Seeking the Baldrige Award and/or ISO 9000 certification are lofty goals even for the best firms. Emerging firms will find their criteria to be useful parameters when developing their total quality programs. Success in the journey to quality excellence, however, ultimately rests with the commitment by management to creating a firm where everyone continually strives to meet each customer's quality expectations.

The journey for excellence has led many firms astray. Many emerging firms have sought or will seek the Malcolm Baldrige Award for the wrong reasons. Their E/CEOs are driven more by their egos than their desire to provide their customers with unparalleled quality. While the Baldrige Award criteria are worthwhile, it is easy to get so wrapped up in the application and reporting process that the firm's energy and resources are devoted more to winning the award than continuing to satisfy its customers. Firms that strive to win the Baldrige Award may miss the point. Firms that strive to provide unparalleled and uncompromising quality for their customers will win something that is far more important than the Baldrige Award; they will win in the marketplace.

If companies are not aggressively pursuing total quality today, they are following a self-liquidating strategy.[21]
FRED SMITH, FOUNDER OF FEDERAL EXPRESS

CHIEF EXECUTIVE GUIDELINES

Name: Raymond Marlow, Chief Executive Officer
Company: Marlow Industries Inc.
Product/Service: Thermoelectric Cooling Modules
Sales: $13,000,000   *Number of Employees:* 150
Awards/Distinctions:

1. Malcolm Baldrige National Quality Award, 1991

2. "One of America's 10 Best Plants," *Industry Week,* 1993

General Guidelines: When it comes to improving the firm's commitment to quality and TQM, the E/CEO should keep the following tips in mind:

1. Total quality must start at the top.

2. You need the "Four Ps" for total quality to work:

   Passion—You have to be dedicated; you have to believe in it. If you do, then your people will respond.
   Persistence—You must meet consistently each week otherwise total quality will not be at the forefront of your company.

Patience—Total quality is like a religion. You don't know who is going to get it or when they are going to get it. You can stress the importance of total quality all the time without success and then all of a sudden people will see the light from a different source.

Pizza—You need to provide rewards and recognition to individuals, groups, teams, and the company as a whole for their part in the total quality system.

Proceed with Caution Guidelines:

1. Don't try to start TQM at the bottom of the firm. I've tried it, and it just doesn't work. You have to start it from the top.

2. Don't let weekly Total Quality Management (TQM) Council meetings slip. Nothing should be allowed to preempt attendance at regular meetings. Attendance needs to be enforced or people will begin to drop out. When things get busy don't consider having meetings every other week. Meetings must be weekly for total quality management to work.

CHIEF EXECUTIVE GUIDELINES

Name: Roger Telschow, President
Company: Ecoprint
Product/Service: Offset Printing
Sales: $850,000   *Number of employees:* 10
Awards/Distinctions:

1. Winner, U.S. Senate Productivity Award for Maryland
2. "Management Plus" Silver Award, National Association of Printers & Lithographers
3. Profiled in *Nation's Business*, 1993

General Guidelines: When it comes to improving the firm's commitment to quality and adopting TQM, the E/CEO should keep the following tips in mind:

1. Absolutely No. 1—Commitment, sincerity from the top. Employees have been conditioned to believe that CEOs practice the "do as I say, not as I do" method of management. Everything—yes, everything—that you do must be consistent with the new quality program or your staff will quickly become disillusioned with it.

2. No magic required. Don't view TQM as some mystical program used only by high-tech companies. It's far easier to change habits in small companies where intrastaff relationships are simpler.

3. Keep it simple. Don't use statistical analysis if a clipboard next to a machine can be used to note "down" times or spoilage.

4. Communicate! Have regular, focused meetings where everyone can participate in solving inter- and intradepartmental problems.

5. Eliminate most titles. Don't emphasize anything that sets one person or department above others in importance. Instead, focus on the team getting results for the customer.

6. Get a little wild, have fun. Stay loose, flexible; take calculated risks; freely admit your mistakes and use them to leverage your learning; maintain a sense of humor; create the sense that your company is on an adventure, and that people are part of a grand experiment.

7. Share profits and open the financials. Nothing communicates trust like showing staff members the P&L. Nothing builds teamwork and profits like making an enterprise everyone's golden goose. About 25 percent of our profits are reinvested in the employees.

Proceed with Caution Guidelines:

1. As CEO, get personal goals straight first. What income and work stress will you accept? Only then decide how and when to implement TQM. You must first believe in a plan and see its benefits before selling it to others.

2. Keep asking if you, yourself, are taking TQM to heart. Do you *really* hear criticisms that customers voice? Do you discount them or act on them?

3. Remember that the customer drives TQM, but that you also must "choose" your customers. You can't be everything to everyone.

4. Remember that market responsiveness and developing a market niche is still paramount. Manufacturing defect-free buggy whips doesn't guarantee a market or a profit.

5. Follow your intuition more. Do not emulate others even if they appear successful if their management style or program doesn't agree with your own sensibilities.

I Would Be Particularly Careful Not to:

1. "Enable" employees who won't buy into the program. Have the courage to remove responsibility from, or let go, employees who

simply cannot embrace the changes that a quality program may create.

2. Judge success by one month's results. Look at the long term and have absolute confidence that incremental changes will make the difference.

3. Forget that TQM is probably the *most vital* in the sales department. Rather than trying to "sell" somebody something, find out how to add value to the relationship: approach customers as partners, learn their business, hear their problems, help make *them* a success.

4. Take everything on at once. Focus on one or at most two key areas so as to not overwhelm yourself or your employees.

19

Going International

Parties who want milk should not seat
themselves on a stool in the middle of a field
in hopes the cow will back up to them.
ELBERT HUBBARD

Emerging firms rarely consider exporting their products or expanding their operations into foreign markets. When they do, it is usually for offensive or defensive reasons. Firms that take the offensive or "proactive" approach do so because they want to capitalize on the opportunities that may lie outside the borders of the U.S. A number of firms, however, approach going international from a defensive or "reactive" stance because their domestic markets have either dried up or competition has become so intense that it is difficult to make a profit. This brings up the first law of going international: "Don't even consider it if your firm doesn't have its domestic act together."

Firms experiencing a healthy rate of growth usually believe their present markets will continue to support additional growth. Their managers focus their attention on present customers and present products-services. While this may be quite natural, this "management by braille" could have a major opportunity cost. Managers who focus their attention on domestic markets may completely overlook the opportunities that may lie outside their country's boundaries.

Some E/CEOs demonstrate their complacency or arrogance by stating, "If people in foreign lands really want our products, then they can contact us to buy them!" This is similar to the executive of a major brewery who was informed by distributors that customers were having difficulty opening the pop-tops of the firm's beer cans. The executive responded, "If they want it bad enough, then they will find some way to open the cans!"

Other E/CEOs have adopted the reactive "field of dreams" philosophy that is captured in the quotation at the beginning of this chapter. They feel that if their firm makes a superior product, then people from all over the world will seek them out. This rarely happens.

E/CEOs need to do a gut check and ask themselves if they want their firms to be "opportunity-driven" or "comfort-driven." If they are committed to being opportunity-driven, then they must investigate every possible avenue for sustained growth. In many cases, E/CEOs find foreign markets may have more lasting value than domestic markets. Foreign markets may be less saturated and consumers may be less price-sensitive. Financial incentives may also be available for exporting and/or expanding operations to other countries.

Procrastination and Rationalization: The Real Reasons for Staying at Home

E/CEOs give numerous reasons why their firms have not explored the opportunities associated with going international. They frequently say they don't have the time to investigate foreign markets. The lack of information and the lack of capital are also cited as reasons for focusing exclusively on domestic markets. A few E/CEOs even bring up trade barriers and red tape as reasons for not going international. A closer look at the reasons, however, usually reveals that they are merely smoke screens or rationalizations. Most E/CEOs don't pursue international opportunities because they do not know what is involved in exporting their products.

Few E/CEOs have an international background. As entrepreneurs, they may have used their engineering background to develop the product that served as the foundation for their new venture. If their background was in sales or finance, then they may have drawn on their experience to help get their firms started. Their lack of experience and education in foreign markets and exporting processes keeps them from pursuing foreign opportunities.

Firms that stay in domestic markets usually are managed by E/CEOs who are unwilling to take the time to learn what is involved in going international. Ironically, the process associated with going international is not very different from the process used when analyzing domestic markets. While the languages and customs may vary from one country to the next, the approach to analyzing potential markets is almost the same.

Going International: Where to Begin?

The E/CEO should not be expected to be the firm's international specialist. The E/CEO is responsible, however, for charting the future direction of the firm. If the E/CEO is not versed in the nature of foreign opportunities and the processes associated with capitalizing on them, then the firm is destined to wear blinders that will limit the firm to domestic markets. If the E/CEO is committed to being at the helm of an opportunity-driven firm, then he or she must recognize that foreign markets may offer even better opportunities than those to be found in domestic markets.

The first step in going international involves the commitment to being an opportunity-driven firm. The second step involves the realization that the United States may not be the center of the universe. The United States constitutes only 5 percent of the world's population and one-third of the world's purchasing power. Numerous economies are growing at a much faster rate than the U.S. economy. It may be logical to focus the firm's attention on developed economies like Canada, Europe, and Japan. Other countries in the Pacific Rim, South America, and the Middle East have economics that are beginning to blossom. The notion of playing "one or two markets ahead" indicates that it may even be worthwhile to investigate the less obvious "up-and-coming" countries.

The third step involves developing some familiarity with what is involved in going international. This includes understanding the various levels of involvement, identifying the countries that represent the best opportunities for exporting, and using the sources of information and assistance that are available. The third step does not require a high level of proficiency. It merely involves developing a feel for the various facets associated with exporting.

As E/CEOs begin to open their eyes to foreign opportunities, they learn exporting is not the exclusive realm of Fortune 500 firms. They learn that smaller, emerging firms are also capitalizing on foreign opportunities. When E/CEOs learn that Weaver Popcorn, a small firm located in Van Buren, Indiana, has garnered 60 percent of the Japanese popcorn market, they begin to realize that almost any type and size of firm can go international.[1] Christopher Bartlett of Harvard University has observed, "The newcomers have the huge advantage [over large firms] of starting fresh."[2] A recent article in *Business Week* noted that the future may belong to younger, smaller companies with nimble feet and a more specific focus. Smaller firms may be able to swiftly seize new markets and develop new products. These attributes will enable emerging firms to gain a competitive advantage in rapidly-evolving global markets.[3]

Learning about international activities is similar to learning linear programming. While E/CEOs may not need to be specialists in linear programming, being familiar with it enables them to know when a business situation can be addressed by it. The key is for E/CEOs to know enough about linear programming so they can converse with people who specialize in linear programming. The same logic applies to going international.

The fourth step involves selecting an individual to be responsible for coordinating the firm's efforts to go international. The person selected for this role should have the time and interest to explore foreign opportunities. This person must be patient yet persistent. Going international takes time and involves numerous frustrations. If E/CEOs are serious about pursuing foreign opportunities, then they should make sure that the job is approached on more than a "time available" basis. This should be a full-time position, but a half-time position may be reasonable in the beginning.

The fifth step involves setting tangible goals for the first year of exploration. The person responsible for analyzing foreign markets should be expected to identify: (1) potential markets, (2) products-services that appear to be the most marketable, (3) changes in packaging, size, labeling, warranties, and the like that may need to be made, (4) avenues for selling and exporting the firm's products-services, and (5) cost-volume-profit-investment-cash flow projections. The irony of the situation is that the firm should be following a similar procedure when it considers expanding its operations and product-service offerings within the United States. The only major difference is that it may take a little more time and resourcefulness to gather and analyze information about foreign markets.

Sources of Information and Assistance Are Readily Available

It has been said that managing an emerging venture can be pretty lonely. This isn't necessarily the case when it comes to going international. Numerous organizations charge little, if any, fee for advice on how to export products-services. E/CEOs and their staffs can go from being complete novices to having a modest level of proficiency in a short period of time if they utilize the services and databases that are available today.

The federal government provides considerable assistance to firms that want to export their products. The government realizes that when U.S. firms export products, more people will be employed. Exports also help the country's balance of payments. It is for these same reasons that little assistance is provided for importing items into the United States from other countries.

Firms interested in exporting need to begin their education by securing a copy of *Export Programs: A Business Directory of U.S. Government Resources* from the U.S. Department of Commerce. This guide can be ordered from the

Trade Information Center by calling 1-800-872-8723. The Commerce Department provides a wealth of information on the mechanics of exporting and the nature of other countries. The following agencies offer assistance:

1. International Trade Administration (ITA). The ITA offers assistance and information to help exporters. It oversees the U.S. and Foreign Commercial Service, which has a network of trade specialists in over 100 U.S. cities and 68 countries. These offices provide information on foreign markets, agent-distributor location services, and trade leads. They also provide counseling on business opportunities, trade barriers, and prospects abroad. Specialists determine a firm's readiness to export and provide suggestions on how to strengthen the firm's export capability. Overseas offices also collect information about trends.

2. The International Economic Policy (IEP) Country Desk Officers. The IEP provides information on trade potential for U.S. products in specific countries. Specialists look at the needs of a particular company in the full context of a country's economy, trade policies, and political situation. Information can be provided on market size and growth as well as other trade data. Their "Business Information Service for Newly Independent States" provides one-stop shopping for firms interested in doing business in what was the Soviet Union. Special assistance is also provided through the Japan Export Information Center, The Eastern Europe Information Center, and the Latin America/Caribbean Business Development Center.

3. Trade Development Industry Officers. These specialists provide assistance to firms as well as manufacturing and service industry associations. Attention is directed to identifying trade opportunities and barriers. This office also develops export marketing plans and coordinates trade missions and fairs.

The Department of Commerce also provides the following reports:[4]

Foreign Trade Report. This monthly report is prepared by the Bureau of the Census. It contains information on the shipments of all merchandise from the U.S. to foreign countries.

Market Share Reports. Data is provided about U.S. manufacturing export activity for the year. This information is useful in monitoring trends and comparing the competitive position of U.S. and foreign exporters. Market share reports may also help identify potential countries for export activity.

Export Statistics Profile. Export activity for various products is compiled. A brief analysis of the export potential for various products is also provided.

Market Research Reports.   These reports analyze the market for a given product in a given country. Marketing practices, trade barriers, and potential buyers are also identified.

The State Department and the U.S. Small Business Administration also provide useful information and assistance. The State Department prepares "Background Notes" for specific countries. These reports summarize a nation's population, economy, government, geography, and foreign policy priorities. The SBA sponsors training programs on exporting. The SBA also coordinates "matchmaking" trade delegations that help firms new to exporting make contacts. Small Business Development Centers cosponsored by the SBA at numerous universities provide counseling.

Large accounting firms and banks usually have international departments or specialists to assist their clients in going international. Accounting firms may be able to provide information on how to report income as well as tax obligations. Accounting firms may also be in a position to offer advice on exporting if some of their clients are already doing business in a targeted country. Most banks have banking "partners" in other countries that can provide information and contacts. The Small Business Foundation of America (1-800-243-7232) offers an export hot line. The *Journal of Commerce* can also be beneficial. It lists export opportunities. AT&T provides assistance for firms seeking export information.

Getting Involved: It May Be Best to Take It One Step at a Time

Going international is not an "all-or-nothing" proposition. Firms usually can select a level of involvement that corresponds with the level of opportunity and the availability of resources. Going international can take place on the following levels:

Level 1—Accepting Orders: This is the most passive approach to exporting. The firm does not market its products-services outside its domestic markets. The firm merely responds to orders on an invoice-by-invoice basis. Under these conditions, the firm develops only a minimal level of proficiency in serving foreign customers and shipping its products.

Level 2—Direct Marketing: The firm may include foreign prospects in its promotional programs. While it may be trying to develop foreign accounts, the firm is not involved in any direct selling efforts. The firm is able to provide better customer service because one or more members of the firm's staff may specialize in handling foreign orders.

Level 3—Export Management Companies (EMCs):   These U.S.-based companies usually specialize in a product group or country. They market and sell the firm's products. These firms may promote products for numerous companies so they should be checked out to be sure they will give the firm sufficient attention.

Level 4—Export Trading Companies (ETCs):   These firms also market and sell products in foreign countries. These firms, however, take title to the firm's products and pay the firm directly. Some countries insist on the use of export management companies or export trading companies. These types of firms may serve as an indicator of the product's marketability. If the products are well received, then the firm may consider moving to the next level.

Level 5—Firm's Sales Force: The first four levels of involvement may not have required much up-front investment by the firm. Except for level two, the firm incurs expenses only when orders come in. Level three and level four can serve as test markets. They may give the firm an idea of: (1) the level of interest in the firm's products, (2) the types of people or organizations that buy the product, (3) price-sensitivity, and (4) what changes should be considered in the product's configuration. If sufficient interest is expressed, then the firm may consider having its own sales staff market its products to prospects rather than relying on a third party. This approach has its trade-offs. While it may be better to have someone on the firm's payroll whose sole focus is the firm's products, EMCs and ETCs usually have established considerable goodwill with prospects. It may take quite a while for the firm's sales staff to establish contacts. Firms considering level five should consider hiring someone who already is familiar with the foreign country and has personal contacts.

Level 6—Establishing Foreign Offices: Level five involves having a salesperson prospect and serve a foreign market. The salesperson then forwards each order to the firm's headquarters. With level six, the firm establishes a foreign office to provide sales support and customer service. This permits the firm to tailor its activities to foreign market(s). Level six may enable the firm to investigate growth opportunities and to provide service after the sale.

Level 7—Licensing: There are two instances when the firm may consider licensing its technology or name to a foreign firm. If the firm finds certain advantages to having its products manufactured in the foreign market, then it may consider licensing the rights to manufacture the product to a firm in that country. This enables the firm to increase its revenue without any major investment. The firm receives a royalty for licensing the rights and/or for each unit manufactured or sold. Licensing is usually for a specified period of time. If the product sells well, then the firm may consider setting up its own production-service facilities or forming a joint venture with that or another firm. The firm may also consider the licensing route if the targeted country prohibits any form of ownership by a firm outside that country.

Level 8—Joint Venture: The firm may decide to expand its manufacturing or service capability outside the United States. The firm may be able to provide higher quality, better service, quicker delivery, and/or more efficient operations. Some countries do not allow a foreign firm to be the sole owner of business property in their countries. In these instances, the firm may consider a joint venture. Firms may consider joint ventures even in countries that allow total ownership because the "local" partner is more familiar with business regulations and labor practices. Joint ventures also reduce the firm's capital requirements and risks.

Level 9—Company Ownership: If the market opportunity looks like it has lasting potential and the firm will be in a position to enjoy a competitive advantage by expanding its operations, management may consider establishing a complete operation in a foreign country. This expansion may take the form of a foreign division or subsidiary. Tax factors and the relative uniqueness of the foreign operation usually affect how such an operation is formally organized.

Level 10—Hybrid: One of the interesting things about going international is that the firm can be a hybrid of almost all nine levels. The firm may promote its products directly to Canada, use export trading companies in South America, have its own sales force in Europe, license its name in Indonesia, do a joint venture in Mexico, and have a subsidiary in Australia. The first few levels offer considerable flexibility. If the market opportunity is expected to be lucrative and lasting, then the firm may consider going to a higher level. Quintile Transnational Corporation of Morrisville, North Carolina, is a good example. In less than 10 years, this firm has opened offices in London, Frankfurt, and Paris. Quintile Transnational has also established a joint venture in Japan.[5]

Beware of Ethnocentrism: When in Rome, Do as the Romans Do!

Foreign markets, like domestic markets, can be seen as "windows of opportunity" that stay open only so long. According to Patricia F. Saiki, former administrator for the U.S. Small Business Administration, the question is no longer "Should I consider exporting?" The question is now, "How soon can I enter the global marketplace?" The zeal to export the firm's products, however, should be tempered with some caution. Management must look before it leaps into foreign waters.

Firms about to embark on their journey into foreign markets should keep the concept of "ethnocentrism" in mind. Ethnocentrism means that the people in one country tend to consider their practices to be the "one best way." While this concept has echoed in the lecture halls of cultural anthropology classes on college campuses for decades, numerous firms have encountered major setbacks when going international because their managers were guilty of ethnocentrism. Firms that exhibit ethnocentrism, that fail to study the unique culture, and that do not calibrate their business practices to the targeted country are destined to offer the wrong marketing mix. They also run the risk of offending foreign prospects.

Patricia Saiki's statement seems to underscore the statement, "He who hesitates is lost." Firms that have studied Japanese business practices, however, know that in negotiations Japanese executives believe, "He who speaks first loses!" The Japanese consider patience to be a sign of strength. Americans are known around the world for their lack of patience and lack of respect for foreign customs. These traits can be particularly detrimental in countries where it may take months to develop a business relationship. In Japan, American managers must avoid discussing business when they first meet Japanese prospects. Moreover, when they get around to finaliz ing any type of agreement, contracts should not be emphasized as they are in the United States. Japanese culture is built on trust rather than litigation.

Firms that want to minimize the likelihood of being ethnocentric should pay particular attention to cultural differences. The greater the differences between the targeted country and the U.S., the greater the need to study that country and to tailor the firm's approach to doing business in that country. Numerous firms have learned that the failure to study the targeted country can lead to disastrous results. Chevrolet has the distinction of committing what may be the corporate world's biggest ethnocentric blunder. Soon after Chevrolet introduced its new midsized Nova to South American markets, customers expressed little interest in it. Management was embarrassed when it learned that the word "Nova" meant "no go" in certain South American countries!

Smaller firms have also been surprised when they offered their products for the first time in certain foreign markets. When Ben and Jerry's opened a store in Russia, the staff was shocked when customers began spitting out their frozen yogurt. It turned out that Russian consumers were not accustomed to having chunks of brownies, cookies, or fruit in frozen products.[6] Another American firm was surprised when it tried to export tennis balls to Japan. Penn Racquet Sports found that while the Japanese may be interested in tennis,

Japanese distributors and consumers expressed little interest in the firm's tennis balls.[7] The Japanese couldn't understand why the can contained three tennis balls. Japanese consumers wanted only two balls. After all, when people play tennis, they only need two tennis balls. The Japanese were not willing to pay for 50 percent more product than they needed.

Domino's found it had to change the size of its pizzas and modify its packaging if it wanted to appeal to Japanese consumers. Domino's downsized its pizzas when it found the Japanese aren't big eaters. Evidently, big portions did not appeal to Japanese consumers, especially female consumers.[8] Domino's also found that Japanese consumers prefer to go out to eat and are accustomed to free delivery. Domino's thereby needed to develop a strategy that was quite different from what had made it a household name in the United States.

Domino's isn't the only firm that has found it necessary to modify its product-service offering and delivery system. Dean Foods Company found that it could not distribute its dairy products in Mexico the same way it does in the United States. Some supermarkets in Mexico turn the electricity off overnight. This practice causes ice cream to repeatedly melt and refreeze. To enter the Mexican market, Dean Foods would have to provide its own refrigerated cases to foster longer shelf life. Dean's management also recognized they would have to pay the store to maintain the electricity through the night.[9] Ben and Jerry's encountered similar problems when it opened its first store in Russia. Russian freezer trucks could not get cold enough.

Going International: Small Steps and Similar Markets May Be Advisable at First

E/CEOs who contemplate entering foreign markets face an interesting dilemma. While they don't want to miss out on the opportunity to penetrate new markets, they also need to be cognizant of the time, money, and risks associated with going where they have not gone before. This may be one of the instances when the short-term incremental approach to doing business may be better than the long-term backwards approach.

Someone once said, "You don't test the depth and temperature of the water by jumping in with both feet." It may be better to test foreign waters on a small scale and to start with markets that are similar to the ones the firm is already serving. When Dick Rennick, president of American Leak Detection Inc., started looking for foreign opportunities for his franchise, he looked for markets that were similar to his domestic markets.

American Leak Detection uses proprietary technology to find leaks that are hidden in concrete and other inaccessible materials.[10] Rennick began his search by identifying the criteria he would use in analyzing alternative foreign markets. Rennick's firm had already been very successful in finding leaks in Southern swimming pools so he looked for countries with a large number of swimming pools. He then narrowed the list of potential markets to include only the ones that placed a premium on water. If water is plentiful and cheap, pool owners don't have a "bias for action" and "sense of urgency" to have a leak fixed. Rennick also placed a premium on English-speaking countries so he would not be faced with a language barrier.

These criteria quickly directed his attention to Australia. Rennick contacted the Australian embassy to request information on the population as well as the number of swimming pools. The Australian embassy also provided leads for trade associations, trade publications, and even a few contractors who knew the nuances of swimming pool repair. The data and networking proved worthwhile. Within a few months, Rennick sold franchise rights for Australia and New Zealand.[11]

Exporter Beware: Even the Most Similar Markets May Present Challenges

Most small firms follow Rennick's approach when taking their first steps into foreign markets. Canada's proximity and relative similarity have made it a logical export target. A closer look, however, reveals that exporting goods to Canadian markets will require a certain level of resourcefulness and resilience. Bending Branches Inc. provides an excellent example of the types of challenges that may be encountered. Bending Branches probably had one of the easiest products to market in Canada. The Minneapolis-based company makes hockey sticks. Nearly 50 percent of the firm's sales are to Canadian consumers. Yet, the additional growth presented an additional challenge. Exporting to Canada affects the firm's profitability because the dollar's value fluctuates.[12]

Other firms have found additional factors need to be included in the exporting equation when doing business in Canada. The most obvious difference is that English is not the primary language in many parts of Canada. This will affect correspondence with distributors and customers. Canada's use of the metric system may also affect labeling and packaging. Finally, the Canadian government may protect certain domestic industries by imposing restrictions on products coming into the country. For example, I Can't Believe It's Yogurt ran into problems when it tried to ship its products to Canada. Canada has placed numerous restrictions on importing dairy products.

The challenges associated with exporting tend to increase at an exponential rate as firms consider countries farther away that have business practices markedly different from those in the United States. This is particularly true when it comes to meeting product standards and collecting accounts receivable. Efforts by the European Community to develop a common set of environmental, health, and safety standards have had an impact on U.S. firms interested in European markets. The new standards may necessitate changes in design and packaging. This effort may be beneficial to U.S. exporters in the long run because the new requirements will be the same for a number of countries. Exporters will not need to meet different standards for each European country.

Collecting accounts receivable represents another challenge. Richard Holcomb of Pioneer Software states, "Companies outside the United States typically pay in 120 to 150 days instead of 30 to 60 days."[13] Holcomb has also found that foreign bad debt write-offs are also about five times greater than domestic write-offs. Fortunately, Pioneer Software's products have a high enough gross margin so the firm can handle a higher level of bad debts than most firms.

Ed Mayorga, CEO of R&E Electronics, demonstrates that whenever there is the will to meet a challenge, there is a way to meet it. His firm not only factors in the higher costs associated with doing business abroad, it also requires its foreign customers to make payments in U.S. dollars directly to its Wilmington, North Carolina, headquarters.[14] This approach to billing is beneficial because it usually means that only U.S. taxes may need to be considered.

Going International May Strengthen the Firm's Position in Domestic Markets

Firms that go international usually find that doing business abroad improves their strength and performance in their domestic markets. Going international encourages management to take an objective look at its assumptions and practices. It also encourages management to learn new ways to do what it has been doing at home.

Foreign distributors and consumers may have much higher standards when it comes to product quality. German and Japanese consumers are known for being more thorough than U.S. consumers. Numerous firms test new products in Japan and Germany before introducing them to their U.S. markets. Firms that sell only to domestic markets tend to assume that if something goes wrong with the product, the customer can send it back to the firm for repair or replacement. Firms that export their products tend to concentrate on building quality into their products rather than relying on service after the sale.

Firms that export to Europe are also far more likely to be familiar with ISO 9000 standards than firms that market their products only to domestic markets. As more firms in the U.S. and abroad require ISO 9000 certification of their suppliers, firms that are already meeting those standards will have an advantage over firms that continue to keep their heads in the sand.

Emerging firms often find that going international provides other dividends. Firms involved in international trade are usually seen in a different light than other small firms. Going international, even on a very limited scale, also affects corporate culture. Firms that export products tend to have more of an external orientation and be more open to new ideas. Their employees also share the excitement and pride associated with selling the firm's products abroad. These firms, in turn, may find it easier to attract talented people.

Going international may also keep foreign firms from entering the firm's domestic markets. Firms that are able to demonstrate their ability to compete on foreign soil send a message that they can compete with any firm—anywhere! Firms that fail to adopt a global perspective are destined to be attacked on their home front by foreign firms that prey on complacent firms that take their domestic consumers for granted. Emerging firms would be well advised to heed military strategists who say, "The best defense is a good offense." Going global may be one way to keep foreign and domestic elephants from trampling emerging firms to death.

Concluding Comments: There Has Never Been a Better Time

This may be the best time for emerging firms to go international. Almost every condition is in place to support exporting the firm's products and expanding the firm's operations to foreign markets. Foreign economies continue to grow at a faster rate than the domestic economy. Technology now enables smaller firms to communicate and transfer funds to almost anywhere in the world. Freight forwarders can expedite the movement of goods. Even the government is trying to help firms.

Going international is not without its risks and naysayers. E/CEOs will hear various concerns expressed by people within their firms about going international. People will be concerned about language differences, trade restrictions, and having to change the way they do business. Yet the risks associated with exporting the firm's products are markedly lower than the risks associated with starting the enterprise or diversifying the firm's product-service offering. The risks of going international can be reduced if management does its homework and paces the firm's expansion. The firm can enter additional markets as it develops additional proficiency.

With time, the firm may shift from the traditional "selling" mode to the more proactive "marketing" mode. In the selling mode, the firm tries to find foreign markets that will buy its present product-service offering. The marketing approach starts with the analysis of foreign markets. Attention is directed to finding needs that are not being met well enough or at all. The firm then develops products-services to meet those needs. Firms that are opportunity-driven and have extensive international experience may even consider "corpreneurial" growth strategies that offer state-of-the-art technology to emerging markets.

Firms that are having difficulty making ends meet should not consider going international. Management needs to be sure it has its act together at home before it enters foreign markets. Firms that are unable to develop a competitive advantage at home are not likely to have the strength to compete away from home. Going international, however, represents an avenue for transforming a healthy firm into an exceptional enterprise. There is no question that the world is becoming a global marketplace. Firms that are positioned to capitalize on emerging global opportunities will be in the driver's seat. Firms that ignore or deny the new global reality will be left in their dust.

The biggest nontariff barrier to Americans in the world is the attitude of the CEO.[15]
KENNETH BUTTERWORTH,
CHAIRMAN OF LOCTITE CORPORATION

CHIEF EXECUTIVE GUIDELINES

Name: Fred Spike, President
Company: Sun International Trading Company
Product/Service: Import/Export Trading Company
Sales: $10,000,000   *Number of Employees:* 65
Awards/Distinctions: North Carolina World Trade Association Import Award

General Guidelines: When it comes to entering foreign markets, the E/CEO should keep the following tips in mind:

1. Enter first the markets with which you are most familiar or from which you have the most customer demand for your product or

service. Don't be influenced too strongly by the siren's call of markets that have the most theoretical potential.

2. Utilize all free and inexpensive means of product introduction including press releases in trade journal, and state and federal government publications.

3. Determine for yourself the marketability of your product in your targeted markets. The opinions of those who "think" they know your market are frequently unreliable even if they have lived in the country you have targeted.

4. Sales strength in the United States indicates virtually nothing about your foreign market potential.

5. Limit your targeted market to a geographical size you can handle.

Proceed with Caution Guidelines:

1. Attend foreign trade shows in order to get a better feel for your targeted market and competition.

2. Get to know your distribution system and the key distributors in your targeted market.

3. Hire employees with export experience. Foreign language skills are desirable at virtually all employee levels.

4. From the beginning, design your products, packaging, and label with the targeted export market in mind.

5. Be prepared to deliver your goods in a timely, cost-effective manner.

And I Would Be Particularly Careful Not *to:*

1. Grant exclusive distributor rights too hastily. Many distributors expect *you* to do all the selling while they collect their profits.

2. Rely too heavily on foreign agents for market advice. They rarely know your products or your customers as well as you do.

3. Waste time on potential distributors who promise you fantastic sales when they know little, if anything, about your products and markets. They are treasure hunters hoping to strike it rich.

CHIEF EXECUTIVE GUIDELINES

Name: David Soderquist, Chief Executive Officer
Company: First Team Sports Inc.
Product/Service: Sporting Goods and Recreational Products
Sales: $38,000,000   *Number of Employees:* 42
Awards/Distinctions: Business Week's "Hot Growth Companies," 1993

General Guidelines: When it comes to entering foreign markets, the E/
CEO should keep the following tips in mind:

1. When you go overseas, despite what some people may tell you about
    working directly with someone in the target country who knows the
    "ins and outs" of that country, it's still your business and no one
    knows your business better than you. You need to be cognizant of
    local laws, customs, and the like—these factors are important and
    you need to incorporate them in your actions.

2. No one will act with the same sense of urgency as someone in your
    firm. For example, many Europeans operate with a multiyear time
    horizon. Your staff will operate in the here and now—they will act in
    the best interests of your company. Europeans are not reviewed on
    their performance in the short term; they like talking about the future
    and trends. Your people will have a greater "sense of urgency" and
    "bias for action." Your people will focus their attention on closing
    deals rather than just developing "relationships." You can't afford to
    "wait" for things to happen. Your staff will need to be in a position to
    "make things happen," and the only way to make things happen is if
    you have your products placed on the retail shelf.

3. Good news! Many Europeans openly welcome dealing "directly" with
    U.S. firms. This is a major change, and it will help U.S. manufacturers.

4. More good news! The Pacific Rim countries are also welcoming U.S.
    products. This is particularly true of the "emerging" Pacific Rim
    countries. They embrace new ideas quicker. The "established" Pacific
    Rim countries still approach doing business in a slower, more "con-
    ventional" manner.

Proceed with Caution Guidelines:

1. If you speak with someone in the "channels," they will want you to go
    the "conventional" way. Beware: this slows distribution time and
    adds to the retail sales price. Try to deal direct—bypass the interme-
    diaries whenever it is possible.

2. Beware of joint ventures or other arrangements that may slow the placement of products before the ultimate consumer.

And I Would Be Particularly Careful Not to:

Get involved in "exclusive distribution" deals. Watch out for them; they can be very dangerous.

20

Other Growth Dimensions to Keep in Mind

SECTION A
DEVELOPING AN EFFECTIVE MANAGEMENT INFORMATION SYSTEM

If you were to ask a first time entrepreneur, "What will it take to succeed?" he or she may say, "Sales and enough money to get up and running." When you pose the same question to E/CEOs who have been managing their firms for a while, their list will usually include, "An effective management information system." Firms that enjoy sustained growth seem to be different in at least one major dimension from firms that faded—they had an effective management information system in place from the beginning that enabled them to manage the firm's growth.

Growth without a solid management information system is like flying at night without instruments. Sustained growth is seldom the result of good luck or a charismatic E/CEO. Sustained growth is the product of the E/CEO and management team consistently making the right decisions. Most emerging firms get into trouble because the management team either does not have the information it needs to make the right decisions or because it chooses to ignore information that is available. In both cases, the E/CEO and management team are flying by the seats of their pants.

Few E/CEOs have a strong financial background or operate with a management information system perspective. This is one of the primary reasons why most emerging firms experience serious growing pains. Their firms may be growing but profits do not follow. Before long, things fall through the cracks. In many cases, record sales levels are quickly followed by a corporate death spiral. Growth-produced elation quickly turns into desperation when receivables fail to come in, when inventory turn slows, when repeat purchases wane, and when the all too typical negative cash flow turns into no cash flow.

Decisions Will Only Be as Good as the Management Information System

Managerial decisions will only be as good as the information that is incorporated in the decision processes. Having the right information at the right time and in the right format gives the firm an edge in the marketplace. Information plays a key role in the strategic direction of the firm as well as in the managing of daily operations.

There is no way for the E/CEO to be in all places at one time. A well-developed management information system can extend management's sight and hearing. The management information system provides an aerial photograph of the firm. It permits management to see what is going on outside the firm as well as what is happening within the firm.

Management information systems are like corporate cultures. Every firm has a unique corporate culture and some sort of management information system. The key to success is having a management information system that enhances performance. One of the things that distinguishes good management information systems from mediocre ones is that the best ones are comprehensive. They focus on financial as well as nonfinancial information. An effective management information system provides information about factors and forces that need to be monitored closely as well as insights into what should be changed.

The management information system can serve as the firm's early warning system. It should function as the firm's radar by scanning the horizon for trends that will keep the firm from being blindsided. Firms that are able to identify opportunities before their competitors will be in a better position to capitalize on them. The same holds true for problems and threats. The sooner the firm identifies them, the easier it will be to prevent or minimize them.

The management information system should also function as the firm's sonar. It should look below the surface to detect cracks in the firm's operating system that tend to be overlooked during rapid growth. In all the excitement of filling sales orders, it is easy for a firm not to notice that receivables are taking a day or two longer to come in, that the gross margin is slipping, that returns are becoming a larger percentage of sales, and that travel expenses are growing at a rate faster than revenue. A properly designed management system is like a CAT scan that identifies things before they are visible—before they become life threatening.

Selectivity Is Crucial

Today's information revolution seems to bring new meaning to the phrase, "Water, water everywhere, but not a drop to drink!" Advances in computer hardware and software have produced mounds of printouts and megabytes of databases. Yet it is the quality and timeliness of the information not the quantity of data that matters. A study by *Inc.* magazine indicated that nearly 40 percent of the CEOs surveyed felt they do not have enough information to run their companies.[1] Most management information systems are designed to provide data and leave it up to the executives to find what they need. Executives have too little time to play hide-and-seek.

Management information systems need to be tailored to the needs of the decision makers rather than software programmers or accountants. Pat Lancaster, who founded Lantech Inc., developed a reporting system to fit his particular needs. He had tried most of the conventional approaches to monitoring his business but found they didn't give him the information he needed. He was particularly frustrated with financial reports. According to Lancaster, "Numbers are great, but they talk about the past."[2] He now has each of the firm's top managers fill out a form each week that provides him with information about product quality, customer status, upcoming deadlines, and other areas that need to be monitored closely. Lancaster has found the reports have another benefit. They also cut down on meeting time.[3]

Management by Exception
Provides Focus

The firm's management information system should incorporate the concept of "management by exception." Once key performance indicators are identified, management should determine what constitutes each factor's green (safety) zone, yellow (caution) zone, and red (intervene) zone. The green zone represents the range of performance for that factor in which everything is going as planned or expected. This means management does not need to change what the firm is doing. The yellow zone constitutes a "caution" zone—management needs to proceed with caution. Performance needs to be closely monitored because a trend may be starting to take shape. If performance stays in the yellow zone for two consecutive periods (months, weeks, or days), then management may need to take action to get the firm back on track. The red zone represents an "exceptional" variance. Exceptional variations may be good (higher-than-expected sales) or bad (higher-than-expected returns). Management needs to quickly modify the firm's strategy or operations when these deviations occur.

The management information system needs to be particularly sensitive to the factors that can jeopardize the firm's growth and survival. Key factors need to be monitored closely and often. Generally speaking, the longer it will take to correct something, the more frequently it should be monitored. The same applies to the size of the yellow and red zones. If small changes in a performance factor can have a major impact on the firm's performance, then the yellow zone needs to be very narrow. Few things go exactly as planned. The sooner deviations are detected, the sooner they can be corrected.

An Effective System Permits "Bifocal" Management

Most effective management information systems are two-dimensional. They permit the management team to monitor performance factors that have a significant impact on the firm's success. They are based on the 80:20 rule. By identifying and monitoring the few (20 percent) factors that make the greatest (80 percent) difference, management can focus its attention.

Some E/CEOs, however, have developed management information systems to make sure no stone goes unturned. They go to great lengths to analyze the 80 percent of their firm's operations that constitute the 20 percent as well. Their systems probe every nook and cranny for anything that can enhance their firm's profitability and cash flow.

Ken Hendricks, founder of ABC Supply Company, has elevated cost-consciousness to the point that it is now an integral part of his firm's culture. Hendricks notes that 3 percent of sales is what separates profit and loss in most firms. His firm has standards for everything. Every P&L item is stated as a percent of sales. By monitoring every expense—from sales per employee all the way down to gasoline expense per truck—Hendrick's firm is able to get the most efficient use of its resources and minimize waste. His management information system gives his firm an edge. According to Hendricks, "When you do all the things we do, you don't have to worry about big companies coming in and eating your lunch."[4]

Cabletron Systems Inc. is another company that has succeeded by staying light on its feet. Cabletron's management team has made a deliberate effort to keep costs under control. Bob Monaco, Cabletron's director of operations, captured the core of his firm's philosophy when he noted, "Run the company as if it's not making money and you'll always make money."[5]

Concluding Comments: Good Information Opens the Doors to Many Possibilities

A comprehensive information system will not only improve the quality of management's decisions, it will also increase the firm's ability to secure debt financing, to offer stock, to acquire other firms, and to form strategic alliances. It may also facilitate the sale of the firm if that is a consideration. Bankers, investors, and other interested parties insist on good information. If management is unable to provide the type of information they seek, then the firm may not be in a position to pass through a window of opportunity when it opens. The interesting thing about opportunities is that they tend to pop up when they are least expected. It is for this reason that it is advisable to establish an effective management information system from day one!

CHIEF EXECUTIVE GUIDELINES

Name: Richard Laine, President, Chief Financial Officer, and Owner
Company: Telechron of North Carolina Inc.
Product/Service: Manufacturer of Timers and Motors Serving the Appliance Industry
Sales: $2,500,000   *Number of Employees:* 14

General Guidelines: When it comes to developing an effective management information system, the E/CEO should keep the following tips in mind:

1. Make sure your management information system people report directly to the finance department. This will keep the cost of getting and maintaining information in perspective.

2. Make sure the information system provides timely and accurate information. Bad data and misinterpreted data lead to bad decisions.

3. The system needs to have a common database to be "shared" by all. It should be an on-line, interactive system whereby people throughout the firm can access the information they need to make better decisions and to provide better service to people inside and outside the firm.

Proceed with Caution Guidelines:

1. Make sure the benefits of having the information are greater than its costs.

2. You need an "overall" system. Keep every department and every person from having their own "unique" PC system. You need to have an interactive system whereby everyone can interact with everyone. You don't want a network of individual "subsystems" that don't share the company's database. Information needs to be shared not splintered!

3. Avoid the "flavor of the month" software and hardware syndrome where everybody wants "their" particular packages and systems. If you offer them 25 flavors, they will want 38 flavors!

4. The information provided by the system needs to be viewed as a "tool" to be used by management. Information is to "help" management; it is not a "substitute" for management. Information is not the "be-all and end-all" of running a business.

5. Remember, the computer will give you what the programmer wants you to see! Information is not an end in itself—and it does not replace "hands-on" management. Information should stimulate inquiry into what is really going on and why it is going on. For example, the data may indicate declining sales. You still need to learn what is behind the numbers—what caused sales to decline. You need to determine if your customers stopped buying because they moved, switched to one of your competitors, went out of business, or are making the product in house. Data is just data until you understand what it means!

SECTION B
FORMING STRATEGIC ALLIANCES

We are seeing the dawn of an era of strategic alliances. Suppliers and customers are now forging alliances that increase their ability to provide better quality, reduce costs, and speed delivery. Alliances are also being formed between firms to enter new markets. Large firms are even establishing mutually beneficial relationships with smaller firms. A number of large firms have demonstrated that it may be better to establish an alliance with a smaller firm than it would be to acquire it. Larger firms may have greater resources, but smaller firms continue to be more entrepreneurial. Alliances permit emerging firms to keep the entrepreneurial focus that is lost in most acquisitions.

IBM has learned that in certain situations it may be better to form alliances with smaller companies than to try to develop products or distribution channels on its own. As president of IBM, Jack Kuehler observed, "Our customers were demanding services and products faster than we could provide them. Not even a company with IBM's resources can afford to go it alone."[1] He further stated, "We enter new markets faster by forming alliances with companies that already have a significant presence in markets where we do not....We avoid having to spend the time and effort duplicating the work of people who are already specialists in a particular area."[2]

Alliances are based on the concept of synergism whereby two or more entities work together to achieve something that is quicker, less expensive, of better quality, and/or more convenient than could be accomplished by the entities acting alone. Corporate alliances demonstrate that the whole can be greater than the sum of the parts.

Alliances are replacing the adversarial nature of traditional business relations. In the past, customers may have tried to squeeze every possible discount or concession from a supplier. Customers frequently played one supplier against another. Large firms often tried to squeeze emerging firms from the market. While these practices are still common, a few firms are finding it more worthwhile to establish "collegial" relationships.

Alliances enable firms to share information, technology, capital, talent, distribution channels, and equipment. They provide win-win opportunities for both parties. Alliances are a far cry from the typical purchase contract where each party tries to gain something at the expense of the other.

Alliances are different from joint ventures. Joint ventures usually occur when two or more firms create a new firm to make and/or market a product or service. Strategic alliances work within the existing firms. They are usually open-ended. They do not have all the legal details associated with supplier-customer contracts. Strategic alliances represent a commitment to share information, to learn from each other, to explore possibilities, and to embark on a journey that will create value. Alliances are built on the premise that the firms will evolve together. Instead of getting caught up in contractual straitjackets, alliances rely on flexibility and resourcefulness. These qualities are rarely found in licensing agreements and joint ventures.

Strategic Alliances May Enable the Firm to Make a Quantum Leap Forward

Most emerging firms spend years trying to achieve a position of strength. This can be a long and frustrating journey. Alliances are like turbochargers; they can provide an emerging firm with considerable strength in a much shorter time. By forming an alliance with a supplier, customer, or another firm, emerging firms are in a position to bridge the gap that keeps them from capitalizing on growth opportunities. What could take years of independent effort may be possible within months if the firm links up with a firm that has the expertise, connections, or resources that it lacks.

Dennis Yablonsky, president of the Carnegie Group Inc., is a firm believer in the value of alliances. His software company has eight strategic alliances or joint ventures with such companies as Boeing, Digital Equipment, and US West. Yablonsky notes, "Relationships with blue chip partners make us more credible in other markets."[3]

Alliances with larger firms may also provide the emerging firm with the capital it needs to operate on a much higher plane. Advanced Magnetics Inc. formed an alliance with Bristol-Myers Squibb Company to develop products targeted at billion dollar markets. According to Jerry Goldstein, Advanced Magnetics' CEO, "Bristol-Myers is a $10 billion company. To it, $10 million is inventory breakage."[4] Alliances with large firms may be particularly beneficial to smaller firms because debt and equity (including venture capital) financing is becoming more difficult to obtain. Alliances may provide "patient capital" emerging firms desperately need.

The ability to enter international markets by forming alliances is also important. James Womack, author of *The Machine that Changed the World*, has definite feelings about the value of alliances to emerging firms. He considers the vision of the entrepreneur trying to compete in a global economy as "naive and romantic."[5] William Bologna, chairman of Columbia Laboratories, seems to share Womack's perception. His $12 million firm has negotiated supply, manufacturing, and licensing agreements with major firms. Bologna states, "We have been able to strike lucrative deals in which we receive 30 percent of our partners' sales income, or a 15 percent royalty rate."[6]

Calyx and Corolla may be one of the best examples of how alliances can enable firms to go from being a concept to a formidable force in an industry. When Ruth Owades came up with the idea of creating a business that would leapfrog the conventional distribution network, she knew she would need to form a revolutionary alliance to make it possible. Owades wanted to establish a catalog business that would bypass the conventional distribution links, markups, and delays by having flowers and plants shipped from the growers directly to the ultimate customers. She believed her new approach to doing business would provide flowers with a longer shelf life at a competitive price.[7]

Owades knew she would need more than the usual shipping arrangement for Calyx and Corolla to succeed. She needed a carrier that would install a computerized package-tracking system at the firm's office and agree to leave packages at the customer's door without a signature. She forged an alliance with Federal Express that has enabled her firm to meet the challenges that have come with her new venture. For example, in designing the boxes Owades enlisted input from the growers, box manufacturers, and Federal Express's packaging lab. Federal Express even sends a team to Calyx and Corolla's headquarters to train Owades's new employees before a busy season.[8]

Mail Boxes Etc. also demonstrates the synergism that can be found in forming alliances. When UPS acquired 9 percent of Mail Boxes Etc.'s stock, it gained access to over thirteen hundred retail outlets for its shipping services. The alliance also meant UPS would have a network of convenient locations for customers to pick up a package if it could not be left at the customer's address. Mail Boxes Etc., in turn, benefited from an infusion of over $11 million. This also reduced the prospect that UPS would become a competitor by setting up its own retail outlets. The alliance saved UPS the years and millions of dollars it would have taken to develop its own retail network.[9]

Concluding Comments: Alliances Are like Marriages–Some Work, Some Don't

Alliances are more likely to succeed when each partner checks out the other and each party gains from the association. Harold Krall, CEO of Cardinal Technologies, has been involved in various alliances. He states, "Usually, the failure occurs either because of a win-lose sense, where a partner thinks he's going to get a lot more than he's going to give, or because of the inability of the two cultures—where the partner sees things in a much different light, and you diverge in your ability to reach an agreement on anything you're going to do."[10] When emerging businesses seek partners for alliances that will let them get to the market quicker, expand their geographic boundaries, and access capital, their E/CEOs should make an extra effort to find partners who share their vision and values. E/CEOs who fail to look before they leap run the risk of being trampled to death by elephants that were supposed to be friendly.

CHIEF EXECUTIVE GUIDELINES

Name: Russell Carter, Chief Executive Officer
Company: Atlantic Corporation/Micro Packaging Inc.
Product/Service: Industrial and Electronic Packaging Materials

General Guidelines: When it comes to forming strategic alliances with other businesses, the E/CEO should keep the following tips in mind:

1. Check the business philosophy of your counterpart. What's the objective? Is it common?

2. Have a solid short-term view as well as a long-term view.

3. The human element is critical. Are your partners compatible person-ally? Business alliances are very personal and personality-driven.

4. Focus on the objectives of products and customers and less on imme-diate personal and company rewards.

5. How big is the vision? It is important for the partners to see the same future.

Proceed with Caution Guidelines:

1. Work out general terms of agreement more independently of legal issues. Business alliance partners must know their comfort level of involvement.

2. Avoid bringing in lawyers and accountants early. They can "spoil the soup" by overdiscussing the highly unlikely scenarios in the contract—this can set a tone of distrust in an environment of trust.

3. Avoid emphasis on competition. Focus on your own objectives.

And I Would Be Particularly Careful Not to:

1. Delegate basic terms of agreement to those other than principals.

2. Limit casual and social contact with the other party. Compatibility of principals partly will determine functional success.

SECTION C
GOING PUBLIC

Emerging firms that maintain a high rate of growth frequently get to the point where "going public" becomes the topic of discussion. Few aspects of growth generate stronger opinions than selling the firm's stock to indi-vidual and institutional investors. Some of the E/CEOs who have taken their firms public are quick to state, "Avoid it at all costs." Other E/CEOs claim the process of going public strengthened their firms.

There are as many reasons for going public as there are pitfalls to avoid. E/CEOs considering the prospect of going public have to answer a series of questions. The first question is rather elementary: "Should the firm go public?" If the answer is "yes," then the "who, what, when, how, where, and how much" questions naturally follow.

Going public is one of the times when the E/CEO cannot go it alone, when entrepreneurial intuition will be totally inadequate, and when mistakes can be disastrous. Going public may be one of the greatest challenges the E/CEO will face. If it is done right, going public may enable the firm to ascend to a higher level of growth and success. If it is not handled well, it can be the straw that breaks the camel's back.

Does the Firm Fit the "IPO" Profile?

Few E/CEOs would object to having a major infusion of cash. There always seem to be more uses for cash than cash on hand. Yet most emerging firms should not consider going public. Only a select group of emerging firms fit the IPO (initial public offering) profile. A firm must have its act totally together before it even considers offering its stock to outsiders. The E/CEO may have started the firm with an excellent product-service and the attitude that changes could be made as things popped up. Going public, however, is like lowering the water level in rapids; obstacles below the surface quickly appear that can jeopardize the whole process. Growth may have provided a buffer for managerial errors. When the firm goes public, however, every dimension of the firm is under the magnifying glass.

The size of the firm, its rate of growth, and the amount of money management seeks to raise have a lot to do with whether it should consider going public. Deloitte & Touche indicates firms should have at least $15 to $20 million in sales, net income of at least $1 million, an annual growth rate of 30 to 50 percent, and the potential to generate $50 to $100 million in annual sales in the near term.[1] A few firms with a strong technology position have also been successful in going public. While they may not have generated the suggested level of sales or profits, their potential to get there quickly attracted sufficient investor interest.

Going public requires more than fitting the financial profile. The firm must have its managerial act together as well as its accounting-information system in place. The management team plays a critical role in two respects. Investors usually insist that a capable management team already be in place. The E/CEO may have been the driving force in the creation of the firm, but investors know a strong management team is essential for sustained growth. Investors also don't want the future of the firm to be tied to the life and sanity of one person! The management team is important for another reason. It will need to fill in for the E/CEO when he or she is tied up in the various stages of going public.

The firm's accounting system will have to be sound and the firm's records will have to be in order. E/CEOs who have operated without a chief financial officer find that it may delay going public for at least two years. They will need to hire someone to serve as CFO to make sure the firm is using generally accepted accounting principles. It may take a year to bring the accounting system up to speed. The second year usually involves

making sure financial records for the last few years meet GAAP requirements as well as any particular requirements set by the Securities and
Exchange Commission. The second year is also spent organizing the multitude of records that must be available when going public.

Timing Plays a Key Role in Going Public

Timing can be seen as a two-dimensional issue. First, a long sequence of
events needs to be followed. Firms usually need to provide audited financial statements for at least the last three years so investors know how the
firm is doing. Firms are usually required to go public within three to four
months after their last annual audit. Data becomes dated quickly and is of
little value for firms that are experiencing rapid growth.

Timing may also be important in terms of the mood that investors may
have toward the stock market in general and new equity offerings in
particular. If the stock market is declining or depressed, then investors tend
to look less favorably at new offerings. In 1987 one firm had the misfortune
of trying to go public in the week the Dow-Jones average dropped by over
five hundred points. The E/CEO decided to sell the business rather than
proceed with the public offering! Conversely, if the market is full of
lucrative yet less risky investment alternatives, then new offerings may
encounter resistance.

The Costs Associated with Going Public Must Be Considered

Firms that decide to raise more than a few million dollars can expect costs
to be anywhere from 10 to 20 percent of the equity offering. An offering of
$4 million may cost $1 million. Underwriter charges average 6 to 8 percent
of the offering. The underwriter's fee will also vary with the type of
agreement that is reached. In a "best efforts" agreement, the underwriter
merely agrees to sell as many shares as possible. If a "firm commitment"
agreement is reached, then the underwriter is committed to the whole
offering. The underwriter buys shares it cannot sell.

Accounting fees can range from $100,000 to $250,000. Legal fees can
be $50,000 to $100,000. Printing fees can exceed $50,000. Some firms even
hire a specialist in investor relations to handle various dimensions of
going public.

Offerings between $2 million and $15 million seem to be an awkward
size. Expenses are a higher portion of the offering with smaller offerings.
Most large underwriters will not even consider offerings of less than $15

million. They feel they don't make enough from the smaller offerings to justify the effort.

There is good news for firms seeking a smaller offering. For years, small firms have had the option of seeking "exempt" offering status. While the Securities Act of 1933 requires considerable documentation and registration requirements, "exempt" status permits smaller firms to do limited offerings. The amount of money raised and the type of investor sought are limited with the exempt status. Any violation of the restrictions usually requires the firm to conform to the regular standards. Fortunately, laws have been enacted recently at the federal and state levels to reduce the amount of restrictions. Regulation "SB" simplifies the process and paperwork for small offerings. It also raises the ceiling on the amount that can be offered.

Small firms seem to be finding ingenious ways to raise capital. John Schaeffer raised $1 million for his Real Goods Trading Corporation by using his computer and customer base. A computer program that is available from the North American Securities Administrators Association helped guide him through SCOR (small corporate offering registration) preparation and documentation. The total bill for the offering was about $130,000. Real Goods sent a notice of the offering (a "tombstone") to a targeted group of its customers. About 5,000 customers requested the prospectus. When all was said and done, the offering was fully subscribed by 750 new shareholders.[2]

Life Will Never Be the Same

Going public changes the E/CEO's life forever. Relationships with friends, board members, and investors must change. Becoming a publicly-traded firm means that the E/CEO can no longer talk to friends about the opportunities the firm plans to pursue. The E/CEO must make sure that the firm's plans are "properly" disclosed so everything is done aboveboard. Going public also means that anyone has access to the firm's financial statements. This means that competitors may learn the firm's operating ratios and expansion plans.

Going public usually means that the firm will need to have a professional board. When the firm was closely held, the board may have been comprised of the E/CEO's friends and relatives. Most E/CEOs recognize the need to put together a value-added professional board before going public. Investors have an impact on board representation after the offering is completed. This is particularly true if a venture capital firm or institutional investor purchases a large block of stock.

Board and investor expectations also add pressure to the E/CEO's job. Meetings will have to be documented better. Salaries and fringe benefit packages for the executives will need to be disclosed, discussed, and justified. The E/CEO will also need to take time throughout the year to field questions from investors, analysts, and the media.

The E/CEO's life will change in two other ways. First, he or she will learn a whole new vocabulary. Going public has its own jargon. The E/CEO will learn about exempt versus nonexempt offerings, green shoes, waiting periods, road shows, blue-sky laws, and various ways of classifying investors. Second, there is a joke on the street that goes, "There is good news and bad news for those who go public. The good news is that you get to meet a whole new group of people. The bad news is that they are attorneys, accountants, and analysts!"

Concluding Comments: Going Public Is a Rite of Passage

Going public offers a number of opportunities that are not available to firms that keep a tight grip on their stock. Firms that are at their debt-to-equity limit may be able to secure additional debt financing by bringing in additional equity. The fact that the firm's stock is traded may elevate its stature in the eyes of its staff. Stock incentives may put the firm in a better position to attract, reward, and keep talent. Firms with traded stock also cast a positive shadow for suppliers, customers, and the public. Going public means that the firm has been able to demonstrate a fairly high level of sophistication in meeting investor expectations. Finally, the E/CEO may also be able to cash in some of his or her stock as long as certain restrictions are met.

E/CEOs need to heed two cautions before going public. First, while the E/CEO may have operated with a reasonable time horizon, going public puts the E/CEO on such a tight timetable that he/she may put strategic thinking on hold. Second, the process of going public redirects the E/CEO's attention away from the marketplace. Instead of directing one's attention to developing innovative products and services, the E/CEO will be trying to meet a whole host of financial inquiries and regulations. It would be a shame if the E/CEO's attempt to create and maintain investors kept the firm from creating and maintaining customers! The E/CEO's dream of having an infusion of new cash could be rudely awakened by the loss of customers, who constitute the ultimate source of capital.

CHIEF EXECUTIVE GUIDELINES

Names: Alan Zimmer, President and Chief Executive Officer and Jim Rouse, CPA, CMA; Treasurer and Chief Financial Officer
Company: Reeds Jewelers
Product/Service: Retail Jewelry Store Chain (70 stores)
Sales: $65,000,000   *Number of Employees:* 694
Awards/Distinctions:

1. Successful 600,000 share IPO at $10/share, 1986

2. Eleventh Largest Jeweler in the United States, *National Jeweler* magazine

3. 1992 National Jeweler Retailer Hall of Fame.

General Guidelines: When it comes to doing an initial public offering, the E/CEO should keep the following tips in mind:

1. Don't take the process too seriously; there is not as much mystique as the players like to perpetuate.

2. The reward is worth the aggravation.

3. You can pay a lot, or you can pay a lot more; stay on top of the bills everyone will be running up.

4. Know, and be able to explain, your business, your niche, and your strategy—thoroughly.

5. Make up your mind to enjoy the process; you're paying the investment bankers, lawyers, and auditors to worry and plan for you.

6. Expect the proposed price of offering to be dropped the night before the deal is done.

Proceed with Caution Guidelines:

1. Select the underwriter(s) with a strong track record in your industry and one you trust and with whom you can enjoy working.

2. Have your operating and financial house in order.

3. Raise the capital you expect to need for the next five years.

4. Get the managing underwriter to solicit analysts' coverage from members of the syndicate.

5. Negotiate and monitor all fees closely.

And I Would Be Particularly Careful Not *to:*

1. Give a blank check to the investment bankers, lawyers, auditors, and printers.
2. Expect the business to run on its own while you are in the IPO process.
3. Believe everything the investment bankers tell you.
4. ˙Expect to eat during breakfasts and lunches while on the road show.

SECTION D
SELLING OUT

It would be a major oversight for a book on managing growth not to address the process of selling out. Some E/CEOs start their ventures with the intent of selling them in a few years for a healthy gain. They look forward to the time when they can cash in on their blood, sweat, and tears. John Wurts, cofounder of Management Decision Systems—which was acquired by Information Resources for $47 million—stated, "We had always intended to go public or sell out in a blaze of glory."[1]

Don Mattrick, who founded Distinctive Software Inc., approached selling his firm in a different manner. When he realized his firm had reached its limits, he sought out a larger firm that would be a complementary fit with his own. He contacted Electronic Arts because he believed it would boost employee morale and provide a strong distribution network for his firm's products. In June of 1991, when the merger was finalized, Mattrick received $13 million for his firm. The merger was particularly beneficial because 90 percent of the proceeds were in Electronic Arts stock. The stock value quadrupled when Electronic Arts became the leading software supplier for Sega Genesis.[2]

Other E/CEOs start and manage their ventures with no real thought about selling out. While their motives for starting and building their ventures may vary, one thing is clear—if the business has demonstrated a solid track record and is positioned to continue its ascent to even higher levels of success, then the firm is destined to be courted by other individuals or firms. Ironically, emerging firms are frequently acquired by larger firms that failed to create their own futures. Some of the dancing elephants find it more promising to acquire emerging firms than to trample them to death.

Look Before You Leap

E/CEOs need to be savvy about the dynamics and nuances associated with selling a firm. The emerging firm may be courted by various suitors over an extended period of time. Some of the suitors may just be window-shopping. It is not unusual for a suitor to appear, drop from the limelight, and then reappear again. The firm may even find itself being courted by numerous suitors at one time.

Some inquiries may not even be from legitimate suitors. They may be tied to a competitor who is using covert tactics to secure information about how the firm works. It is for this reason that confidential information needs to be carefully monitored. Confidentiality is important for another reason. If word gets out that the firm is up for sale, employees, suppliers, customers, and creditors may start distancing themselves from it. Some suitors may also seek confidentiality. They may not want to identify themselves at first. If the suitor is from outside the United States, it may be difficult to learn its true identity.

E/CEOs need to recognize that once the courtship begins, they are no longer the masters of their time. Selling the venture is like everything else in managing an emerging business. It will take more time, more information, more people, more money, and more patience than the E/CEO first imagined. Documents will need to be drafted and regulations will need to be met. The sale of the firm may also require a waiting period before the deal can be finalized.

It usually takes three to eight months to sell a business—if the deal goes through! Yet this may actually be only the tip of the iceberg. A firm may be for sale for years before a deal is finally closed. The process of selling the firm has considerable opportunity cost for the E/CEO. The E/CEO will enlist the services of the firm's accounting firm, legal counsel, and appraisers as well as a broker, matchmaker, or investment banking firm in the selling process. The E/CEO should plan on committing at least three hundred hours of time to it as well. The firm will only have a "part-time" CEO during this period. There will be times when the E/CEO is so wrapped up in negotiations, the firm will have to operate without his or her services.

The strategic direction of the firm is certain to suffer from the time the E/CEO devotes to selling the firm. As data gathering, projections, and negotiations escalate, firms tend to put major initiatives on hold. If the deal falls through, then the firm may have missed an irretrievable window of opportunity. This in turn, may lower the firm's profits, marketability, and overall value.

Have the Firm's Act Together

The E/CEO needs to be sure business continues as usual. This is one of the times when having a solid management team is essential. A strong management team can provide two significant dividends for the time the E/CEO invested in developing it. First, the team should be able to address strategic and operational issues on its own. Second, firms with strong management teams usually can command a higher selling price. Since most E/CEOs do not stick around for long after the sale, suitors usually look for firms that already have a chief operating officer or an experienced management team.

E/CEOs also need to be sure the firm's accounting records are up to date. The firm will need to provide data on past years' profitability, present assets (including receivables, inventory, equipment and the like) as well as future projections. The firm will be expected to provide a business plan for the next few years that projects trends, investment requirements for expansion, and profitability. The firm will also need to identify litigation that may be pending, warranties that need to be honored, and proof that the property it is using is in compliance with environmental standards.

E/CEOs who have been committed to professionalizing the firm's operations from day one will encounter fewer setbacks and challenges. E/CEOs should include the question, "How would this look to a suitor?" when making decisions as the firm evolves. Too many E/CEOs paint their firms into a corner by compromising their people, accounting systems, and associated liabilities. The more the firm represents a "turnkey" operation, the more the suitor will pay for it. A firm that has been run by the seat of the E/CEO's pants will be valued less than a professionally managed firm.

Timing Plays a Crucial Role

To paraphrase the folk song, "For every thing there is a season and for every thing there is a reason." There are two cardinal rules to follow when selling a business. First, sell it at the right time. Second, sell it for the right reasons. Too many E/CEOs wait until their businesses are in trouble before they put them up for sale. Businesses that are doing very well and are trending up command the highest prices. Firms that are in trouble and trending down are usually relegated to being sold for the liquidation value of the assets.

Suitors usually court businesses that have a promising future and that fit their corresponding corporate strategy. Firms that are positioned to capitalize on emerging opportunities tend to command a higher price-earnings multiple. Firms in saturated markets usually garner a much lower price-earnings ratio. E/CEOs who are interested in selling their firms should guard themselves against the natural desire to ride the growth wave until it crests. If the E/CEO waits too long before putting the firm on the market, then last year's income statement may not generate much interest. Most suitors prefer to get on the wave as it begins to grow rather than after it crashes.

There are two other quirks to the timing issue. First, suitors usually don't appear on schedule. Suitors frequently express their interest before the E/

CEO puts out the welcome mat. Offers, like drop-in visitors, have a habit of showing up at the strangest times. Second, E/CEOs who start their ventures with the philosophy "My business is for sale if the price and terms are right" will be better prepared to evaluate the merits of an offer whenever it is tendered.

Structuring the Deal

It is ironic that even with all the sophisticated software packages floating around, there is no universally accepted basis for valuing a business. Some valuation techniques look at annual sales. Other valuation techniques use a multiple of after-tax profits (price-earnings ratio) or the market value of the assets. The value of the business will also be affected by the state of the economy, the nature of the industry, the prime rate, the stock market, and other factors. Most accounting firms and investment bankers use numerous formulas and incorporate various factors when valuing a business.

The nature and terms of the deal will also affect the final price. A straight cash sale usually elicits a lower price. If the sale is set up with the seller providing some of the financing, then the seller may be able to command a higher price. The same may be true with a leveraged buyout if the seller is expected to be part of the debt financing. Stock swaps tend to command a higher price if the seller is restricted from selling all or part of the acquiring company's stock for a period of time. The nature of the deal also affects tax obligations. A cash sale usually creates an immediate tax obligation for the seller. A stock swap, however, may postpone a tax obligation until the buyer's stock is sold. Buyers also tend to prefer firms that have tangible assets rather than just goodwill. Tangible assets are easier to leverage and depreciate.

Three other aspects of the deal cannot be ignored. First, the E/CEO needs to know from the beginning if he or she wants to stay on with a "management contract." If so, then the responsibilities, duration, and salary-fringe package may become key negotiating points. Second, the E/CEO needs to have a position regarding a "noncompete" clause. The nature, scope, and duration of the clause may be critical. Third, the E/CEO may want to negotiate a clause that gives him or her the first shot at buying back the business if the acquiring firm wants to unload the business at a later date.

E/CEOs should have a specific idea of what they are willing to sell the business for before suitors appear on the scene. When the right offer comes along, the E/CEO needs to be able to move quickly toward closure. The longer things drag on, the greater the likelihood the sale will fall through. Also, the longer the negotiations, the more the E/CEO may get caught up in a "selling mindset." If the suitor senses the seller's vulnerability, then the buyer may exit from the process and come back later with a take-it-or-leave-it "lowball" offer.

John Wurts approached the selling situation in an interesting fashion. He noted, "If someone offers me a fair price for the company, I'm going to turn it down. I'm going to be prepared to wait [and keep it profitable] until someone comes along who's willing to pay a ridiculous price, then I'm going to take it on the spot."[3]

Don't Underestimate the Emotional Side of Selling Out

Few E/CEOs take the sale of their firm in stride. E/CEOs who do not have something to do that will challenge them after the sale usually experience serious withdrawal. Some E/CEOs, however, find the sale of their firm to be a liberating experience. True entrepreneurs have more ideas than time and capital. The sale of one business may give them the time and the money to pursue other market opportunities. For example, Mel and Patricia Ziegler used the proceeds from the sale of their Banana Republic safari-theme retail stores and catalog business to fund their Republic of Tea.[4]

Most E/CEOs learn it is not healthy to stay emotionally attached to their firms after the sale. Most buyers will modify the direction, operations, personnel, and culture of the firm. When the buyer acquires the firm, the buyer is paying for the right to make wholesale changes. If the E/CEO is concerned about what will happen to the people who helped the firm grow, then he or she should have given them the opportunity to buy stock in the firm from the beginning so they could also profit from the sale. An ESOP also could have given them the opportunity to influence their future when the E/CEO wanted to cash in.

If the E/CEO is not prepared to let go, then he or she should seek out a buyer who will serve as a holding company. Conglomerates and high-tech firms frequently acquire emerging firms and keep the E/CEO on as the president of that division or subsidiary. To some E/CEOs, this is like having their cake and eating it too. They have the opportunity to stay involved, and they can fund growth by tapping the larger firm's resources.

Concluding Comments: It Isn't Over until It's Over

Murphy's Law, "If anything can go wrong, it probably will," frequently applies to selling the firm. Yet, even if the courtship falls through, the firm may be better off. Many E/CEOs have found that they come away with a more objective view of their firm. They also find they are more willing to make personnel and operational changes that they had been unwilling to make earlier. Some E/CEOs who had grown tired of their ventures even find they are such an integral part of their lives that they would be lost without them.

CHIEF EXECUTIVE GUIDELINES

Name: William M. Rowe III, Former President and Stockholder
Company: South Atlantic Services Inc.
Product/Service: Contract Chemical Formulating and Packaging
Number of Employees: 45

General Guidelines: When it comes to selling the firm, the E/CEO should keep the following tips in mind:

1. In the years before considering a sale, treat your employees fairly and honestly. Any reasonable purchaser will ask your employees to confirm your professed data. This is no time to have your employees "vent" at the suitor.

2. Create an environment where employees have a kind of psychological ownership and a stake in the business. This has a lot to do with whether the firm will grow to the point where the sale of the business will be possible and worthwhile. Keeping things "close to the chest" (very private with information) will work to the owner's detriment. When the employees find out the owner is considering selling the business (or worse, when they find that a suitor is touring the premises) and they have not been told, trust goes out the window right away. Confidentiality is just not possible or fair.

3. The "big meeting" to discuss the situation must be handled delicately. My own opinion is not to have a big meeting, at least not at first. Private individual meetings with all the top personnel (and the more who can be included in this group, the better) will seem more considerate on the part of the owners. This will yield better results in the end.

4. Generally speaking, the lower the gross sales price, the less the sophistication of the selling process. If a lending institution is to be involved, then significant amounts of data will have to be formal enough to be read and understood by many who will never visit the plant site.

5. Records, records, and more records. A first-time seller of a $1 million-plus business will never believe how much information a suitor and/or bank can request. Audited financials are a minimum. The more the better. This can hardly be overstated. The original cost will be more than made up by two factors. First, the cost to reconstruct data is very high. Second, reconstructed data never has quite the same power or believability as timely captured data.

6. Make 10 copies of every legal document in effect. This also applies to personnel policies, audited statements, and the like. This will save considerable time and speed the process.

7. Boy Scoutism. Pay your taxes. Don't cheat the government, your customers, or your suppliers. There is no investigation like that of a suitor. Make sure your personal life (tax-wise) is in order. An audit by the IRS may take place as a result of the sale.

8. Remember, that which is not in writing does not exist. One should not count on something that is not spelled out completely in a binding document. Put those things that are significant to you in writing. At first, put your "dream sheet" down. When the time arrives for you to submit your first draft, include just about everything you could possibly want. It is most probable that a number of these items will be negotiated away by you in order to make the deal.

9. Do not get impatient. If you are having a fire sale, that's different. If you are asking the highest reasonable price you feel your business might yield, then prepare for it. This gets back to having your employees on your side. The time between first announcement and final consummation can be difficult for the owners and the employees. They need to be on the team. Put them there.

10. Time and frustration are related to how common one's business is. The more complex and unusual the business, the longer it will take people to understand your business. This same "esoterica" will probably eliminate using a broker to sell the business. The more unusual one's business, the more the owners will find they will have to do the explaining and selling of the business to the prospect. If you use a broker, then be sure the fee reflects the work expected to be done.

11. Do not underestimate the agony of dealing with a "looker." Insist on a Letter of Intent. Try to have the letter be as definitive as possible. This will keep as many "lookers" from bothering you and your employees. Preferably, the letter will form a basis for the actual sales agreement that will come later. Be careful, however, with the Letter

of Intent. Do not underestimate its binding potential. Just because it is called a Letter of *Intent* does not mean that it cannot be binding. It can rarely be binding on the buyer, but the seller can get stuck if he or she isn't serious about selling in the first place. A letter of intent can be enforced against you.

12. Do not put your business on the market unless you really intend to sell.

Epilogue

This is what the world looks like to the emerging firm that is not nimble enough to dance with the elephants!

This elephant was drawn by Taylor C. Harper. Reprinted with permission of the artist.

References

Chapter 1

1. John Sculley, *Odyssey*, Perennial Library, New York, 1988, p. 90.
2. Warren Bennis, *On Becoming a Leader*, Addison-Wesley, Reading, Mass., 1989, p. 134.
3. "How Can Somebody Not Be So Optimistic?" *Business Week*, "Reinventing America," special edition, 1992, p. 184.
4. "Sam Walton in His Own Words," *Fortune*, June 29, 1992, p. 106.
5. Thomas J. Watson, Jr., *A Business and Its Beliefs*, McGraw-Hill, New York, 1963, p. 79.

Chapter 2

1. Theodore Levitt, "Marketing Myopia," *Harvard Business Review*, July-August 1960, p. 26.

Chapter 3

1. William E. Sheeline, "Avoiding Growth's Perils," *Fortune*, August 13, 1990, p. 55.
2. Lawrence J. Peter, *The Peter Principle*, Bantam Books, New York, 1969, p. 8.
3. Peter F. Drucker, *Managing in Turbulent Times*, Harper & Row, New York, 1980, p. 45.
4. John W. Gardner, *No Easy Victories*, Harper Colophon Books, New York, 1968, p. 42.

Chapter 4

1. William E. Sheeline, "Avoiding Growth's Pitfalls," *Fortune*, August 13, 1990, p. 58.
2. Ibid., p. 55.

Chapter 5

1. Tom Richmond, "Growing Steady," *Business Strategy: Planning for Growth, Inc.* magazine, Boston, 1987, p. 3.
2. Craig R. Hickman and Michael A. Silva, *Creating Excellence*, New American Library, New York, 1984, p. 199.
3. William E. Sheeline, "Avoiding Growth's Perils," *Fortune*, August 13, 1990, p. 55.

Chapter 6

1. Taken from an excerpt of Anthony Carnevale's "Putting Quality to Work: Train America's Workforce." Carnevale's thoughts originally appeared in *America and the New Economy*, American Society for Training and Development, Washington, D.C., 1990.
2. Theodore Levitt, "Marketing Myopia," *Harvard Business Review*, July-August 1960, p. 26.
3. Rosabeth Moss Kanter, *The Change Masters*, Simon and Schuster, New York, 1983, p. 64.

Chapter 7

1. Robert G. Cooper, "Stage-Gate Systems: A New Tool for Managing New Products," *Business Horizons*, May-June 1990, p. 44.
2. This material originally appeared in H. Igor Ansoff's book, *Corporate Strategy*, McGraw-Hill, New York, 1965, p. 109. Used with permission of the author.
3. "Are You Ready?" *Success*, July-August 1991, p. 51.
4. "100 Ideas for New Businesses," *Venture*, November 1988, p. 67.
5. Donald W. Brinkman, "On the Path to Opportunity," *Success*, June 1992, p. 16.

Chapter 8

1. Richard Poe, "Their Uncanny Think Tank," *Business Month*, November 1989, p. 62.
2. Kenichi Ohmae, "Getting Back to Strategy," *Harvard Business Review*, November-December 1988, pp. 152–153.
3. Robert J. Allio, *The Practical Strategist*, Harper & Row, New York, 1988, p. 134.
4. Ibid., p. 134.
5. William H. Davidow and Michael S. Malone, "Instant Profits," *Success*, January/February 1993, p. 80.
6. H. Skip Weitzen, "Billion Dollar Growth," *Success*, April 1993, p. 14.

7. "How Can Somebody Not Be Optimistic?" *Business Week,* "Reinventing America," special edition, 1992, pp. 104–105.

8. Ibid., p. 114.

9. Mark Roman, "New Niches for the 90s," *Success,* April 1989, p. 51.

10. Robert B. Reich, "The Real Economy," *Atlantic Monthly,* February 1991, p. 36.

11. Ibid., p. 37.

Chapter 9

1. Kenneth N. Dayton, "Corporate Governance: The Other Side of the Coin," *Harvard Business Review,* January-February 1984, p. 34.

2. Leon A. Danco, "Most Family Businesses Need Outside Directors," *Nebraska Business Center Report,* May 1987, p. 2.

3. Richard H. Mimick, "The New Age Board of Directors," *Business Quarterly,* Winter 1985, p. 49.

4. Ahmad Tashakori and William Boulton, "A Look at the Board's Role in Planning," *The Journal of Business Strategy,* Winter 1985, p. 69.

5. Dayton, *Harvard Business Review,* p. 34.

6. Richard Behar and Mark Clifford, "Kibitzing in the Boardroom," *Forbes,* February 10, 1986, p. 74.

7. Dayton, *Harvard Business Review,* p. 35.

8. Behar and Clifford, *Forbes,* p. 74.

9. John F. Persinos, "The Advice Squad," *Inc.,* January 1986, p. 82.

10. Ibid., p. 82.

11. Mimick, *Business Quarterly,* p. 53.

12. Persinos, *Inc.,* p. 80.

13. Behar and Clifford, *Forbes,* p. 74.

14. Sharon Nelton, "Bringing an Outside Board Aboard," *Nation's Business,* May 1985, p. 31.

15. Dayton, *Harvard Business Review,* p. 35.

16. Ibid., p. 37.

17. John A. Gardner, *No Easy Victories,* Harper Colophon Books, New York, 1968, p. 42.

18. Graef S. Crystal, "Do Directors Earn Their Keep?" *Fortune,* May 6, 1991, p. 79.

19. Thomas J. Watson, Jr., *A Business and Its Beliefs,* McGraw-Hill, New York, 1963, p. 79.

Chapter 10

1. John W. Gardner, *No Easy Victories,* Harper Colophon Books, New York, 1968, p. 42.

2. Craig R. Hickman and Michael A. Silva, *Creating Excellence*, New American Library, New York, 1984, p. 176.

3. Michel Robert, *The Strategist CEO*, Quorum Books, New York, 1988, p. 22. Copyright 1988 by Michel Robert. Used with permission of Quorum Books, an imprint of Greenwood Publishing Group Inc., Westport, Conn.

4. James L. Adams, *The Care and Feeding of Ideas*, Addison-Wesley, Reading, Mass., 1986, p. 2.

5. Ibid., p. 205.

6. Hickman and Silva, *Creating Excellence*, p. 151.

7. Rosabeth Moss Kanter, *The Change Masters*, Simon and Schuster, New York, 1983, p. 369.

8. Harold Fearon, William Reif, William Ruch, and William Werther, "Management and the Year 2000," *Arizona Business*, April 1981, p. 3.

9. R. M. Narchal, K. Kittappa, and P. Bhattacharya, "An Environmental Scanning System for Business Planning," *Long Range Planning*, December 1987, p. 97.

10. Selected excerpt from *Leaders: The Strategies for Taking Charge* by Warren Bennis and Burt Nanus. Copyright © 1985 by Warren Bennis and Burt Nanus. Reprinted with permission of HarperCollins Publishers, Inc., pp. 167–180.

11. Peter Drucker, *Managing in Turbulent Times*, Harper and Row, New York, 1980, p. 41.

12. Pierre Wack, "Scenarios: Uncharted Waters Ahead," *Harvard Business Review*, September-October 1985, p. 73.

13. Burt Nanus, *Visionary Leadership*, Jossey-Bass, San Francisco, 1992, p. 85. Used with permission of Burt Nanus and Jossey-Bass Publishers.

14. Robert Townsend, *Up the Organization*, Alfred A. Knopf, New York, 1970, p. 129.

15. Kanter, *The Change Masters*, p. 278.

16. Hickman and Silva, *Creating Excellence*, p. 159.

17. Ibid., p. 150.

Chapter 11

1. Peter F. Drucker, "Strategic Planning: The Entrepreneurial Skill" in *Management: Tasks, Responsibilities, Practices*, Harper & Row, New York, 1974, p. 123.

2. Reprinted from April 28, 1975 issue of *Business Week* by special permission, copyright © 1975 by McGraw-Hill, Inc.

3. Michael E. Porter, "Know Your Place," *Inc.*, September 1991, p. 93.

4. Ibid., p. 93. The five mistakes reprinted with permission of *Inc.* magazine.

5. Ibid., p. 93.

6. Donna E. Vinton, "A New Look at Time, Speed, and the Manager," *The Academy*

   of Management EXECUTIVE, November 1992, p. 7.
7. Robert J. Allio, *The Practical Strategist,* Harper & Row, New York, 1988, p. 139.
8. Ibid., p. 4.

Chapter 12

1. Brian Dumaine, "Creating a New Company Culture," *Fortune,* January 1990, p. 127.
2. John K. Clemens, "A Lesson from 431 B.C.," *Fortune,* October 13, 1986, p. 164.
3. Heinz Weihrich, "How to Achieve Excellence by Managing the Culture in Your Company," *Industrial Management,* September/October 1989, p. 28.
4. Ibid., p 28.
5. Daniel R. Dennison, *Corporate Culture and Organizational Effectiveness,* John Wiley & Sons, New York, 1990, p. 2.
6. Ibid., p. 3.
7. John P. Kotter and James L. Heskett, *Corporate Culture and Performance,* The Free Press, New York, 1992, p. 35.
8. Craig R. Hickman and Michael A. Silva, *Creating Excellence,* New American Library, New York, 1984, p. 82.
9. Robert J. Allio, *The Practical Strategist,* Harper & Row, New York, 1988, p. 94.
10. Hickman and Silva, *Creating Excellence,* p. 80.
11. Allio, *Practical Strategist,* p. 97.
12. Terrance E. Deal and Allan A. Kennedy, *Corporate Cultures,* Addison-Wesley, Reading, Mass., 1982, p. 8.

Chapter 13

1. Robert J. Allio, *The Practical Strategist,* Harper & Row, New York, 1988, p. 139.
2. Leslie Brokaw, "The Secrets of Great Planning," *Inc.,* October 1992, p. 151.
3. Steve Kaufman, "Going for the Goals," *Success,* January 1988, p. 40.
4. Peter F. Drucker, "Strategic Planning: The Entrepreneurial Skill," in *Management: Tasks, Responsibilities, Practices,* Harper & Row, New York, 1974, p. 123.
5. Ibid., pp. 123, 126.
6. Allio, *Practical Strategist,* p. 145.
7. Ibid., pp. 145–146.
8. Teri Lammers, "The One-Page Strategy Guide," *Inc.,* September 1992, p. 135.
9. Malcolm Forbes, *The Forbes Scrapbook of Thoughts on the Business of Life,* Forbes Inc., New York, 1976, p. 33.

Chapter 14

1. Tom Post, "Firing Up for the Future: An Interview with Steven Brandt," *Success,* January/February 1989, p. 59.
2. Ibid., p. 58.
3. Robert Townsend, *Up the Organization,* Alfred A. Knopf, New York, 1970, p. 144.
4. Leslie Brokaw, "Playing for Keeps," *Inc.,* May 1992, p. 41.
5. Mary Rowland, "Competing for Workers," *Success,* June 1993, p. 16.
6. Ibid., p. 60.
7. Matt Rothman, "Into the Black," *Inc.,* January 1993, pp. 59–60.
8. Ibid., pp. 60–64.
9. Post, "Firing Up," p. 59.
10. Roger Fritz, "The Competitive Edge," *Success,* August 1992, p. 50.
11. Ibid., p. 50.
12. Post, "Firing Up," p. 58.
13. Rothman, "Into the Black," p. 64.
14. Martha E. Mangelsdorf, "Ground-Zero Training," *Inc.,* February 1993, p. 83.
15. Dominic Bencivenga, "Some Employers Change Approach to Employee Pay," *Wilmington Morning Star,* December 27, 1992, p. E-1.
16. Brokaw, "Playing for Keeps," p. 38.

Chapter 15

1. Warren Bennis and Burt Nanus, *Leaders,* Harper & Row, New York, 1985, p. 86.
2. Stephen C. Harper, "Real Managers Eat Last," *Business,* October 1983, p. 52.
3. George Odiorne, "How to Manage by Objectives," *Industry Week,* June 8, 1970.
4. Rahul Jacob, "Thriving in a Lame Economy," *Fortune,* October 1992, p. 44.
5. Thomas J. Peters and Robert H. Waterman, *In Search of Excellence,* Harper & Row, New York, 1982, p. 15.
6. Teri Lammers, "The Essential Employee," *Inc.,* December 1992, p. 160.
7. Leslie Brokaw, "Playing for Keeps," *Inc.,* May 1992, p. 38.
8. "Modernizing the Suggestion Box," *Inc.,* October 1992, p. 34.
9. Joshua Hyatt, "Ideas that Work," *Inc.,* May 1991, p. 64.
10. "Modernizing," *Inc.,* p. 34.
11. Jacob, "Lame Economy," p. 44.
12. John W. Gardner, *No Easy Victories,* Harper Colophon, New York, 1968, p. 40.

Chapter 16

1. Joseph Mancuso, "Secrets from CEOs," *Success,* October 1985, p. 20.
2. Robert McGarvey, "Only the Best Will Do." *Entrepreneur,* December 1992, p. 160.
3. Ibid., p. 163.
4. Ibid., p. 162.
5. Michael P. Cronin, "Ongoing Sales Rewards," *Inc.,* April 1992, p. 119.
6. "Making Employees Owners," *Inc.,* December 1992, p. 34.
7. Mark Henricks, "The Golden Handcuff," *Entrepreneur,* December 1992, p. 118.
8. Rosalind B. Resnick, "ESOPs for Everyone," *CFO,* July 1992, p. 50.
9. Henricks, "Golden Handcuff," p. 118.
10. "How to Retain Key Employees," *Inc.,* November 1992, p. 36.
11. "The Expanding Range of Employee Benefits," *Business Week,* Small Business Supplement, June 21, 1993.
12. Roger Fritz, "The Competitive Edge," *Success,* August 1992, p. 50.
13. Leslie Brokaw, "Playing for Keeps," *Inc.,* May 1992, p. 38.

Chapter 17

1. Tom Peters, *Thriving on Chaos,* Harper & Row, New York, 1988, p. 82.
2. Ibid., pp. 111–112.
3. Jan Carlzon, *Moments of Truth,* Harper & Row, New York, 1987, p. viii.
4. Ibid., p. 3.
5. Jenny C. McCune, "The Perfection Principles," *Success,* April 1991, p. 28.
6. Peters, *Thriving on Chaos,* p. 112.
7. Carlzon, *Moments of Truth,* p. 3.
8. Peters, *Thriving on Chaos,* p. 112.
9. Jay Finegan, "Taking Names," *Inc.,* September 1992, pp. 129–130.
10. John Case, "Customer Service: The Last Word," *Inc.,* April 1991, p. 91.
11. McCune, "Perfection Principles," p. 28.
12. Paul Hawken, "The Ecology of Commerce," *Inc.,* April 1992, pp. 96, 98. Reprinted with permission of *Inc.* magazine.
13. Lisa Benenson, "Bull's Eye Marketing," *Success,* January/February 1993, pp. 46, 48.
14. Ibid., p. 43.
15. Edward O. Welles, "How're We Doing?" *Inc.,* May 1991, pp. 80–82.
16. Finegan, "Taking Names," p. 129.

17. Karl Albrecht and Lawrence J. Bradford, *The Service Advantage,* Dow Jones–Irwin, Homewood, Ill., 1990, p. 229.

18. Leslie Brokaw, "The Mystery Shopper Questionnaire," *Inc.,* June 1991, pp. 94–97.

19. Albrecht and Bradford, *Service Advantage,* pp. 214, 216.

20. George R. Walther, "Your Secret Opportunity," *Success,* May 1992, p. 12.

21. "Turning Inquires/Complaints into Sales," *Small Business Report,* October 1985, p. 54.

22. Peters, *Thriving on Chaos,* p. 112.

23. Walther, "Secret Opportunity," p. 12.

24. Brian Dumaine, "Creating a New Company Culture," *Fortune,* January 15, 1990, p. 128.

25. Michael Hammer and James Champy, *Reengineering the Corporation,* Harper Business, New York, 1993, p. 61.

26. Peters, *Thriving on Chaos,* p. 138.

27. Hammer and Champy, *Reengineering the Corporation,* p. 39.

28. Mark Henricks, "Satisfaction Guaranteed," *Entrepreneur,* March 1992, p. 48.

29. Case, "Customer Service," p. 93.

Chapter 18

1. Jerry G. Bowles, special advertising supplement on quality, *Fortune,* September 1992.

2. Otis Port and Geoffrey Smith, "Beg, Borrow—and Benchmark," *Business Week,* November 1992, p. 74.

3. Ronald Henkoff, "The Hot New Seal of Quality," *Fortune,* June 28, 1993, pp. 116–117.

4. Michael Barrier, "Small Firms Put Quality First," *Nation's Business,* May 1992, p. 24.

5. Jerry G. Bowles, "The Quality Imperative," *Fortune,* special advertising supplement, 1986.

6. Otis Port et al., "Quality," *Business Week,* November 30, 1992, p. 72.

7. Mark Henricks, "Quest for Quality," *Entrepreneur,* September 1992, p. 42.

8. Port and Smith, "Beg, Borrow," pp. 71, 72.

9. Ibid., p. 74.

10. Ibid., p. 68.

11. Otis Port, "Questing for the Best," *Business Week,* October 25, 1991, p. 11.

12. Port, "Quality," pp. 70, 71.

13. Michael Hammer and James Champy, *Reengineering the Corporation,* Harper Business, New York, 1993, pp. 2–3.

14. Ibid., p. 3.

15. Frank Rose, "Now Quality Means Service Too," *Fortune,* April 22, 1991, p. 100.

16. Port, "Quality," p. 71.

17. Hammer and Champy, *Reengineering,* p. 52.

18. Port, "Questing for the Best," p. 14.

19. Michael Barrier, "Small Firms," pp. 24–25.

20. William D. Marbach, "Quality: What Motivates American Workers?" *Business Week,* April 12, 1993, p. 93.

21. Richard J. Schonberger, "Total Quality Management Cuts a Broad Swath—Through Manufacturing and Beyond," *Organizational Dynamics,* Spring 1992, p. 27.

Chapter 19

1. Tom Peters, *Thriving on Chaos,* Harper & Row, New York, 1988, p. 161.

2. Stephen Baker, Kevin Kelly, Richard D. Hof, and William J. Holstein, "Mini-Nationals Are Making Maximum Impact," *Business Week,* September 6, 1993, p. 66.

3. Ibid., pp. 66–67.

4. Deloitte, Haskins & Sells, *Expanding Your Business Overseas: An Entrepreneur's Guidebook,* Deloitte, Haskins & Sells, New York, 1985, pp. 22–23.

5. Martha E. Mangelsdorf, "Building a Transnational Company," *Inc.,* March 1993, p. 93.

6. Ben Hiatt, "Ben and Jerry's Succeeds in Russia despite Small Setbacks," *Wilmington Morning Star,* June 23, 1993, p. 5-C.

7. Guen Sublette, "When in Rome...," *Entrepreneur,* September 1992, p. 133.

8. Greg Matusky, "Going Global," *Inc.,* April 1993, p. 11.

9. Lois Therrien, "Market Share Con Leche?" *Business Week,* "Reinventing America," special issue, 1992, p. 122.

10. Matusky, "Going Global," p. 59.

11. Ibid., p. 60.

12. Albert Warson, "Tapping Canadian Markets," *Inc.,* March 1993, p. 90.

13. Jill Andresky Fraser, "On the Road," *Inc.,* March 1993, p. 94.

14. Jill Andresky Fraser, "Pricing to Cover Export Costs," *Inc.,* March 1992, p. 104.

15. Tim Smart, "Why Ignore 95% of the World's Market?" *Business Week,* "Reinventing America," special issue, 1992, p. 64.

Chapter 20

Section A

1. Christopher Caggiano, "Are You Too Busy to Be Smart?" *Inc.*, May 1992, p. 24.
2. Elizabeth Conlin, "The Vital-Signs Assessment," *Inc.*, April 1993, p. 127.
3. Ibid., p. 127.
4. "Waste Not, Want Not," *Inc.*, March 1991, p. 34.
5. Joshua Hyatt, "Born to Run," *Inc.*, January 1991, p. 44.

Section B

1. David E. Gumpert, "Big Company-Small Company: The New American Partnership," *Inc.*, special advertising supplement, July 1992, p. 7.
2. Ibid., p. 7.
3. Ibid., p. 4.
4. Robert A. Mamis and Edward O. Wells, "Small Is, Finally, Beautiful," *Inc.*, May 1992, p. 132.
5. Ibid., p. 132.
6. Jill Andresky Fraser, "Negotiating Better Licensing Deals," *Inc.*, December 1992, p. 43.
7. Leslie Brokaw, "Twenty-Eight Steps to a Strategic Alliance," *Inc.*, April 1993, p. 101.
8. Ibid., p. 104.
9. George Gerndon, "A Sweet Deal," *Inc.*, March 1991, p. 12.
10. Leslie Brokaw, "Guaranteed Success," *Inc.*, March 1993, p. 67. Reprinted with permission of *Inc.* magazine.

Section C

1. Leslie Wat, *Strategies for Going Public*, Deloitte, Haskins & Sells, New York, 1983, p. 21.
2. Leslie Brokaw, "Where Great Ideas Come from," *Inc.*, January 1993, pp. 76–77.

Section D

1. "After the Sale," *Inc.*, August 1990, pp. 39–40.
2. Ingrid Abramovitch, "Cashing Out," *Success*, March 1993, pp. 30, 32.

3. "After the Sale," p. 42.
4. Russell Mitchell and Sandra D. Atchison, "You Are Relaxed. You Are Content. You Are Approaching Tea Mind," *Business Week,* November 30, 1992, p. 44.

Index

About the Author

Stephen C. Harper is president of Harper and Associates Inc., a management consulting firm, and a professor of management in the Cameron School of Business at the University of North Carolina, at Wilmington, where he directs the Small Business Institute. He is editor and coauthor of *Management: Who Ever Said It Would Be Easy?* His most recent book, *The McGraw-Hill Guide to Starting Your Own Business* was a featured selection of the Fortune Book Club. He earned his Ph.D in management from Arizona State University.